5/09 0-0 LAD n/a

International
Dictionary of Gastronomy

THE HIPPOCRENE COOKBOOK LIBRARY

International Dictionary of Gastronomy

Guido Gómez de Silva

HIPPOCRENE BOOKS, INC.
New York

Book design by K & P Publishing Services.
Jacket design by Acme Klong Design, Inc.

For more information, address:
HIPPOCRENE BOOKS, INC.
171 Madison Avenue
New York, NY 10016

ISBN 0-7818-0876-6

Cataloging-in-Publication Data available from the Library of Congress.

Printed in the United States of America.

To the memory of my sister,
Manuela Gómez de Silva,
a sweet girl

Table of Contents

Menu Words A to Z

Basic Five-Language Gastronomy Dictionary

agar allspice asparagus aglio amaranth anchovy avgolemono

a, in Italian and Spanish (*à* in French) means "in [a certain fashion]," see **a la**.

abacate, Portuguese for **avocado**.

abacaxi, Portuguese for **pineapple**.

abadejo, Spanish for **codfish**.

abaisse [French, from *abaisser* "to lower, press down,"], a thin undercrust of pastry, the dough having been made thinner with the rolling pin.

abalone [from Spanish *abulón*, from an American Indian word (California)] or **sea-ear** or **Venus's ear**, a certain mollusk (shellfish) and its flesh.

abulón, Spanish for **abalone**.

Abyssinian banana, another name for **ensete**.

accompaniment [from French *accompagnement*], a complement (to meat, fish, shellfish), such as a sauce, relish, broiled fruit, parsley.

achar (India), a pickle, relish.

achara or **atsara** (Philippines), a pickle, relish.

achiote [Spanish, from Náhuatl *achiotl*], a preparation made from the seeds of the **annatto** tree, used to flavor and impart a yellow or reddish color to various foods (Venezuela, Mexico).

achira [Spanish, from Quechua], a plant from whose tubers an **arrowroot** is made (Peru).

acid drop, a tart piece of candy.

ackee, variant of **akee**.

acorn squash, a dark green **winter squash** with yellow to orange flesh.

ade, a drink made from water, fruit juice, and sugar.

-ade, as an ending, indicates "a sweetened drink of"; examples: lemonade, limeade, orangeade.

adobo [Spanish], a dish of Spanish origin consisting of meat or fish (e.g., chicken, pork, tuna fish) marinated in a sauce, browned in fat, and then simmered in the marinade; the sauce usually contains vinegar, salt, oregano, garlic.

adzuki bean or **adsuki bean** [from Japanese *azuki* "red bean"], a certain plant and its seeds; the plant is widely cultivated in the Orient for the flour that is made from its seeds.

aebleskive [Danish "apple slice,"], a pastry made of batter baked in a muffin-shaped pan.

Afghanistan. Lamb kabob and lamb pilaf are representative dishes of Afghanistan.

African pepper, another name for **cayenne pepper**.

agar or **agar-agar** [Malay "jelly, gelatin"] or **Japanese gelatin**, a material prepared from certain red algae, used as a gelling and thickening agent in certain foods (e.g., jellies). It resembles gelatin (sense 1).

agaric [from Latin *agaricum*, from Greek *agarikon*, a fungus], the common cultivated mushroom (other fungi are also called *agaric*). Agarics include blushers, honey mushrooms.

agave worm or **maguey worm** [Spanish: *gusano de maguey*], the larva of various butterflies that is fried and eaten, especially in Mexico and the southern United States.

agnolotti [from the plural of Italian *agnolotto*, from *agnellotto*, "large lamb", from *agnello* "lamb"], a crescent-shaped dumpling (made of pasta) usually filled with cooked meat, ricotta cheese, or seasoned vegetables.

aguacate [from Nahuatl *ahuacatl* "testicle," from the shape of the fruit], Mexican Spanish for **avocado**.

aglio, Italian for **garlic**.

ahi [Hawaiian], the same as **tuna**.

aholehole or **ahole** [Hawaiian], a small, tropical food-fish.

ahuatle [Mexican Spanish *ahuautle*, from Nahuatl *ahuautli*, from *atl* "water" + *huautli* "wild amaranth"], the eggs of certain water insects, that are dried and used as food (Mexico).

ai [Japanese], variant of **ayu**.

aiguillette [French "small needle"], long, narrow strip of rump steak or fowl (especially duck).

ail, French for **garlic**.

aioli [Provencal (French *ailloli* or *aïoli*), "garlic oil"], a garlic mayonnaise, i.e. a sauce made of crushed garlic, olive oil, egg yolks, and lemon juice.

aji [from American Spanish *ají*, from Taino *axí*], hot pepper, chili; also, a chili sauce.

ajiaco [American Spanish, from *ají* "hot pepper, chili"], a stew (especially Colombian and Cuban) with broth and pieces of (chiefly) meat or chicken, potatoes, Indian corn, onion, and hot peppers, as well as certain rhizomes and tuberous roots (sweet potato, yuca, malanga, yam), and leaves of a plant called *guasca*.

ajo, Spanish for **garlic**.

ajonjoli [from Spanish *ajonjolí*], the same as **sesame**.

akee or **ackee** [from a native name in Liberia (Kru *a-kee*)], the spongy flesh, used in tropical cooking, of the aril (covering) enveloping the seeds, contained in capsules, of a certain tropical tree native to Africa (likewise called *akee*). It is used in the Jamaican dish *saltfish and akee*.

akhrot [Hindi], the English walnut tree (India).

a la or **à la** [from French *à la* "after the fashion (of), in the manner (of); with," followed by a feminine singular noun, as in *à la grecque* "in the

Greek manner"], in the manner or style of; with. In French, this expression varies in form according to the gender and number of the noun that follows and according to whether that noun begins with a vowel or a consonant: *à l"* is followed by a vowel (e.g., à l"orange), *au* by a masculine singular (e.g., au beurre, au jus), *aux* by a plural (e.g., *aux amandes* "with almonds"). The Italian equivalents are, respectively, *alla, all", ai* (e.g., all"arrabbiata "in haste [with high heat]; in anger"); *a la* is also used in Spanish (e.g., *a la española, a la francesa, a la italiana, a la madrileña, a la mexicana* "in the Spanish [French, Italian, Madrid, Mexican] fashion"). In French, Italian, and Spanish, the form is *à la, alla, a la* (all three, feminine) when followed by an adjective (and the adjective too is in the feminine), because the word for "manner" or "fashion" is a feminine noun (French *manière, façon, mode;* Italian *maniera, moda;* Spanish *manera, moda).*

a la carte [from French "by the menu"; the opposite is *au menu, à prix fixe*], according to the bill of fare, in which each dish has a separate price. Distinguished from **table d'hôte** or **prix fixe** (a meal of several courses offered at a fixed price).

à la grecque [French "in the Greek manner"], served in a sauce of olive oil, lemon juice (or wine), and seasonings (e.g., coriander, fennel, sage, thyme). Usually said of vegetables, served cold.

a la king, prepared in a white cream-sauce with green or red peppers and mushrooms (e.g., cut-up chicken or turkey a la king). Sometimes flavored with sherry.

alalauwa [Hawaiian], a tropical food-fish.

alalonga or **alalunga** [Italian, "long fin"], an **albacore**.

à l'américaine, see **lobster**.

a la mode [French "in the fashion"], *1.* served with ice cream (e.g., pie a la mode); *2.* braised with vegetables and served in a brown sauce. In French, the phrase is used more widely than in English, as in *boeuf à la mode* "larded beef cooked with carrots and onions", often abbreviated to *mode (boeuf mode),* or in *tripes à la mode de Caen* "tripe in the fashion of Caen, braised tripe and onions."

à l'armoricaine, see **lobster**.

albacore [from Portuguese *albacor* (Spanish *albacora),* from Arabic *al-bakurah*], or **long-finned tuna** or **white-meat tuna**, a large fish of the tuna family; it is the source of most canned tuna.

albahaca [from Arabic *al-habaqah* "the basil"], Spanish for **basil** (plant with aromatic leaves).

Albania. Lamb kabob is popular in Albania.

al burro, [Italian "with butter"] (said of pasta).

al dente [Italian *al dente* "to the tooth"], incompletely cooked, cooked just enough to retain a somewhat firm texture. The phrase is used especially of pasta and of rice.

alegria [from Mexican Spanish *alegría*, "happiness, gaiety," from Spanish *alegre* "happy, gay"], a certain plant (a coarse herb) and its seed. The plant is also called **amaranth**.

alewife or **spring herring** or **Tauton turkey**, a certain fish of the herring family.

11

alfalfa [Spanish] or **lucerne**, a certain plant (a legume).

alga [Latin "seaweed"], any of various chiefly aquatic plants (e.g., kelps and other seaweeds). Among edible marine algae: Irish moss, red laver, sea lettuce.

algarroba or **algaroba** [from Spanish *algarroba* "carob", from Arabic *al-kharrubah* "the carob"], *1.* Spanish for **carob** (algarroba bean, the long pod of the carob tree, containing a sweetish pulp); *2.* (Mexico) the sweet, bean-like, pulpy pod of the mesquite (see **mesquite bean**).

Algeria. The following are among representative dishes and products of Algeria: couscous, roast mutton (Arabic *mashwi*, "roast"), goat, chickpeas, dates, citrus fruit, grapes. Beverage: sweet mint tea.

algin [from *alga*], a gelatinous substance obtained from various marine brown algae, especially the giant kelp, and used as a thickener and emulsifier in certain foods (e.g., ice cream).

alimentary paste [translation of Italian *pasta alimentaria*, "food paste, food dough"], another name for **pasta**.

alla, Italian for **a la**.

all'amatriciana, see **amatriciana**.

all'arrabbiata, see **a la**.

allemande [from French *(sauce) allemande*, "German (sauce)"], or **allemande sauce**, a yellow sauce made by adding egg yolks to velouté (which is usually a white sauce).

alligator button, the fruit of the water chinquapin (a lotus and its edible seed).

alligator juniper [called "alligator" from the ridged appearance of the tree's bark], a shrub or small tree of northern Mexico and the southwestern United States having a sweet fruit.

alligator pear, another name for **avocado**.

allium, any of various plants characterized by their pungent odor (e.g., chives, garlic, leek, onion, shallot).

all-purpose flour or **family flour**, flour made from a blend of wheats, useful for all cookery except the finest cakes.

allspice [so called because it seems to combine the flavors of several spices (cinnamon, cloves, nutmeg)] or **Jamaica pepper** or **clove pepper** or **pimento**, the dried, aromatic berry of the allspice tree (a West Indian tree) used whole or ground as a spice, and the ground spice itself.

allspice oil, see **pimento oil.**

almond [French *amande*, Italian *mandorla*, Spanish *almendra*], the nut (stone, kernel) contained in the fruit of a certain small tree (likewise called *almond*) of the rose family, native to the Mediterranean region. Compare **amaretto**.

almond extract, the concentrated liquid from kernels (of almonds, apricots, peaches) soaked in alcohol, used for flavoring.

à l'orange [French, "with orange"], prepared or served with oranges (e.g. canard à l'orange "duck in an orange sauce").

alpine dock, a dock (plant used as table greens) of the Alps.

aman [Hindi], a certain long-stemmed rice (India).

amande, French for **almond**.

amandine [French, from *amande* "almond"], prepared or served with almonds (e.g., snap beans amandine, (fish) fillet amandine). In English, it is sometimes spelled *almondine*.

amanori [Japanese], a gelatinous seaweed that is prepared by drying and pressing in Japan. Also called simply **nori**, as well as **laver**.

amaranth (from Greek *amaranton*, a certain flower, from *amaranton*, neuter of *amarantos* "unfading"], any of certain herbs that can be used as table greens and have edible seeds. Compare **alegria**.

amarelle [ultimately from Latin *amarus* "bitter; sour"], a type of sour cherry.

amaretto [from Italian "little bitter one"], a small cookie with almond flavor.

amate [Spanish, from Nahuatl *amatl* "paper," a tree used by ancient Mexicans to make a material on which to write their codices], a Mexican and Central American tree with edible fruits.

amatriciana [Italian, from *Amatrice*, town 100 km NE of Rome] or **matriciana** [from dividing *all"amatriciana* "in the Amatrice manner" as if it were *alla matriciana*], with a tomato and salt pork (or bacon) sauce, usually with grated cheese (pecorino [e.g., Romano] or Parmesan), onions, and olive oil added.

ambrette [French, "little amber," from *ambre* "amber"], a French dessert pear with the odor of musk.

ambrosia [Greek, "immortality" (in Greek and Roman mythology, the food of the gods)], a dessert of a fruit (e.g., orange, pineapple) or of mixed fruits (such as apples, bananas, oranges, pineapple) topped with shredded coconut (plain or toasted).

American cheese, a smooth, mild cheddar cheese originally made in the United States.

American cherry, another name for the **sweet cherry**.

American fried potatoes, another name for **hashed brown potatoes**.

American mint, another name for **peppermint** (sense 1).

anadama bread, a leavened bread made with flour and flavored with cornmeal and molasses.

analogue ["something similar"], a product made of vegetable matter (e.g., soybeans) and used as a meat substitute.

ananas, French for **pineapple**.

anato, see **annatto**.

anchoa, Spanish for **anchovy**.

anchoveta or **anchovetta** [from Spanish *anchoveta*, diminutive of *anchova*, variant of *anchoa* "anchovy"], a small **anchovy**.

anchovy [from Spanish *anchova*, variant of *anchoa* "anchovy"], certain small, herring-like, marine fishes caught for preserving (with salt and some of their blood) and for making sauces and relishes. Anchovy paste can be used with cream cheese to make a spread, and in velouté sauce when it is prepared with fish stock instead of chicken or veal stock.

anchovy pear or **river pear** ("anchovy" from its use as an hors d'oeuvre], the fruit of a certain West Indian tree (likewise called *anchovy pear),* resembling the mango in taste and often eaten as a pickle.

13

Andorra. Spanish dishes such as gazpacho and paella and French dishes such as vichyssoise are popular in Andorra.

andouille [French, ultimately from Latin *inductus* "inserted"], a spiced, smoked pork sausage. Sometimes pork or veal tripe, beef, veal, or mutton are added. Certain well-known ones are: *andouille de Vire*, *andouille de Bretagne*.

andouillette [French *andouillette* "small andouille"], a fresh pork sausage made with tripe or chitterlings; a specialty of Lyon (town in eastern France).

angel cake or **angel food** or **angel food cake** [named for its color], a white sponge cake made of flour, sugar, and egg whites (often with vanilla and almond flavoring; sometimes with cocoa added, then called *chocolate angel food*). Compare **devil's food cake.**

angelfish, any of several fishes of warm seas.

angel-hair pasta [part translation of Italian *capelli d"angelo*, literally = "hairs of angel," also called *capellini* "little hairs"], long pasta of a diameter smaller than that of vermicelli.

angelica [Late Latin, "angelic, heavenly"; French *angélique*], an herb of the carrot family and its stems (leafstalks and rootstalks) that are candied and used in decorating cakes, candies, desserts.

angelot [Old French *angelot* "little angel,"], a small cheese made in Normandy.

angel pie, a dessert consisting of a baked shell of meringue filled with strawberries or other crushed fruit and whipped cream, or with another filling (as that of a lemon torte).

angels on horseback, a dish (an *hors d'oeuvre*) consisting of oysters wrapped in bacon and baked or grilled (or skewered and then broiled) and served on toast or toast points. Compare **devils on horseback.**

anglaise [from French *à l'anglaise*, "in the English manner"] *1.* boiled or steamed and served without sauce (as in French *pommes à l"anglaise* "potatoes anglaise"); *2.* breaded (as in *cutlets anglaise).* See also under **consommé.**

Angola. Dishes made with peanuts and dishes made with sesame are popular in Angola.

angostura bark or **angostura** [from *Angostura*, former name of Ciudad Bolívar, eastern Venezuela], an aromatic bitter bark used as a flavoring, for instance in angostura bitters.

angostura bitters, a bitter aromatic tonic made from water, angostura bark and other ingredients.

anguila, Spanish for **eel.**

angula, Spanish for *baby eel.*

anise (French *anis*, Italian *anice*, Spanish *anís)* or **aniseed**, the aromatic seed of a certain plant (likewise called *anise)* of the carrot family, used as a flavoring in cooking.

aniseed [from *anise seed*], see **anise.**

aniseed star, the fruit of the star anise tree; used as a spice.

anise oil or **aniseed oil** or **star anise oil**, an oil obtained from the dried fruits of the anise plant and used as a flavoring.

aniseroot, another name for **sweet chervil.**

annatto or **anato** [from Carib *annoto*], a yellowish red dyestuff prepared from the pulp surrounding the seeds of the annatto tree (a tropical American tree) and used in cooking. Compare **achiote**.

anon, another name for **sweetsop**.

anona, Spanish for **sweetsop**.

Antigua and Barbuda. The following are among representative dishes and products of Antigua and Barbuda: seafood, vegetables, fruits, ¹**pepper pot**; a mixture of cornmeal and okra *(fungee);* dumplings *(dumplins), a* sweet pudding made from grated sweet potato and coconut mixed with pumpkin, spices, and sugar boiled in a banana leaf *(ducana)*

antipasto [Italian "before the food"], assorted **appetizers**, usually including peppers, tomatoes, olives, cheese, fish, cold cuts. The word is often used as synonymous of **hors d'oeuvre**.

apio, Spanish for **celery**.

appetitost [Danish "appetite cheese,"], a soft Danish cheese made from sour buttermilk.

appetizers or **relish**, small portions of food (e.g., cheese, cold cuts, fish, olives, peppers, tomatoes) served before a meal to stimulate the appetite; see **antipasto, canapé, hors d'oeuvre, smorgasbord.** Tomato juice, and the blended juice of several vegetables are also considered appetizers.

apple, the rounded fruit of a certain tree (likewise called *apple)* of the rose family. Dishes made with apples include biffins, crisps, dumplings, fritters, grunts, pies, strudels, turnovers; baked apples; cakes, muffins, pandowdies, puddings, salads, stuffings.

apple banana, a banana having fruit smaller than that of the common banana, with a very thin skin and apple-like flavor.

appleberry, the fruit of an Australian vine (likewise called *appleberry).*

apple butter, a thick brown spread made of apples stewed down with sugar and spices usually in cider.

apple grunt, a deep-dish apple pie.

apple honey, apple syrup used as a sweetening agent.

apple pandowdy, a kind of apple pie, see **pandowdy**.

applesauce, a relish or dessert made of apples sweetened, stewed to a pulp, and sometimes spiced. It is used with roast pork or duck.

apricot [from French *abricot*, from Arabic *al-birquq*], a certain oval, juicy fruit. Dishes made with apricots include cakes, cobblers, mousse, pies, purées, salads, sauces. Apricots are also used in ice cream.

apricot palm, a small palm that bears apricot-flavored fruits.

à prix fixe, see **a la carte**.

Arabian coffee, seeds which form most of the coffee of commerce.

Arabica coffee, or **Arabica**, coffee seeds produced from the Arabian coffee plant. Compare **mocha** (sense 2).

arachide, French and Italian for **peanut**.

araucaria [from *Arauco*, an area of Chile], a certain tree (that resembles a pine) with edible seeds.

arctic char, a char (fish) of arctic waters, called also **arctic trout** (in French, *omble de l'Arctique).* It is often served grilled.

areca or **areca palm**, another name for **betel palm**.

areca nut, another name for **betel nut**.

argan oil, an oil obtained from the seeds of the Moroccan argan tree and used in cooking.

Argentina. The following are among representative dishes and products of Argentina: churrasco, carbonado (Spanish *carbonada),* chicken puchero *(puchero de gallina),* empanada, chorizo (but *bife de chorizo* is a beefsteak), steak topped with two fried eggs *(bife a caballo,* "beefsteak on horseback"); grilled meat *(asado* or *parrillada)* including variety meats *(achuras)* and sausages; fried fish, shellfish; a dish *(humitas)* of cornmeal dough wrapped in corn husks *(hojas de chala),* the dough being seasoned with a fried preparation of hot pepper, tomato, and onion; armadillo *(peludo);* a dish *(locro)* of ground Indian corn with meat, beans, pumpkin, and potatoes, served with a sauce made with fried onion; evaporated milk sweet *(dulce de leche).* Beverage: mate.

aricuri, see **ouricury**.

aril, an outer covering of certain seeds. It is often fleshy, as in the **akee**.

Arizona walnut, a tree with a thin-shelled edible nut found in northern Mexico and the southwestern United States.

armadillo [Spanish,"the little armed one," diminutive of *armado* "armed," so called because it has a covering of small bony plates], a mammal found in the Americas from the southern United States to Argentina. In Argentina, it is also called *peludo*.

Armenia. Some representative dishes and products of Armenia are shish kebab (Armenian *khorovats,* "roasted"), dolma, pilaf, meat balls in broth *(kufta),* lentils, barley, split peas, eggplant, baklava.

aromatic, a sweet-smelling or spicy plant or substance (e.g., cinnamon, ginger, spices).

arrabbiata, see **a la**.

arracacha [Spanish, from Quechua *rakkacha*], a tropical American herb related to the carrot; its root is eaten in parts of South America.

arrayán [Mexican Spanish, from Spanish *arrayán* "myrtle"], a Mexican tree having an edible fruit that is often candied.

arrowroot, a starch used in foods, obtained from the tuberous roots of a certain tropical American plant (likewise called *arrowroot).* Compare **achira**.

arroyo grape, another name for the **chicken grape**.

arroz, Spanish for **rice**.

arroz con pollo [Spanish "rice with chicken"], a casserole of rice with chicken seasoned usually with saffron, garlic, and other condiments.

artichoke or **globe artichoke**, a plant having a large flower head that when immature (unopened) is cooked as a vegetable. Compare **Jerusalem artichoke**.

arugula or **rocket** or **garden rocket** or **rugola**, an herb of the mustard family whose foliage is used in salads.

asafetida, a bitter resinous material obtained from the roots of several West Asian plants. It is strongly scented and when dried is used sparingly in Asian cooking, particularly curried fish, lentil soup, and certain vegetarian dishes.

ashcake, a cake of cornmeal, baked in hot ashes.

asiago [from *Asiago*, town in northeastern Italy, where it originated], a pungent, hard, sweetcurd, semicooked Italian cheese. It is suitable for grating.

asparagus [French *asperge*, Italian *asparago*, Spanish *espárrago*], the tender young shoots of the asparagus plant, cooked and eaten as a vegetable.

asparagus bean or **yard-long bean** [from the pod measuring up to 1 yard (30 to 90 cm)], the long, succulent pod of a South American plant likewise called *asparagus bean*.

asparagus lettuce, a variety of the common lettuce having a thick edible stem.

asparagus pea, another name for the **Goa bean**.

aspartame, a protein used as a low-calorie sweetener.

asperge, French for **asparagus**.

aspic, a jelly (e.g., of concentrated fish or meat stock with gelatin) used either as a garnish or to make a cold dish of meat, fish, vegetables, or fruit set in a gelatin mold. The aspic may be made of chicken or beef broth, cooked down until it jells naturally, or of tomato juice and gelatin. The aspic as a cold dish may be made with fowl (French *aspic de volaille*), foie gras (French *aspic de foie gras*); it may contain crab meat, shrimp, chopped raw vegetables, eggs.

assai, *1*. the fleshy fruit of the assai palm (a tropical South American tree); desserts and ice cream are flavored with the fruit; *2*. a Brazilian beverage (Portuguese *assaí*) made by infusion from this fruit with the addition of cassava.

assiette [French "plate (individual serving)"], a dish of cold cuts or hors d'oeuvres. In French, this is called *assiette anglaise*, "English plate".

atemoya [from the beginning of Tagalog *ates* "sweetsop" + Spanish *chirimoya* "cherimoya"], a tropical fruit produced by crossing the sweetsop and the cherimoya.

Atlantic croaker, or **hardhead**, a small fish of the Gulf and the Atlantic coasts of the United States south of Cape Cod.

Atlantic sailfish, a sailfish of the warmer parts of the Atlantic Ocean and the Gulf of Mexico. Its flesh is often served smoked.

Atlantic salmon, a fish of northern Atlantic waters. Also called **salmon**.

atole [Spanish, from Nahuatl *atolli*], a thin gruel of cornmeal cooked in water or milk and served hot. In some Spanish-American countries it is called *atol*.

atsara, Tagalog and Pilipino for **achara**.

atta [from Hindi *ata*], wheat flour (India).

atún [from Arabic *at-tun* "the tuna"], Spanish for **tuna**.

aubergine, French and mostly British English for American English **eggplant**.

au beurre [French "with butter"], cooked or served with butter (e.g., peas au beurre).

au beurre blanc [French "with white butter"], cooked or served (e.g., sea urchin) with a certain sauce made with softened butter; see **beurre blanc**.

au beurre noir [French "with black butter"], cooked or served with a cer-

asiago
———————
au beurre noir

17

tain sauce seasoned with browned butter (e.g., *raie au beurre noir* "ray (fish) in a browned butter sauce"); see **beurre noir**.

au bleu [French "to the blue": the skin of fish cooked in this manner turns blue], cooked by boiling in water with vinegar, either immediately after being killed, or when still alive. This method of preparing certain fishes, especially trout, in a court bouillon is called in French *cuisson au bleu* "cooking to the blue". See also **bleu**.

au court-bouillon, see **court bouillon**.

aufait, brick ice cream with candied fruit between layers.

au gratin [French "with a crust of bread crumbs"], covered with bread crumbs and grated cheese (or with only bread crumbs) and browned in an oven. Casserole dishes au gratin include crabmeat, macaroni, potatoes, sweetbreads, whiting, zucchini). Compare **gratin**, ²**scallop**.

au jus [French "with juice"], served in the natural meat juices or gravy obtained from roasting (e.g., chateaubriand, leg of mutton, roast beef au jus).

au menu, see **a la carte**.

au naturel [French "in the natural (manner)"], cooked or served plainly, without dressing, without seasoning (e.g., caviar, oysters, tuna fish au naturel).

au poivre [French "with pepper"], prepared (e.g., steak) with coarsely ground black pepper. Compare **steak au poivre**.

aurore [French "dawn"], with a pink or golden yellow color given a white sauce by the addition of tomato puree, lobster coral, or egg yolks.

Australia. The following are among representative dishes and products of Australia: beef, lamb, mutton, fish (e.g., rainbow trout), shellfish (mollusks and crustaceans), kangaroo tail soup, toad-in-the-hole, barbecued fruits. Beverage: tea.

Australian millet, an Australian grass with edible seeds.

Australian salmon, or **kahawai**, a certain fish that occurs along the coasts of New South Wales and Tasmania in Australia, and of New Zealand.

Austria. The following are among representative dishes and products of Austria: veal cutlet (German *Wienerschnitzel),* sauerkraut, sauerbraten, goulash, roast suckling pig, roast boar, dumpling *(Knödel* or *Nockerl),* strudel, Sacher torte, Linzer torte, Gugelhupf, fish. Beverage: coffee.

autumnal tea, a black tea grown during the autumn in certain areas of northeastern India.

aux amandes, see **a la**.

avellana, Spanish for **hazelnut**, **filbert**.

avena, Italian, Latin, and Spanish for **oats**.

avgolemono (modern Greek *augolémono*, from *augó* "egg" + *lemónion* "lemon"], a soup or sauce made of chicken stock, egg yolks, rice, and lemon sauce.

avocado [Portuguese *abacate*; Mexican Spanish *aguacate* (from Nahuatl *ahuacatl* "testicle," from the shape of the fruit)] or **avocado pear** or **alligator pear** or **midshipman's butter** or **palta** or **Spanish pear** or **vegetable butter** or **butter pear**, the fruit of certain tropical American trees; it has greenish-yellow pulp. Dishes made with avocado include guacamole.

awa [Hawaiian] or **milkfish**, a certain food-fish.

awabi [Japanese], a certain abalone (shellfish).

Ayrshire, an animal of a breed of dairy cattle originating in Ayrshire (also called Ayr), former county of southwestern Scotland.

ayu or **ai** [Japanese] or **sweetfish**, a small, salmon-like fish of Japan.

azarole [French, from Spanish *acerola*, from Arabic *az-zu'rūr*], the somewhat sour fruit of a southern European shrub (likewise called *azarole*); a jam is made with it.

azyme or **azym** [from Greek *azymos* "unleavened"], unleavened bread (eaten by Jews at the Passover).

bollo   bonefish

brochette   babka

bannock

béchamel

blancmange

baba or **baba au rhum** [French "baba with rum"], a yeast-leavened rum cake usually made with raisins; the cake is soaked (after cooking) in a rum and sugar syrup before serving. Fruit juice or kirsch may be used instead of rum.

babassu or **babaçu** [from Brazilian Portuguese *babaçú*], a palm tree of northeastern Brazil with hard-shelled nuts that yield an oil similar to coconut oil.

babassu oil or **babaçu oil**, an oil obtained from kernels of babassu nuts that is used in food and is similar to coconut oil.

babka [Polish "little old woman, grandmother"], a Polish glazed coffee cake flavored with orange rind, rum, almonds, and dried fruit (often raisins).

baby beef, meat from a fat young beef steer or heifer.

bacalao, Spanish for **codfish**. In Spain, codfish is usually cured and salted. *Bacalao al pil-pil* is a dish typical of the Basque Provinces (northern Spain) made in an earthen pot, with codfish, oil, hot peppers, and garlic.

bacca, another name for **berry** (sense 1).

backsey, a cut of meat usually including all or most of the loin (Scotland). Compare **foresey**.

backwater, a large ray (fish) of the western Pacific Ocean.

bacon, the salted and smoked meat from the back and sides of a pig after removal of spareribs. It is usually served fried or broiled, in narrow strips, with eggs; it is also used to wrap around certain hors d'oeuvre. Compare **Canadian bacon**.

bacon hog or **bacon pig**, a hog raised for bacon and other cured products.

bacon square, the smoked jowl of a pig trimmed square.

bacury or **bacuri** [from Brazilian Portuguese *bacurí*], the fruit of a tropical South American tree (likewise called *bacury*).

badderlocks, a large seaweed having long fronds eaten as a vegetable.

bagel [from Yiddish *beygel*], a ring-shaped roll that is made of raised dough and cooked by dropping it briefly into nearly boiling water and then baked to give it a glazed, brown outside over a white inside.

bago [Tagalog], an Asiatic shrub having edible young leaves and seeds.

bagoong [Tagalog], a seasoning consisting of a paste of salted small fish and prawns which have been fermented (Philippines).

bag pudding, a dessert pudding cooked (boiled or steamed) in a bag.

bagre, Portuguese and Spanish for **catfish**.

baguette [French "rod"], a loaf of French bread with an oblong shape.

Bahamas. The following are among representative dishes and products of the Bahamas: turtle pie, turtle soup, conch chowder, fish chowder, fish (grouper, kingfish), fish stew, soursop, mango, coconut pie.

Bahrain. Lamb kabob, hummus, and lamb pilaf are among representative dishes of Bahrain.

bain-marie, see **double boiler**.

bake (to), to cook (e.g., bread, cakes, pastry) with dry heat, especially in an oven but also on heated stone or metal or under coals. Fruits (such as apples, bananas, pears, quinces) and vegetables (such as eggplant, potatoes, squash) are often baked. Notes: The term *roasting*, originally applied to meat cooked on a spit before an open fire, is now applied to food, usually meat, baked in an oven. *Casserole cooking* is baking in the oven in a covered dish of glass or pottery. Compare **casserole** and **au gratin**.

baked Alaska, a dessert consisting of sponge cake topped with ice cream, completely covered with meringue (so the ice cream will not melt in the oven) which then is quickly browned in an oven.

baked apple or **baked-apple berry**, another name for the **cloudberry** (fruit).

baked beans, beans softened by soaking (in cold water) and boiling and then baked (in an earthen pot) usually with salt pork and seasonings (often including molasses). Compare **Boston baked beans**.

baker's cheese, soft, uncooked cottage cheese. It may be used for cheese pie or cake.

baking powder, any of various powdered mixtures of a carbonate (e.g., baking soda), at least one slightly acidic compound (e.g., cream of tartar), and starch or flour, used as leavening agents in making baked goods (e.g., quick breads, cake); when the mixture is moistened the carbonate and acid react, liberating carbon dioxide which raises the dough.

baking soda, another name for **sodium bicarbonate** (a chemical compound used in baking powders).

baklava [Turkish], a dessert of very thin layers of puff pastry filled with chopped nuts and honey or a sugar syrup, and cut usually in diamond-shaped pieces for serving.

bakupari [from Portuguese *bacoparí, bacuparí*], a Brazilian tree producing an edible fruit with a very white pulp.

ball, a roundish mass, as of minced fish or meat or of vegetable.

balut [from Tagalog *balót, balút*], boiled duck eggs that had been incubated almost to the point of hatching (Philippines).

bamboo shoot, one of the young and tender, slightly acid, buds from the rhizome of bamboo (a woody grass), cut as soon as it appears above the ground (winter shoots are preferred), and used as a vegetable (China, Japan). Usually only the inner, most tender parts of the shoots are employed; they can be served by themselves, stir-fried, or with pork or chicken or mushrooms.

bagoong

bamboo shoot

banana [Portuguese or Spanish, of West African origin] or **platano** or **saging** (Philippines), the crescent-shaped fruit of a plant (likewise called *banana),* having white, soft flesh and an easily removed rind that is usually yellow or reddish when ripe and dark brown at full maturity. Compare **plantain**.

banana fish, another name for **bone fish**.

bananas Foster, a dessert of flamed bananas served with ice cream.

banana split, a dessert made with a banana split lengthwise, topped with vanilla ice cream, and garnished with whipped cream, chopped nuts, and a maraschino cherry.

banana squash, a winter squash having fruits that are long and slender and that become gradually smaller at both ends.

Banbury tart [from *Banbury*, town in southern England, noted for its cakes], a small, triangular, baked tart with a fruit filling (especially of raisins), or filled with **mincemeat** (sense 1).

bandoleer fruit, the berrylike fruit of a certain East Indian vine.

Bangladesh. The following are representative dishes and products of Bangladesh: curries (Bengali *tarkari;* chicken, mutton, beef, fish, prawns), kabobs, pilafs *(pulao),* biryani, shellfish, fish (especially bekti [pomfret], hilsa), pulses, mangoes, bananas, pineapples, jackfruit, watermelon, coconut, guava, litchi, papaya, oranges. Desserts (based on yogurt, rice, milk, nuts). Beverages: tea *(cha),* lassi (made of yogurt), green-coconut water.

bannock, *1.* a pancake, usually unleavened, made of oatmeal, barley, or wheat flour, baked in flattish loaves (Scotland); *2.* a thin corn cake baked on a griddle (New England).

bar, a solid piece of candy longer than it is wide.

barbacoa, see ¹**barbecue** (sense 2).

Barbados. The following are among representative dishes and products of Barbados: black pudding (sausage stuffed with sweet potatoes; served with souse [sense 1]), eddo, roast suckling pig, flying fish (e.g., steamed or in a pie), sea urchins, bean and pumpkin soup; coo-coo (pudding of salt beef and cornmeal or breadfruit), ¹pepper pot, jug-jug (a mold of green peas, corned beef, and pork), guava, mango, avocado, shaddock, orange, coconut, cornmeal pone (sense 3; with pumpkin and grated coconut).

Barbados cherry or **West Indian cherry** [from *West Indian* "of the West Indies" (the islands bordering the Caribbean)], the berry of certain West Indian shrubs (likewise called *Barbados cherry)* somewhat resembling a cherry in flavor.

Barbados gooseberry or **lemon vine**, the fruit of a certain West Indian cactus (likewise called *Barbados gooseberry).*

Barbary fig, another name for **prickly pear**.

¹**barbecue** [from American Spanish *barbacoa*], *1.* a hog, steer, or other large animal (or pieces of meat, chicken, or fish) roasted or broiled whole or in large pieces, on a spit, over an open fire or over a fire in a pit; *2.* goat or sheep roasted in this fashion (Mexico, where it is called *barbacoa).*

²**barbecue (to)**, *1.* to roast or broil (e.g., beef or fish) on a rack over hot

coals or on a spit over a fire, basting the meat with a seasoned sauce, often made from the drippings; 2. to cook (e.g., beef or fish) in a vinegar sauce.

barbecue sauce, a sauce made chiefly of vinegar, condiments, spices, vegetables, sugar, that may be used in cooking, basting, or serving meat or fish. Frequent ingredients are brown sugar, paprika, dry mustard, cayenne pepper, tomato juice.

barbudo [American Spanish, from Spanish "bearded," from *barba* "beard"], any of several threadfins (fishes).

Barcelona nut [from *Barcelona*, city in northeastern Spain, in Catalonia], a Spanish variety of hazelnut, kiln-dried.

bard or **barde** [from French *barde*, from Spanish *barda* "horse armor"], a thin slice of bacon or of salt pork used to cover meat or fowl for cooking.

bardé [French "covered with bacon",] (of meat or fowl) covered with salt pork or slices of bacon for cooking.

bardee, a borer that is the larva of a beetle (Australia).

barfish [from English *bar* "band, stripe"; from the stripes on the back], another name for the **white bass** (fish).

Barleduc [from French *Bar-le-Duc*, town in northeastern France where it was originally made], a savory preserve or jam of whole white currants or of gooseberries from which the seeds have been removed (laboriously). It is usually made with honey and served with roast meat or used in pies.

barley, the seed or grain of a certain cereal grass (likewise called *barley),* also called *barleycorn.*

barley candy, another name for **barley sugar**.

barley sugar or **barley candy** [so called because formerly an extract of *barley* was added], a clear, hard candy made by boiling down cane sugar until it melts and then cooling it.

baron [French], a cut of meat (usually beef) consisting of two loins or sirloins not cut apart at the backbone. In French, *baron d'agneau* "lamb baron" is a cut consisting of both legs and both fillets of the lamb.

barracuda [Spanish], any of various fishes, mostly tropical and marine, having a long narrow body. It is a fat fish, and is therefore best for baking, broiling, planking.

barramunda or **barramundi** or **Burnett salmon**, any of several river fishes of Australia.

basella, a vine native of tropical Asia and Africa, used as a potherb.

basil [French *basilic*, from Greek *basilikon*, an aromatic plant, from *basilikon*, neuter of *basilikos* "royal," from *basileus* "king"; Italian *basilico*, Spanish *albahaca*], a plant having aromatic leaves used as seasoning. The word normally refers to *sweet basil* (a species of basil). Dishes using basil include pesto, pistou.

basil oil, an oil (a flavoring) obtained from the flowering tops of sweet basil.

bass, any of several fishes. The bass is a lean fish and therefore best for boiling or steaming. Compare **channel bass**, **sea bass**, **striped bass**, **white bass**.

bastard trout or **bastard weakfish**, other names for the **silver squeteague** (a certain weakfish).

¹**baste (to)**, to moisten food at intervals while it is cooking (as meat while roasting) by spooning over it sauce, pan drippings, melted butter, or fat, in order to prevent drying and to add flavor.

²**baste**, the liquid used to moisten food while roasting.

batata, Spanish for **sweet potato**.

Batavia cassia or **Batavia cinnamon** [from *Batavia*, former name of Jakarta, Indonesia], other names for **fagot cinnamon** (a cinnamon bark).

Bath asparagus [from *Bath*, city of southwestern England], the shoots of a certain star-of-Bethlehem (plant).

Bath bun [from *Bath*, city of southwestern England], a round bun made of yeast dough containing currants and usually decorated with nuts or pieces of candied fruit.

baton [from French *bâton* "stick"], *1.* a long, rigid loaf of bread; *2.* a sometimes flavored stick made of bread dough.

batter, *1.* a beaten liquid mixture (as for cakes or waffles) that consists of flour, milk (or water), and eggs; it is thin enough to pour or drop from a spoon. Compare **dough**; *2.* a mixture (e.g., flour and egg) used as a coating for food that is to be fried; fish, tripe, chicken, vegetables, fruits, may be dipped in batter or coated with it and fried in deep fat previously heated.

batter bread, another name for **spoon bread**.

battercake, another name for **pancake**.

batter pudding, a boiled pudding of eggs, flour, and milk or cream.

bauno [Cebuan], a wild mango (Philippines).

bauple nut, another name for **macadamia** (tree and nut).

Bavarian cream or **Bavarian**, a cold dessert of a flavored (as with lemon, lime, orange, pineapple, raspberry, strawberry) whipped gelatin mixture into which whipped cream is folded.

bayberry, see **bay leaf**.

bay leaf, the dried aromatic leaf of the bay tree (also called *laurel*, *bay laurel*), or of the bayberry (also called *black cinnamon*), used as an herb (seasoning) in cooking.

bay plum, another name for **guava** (fruit and tree).

bay tree, another name for **laurel**.

beach plum, the plum-like fruit of a certain North American shrub (likewise called *beach plum*). It is often used for jam.

beaked parsley, another name for **chervil** (aromatic herb used in soups and salads).

bean, *1.* the seed of various plants (likewise called *bean);* see also **broad bean**, **green bean**, **kidney bean**, **lima bean**, **sieva bean**, **snap bean**, **string bean**, **wax bean**; *2.* a bean pod used as a vegetable; *3.* any of various seeds or pods that resemble beans (e.g., a coffee bean; the vanilla bean). Beans are also used as the main ingredient in such dishes as **baked beans**, **Boston baked beans**, bean salad, bean soup, **refried beans**.

bean curd or **bean cheese** or **tofu** [from Japanese *tofu*, from Chinese *dòu* *fù*, "bean" + "curdled"], a soft, pressed, soybean-milk cheese (China, Japan) made with certain coagulants. It can be served with bean sprouts or mixed vegetables or in soup. In Chinese, it is called *fuyü*.

bean flour, a ground bean meal.

bean sprout, a young, tender shoot (or sprout) of certain bean seeds, such as the soybean or the mung bean, germinated in humid darkness, used in Chinese cooking.

beardie [from English *beard*], an Australian codlike fish with bristly gills under the lower lip.

béarnaise, or **béarnaise sauce** or **sauce béarnaise** [French "of Béarn (feminine)," from *Béarn*, region of southwestern France], hollandaise sauce (a thick sauce made with eggs and melted butter) flavored with tarragon, shallots and chervil, and served with meat (e.g., tournedos) or fish.

beat (to), to whip (batter, eggs), to mix rapidly to a frothy consistency by stirring with an instrument (spoon, beater, whip), in order to make smooth or to incorporate air.

beaten biscuit, a biscuit made of dough lightened by beating.

beccafico [Italian "pecks fig, figpecker," from *beccare* "to peck" (from *becco* "beak" + *fico* "fig")], any of various European songbirds or warblers eaten as a delicacy in Italy when fat on fruit and grains in autumn.

béchamel or **béchamel sauce** [French, for 18th-century French courtier, Louis de *Béchamel*, who invented this sauce], a white sauce of milk or cream, browned butter, and seasonings.

bêche-de-mer, another name for **trepang**.

beech, a certain tree having edible nuts (called *beech nuts)* partly enclosed in burs.

beech agaric, a certain edible mushroom that is a parasite on the beech.

beech fungus, a certain edible fungus of South America.

beech nut, the nut of the beech.

beef, the flesh of a slaughtered full-grown steer, bull, ox, or cow. The following are among choice cuts of beef: standing rib or rolled rib (for roast beef); fillet of beef tenderloin; steak (club, T-bone, porterhouse, tenderloin [filet mignon], sirloin). Steak can be served broiled, planked; other beef dishes include pot roast, short ribs, stew, round steak, minute steak (often the same as cube steak), flank steak, brisket, beef bourguignon, beef Stroganoff, beef Wellington, boiled dinner, Swiss steak; from ground beef: meat loaf, hamburger, meat balls, Salisbury steak. The variety meats include liver, heart, tongue, kidney.

beefalo [from *beef* + *buffalo*], a hybrid between cattle suitable for beef and the North American buffalo.

beef bacon, beef plate or brisket cured like pork bacon.

beef bourguignon [French *boeuf bourguignon*, "beef, ox Burgundy style," from *Bourgogne* "Burgundy," a region of eastern France], braised beef cubes simmered in a seasoned red-wine (especially red Burgundy wine) sauce with onions, mushrooms, and carrots. In French, *boeuf bourguignon* is also called simply *bourguignon*.

beef bread, the pancreas of a mature beef; compare **sweetbread**.

beef breed, any breed of cattle developed primarily for the production of

25

meat rather than milk (e.g., Angus, Hereford, Shorthorn). Compare **dairy breed**.

beefburger, another name for **hamburger**.

beef juice, the juice of beef extracted not by cooking but by pressure.

beef Provençal, a French stew in red wine, first marinated and then cooked.

beefsteak, a slice of beef usually cut from the loin or the hindquarters and suitable for broiling or frying. Beefsteaks include club steaks.

beefsteak fungus or **beefsteak mushroom** or **beeftongue**, an edible fungus growing on dead trees and having a reddish cap.

beef Stroganoff [for Count Paul *Stroganoff*, 19th-century Russian diplomat], thinly sliced beef fillet sautéed in a sour-cream sauce with mushrooms (and often with onions).

beef tea, a broth made by boiling pieces of lean beef. Compare **bouillon**.

beef tongue, see **beefsteak fungus**.

beef Wellington, a fillet of beef covered with pâté de foie gras and baked in a casing of pastry.

beet, *1.* a certain plant with large thick leaves (used when young as greens) and with a thickened fleshy root; *2.* (also called *beetroot)* the enlarged, dark red root of this plant eaten as a vegetable. The beet root is also a source of sugar. Compare **chard**, **sugar beet**. Beets can be eaten buttered, glazed, pickled, in salads; and beet greens likewise in salads. Beet dishes include borsch, Harvard beets.

beetroot, see **beet** (sense 2).

beet sugar, sugar made from the crystallized juice of beet roots.

beggar's chicken, a Chinese dish of marinated and stuffed chicken wrapped in lotus leaves, roasted in a shell of clay.

begti or **bekti** [Bengali] or **giant perch**, a large fish of Asia and the Pacific area.

beignet [French], another name for **fritter**.

bel [Hindi], the fruit (also called *Bengal quince)* of a certain thorny tree of India (likewise called *bel).*

Belgium. The following are among representative dishes and products of Belgium: mussels with fried potatoes *(moules frites)*, kidney stew *(choesels)*, waterzooi, witloof (endive; in Belgian French, *chicon)*, asparagus (especially in May and June), smoked ham, sausages (including blood sausage [*boudin*]), fish (for instance, filet of sole, eels [e.g., in green sauce], trout [e.g., en papillote]), shellfish (e.g., crayfish, lobster, shrimp), Flemish-style braised beef *(carbonnade* [or *carbonade] flamande)*, goose, pastries.

bell pepper, another name for the **sweet pepper** (a certain bell-shaped fruit of a pepper plant). It is red when ripe but is eaten green, too.

bel paese [from Italian *belpaese* "beautiful country"], a mild, soft, cheese of Italian origin. It is a good cheese for cooking and is used in many dishes in which mozzarella can also be used (e.g., fried eggs with cheese [*uova al tegame al formaggio*]).

beluga [from Russian *byeluga*, from *byelyy* "white" + *-uga*, augmentative suffix], *1.* a large white sturgeon (also called *beluga sturgeon)* of the Black sea, the Caspian sea, and their tributaries, whose roe is used for caviar and whose swim bladder is used to make *isinglass* 2. caviar processed from beluga roe.

benne or **bene** [West African], another name for **sesame** (senses 1 and 2).

benne cake, a small cake of benne seeds boiled with sugar.

ben or **behen** [from Arabic *ban*], the seed of a certain African and southeastern Asian tree, used to make ben oil.

ben oil or **behen oil**, an oil obtained from ben, used in cooking.

Bercy, or **Bercy sauce** [from French *Bercy*, quarter of Paris, France, on the right bank of the Seine], velouté sauce (flour, batter, stock) with minced shallots, parsley, lemon juice, and white wine (dry or vermouth). It can be served on fish.

bergamot, any of several mints used as seasoning.

Bermuda. The following are among representative dishes and products of Bermuda: lobster, cassava, sweet potatoes, fish chowder, baked onions.

Bermuda chub, a gray fish striped with blue or yellow of Bermuda and southern Florida.

Bermuda lobster, a large spiny lobster.

Bermuda onion, a large, mild-flavored, yellow-skinned variety of onion, that probably originated in Italy or the Canary Islands.

berrugate [probably from Spanish *verruga* "wart"], a tripletail fish found along the Pacific coast of Panama and of certain countries of Central America.

berry or **bacca**, *1.* any of various usually edible fruits of small size (such as the blackberry, checkerberry, raspberry, rose hip, strawberry); *2.* a simple pulpy fruit (such as the banana, blueberry, cranberry, currant, gooseberry, grape, tomato); *3.* any of various seeds or dried kernels, such as that of the coffee plant. Berries (senses 1 and 2) are used for pies, chiffon pies, muffins.

berry sugar or **castor sugar**, granulated sugar.

betel or **betel pepper** [from Portuguese *bétele, bétel*, from a Dravidian word], a climbing Asiatic pepper whose dried leaves are chewed with the betel nut (together with lime made from burnt coral).

betel nut [called *betel* from its being chewed with betel leaves] or **areca nut** or **Indian nut** or **supari** or **bonga** or **bunga**, the seed of the fruit of the betel palm used in eastern Asia for chewing (with betel leaves and lime).

betel palm or **areca** or **areca palm**, a tropical southeast Asia palm tree having egg-shaped nuts; see **betel** and **betel nut**.

Betty [from *brown Betty*], a baked dessert made of alternate layers of fruit (e.g., cranberries) and buttered crumbs, with sugar and spices. Compare **brown Betty** (which is made with molasses or brown sugar).

beurre, French for **butter**. See **au beurre**. In French, such phrases as *beurre d'anchois, beurre d'écrevisse* stand for a paste made from the flesh of these animals (anchovy, crayfish) squashed in butter.

beurre blanc [French "white butter"], a sauce of softened butter, with lemon juice, vinegar, or wine cooked down and flavored with herbs (and often stock). Sea urchins may be served au beurre blanc.

beurre noir [French "black butter"], a sauce made from butter browned and often seasoned with vinegar and parsley.

beverage, any of various liquid refreshments other than water (as fruit juice, fruit drinks and punches, lemonade, limeade, orangeade, cocoa and chocolate, coffee, tea, milk, milk shake, eggnog, ice cream soda).

bialy [Yiddish, short for *bialystoker*, "of Bialystok," from *Bialystok*, city in northeastern Poland], a flat roll that has a depressed center and is ususaly covered with onion flakes.

Bibb lettuce [for *Bibb*, 19th-century grower], a kind of lettuce of a variety that has a small head and tender dark-green leaves.

bichir, a large fish of the upper Nile river.

biffin, a baked apple pressed into a flat, round cake.

Bigarreau cherry or **Bigarreau** [French, from *bigarrer* "to variegate"], any of several varieties of sweet cherry with rather firm, often light-colored flesh (red and white).

bigeye, any of several marine fishes (catalufas) of tropical seas, having large eyes and reddish scales.

bigeye bass or **big-eyed bass**, a small fish of the coast of California.

bigmouth buffalo, a certain large fish.

bilberry, the sweet blue or blackish berry of a certain plant (likewise called *bilberry*) similar to a blueberry.

bilimbi or **bilimbing**, the acid fruit of a certain eastern Asia evergreen tree (likewise called *bilimbi*, or *cucumber tree*, and that resembles the carambola) that is used for preserves or pickles.

billi-bi or **billy-bi**, a soup consisting of mussel stock, white wine, and cream.

bill of fare, see **menu** (sense 1).

biltong [Afrikaans "buttock tongue"], narrow strips of meat, dried in the sun; especially jerked beef, venison, or ostrich.

bind (**to**), to unite into a whole, give a thickened consistency.

binny, a large fish of the Nile river.

bird, *1.* any member of a class of vertebrate animals distinguished by having feathers and the forelimbs modified to form wings. Birds that are eaten (baked, pan-broiled, stewed) include beccafico, chicken, grouse, ostrich, pheasant, partridge, turkey; *2.* a thin piece of meat rolled up with stuffing and skewered, browned, and braised. Compare **veal bird**.

bird pepper or **bush pepper**, the small, narrow, red, very pungent fruit of a certain pepper plant likewise called *bird pepper*.

bird's nest, or **edible bird's nest**, the nest of various small swifts of southern Asia, made chiefly of the gelatin-like saliva of the birds (thickened by evaporation) and used in making soup (see **bird's nest soup**).

bird's nest soup [translation of Chinese *yàn wó táng*, "swift nest soup"], a soup of Chinese origin made from a gelatinous coating on the nests of certain small swifts. These cave-nesting swifts build their nests using a glutinous secretion from their salivary glands. The nests are cooked in chicken stock to make the soup. Compare **bird's nest**, **salangane**.

biryani or **biriani** [probably from Persian *biryan* "roasted"], a spiced dish of meat, fish, or vegetables (often brown lentils) cooked with rice flavored with saffron or turmeric (Bangladesh, India, Pakistan).

biscotto [Italian "twice cooked" (it was formerly placed in the oven a second time, to remove any moisture); compare **biscuit**], a crisp cookie or biscuit of Italian origin, usually flavored with anise.

biscuit [French "twice cooked" (it was formerly placed in the oven a second time, to remove any moisture); compare **biscotto**], *1.* a small cake of shortened bread (from dough that has been rolled and cut or dropped) leavened with baking powder or soda; many biscuits (sense 1) are made with flour, sugar, shortening, and may be flavored with coconut, anise, vanilla, or cheese. Compare **galette**; *2.* a thin, crisp cracker of unleavened bread; *3.* any of certain hard or crisp, dry, baked products (cracker; cookie).

biscuit tortoni, see **tortoni**.

biskop [Afrikaans "bishop"], either of two large marine fishes of southern Africa. Compare **black biskop**, **white biskop**.

bismarck, a raised doughnut shaped like a ball, fried, with filling usually of jelly.

Bismarck herring [translation of German *Bismarckhering*, for the German 19th-century prince Otto von *Bismarck*], filleted herring marinated in vinegar and spices, served with raw onion and lemon.

bisnaga or **biznaga** [from Mexican Spanish *biznaga*, alteration of *vitznauac* (by confusion with Spanish *biznaga* "parsnip"), from Nahuatl *huitznahuac*,"thorn-surrounded"] or **visnaga**, any of several thorny cacti of Mexico and the southwestern United States. It is eaten candied in Mexico (minus the thorns, of course).

bisque [French, perhaps from *Biscaye* (province of northern Spain on the Bay of Biscay) (Spanish *Vizcaya*)], *1.* a thick cream soup made from crayfish or other shellfish (clam, crab, lobster, oyster, shrimp), fish, or game (with milk and seasonings); *2.* a creamed soup of pureed vegetables (usually tomatoes with milk and seasonings); *3.* ice cream containing crushed nuts or macaroons.

bitter, of one of the four basic taste sensations; the others are salty, sour, and sweet.

bitter cassava, a variety of cassava used to make the flavoring cassareep.

bitter chocolate, another name for ¹**chocolate** (sense 1).

bitter cress or **land cress**, any of certain plants having edible leaves.

bitter gourd, a certain edible gourd of Australia and Asia.

bitter herb, a horseradish salad eaten by Jews during the Seder of Passover. Compare **maror**.

bitter orange, another name for the **sour orange**.

bitterroot, the starchy, edible root of a certain plant (likewise called *bitterroot*) of western North America (Rocky Mountains).

bitters, see **angostura bitters**.

bittersweet, bitter and sweet at the same time; bitter chocolate, for instance, is one that contains little sugar.

bitty cream, bacteria-curdled cream.

biznaga, see **bisnaga**.

black abalone, a dark-shelled abalone.

black angelfish, a dark-colored angelfish of the western Atlantic Ocean.

black bean, any of several black-seeded beans (e.g., a black kidney bean used in Latin American cooking, and a black soybean used in Oriental cooking).

blackberry, any of various usually black, glossy, edible berries of certain plants (brambles, likewise called *blackberries)*, that are usually larger than the related raspberries. Dishes using blackberries include pies, cobblers.

black biskop, a large, dark biskop (fish).

black-bordered oyster, an oyster of northern Australia with a bluish black shell.

black bread or **schwartzbrot** [German], a dark-colored, coarse bread, usually of rye flour; especially a sour rye bread of central and northern Europe.

black bream or **luderick**, any of several Australian and African fishes.

blackcap or **blackcap raspberry**, other names for the **black raspberry**.

black cherry, another name for the **sweet cherry**.

black cinnamon, another name for the bayberry (see **bay leaf**).

black cod, another name for the **sablefish**.

black crab or **mountain crab**, a certain crab of southern Florida and the West Indies.

black crappie or **speckled perch** or **strawberry perch**, a sunfish of North America having dark, mottled coloring on a silvery ground.

black currant, the black fruit of a European bush (likewise called *black currant*, and also **cassis**).

black-eyed pea, the seed of the cowpea plant (West Indies) that, despite the second part of its name, is more nearly related to the bean than to the pea.

blackfin, a whitefish of the Great Lakes.

blackfish or **luderick**, any of various dark-colored fishes.

Black Forest cake [from *Black Forest*, region in southwestern Germany (German *Schwarzwald)*], a chocolate layer-cake with cherries.

black ginger, or **coated ginger**, the rootstock of ginger dried and unscraped; distinguished from white ginger (which is scraped).

black grouper or **bonaci**, a large, dark grouper of the warmer waters of the Atlantic.

black guava, the black fruit of a certain tree (likewise called *black guava)* of Guyana and Jamaica.

black heart, a certain sweet cherry (a heart cherry) having a dark flesh and skin.

black hickory, another name for the **black walnut**.

black huckleberry, the shining black fruit of a certain shrub (likewise called *black huckleberry).*

black mustard or **brown mustard** [so called from the dark-colored seeds] or **red mustard**, a certain plant having pungent seeds that ground to a powder are the principal source of table mustard (compare **white mustard**).

black pepper or **pepper**, a pungent condiment (a spice) consisting of the fruit of a certain plant (likewise called *black pepper)* of eastern Asia, ground with the black husk still on (compare ¹**pepper** [sense 1]).

black raspberry, the fruit of a certain shrub (likewise called *black raspberry*, and also *blackcap).*

black rockfish, a certain dark rockfish.

black ruff, another name for certain **blackfish**.

black salmon, any of various dark-colored salmons.

black salsify or **scorzonera** or **vegetable oyster**, a certain plant whose root (called *scorzonera*) and greens are eaten. The root is black on the outside.

black sapote [Mexican Spanish *zapote negro*], a dark-fleshed Mexican persimmon (fruit). The tree is likewise called *black sapote*.

black snapper or **schoolmaster**, a certain dark-colored snapper (fish).

blacktail, the name of both a young salmon trout and a dassie (fish).

black-tailed shrimp, a certain dark-colored shrimp of western North American coasts.

black tamarind, another name for the **velvet tamarind** (tree).

black tea, tea that is dark due to the leaf's being fully fermented or oxidized before drying. Compare **green tea** (that is not fermented), **oolong** (that is partially fermented). In Chinese, black tea is called "red tea."

blackthorn, a certain tree or shrub (also called **sloe**) that bears small purplish or blue black fruits called sloes that are used for preserves.

black walnut or **black hickory**, the edible nut of a tree (likewise called *black walnut*) of eastern North America.

bladder kelp, any of various brown algae with prominent floats (sacs buoying up their bodies).

blanch (to) [from French *blanchir* "to whiten," from *blanche* "white (feminine)"], *1.* to whiten (e.g., celery) by covering (earthing, boarding, wrapping) to cut off light; *2.* to loosen the skin (e.g., of almonds before they are roasted and salted, or of peaches before canning) or to whiten (e.g., kidney, brains, sweetbreads, before their final preparation) by scalding in boiling water or steam.

blancmange [French *blanc-manger*, "white food"], a flavored (e.g., with cocoa) and sweetened milk pudding, thickened with cornstarch or other gelatinous or starchy ingredients, and shaped in a mold. Almonds are often added.

blanquette [French, from Provencal *blanqueto*, from *blanc* "white"], a stew of light meat (e.g., veal or breast of chicken) or seafood (e.g., lobster) in a white sauce.

blanquillo [Spanish "the little white one"; (in Mexican Spanish, "egg"), diminutive of *blanco* "white"], a certain marine fish.

blend (to), to mix thoroughly, combine (e.g., flour with broth to thicken gravy).

bleu (French "blue"), French for "rare" (e.g., French *bifteck bleu* = "rare steak"). See also **au bleu** and **bleu cheese**.

bleu cheese [from French *bleu* "blue"], another name for **blue cheese**. In French, when *bleu* refers to a cheese, the adjective may become a noun (e.g., *bleu de Bresse, bleu d'Auvergne*).

blewits [probably from *blue*], an edible agaric that is bluish (actually, lilac) when young.

blin (plural *blini*) [Russian "pancake"], a small, thin, often buckwheat, pancake, usually served with caviar or filled with sour cream and folded. Compare **blintze**.

blintze or **blintz** [from Yiddish *blintse*, from Russian *blinets*, diminutive

black salmon
———————
blintze

31

of *blin* "pancake"], a thin, usually wheat-flour, rolled pancake with a filling usually of cream cheese (also of cottage cheese, fruit, or seasoned mashed potatoes) and often served with sour cream. It is sautéed or baked. Compare **blin**.

blood orange or **Malta orange**, a variety of orange with red pulp.

blood sausage or **blood pudding** or **boudin**, sausage containing a large proportion of blood (with pork fat and seasonings) so that it is very dark.

BLT, a sandwich with bacon, lettuce, and tomato.

blueback salmon, a salmon of a species that includes the sockeye or red salmon.

blueberry, the sweet juicy blue, purplish, or blackish berry of certain shrubs likewise called *blueberries*. Blueberries are used in pies, buckles, muffins, pancakes, waffles, teacakes.

blueberry ash or **blueberry tree** or **whitebark**, any of several Australian trees that bear an edible **drupe**.

blue cat or **blue catfish**, a large, bluish catfish of the Mississippi valley.

blue cheese [translation of French *fromage bleu*] or **bleu cheese**, a semi-soft cheese usually made of cow's milk and characterized by veining of greenish blue mold.

blue cod, a fish of the Pacific coast of North America.

blue crab, any of various, largely blue, crabs of the Atlantic and Gulf coasts of the United States; they provide the soft-shell crabs. Also a crab of Australia.

blue fig, another name for **Brisbane quandong**.

bluefin or **bluefin tuna** or **leaping tuna**, a certain very large tuna.

bluefish, any of various food fishes that are predominantly blue.

bluegill or **bluegill bream** or **coppernosed bream** or **coppernosed sunfish**, a sunfish of North American lakes and streams; it is a ¹**panfish**.

blue huckleberry, another name for the **dangleberry** (a sweet fruit).

blue parrot fish, either of two Australian fishes.

blue plum, a certain Australian tree having an edible fruit like a plum.

blue runner or **yellow mackerel**, a fish of the western Atlantic, that is bluish green above (and yellow below).

Blue Vinny, or **Dorset**, a white cheese made of cow's milk, marked with blue veins.

blusher or **blushing mushroom**, an edible mushroom that is yellowish but turns red when touched.

boar, a wild **hog**.

bobotie [Afrikaans], a dish of minced meat with curry and condiments, of southern African origin.

bocon [from Spanish *bocón*, "big-mouthed," augmentative of *boca* "mouth"], any of several Caribbean anchovies having very large mouths and eyes.

boeuf bourguignon, French for **beef bourguignon**.

boil (**to**), to generate bubbles in a liquid by the application of heat, to cook by boiling. Under standard atmospheric conditions (at sea level, 760 millimeters of mercury), water boils at the temperature of 100°C (212°F); at high altitudes the boiling point is appreciably lower (i.e., a liquid boils at lower temperatures) and food takes longer to cook. Boiling water is used in making beverages as tea and coffee, and in cooking vegetables, cereals, and pasta; it is used in the under part of double boilers and in pressure cookers; most top-of-the-stove cooking is done at boiling point or a few degrees below. Five words of similar meaning: *stew* = "cook slowly in a little liquid, preferably at 85°C (185°F) on the stove or in the oven (with the addition of spices or flavorings)"; *simmer* = "heating to or near the boiling point or at 85°C (185°F; agitated state)" (this is the best temperature for "boiled" meat and eggs; stock is made by cooking meat, poultry, fish, vegetables, and seasonings in water at this temperature); *seethe* = "steady boiling at high temperature (even more agitated state)"; *parboil* = "boiling partly or cooking partially in water or (for shellfish) in their own juices"; *scald* = "heating just below boiling point, usually in the top of a double boiler (milk is scalded at 91°C [196°F])."

boiled dinner or **New England boiled dinner**, a dinner of boiled meat (usually, corned beef or ham) prepared and served with boiled vegetables (e.g., potatoes, carrots, onions, turnips, cabbage).

bok choy, another name for **Chinese cabbage**.

boldo [American Spanish, from Araucan *boldu*], a Chilean evergreen shrub with sweet fruit.

Bolivia. The following are among representative dishes and products of Bolivia: small meat pies with raisins and olives (Spanish *salteñas)*, potato, quinoa, chicken and vegetable soup *(sajta)*, charqui, chuño, Indian corn, sweet potatoes, heart of palm *(palmito)*, pork fricassee, corn kernels *(mote)*, lake fish, cavy (guinea pig), peanut soup, peanut sauces; crisp, fried pork *(chicharrón);* cornmeal steamed with raisins and nuts *(humintas)*.

bollito misto [Italian "mixed stew"], a dish of Piedmontese origin, of mixed meats (e.g., beef, a calf's head and calves' feet, pork sausage, and a capon; or beef, lamb, veal, and sausage) boiled (all in the same pot) with vegetables (e.g., haricot beans, potatoes, cabbage, a tomato sauce).

bollo [American Spanish "fritter," from Spanish "bun, muffin"], a seasoned fritter of black-eyed-pea flour.

bologna [from *Bologna sausage*, from *Bologna*, city of northern Italy] or **Bologna sausage**, *1.* a large, seasoned, smoked sausage made of mixed meats (e.g., beef, veal, and pork) chopped fine; *2.* a sausage (e.g., of turkey) made to resemble the bologna of mixed meats.

Bolognese sauce [Italian "of Bologna," from *Bologna*, city of northern Italy], a meat sauce with milk added. In Italian it is also called *ragù* [from French *ragoût*; compare **ragout**]. It is used, for instance, on spaghetti.

bolti or **bulti** [from Arabic *bulti*], a fish (scientific name: *Tilapia nilotica)* of the Nile and other rivers of Africa and of certain rivers of Asia Minor.

Bombay duck, the dried flesh of a small marine fish (likewise called *Bombay duck)* of India, eaten with curry, or used as a relish.

bombe [French "bomb," because of its shape], a round or melon-shaped frozen dessert, consisting of frozen mixtures (two or more layers of ice cream of different flavors), prepared in a mold.

bon, another name for the **broad bean** or the **kidney bean**.

bonaci, another name for the **black grouper**.

bonbon [French *bon* "good"], a piece of candy, and specifically one having a center of fondant, fruit, or nuts, and coated with chocolate or fondant. In French, a *bonbon* is any small candy.

bone (**to**), to remove the bones from (e.g., fish, chicken, duck).

bonefish or **banana fish** or **o'io**, any of several slender, silvery, marine fishes of warm waters.

bone marrow, see **marrow** (sense 1).

boner, a low-grade beef animal; its bones are removed to prepare canned meats or sausage.

bonga or **bunga** [from Tagalog *bunga*], another name for the **betel nut** (Philippines).

bonito [Spanish "beautiful, pretty"], any of various marine fishes resembling the mackerel and the tuna.

bonito shark, another name for **mako**.

bonne femme [French "(in the manner of) a good housewife"], prepared in home-style cooking. For instance, *filet de* [or *of*] *sole bonne femme* is baked with melted butter, lemon juice, and chopped onion.

bonnet pepper, another name for the **pimiento**.

borage [from French *bourrache*], a plant whose young leaves are used as a salad herb.

Bordelaise or **Bordelaise sauce** or **sauce bordelaise** [French "with Bordeaux (feminine)," from *Bordeaux* "a wine from the area of Bordeaux," from *Bordeaux*, city of southwestern France], a brown sauce flavored with Bordeaux wine, often prepared with garlic, chopped mushrooms, and onion, and usually employed on beef.

borecole [from Dutch *boerenkool*, "peasant's cabbage"], another name for **kale** (sense 1).

Borneo tallow, a fat obtained from nuts of certain Indonesian trees and used as a substitute for cocoa butter in the manufacture of chocolate candy.

borsch or **borshch** [from Russian *borshch*, "cow parsnip" (the original base of the soup)], a beet soup of eastern European origin, served hot or cold, often with sour cream or sour milk. It is also made with a variety of vegetables (e.g., carrots, onions, celery).

Boston baked beans, beans (e.g., navy beans or pea beans) seasoned with molasses and salt pork, baked in an earthen pot.

Boston brown bread, another name for **brown bread** (sense 2).

Boston butt, the upper, lean, portion of a pork shoulder.

Boston cracker, a round, thick, unsalted cracker.

Boston cream pie, a round cake that is split in half horizontally (i.e., it has two layers) and then filled with a custard or cream filling, and often frosted with chocolate.

Boston lettuce, any of several lettuces forming a rounded head and having yellow-green leaves.

boucan, see **buccan**.

bouchée [French "mouthful," from *bouche* "mouth"], a small patty or cream-puff shell filled with creamed meat (usually white) or fish; it is similar to a vol-au-vent and in French is often called *bouchée à la reine* ("mouthful, queen style"). In French, the word is also used for a piece of chocolate with a filling.

boudin [French], *1.* another name for **blood sausage**; *2.* forcemeat (usually white meat from chicken or turkey) shaped like a sausage and served as an entree (in French, this second sense is also called *boudin blanc*).

bouillabaisse [French, from Provençal *bouiabaisso*, "boil (and) settle (both verbs are in the imperative)," from *boui* "boil" + *abaisso* "lower, settle"], a fish stew or chowder of French origin (particularly associated with Marseilles) made of several kinds of fish (e.g., white fish, red fish, mullet, whiting, sole) and shellfish (e.g., shrimp, crab, lobster meat, oysters, mussels), seasoned with onions, garlic, saffron, tomatoes, herbs, and olive oil. It is often served in its broth, and with bread slices.

bouillon [French, from *bouillir* "to boil"], a broth made typically by simmering lean beef in water with seasonings; it is served as a soup. Bouillon can also be made from clams (in the shell), chicken, vegetables (e.g., tomatoes), and it can be jellied, too. When a distinction is made between a bouillon and a consommé the main difference is that the meat for a consommé is browned before simmering. Compare **stock**.

bouillon cube, a small cube of evaporated stock for making bouillon.

boulangère [French, "(the) baker's (way)," from *boulangère* "baker (feminine)" (the masculine is *boulanger*)], cooked in a casserole with sliced onions.

boulder raspberry, the dark purple fruit of a shrub of the Rocky mountains.

bouquet garni [French "garnished bouquet"], an herb mixture (e.g., thyme, bay leaf, parsley, and marjoram) that is either tied together or enclosed in a porous container (e.g., cheesecloth, muslin bag) and is cooked with a dish (e.g., soup, stew, roast) but removed before serving. Compare **fines herbes**.

bouquetière [French "the flower seller's (way)," from *bouquetière* "flower seller (feminine)," from *bouquet* "bouquet, flower bunch"], garnished with vegetables (e.g., pork, beef, roast chicken, rack of lamb bouquetière).

bourguignonne [French "in the Burgundy (way)," from *bourguignonne* "of Burgundy, Burgundian (feminine)," from *Bourgogne* "Burgundy (region in eastern France)"], prepared or served (e.g., sweetbreads, brains, chicken, sautéed beef) in the manner of Burgundy (e.g., prepared with a sauce made with red Burgundy wine and usually bacon, mushrooms, and braised onions). Snails so prepared are called in French *escargots à la bourguignonne*. Compare **beef bourguignon, coq au vin**.

bourride [from Provençal *bourrido*, *boulido*, "something boiled"], a fish stew of Provençal origin similar to bouillabaisse that is usually thickened with egg yolks and flavored with garlic (often one pureed clove

boysenberry

Brazilian sassafras

per person), i.e., it is a kind of bouillabaisse with aioli added. In the South of France, they also speak of *poulet en bourride*, i.e. a bouillabaisse of chicken, with aioli sauce.

boysenberry [for Rudolph *Boysen*, 20th-century horticulturist who developed the plant], the large, wine-red fruit (with a flavor like a raspberry) of a certain prickly bramble (likewise called *boysenberry*). It is used in pies and cobblers.

braciola [Italian, from *brace* "live coal"], a thin slice of meat (e.g., veal) that is often wrapped around a filling of meat (e.g., ham), chopped vegetables (parsley, pine nuts, raisins), and seasonings and sometimes cooked in wine. In Italian, the word stands for any slice of beef or pork cooked on live coals or in a frying pan, while the stuffed kind is called *bracioletta* (or *braciolina*) *ripiena*.

brain, a variety meat often served breaded.

[1]**braise (to)** [from French *braiser* "to braise," from *braise* "live coals, hot charcoal"], to cook (meat [e.g., beef], vegetables [e.g., lettuce, carrots], squab, a fish) by browning in fat, then simmering in a small quantity of liquid (usually water) in a tightly covered pot on top of the stove or in the oven. Meat cooked in this way is often called a pot roast. Compare [2]**roast**.

[2]**braise**, an item of braised food.

bramble, any of certain prickly plants or shrubs of the rose family, especially the blackberry or the raspberry, and its fruit.

bran, the broken coat of the seed of cereals, such as wheat, rye, and oats, separated from the flour.

brandade [French, from Provençal *brandado* "shaken," from *brandar* "to shake, agitate"], a puree of salt cod, prepared the Provençale way, with olive oil and garlic, and sometimes tomatoes.

bratwurst [German, Old High German "meat" + "sausage"], a sausage made with finely chopped, seasoned fresh pork, and usually fried.

braunschweiger or **Braunschweiger** [German "Brunswick (sausage)," from *Braunschweig* "Brunswick (region and city in Germany, west of Berlin)"], a smoked liver sausage. Some cooks combine it with canned tomato soup, then spread the mixture on hot toast.

brawn, a pickled or preserved preparation made from chopped, cooked, and molded meat of pig's head, feet, legs, and sometimes tongue.

Brazil. The following are among representative dishes and products of Brazil: feijoada, churrasco, shrimp (Portuguese *camarão*, plural *camarões*) and other seafood, *vatapá* (typical of Salvador [formerly *Bahia*]; it consists of fish or shrimp cooked in palm oil [*azeite-de-dendê*] and coconut milk [*leite de côco*]), sausages *(linguiças)*, coconut *(côco)*, papaya *(mamão)*, mango *(manga)*, pineapple *(abacaxi)*, heart of palm *(palmito)*, avocado *(abacate)*, cheese with guava paste *(queijo com goiabada)*, pumpkin sweet *(doce de abóbora)*. Beverage: coffee *(cafezinho* "small coffee").

Brazilian arrowroot, a starch obtained from the bitter cassava. Compare **tapioca**.

Brazilian sassafras, a South American tree whose seed is the **pichurim bean** (a flavoring agent).

Brazilian shrimp or **brown shrimp** or **red shrimp** or **redtail**, a large, reddish brown shrimp of the Gulf of Mexico.

Brazilian tea or **Brazil tea**, another name for **maté** (beverage, and plant).

Brazilian teal, a wild duck of South American tropical forests.

Brazil nut or **cream nut** or **Para nut**, the roughly triangular, brown-shelled, white-fleshed nut of a certain tree (called *Brazil-nut tree* or *Brazil nut,* too) of tropical South America.

¹**bread**, or **pain** (French) or **pan** (Spanish) or **pane** (Italian), a staple food made from flour or meal mixed with a liquid, usually leavened, kneaded, and baked. Much bread is made from enriched white wheat flour with salt, sugar, fat, and water or milk; a part of the wheat flour may be replaced by whole-wheat flour, rye flour, soybean flour, corn meal, rolled oats, bran, and other cereals, or cooked potato. Sometimes some of the following are added: raisins, prunes, nuts, eggs, cheese, cinnamon or other spices, cardamom and caraway seeds. Stale bread with fat, seasoning and water or other liquid is used for stuffing veal, lamb, poultry, and fish; other ingredients (e.g., sausage meat, mushrooms, oysters) are often added to the stuffing. Yeast breads include buns, challah, kolacky, kuchen, limpa, pumpernickel, ¹roll, streuselkuchen. Some are fried, like bismarck, cruller, fritter, raised doughnut; others are not fried, like English muffin, hot cross bun, Sally Lunn, stollen. Bread with yeast (obtained from wine) began some 5000 years ago (without yeast, in the Stone Age). The Romans installed water mills along rivers in the fourth century of the Christian era; the first windmill was built A.D. 833. Some other breads: anadama bread, bagel, baguette, baton, bialy, black bread, focaccia, French bread, grissino. See also **quick bread, bread crumbs, crouton**.

²**bread (to)**, to cover (e.g., a pork chop) with bread crumbs (with flour and egg), especially before cooking.

bread and butter, bread (usually sliced) spread with butter.

bread-and-butter pickle, a pickle relish of sliced onions and cucumbers.

bread crumbs, dry bread forced through a food chopper or grater. When mixed with melted fat, bread crumbs are called *buttered crumbs* and used as a coating on baked dishes. Au gratin dishes are covered with bread crumbs.

bread flour, a flour for bread dough, of a good quality of gluten. For bread, it is better than all-purpose flour or cake flour.

breadfruit or **rimas** or **cmansi** or **kamansi**, *1.* a round, starchy, usually seedless tropical fruit (especially of South Pacific islands) that has a greenish yellow rind and light yellow flesh when ripe, and is deemed to resemble fresh bread in texture and color when baked or roasted (it is not edible until cooked); in Seychelles Creole, it is called *friyapen* [from French *fruit à pain*]; see also **popoi**; *2.* an African tree that yields seeds used for making meal.

bread grain, cereals (e.g., wheat and rye) that yield flour from which bread can be made.

breadnut, the round, nutlike fruit of a tree (likewise called *breadnut)* of Central America and the West Indies, that is roasted and ground into a flour to produce a substitute for wheat flour.

bread pudding, a sweet dessert made with bread crumbs (or pieces of dry bread), milk and sugar, often eggs, with chocolate pieces or raisins or broken nuts (sometimes also dates) added.

breadroot or **prairie turnip**, the starchy root of a certain plant (likewise called *breadroot)* of the central North American plains.

bread sauce, a milk-and-butter sauce thickened with bread crumbs; onion and whole cloves are often added. It is usually served with small roasted wild birds or roast meat.

breadstick, a long, slender piece of bread dough baked until crisp, often served with soup. Compare **grissino**.

breadstuff, grain, flour, or meal used in the baking of bread.

bread wheat, wheat suitable for making bread.

breakfast food, anything eaten at the first meal of the day.

bream, any of several fishes.

breast, the fore part of the body of an animal (e.g., calf, lamb, fowl) dressed as meat.

breba [from Spanish *breva*], a fig of the first annual crop of fig trees that bear twice a year.

bredi [from Afrikaans *bredie*], a meat stew containing a vegetable (e.g., cabbage, spinach; southern Africa).

Bretonne sauce [French "sauce from Brittany"], a brown sauce with fried red onions.

brew (to), to prepare (e.g., tea) by infusion (steeping) in hot water.

brewis, *1.* a broth (regional); *2.* bread soaked in gravy, broth, or hot milk (regional).

brick cheese, a brick-shaped, sweet-curd, semisoft cheese.

brick sugar, another name for **cube sugar**.

brick tea, a small brick of tea leaves and stalks made in China. Compare **tablet tea**.

bridecake or **bride's cake**, other names for **wedding cake**.

Brie or **Brie cheese** [French, from *Brie*, district in northeastern France, where it was first made], a mold-ripened, cow-milk cheese; its rind is whitish, its interior pale yellow.

brill, a flatfish of European waters, related to the turbot.

brine, a salt solution (water with salt) used to preserve and pickle food.

brine shrimp, any of various small crustaceans that can exist in highly saline water.

brinjal or **brinjaul** [from Portuguese *brinjela, berinjela*], a name used in India and Africa for the eggplant.

brioche [French], a soft, light-textured, slightly sweetened roll or bun made from eggs, butter, flour, and yeast baked in muffin tins or cups. Its yeast dough is also used as a pastry wrap for such foods as fish (e.g., pike, then called in French *brioche de brochet)* or oysters.

Brisbane quandong, or **blue fig**, an Australian tree with edible fruit.

brisket, the chest of an animal (e.g., beef) with bones removed. It is often braised. When cured like pork bacon, it is called *beef bacon*.

brisling [Norwegian], another name for the **sprat** (a small herring).

brittle, a hard candy made by boiling sugar to the point of caramelization, adding nuts (e.g., peanuts), and cooling in thin sheets.

broad bean or **fava bean** or **faba** or **field bean** or **haba** or **bon** [French *fève*, Italian *fava*, Spanish *haba*], the large flattened seed (in long, edible pods) of a certain plant likewise called *broad bean.*

Broad-Breasted Bronze, a large strain of the **Bronze turkey**.

broccoli or **brocoli** [from Italian *broccoli*, plural of *broccolo* "cabbage or turnip sprout," diminutive of *brocco* "shoot, sprout; small nail"] or **heading broccoli** or **winter cauliflower**, the greenish flower head of a certain plant (likewise called *broccoli)* related to the cabbage and to the cauliflower, eaten as a vegetable before the green buds have opened.

broccoli rab, see **Italian turnip**.

brochette [French "skewer," diminutive of *broche* "spit; pointed tool"], *1.* a small spit, skewer; *2.* food (e.g., meat [liver, kidneys], fish, vegetables) broiled or roasted on a skewer.

¹**broil (to)** [from French *brûler* "to burn"], to cook by direct exposure to radiant heat, to grill (e.g., on a wire grill over live coals or under an electrically heated metal coil or under a gas flame); food is seared first on one side and then on the other, then cooked more slowly to the desired condition. Broiling is considered the best method for cooking tender cuts of meat (e.g., beefsteak) and slices of fish (e.g., buffalo fish, cod, gar, salmon, shad). Fowl, tomatoes, some fruits and sliced cooked vegetables may also be prepared in this way. Bread is toasted or browned by broiling. Compare **pan-broil**, ¹**grill**. Broiling can be called the oldest method of cooking, since it antedates the invention of stewpots and turning spits (roasting). The high heat quickly sears the outer surface and makes a seal which holds the juices inside; rubbing with some olive oil helps recapture the old-fashioned, slightly burned taste.

²**broil**, something broiled, a ²**grill**.

broiler, a young chicken (fit for broiling).

Bronze, or **Bronze turkey**, a large domestic turkey.

bronze bream, a fish of southern Africa that is bronzy above.

brook trout or **speckled trout**, a speckled char (fish) of eastern North America.

brose, a dish made by pouring some boiling liquid (e.g., water or beef stock) on meal (e.g., oatmeal) and stirring it (Scotland).

brötchen [German, diminutive of *Brot* "bread"], a ¹**roll** (baked yeast dough).

broth, *1.* stock, the water in which meat, fish, vegetables, or cereal grains have been cooked; compare **beef tea**, **bouillon**; *2.* a thin, clear soup based on stock, to which rice, barley, meat, or vegetables can be added; compare **consommé**. Meat broth is made from beef, lamb, or chicken cut in small pieces; cooking is started in cold water and completed by simmering.

brown (to), to cook (e.g., flour, meat) until of the color brown, by scorching slightly.

brown Betty [from *Betty*, pet form of *Elizabeth*], a baked pudding made of alternate layers of sliced or chopped apples and bread crumbs, with raisins, butter, and spices, usually sweetened with molasses or brown sugar. Compare **Betty**.

brown bread, *1.* bread made of whole wheat flour; *2.* or **Boston brown**

bread, a dark brown, steamed (in a tightly covered tin surrounded with boiling water) bread made usually of cornmeal, white or whole wheat flours, molasses, soda, and milk or water.

brownie, a small square or rectangle of moist chocolate cake often containing broken nuts.

brown mustard, another name for both **black mustard** and **Indian mustard**.

brown rice, rice grains removed from the hulls but not polished, so that they retain the germ and the yellowish outer layer containing the bran.

brown sauce or **espagnole sauce** or **sauce espagnole** or **Spanish sauce**, a foundation sauce made typically of stock thickened with flour browned in fat (the fat and flour are well browned before the liquid is added) with added seasonings; **Bordelaise** and **Provençale** are brown sauces (compare **a la mode**, sense 2).

brown shrimp, another name for the **Brazilian shrimp**.

brown stock, stock typically made from beef.

brown sugar, unrefined or partially refined sugar.

brown trout, a freshwater fish having yellow-brown sides speckled with various colors.

Brunswick stew [from *Brunswick* county, Virginia, where these stews originated], *1.* a stew of squirrel or rabbit meat and onions; *2.* a stew of two or more meats (e.g., chicken and squirrel) with vegetables (e.g., corn, okra, and tomatoes).

brush (to), to spread thinly, as with a brush or with a crumpled paper (e.g., to spread butter on loaves of bread after they are taken from the oven).

brush cherry or **rose apple**, the fruit of an Australian tree likewise called *brush cherry*.

Brussels sprout or **sprout** or **thousand-headed cabbage**, any of the small, green, budlike heads resembling small cabbages and borne on plants (likewise called *Brussels sprouts)* related to the cabbage and cauliflower.

bubble and squeak [so called from the sounds made in cooking the dish], a dish of British origin consisting of cabbage (or other greens) and potatoes fried together.

bucatini, another name for **perciatelli**.

¹**buccan** or **boucan (to)**, to expose meat in strips to fire and smoke upon a wooden frame or grid for roasting.

²**buccan** or **boucan**, *1.* a wooden frame or grid (first used by the Caribs of the West Indies) for roasting, smoking, or drying meat or fish over a fire; *2.* meat or fish smoked or roasted on such a frame.

buckie, a smoked alewife (fish).

buckle, a coffee cake baked with berries (e.g., blueberries) and a crumbly topping.

buckthorn, a certain tree of the sapodilla family.

buckwheat, *1.* the small triangular seeds of a certain plant, native to Asia, cracked or ground for flour or cereal; *2.* the flour itself.

buckwheat cake, a pancake made with buckwheat flour.

buckwheat honey, a dark honey produced from buckwheat, especially in the northeastern United States.

Buddha's-hand, another name for **fingered citron**.

buffalo, *1.* any of several oxen (e.g., the water buffalo, originally from India); *2.* the flesh of a buffalo (e.g., buffalo carpaccio with marinated mushrooms). See also **buffalo fish**.

buffalo berry, the scarlet berry of either of two shrubs of western North America, likewise called *buffalo berries*.

buffalo fish, or **buffalo**, any of several North American freshwater fishes of the Mississippi valley, having a humped back. It is a lean fish, and therefore best for boiling and steaming; it is also served as broiled steaks.

buffalo gourd [so called from its location in *buffalo* country] or **calabazilla** or **prairie gourd**, a plant of the gourd family, with seeds rich in an oil used in cooking.

buffet [French "sideboard, counter"], a meal at which guests serve themselves from various dishes (e.g., cold cuts, cheeses, pastry) displayed on tables or counters.

buisson [French "bush"], a fruit tree with a closely pruned head; in French, *buisson* also means a food (especially, crustaceans [e.g., crayfish]) arranged in the form of a pyramid.

bukayo or **bucayo** [Tagalog], a confection of grated coconut fried in brown sugar (Philippines).

Bulgaria. The following are among representative dishes and products of Bulgaria: kabob, cabbage or grape leaves stuffed with minced meat and rice (Bulgarian *sarmi)*, minced meat or sausages grilled on charcoal or roasted in an open fire *(kebabcheta)*, moussaka, chilled whipped-yogurt-and-cucumber soup *(tarator)*, other yogurt *(kisselo mliako)* dishes, meat and vegetable (especially green beans, tomatoes, eggplant, peppers, potatoes) stew *(gyuvech)*, mixed salad with grated white cheese *(shopska salata)*, watermelon, peaches, walnuts.

Bulgarian milk, a fermented milk (especially, yogurt).

bulgur [Turkish], parched (boiled, and then sundried) cracked wheat (Turkey).

bullamacow or **bullamacau**, canned beef (Pacific Islands).

bull grunter, a certain marine fish of the eastern coast of southern Africa.

bullhead, *1.* any of various freshwater catfishes of the United States; *2.* any of several large-headed fishes (e.g., the sculpin).

bullnose pepper, another name for the **sweet pepper**.

bullock's-heart or **bullock heart** [so called from its size and appearance], a tropical American fruit related to the soursop and sweetsop.

bun or **sweet roll**, any of a variety of sweet or plain small breads that are leavened with yeast or baking powder, especially a round roll. Buns are sometimes spiced. Compare **hot cross bun**. Buns include Bath buns.

buñuelo [Spanish], a flat, semisweet cake made mainly of flour, eggs, and milk (the dough must be well beaten), fried in deep fat and usually served with sugar and cinnamon or cane syrup; in Spanish, a *buñuelo de viento* is one that has a cream or other sweet filling.

bunya bunya, or simply **bunya**, an Australian evergreen tree bearing seeds that have the flavor of roasted chestnuts when ripe.

burbot, a freshwater fish of the cod family.

Burdekin plum [from *Burdekin* river, eastern Queensland, northeastern

Australia] or **sweet plum**, the fruit of a certain Australian tree (likewise called *Burdekin plum*).

Burdekin vine, an Australian vine bearing edible tubers.

burgao [American Spanish], a marine snail of the West Indies.

burger, *1.* a flat cake of ground or chopped meat fried or grilled; *2.* an informal name for a **hamburger** (sense 3, a sandwich containing a burger [sense 1]).

-burger [from the ending of *ham<u>burger</u>*], as an ending it means *1.* a patty of a specified kind of ground food (e.g., porkburger); *2.* a sandwich made from such a patty; *3.* a sandwich with a filling consisting of a hamburger (sense 2, a patty of ground beef) topped with a specified food (e.g., cheeseburger).

burgoo, *1.* a thick oatmeal gruel; *2.* hardtack and molasses cooked together; *3.* a thick, spicy soup or stew of several kinds of meat and vegetables.

buriti [Portuguese], another name for the **muriti palm**.

burnet [from French *brun* "brown," from the brownish-red flowers of the plant], *1.* any of several plants of the rose family, having cucumber-flavored leaves; *2.* the same as **salad burnet**.

burnet bloodwort, another name for the **salad burnet**.

Burnett salmon [from *Burnett* river, Queensland, northeastern Australia], the same as **barramunda**.

burnt almonds, roasted almonds.

buro [Tagalog], a dish of Philippine origin consisting of fish prepared with boiled rice and seasonings.

burrito [Mexican Spanish, "little donkey," diminutive of Spanish *burro* "donkey"], a Mexican dish consisting of a flour tortilla rolled or folded around a savory filling (e.g., of beef, chicken, refried beans, or cheese) and usually baked.

burro, Italian for **butter**; compare **al burro**.

bush bean, a plant that is a variety of the string bean (= **snap bean**, green bean).

bushberry, any of several berries (or fruits resembling berries) borne on bushes (e.g., currants, gooseberries, raspberries).

bush fruit, a small fruit (e.g., currant, gooseberry) growing on a bush.

bush marrow, a certain squash.

bush nut, another name for the **macadamia nut**.

bush pepper, another name for the **bird pepper**.

bush pumpkin or **bush squash**, a certain pumpkin.

bush tea, the leaves of a certain southern African plant (likewise called *bush tea*) used as a beverage.

butt, *1.* a lean upper cut of the pork shoulder; *2.* the large end of a beef loin.

butter [French *beurre*, Italian *burro*, Spanish *mantequilla*], *1.* a soft, yellowish or whitish emulsion of fat, air bubbles, and water droplets made by churning the cream obtained from milk and used in cooking or as a spread; *2.* a spread made from fruit (e.g., apple), nuts (e.g. ground and roasted peanuts), or other foods.

butter bean, another name for the **wax bean**.

butter cake, a cake made with shortening as distinguished from **sponge cake** (that contains no shortening); butter cakes include **gold cake**, **white cake**.

butter clam, either of two species of large clams of the Pacific coast of North America.

buttercream, *1.* a fondant (sense 1) to which butter is added before creaming (= beating); *2.* a cake filling or frosting made by creaming butter, cream, and sugar (a flavoring may be added).

buttercup squash, a turban squash; its flavor resembles that of sweet potatoes.

buttered crumbs, see **bread crumbs**.

butterfat, the natural fat of milk and chief constituent of butter.

butterfish [from its slippery mucous coating], a small marine fish of the North American Atlantic coast.

buttermilk, *1.* the liquid left after the butterfat has been removed from whole milk or cream by churning; *2.* milk soured by the addition of suitable bacteria.

butternut [so called from the oil in the nut] or **gray walnut** or **lemon walnut** or **white walnut**, the sweet-flavored, egg-shaped, oily nut of a certain tree of eastern North America. Compare **oil nut**.

butter oil, butterfat melted and clarified (freed from impurities). Compare **ghee**.

butter pear, another name for the **avocado**.

butter sauce, a seasoned sauce made of butter and water or broth, sometimes thickened with flour; it may be employed as a basis for the making of other sauces. It can be used on eggs, fish, pasta, vegetables. Compare **hollandaise sauce**, **maître d'hôtel**.

butterscotch or **toffee**, *1.* a hard candy made by boiling together brown sugar, butter, corn syrup, and water; *2.* a syrup, sauce, or flavoring made by melting butter and brown sugar (it can be used for pies and cookies, for ice cream and frozen desserts).

button cactus, a small cactus of northern Mexico and of Texas having edible fruits.

button onion, an onion picked before it has reached full size; it is used for pickling or as a garnish.

cabbage [from French *caboche* "head (informal); large-headed nail"], *1.* a plant having a short stem and a large head formed by tight green, reddish, or purplish leaves. May be served au gratin, buttered, creamed, scalloped, with Hollandaise or cheese sauce, in salads; *2.* a terminal bud of certain palm trees eaten as a vegetable.

cabbage lettuce, another name for **head lettuce**.

cabbage palm or **palmito** [Spanish], a tropical American palm tree (e.g., cabbage palmetto) whose terminal bud (see **cabbage**, sense 2) is eaten (when young) like cabbage as a vegetable.

cabbage tree or **cabbage palmetto**, any of several palms (one of which is also called *cabbage palmetto)* having a terminal bud that can be eaten as a vegetable.

cabezone or **cabezon** [from Spanish *cabezón* "large-headed," augmentative of *cabeza* "head"], a large, green-fleshed sculpin (fish) of North American Pacific coastal waters.

cabinet pudding [from *cabinet* "advisory council to head of state"], a pudding of bread or cake (e.g., diced sponge), with candied or dried fruit (e.g., currants, cherries, candied peel, candied kumquats), milk, and eggs, often molded and usually served hot with custard or fruit sauce.

cabrilla [Spanish "little goat"], any of various sea basses. Compare **red hind**.

cabrito [Spanish "young, unweaned kid," masculine diminutive of *cabra* (feminine) "goat"], the flesh of a young kid roasted or stewed. Roast kid *(cabrito al horno)* is a great favorite in northern Mexico, where it is served with wheat as well as corn tortillas, guacamole, black beans, and either a green-tomato and hot pepper sauce *(salsa verde)* or an uncooked tomato sauce *(salsa cruda).*

cacao [Spanish, from Nahuatl *cacahuatl* "cacao beans"] or **cacao bean** or **cocoa bean**, the dried and usually partly fermented fatty seeds (that are contained in seed pods) of a certain tropical American tree (called *cacao tree, chocolate tree,* or simply *cacao),* used chiefly in making cocoa (chocolate pulverized), chocolate, and cocoa butter. Compare ¹**chocolate, cocoa**.

cacao butter, another name for **cocoa butter**.

cacciatore or **cacciatora** [from Italian *(alla) cacciatora* "(in the manner of) hunters" (feminine because *maniera* "manner" is feminine), from *cacciatore* "hunter"], simmered or stewed with tomatoes, herbs (sage, rosemary, garlic) and other seasonings (vinegar, sometimes wine). Dishes prepared in this manner include rabbit, pasta, steak, chicken, lasagna.

caciocavallo, [Italian "horse cheese," perhaps originally called *cacio a cavallo* ("cheese on horseback") because of the way two of them are strung together as if astride a horse (or from a design of a horse?)] or **caciocavallo cheese**, a cow-milk (perhaps originally a mare-milk) hard cheese originating in southern Italy and made from matted curd worked by hand in hot water or whey (it is a pasta filata cheese) and often molded into the shape of a long pear, large squash, or a spindle.

caerphilly [from *Caerphilly*, urban district in Wales], a mild, friable cheese of Welsh origin.

Caesar salad [from *Caesar's*, restaurant in Tijuana, northwestern Mexico, where it originated], a salad usually made with romaine, garlic, fillets of anchovy, and croutons and dressed with olive oil, coddled egg (or a raw egg), lemon juice, and grated cheese (e.g., Parmesan). Salt, dry mustard, and black pepper are often added.

café au lait [French "coffee with milk"], coffee with hot milk in about equal parts poured into the cup at the same time.

café filtre [French], coffee (or a cup of coffee) made by passing hot water through ground coffee and a filter.

café noir [French "black coffee"], *1.* black coffee, coffee served without milk or cream; *2.* another name for **demitasse** (small cup of black coffee).

caffè espresso [Italian "pressed out coffee"], the original Italian name for **espresso**.

caffeine (from German *Kaffein*, from *Kaffee* "coffee"] or **theine**, a bitter alkaloid (an organic base) found in coffee, tea, and kola nuts.

caimito [Spanish, from Taino *caymito*], another name for the **star apple** (which is not the same fruit as the **starfruit** or **carambola**).

Cajun [from *Acadian* "of Acadia," from *Acadia*, an early name of Nova Scotia, southeastern Canada], prepared in a style of cooking originating among the Cajuns (Louisianians descended from French-speaking immigrants from Acadia), i.e. with spices. Dishes prepared in this manner include Cajun chicken breast, swordfish, grouper. Compare ²**creole**.

cake, *1.* a sweet baked food made from a dough or thick batter usually containing flour and sugar and often shortening, eggs, and a raising agent (e.g., baking powder) in loaf or rounded layer form; *2.* a flattened usually round mass of food (a patty) that is baked or fried (e.g., fish, potato, hashed meat); *3.* a flat, thin mass of dough or batter, baked or fried (e.g., a pancake). Cakes in the first sense include Lady Baltimore cake, angel cakes (these are egg-white cakes), Lord Baltimore cake (an egg-yolk cake or gold cake), and whole-egg cakes; Black Forest cakes, butter cakes, chiffon cakes, chocolate cakes, cream cakes, devil's food cakes, fruit cakes (in which raisins, currants, dates, or figs are added to the mixture), pound cakes, spice cakes, sponge cakes (including jelly rolls). In molasses cakes, molasses is used instead of, or in addition to, part of the sugar. The main decorations used on cakes are nuts, candies, and frosting forced through a pastry bag with a tube in the end; a variety of sweet mixtures (fillings) is used between layers of cake and in cream puffs. Icings are uncooked, frostings are cooked and made of egg white. Compare **gâteau**.

cakebread, *1*. bread made in flattened cakes; *2*. bread of the finer or more dainty quality of cake.

cake flour, flour ground to a refined texture (made from soft wheat).

cala, a rice cruller, a creole (especially from New Orleans) fried-cake made mainly of rice (with eggs, sugar, vanilla, nutmeg, flour).

calabash [from Spanish *calabaza* "gourd"], the rounded fruit of a certain tropical American tree likewise called *calabash*.

calabaza, Spanish for **gourd**.

calabazilla [Mexican Spanish *calabacilla* "small gourd," diminutive of *calabaza* "gourd", from Spanish *calabacilla* "squirting cucumber,"], another name for **buffalo gourd**.

calabrese [Italian "from Calabria (region of southern Italy)"], a variety of broccoli.

calamar, Spanish for **squid**.

calamari [Italian "squids," plural of *calamaro*, from Medieval Latin *calamarium* "pen-case," from Latin *calamus* "reed pen"; so called from the shape of the squid shell and from the inky substance that the squid secretes], squid used as food. In Italy, a *calamaretto* ("little squid") is a small squid, also used as food.

calamaro, Italian for **squid**.

calamary or **calamar**, another name for the **squid**, and especially for the giant squid.

calamondin [from Tagalog *kalamunding*] or **China orange**, the fruit, resembling a small orange, of a small citrus tree (likewise called *calamondin*) of the Philippines.

caldo verde [Portuguese "green broth"], a soup that is a puree of potatoes and greens, often with smoked sausages. In Portugal, caldo verde is made from finely shredded leaves of a large cabbage called *couve*.

calf, a young cow or bull not yet mature enough to be considered beef. Calf meat is usually called **veal**. Calf liver is a variety meat.

calf's-foot jelly or **sulze**, a gelatinous food made by boiling calves" feet.

calico bean [from *calico* "multicolored," from *calico* "cotton cloth with figured patterns"], another name for the **kidney bean**.

calico corn [from *calico* "multicolored," from *calico* "cotton cloth with figured patterns"], Indian corn having mottled kernels.

calico crab [from *calico* "multicolored," from *calico* "cotton cloth with figured patterns"], a certain brilliantly spotted crab.

calico salmon [from *calico* "multicolored," from *calico* "cotton cloth with figured patterns"], another name for **dog salmon**.

California black walnut, a certain tree with edible nuts.

California mussel, a certain mussel.

California orange, another name for the **navel orange**.

California pompano, a certain butterfish (a slippery fish) of the United States Pacific coast.

California sardine, a certain sardine of the United States Pacific coast.

California sea trout, a certain greenling (fish) of the United States Pacific coast.

calimyrna fig [from *California* + *Smyrna*], the Smyrna fig when grown in California.

calisson, in French, name of an almond-paste tea cake from Aix-en-Provence (city, southeastern France).

¹**callaloo** or **calalu** [from Spanish *calalú*], a tropical American plant whose leaves are used as greens, especially in the West Indies and in ²callaloo.

²**callaloo** or **calalu** [from Spanish *calalú*, plant (see ¹**callaloo**)], a soup or stew made with greens (e.g., callaloo or spinach), okra, and often crabmeat. Pumpkin, amaranth, purslane are sometimes added, as well as salt, vinegar, lard (West Indies).

callop, or **golden perch**, a certain fish of Australian inland waters.

calumpit, another name for **kalumpit**.

calzone [Italian, singular of *calzoni* "trousers, pants," from the shape of this turnover], a baked or fried turnover of pizza dough, usually filled with cheese and ham.

camachile or **huamuchil** or **guamuchil** [from American Spanish *guamúchil, huamúchil*, from Nahuatl *cuauh-mochitl*], a certain tropical American tree bearing an edible fruit.

camagon [from Spanish *camagón*, from Tagalog *kamagóng*] or **mabolo**, a certain tree of the Philippines that bears an edible fruit.

camansi or **kamansi** [from Tagalog *kamansi*], a name for the **breadfruit** (sense 1) in the Philippines.

camarón, Spanish for **shrimp**.

camas or **camass**, a certain plant of the lily family, of the western United States, with edible bulbs.

Cambodia. Rice, pork and poultry, peas, potatoes, sweet potatoes, are among the main foods of Cambodia.

cambric tea [from *cambric* "a thin white fabric" (from *Cambrai*, city of northern France), from the drink being thin and white], a drink for children, made of hot water, milk, sugar, and often a small amount of tea.

Camembert [French, from *Camembert*, town in Normandy, region of northwestern France, where it was first made] or **Camembert cheese**, a cow-milk, creamy, blue-mold-ripened French cheese with a thin grayish white rind.

camomile, variant of **chamomile**.

camote [from Nahuatl *camotli* "yam"], the Mexican Spanish name for **sweet potato**.

Canada. The following are among representative dishes and products of Canada: fish (e.g., salmon, cod, arctic char), shellfish (e.g., lobster, oysters), beef, bacon, cheese, potatoes, maple syrup. In the province of Quebec, also pea soup (French *soupe aux pois*), onion soup *(soupe à l'oignon)*, pork-and-beef pie *(tourtière)*, crêpes.

Canada blueberry, a shrub of northeastern North America having bluish black fruit.

Canada buffalo berry, a certain **buffalo berry**.

Canada field pea, another name for the **field pea**.

Canadian bacon, cured, smoked bacon cut from the loin of a pig.

canapé [French "sofa, couch, seat," from the idea that the bread or other base is a seat for the topping], a cracker or small, thin piece of bread or toast, used as a base, spread or topped with cheese, meat, or relish, and served as an appetizer. Some other bases: tiny yeast rolls; toasted split English muffins; melba toast; crisp, thin pastry in small shapes; cucumber, zucchini, dill pickle slices. Some other toppings: deviled ham, caviar, anchovy, tomato-and-shrimp, mushroom (fried and chopped), crabmeat, clam, shrimp, avocado mashed with cream cheese and some mayonnaise, mashed sardine. The following, if very small (miniatures), are also called canapés: biscuits, cream puffs, pizzas.

canard, French for **duck**.

Canary banana [from the *Canary* Islands (in the Atlantic Ocean off north-western Africa)], another name for **dwarf banana**.

candied, coated or encrusted with sugar or syrup, or cooked with sugar. Candied sweet potatoes or carrots are first boiled and then cooked further in a sugar sauce; candied fruits may or may not be cooked before the addition of the sauce. Compare ¹**glaze**.

candlefish, an oily, edible fish related to the smelt, of northern Pacific waters, formerly dried and used as a candle by American Indians.

¹**candy**, *1.* any of numerous kinds of sweet confections made with sugar, corn syrup, or similar substances, often combined with chocolate, dairy products, fruits, or nuts; *2.* a single piece of such a confection. Candies include bars, barley sugar, benne cake, crème caramel, divinity, fudge, penuche, toffee. Uncooked candies require confectioners' sugar combined with egg white or fruit juice. Hard candies include butterscotch, nut brittle, and glacéed fruits and nuts, dipped in syrup.

²**candy (to)**, to cook or coat with sugar or syrup. Compare **candied**.

cane, another name for **sugarcane**.

canela, Spanish for **cinnamon**.

¹**canella**, Italian for **cinnamon**.

²**canella** [from Medieval Latin *canella*, "small reed," diminutive of Latin *canna* "reed," from the shape of the rolls of the prepared bark] or **canella bark** or **white cinnamon**, the aromatic inner bark of a certain tree (the cinnamon), used as a condiment.

cane sugar, sucrose, i.e. a sugar yielded by sugarcane.

cangrejo, Spanish for **crab**.

canistel [American Spanish] or **eggfruit**, the orange-yellow fruit of a certain tropical American tree.

canna, see **edible canna**.

cannelloni [Italian, plural of *cannellone* "tubular soup noodle," from *cannello* "segment of a stalk of cane," diminutive of *canna* "cane, reed, tube"], an Italian pasta dish of large-sized, tube-shaped macaroni stuffed with forcemeat or some cheese mixture, baked, and served with tomato sauce. Cannelloni can also be filled with a vegetable mixture or fish. One way to prepare them is *cannelloni fiorentina* ("Florence-style"), i.e., with a filling of meat, chicken livers, eggs, and spinach, and covered with béchamel.

cannelon [from Italian *cannellone* "tubular soup noodle," from *cannello* "segment of a stalk of cane," diminutive of *canna* "cane, reed, tube"], a hollow roll or cone of puff paste stuffed with finely chopped meat or some sweet filling (e.g., cream) and baked or fried.

cannoli [Italian, plural of *cannolo* "small cylinder, tube," diminutive of *canna* "cane, reed, tube"], a dessert of Sicilian origin consisting of a tube of pastry (or a horn-shaped pastry shell) fried in deep fat (or baked) and filled with a sweetened (with sugar) mixture of whipped ricotta cheese, cream, and flavoring. Bits of chocolate and candied citron can also be added.

canola [from *Canada oil-low acid*] or **canola oil**, an oil obtained from the seeds of a rape plant of an improved variety (likewise called *canola*) that is high in monounsaturated fatty acids. The seeds are low in erucic acid.

Cantal [French, from *Cantal*, region in south central France, where it is made], a French cow- or goat-milk, hard, cheddar-type cheese.

cantaloupe or **cantaloup** [from *Cantalupo*, former papal villa near Rome, Italy, where it was first grown in Europe] or **rock melon**, a round muskmelon having a ribbed or warty rind and reddish orange flesh that is eaten raw as a fruit.

Canton ginger [from *Canton* (now Guangzhou), China], a fine grade of preserved or crystallized ginger.

Cape Cod turkey [from *Cape Cod*, a peninsula in southeastern Massachusetts], a name of the **codfish**.

Cape crayfish or **Cape crawfish** [from the *Cape* of Good Hope, a cape in southern South Africa] or **kreef**, the **spiny lobster** of the coast of southern Africa.

Cape fennel [from the *Cape* of Good Hope, a cape in southern South Africa], a southern African plant having an edible root.

Cape gooseberry [from the *Cape* of Good Hope, a cape in southern South Africa], a plant native to tropical America but extensively cultivated in South Africa, having edible yellow berries.

capelin or **capelan** [Canadian French *capelan*, from French *capelan* "codfish"], a small, salmonoid, northern, marine fish related to the smelts.

Cape lobster, a small lobster from the Cape of Good Hope in southern South Africa.

¹**caper**, a greenish flower bud or a young berry of a certain shrub (likewise called *caper*) pickled and used as a condiment in sauces and dressings.

²**caper**, a piece of buttered bread or oatcake usually with a slice of cheese on it (Scotland).

caper berry, the small berrylike fruit of the caper shrub.

capercaillie or **capercailzie**, a large grouse of northern Europe.

Cape rock lobster and **Cape spiny lobster** [from the *Cape* of Good Hope, a cape in southern South Africa], two other names for the **Cape crayfish** or **spiny lobster**.

capibara, variant of **capybara**.

49

capitaine [French "captain"], another name for **Nile perch**.

capocollo [Italian "head" + "neck"], a cured and smoked pork product (from the fleshy part around the neck) cased like a sausage.

capolin, variant of **capulin**.

capon, *1.* a castrated male chicken (compare **poularde**, which is a sterilized female pullet); *2.* a castrated male rabbit.

caponata [from Sicilian *capunata*], a relish of chopped eggplant and other vegetables (e.g., celery, olives, capers, onion, tomato puree, parsley). Anchovies and pine nuts may be added.

cappelletti [Italian, plural of *cappelletto* "little hat," diminutive of *cappello* "hat," from their shape (little peaked hats)], small cases of dough (pasta) usually filled with a savory meat or cheese mixture (compare **ravioli**).

cappuccino [Italian "Capuchin (monk)," from the likeness of its color to that of a Capuchin's habit], espresso coffee topped with a little frothed hot milk or cream and often flavored with cinnamon.

capretto [Italian "kid," diminutive of *capra* "goat"], the meat of a kid.

capulin or **capolin** [from American Spanish *capulín*, from Nahuatl *capulin*], a certain Mexican tree having edible cherries.

capybara or **capibara** [from Portuguese *capibara*], a large rodent of tropical South America related to the guinea pig.

¹**carabao** or **carabao mango**, a Philippine variety of the **mango** (sense 1).
²**carabao**, another name for **water buffalo**.

carambola [Portuguese] or **starfruit** [its cross section has the shape of a five-pointed star] or **Coromandel gooseberry** [from the *Coromandel* Coast, the southeastern coast of India] or **thrumwort**, the five-angled fruit of a certain tree of eastern Asia, used in Chinese cookery. It is not the same fruit as the **star apple** or **caimito**.

caramel [from Spanish *caramelo* "caramel," from Portuguese *caramelo* "icicle; caramel"], *1.* a smooth, chewy candy made with sugar, corn syrup, butter, and cream (or milk) and flavoring, cooked to a firm ball and cut in small blocks (which may be called *cream caramels; in French, when they are soft, they are called *caramels mous); 2.* a brittle, brown substance obtained by heating sugar, used for coloring and sweetening foods (e.g., carbonated beverages, bakery products, confections). A caramel sauce (made with caramelized sugar) can be used as topping on cakes, puddings, fruit (peaches, baked apples, seedless grapes). The French *crème au caramel* (or *crème caramel*) is a caramel custard.

caramel custard, custard topped with caramelized sugar.

caramel sauce, caramelized sugar.

caramelize (to), to change (e.g., sugar) into caramel, to melt (e.g., granulated sugar) over medium heat to a golden brown syrup (burnt sugar).

caraway or **caraway seed**, the pungent fruit of a certain herb (likewise called *caraway)* of the carrot family used in seasoning.

caraway oil, an oil obtained from caraway seeds, used as a flavoring agent.

carbonado [from Spanish *carbonada*, from *carbón* "charcoal"], a piece of scored and broiled or grilled fish, fowl, or meat. In South America (especially Argentina, Chile, Peru, and Uruguay) a *carbonada* is a dish made of small pieces of meat, Indian corn, squash, potatoes, and sometimes rice.

carbonara [Italian "from the charcoal grill; in the manner of a charcoal maker," from *carbonaro* "of a charcoal maker," from *carbonaio* "charcoal maker, charcoal seller" from *carbone* "charcoal"] (of a pasta dish; e.g., linguine carbonara, spaghetti carbonara) made with a white cheese sauce (usually Parmesan and cream) with eggs and bits of bacon and ham; green peas are sometimes added.

carbonated beverage, a soft drink combined with carbon dioxide gas (and therefore effervescent).

carbonated water, another name for **soda water**.

carbonnade [French *carbonnade* or *carbonade* "grilled (meat)," from Italian *carbonata* "pork cooked on charcoals," from *carbone* "charcoal"], a stew usually of beef or pork cooked in beer.

cardamom, the aromatic, capsular fruit of a tropical Asiatic plant (likewise called *cardamom*) of the ginger family, the seeds of which are used as a condiment. It is the second most expensive spice (next to saffron). The pods are discarded after baking or cooking. The black pod variety is used in soups and stews, the others for desserts and beverages. Cardamom seeds are used in certain northern European baked goods and meat dishes, and in North African specialties.

cardoncillo, a cactus of tropical America.

cardoon or **cardon** [from French *cardon*, from Latin *carduus* "thistle; artichoke"], a large thistlelike plant of southern Europe related to the artichoke, having edible leafstalk and roots.

caribou, see **deer**.

carnauba [from Portuguese *carnaúba*], a fan palm of Brazil that has an edible root.

carob [from French *caroube*; Italian *caruba*, Spanish *algarroba*] or **carob bean** or **algarroba** or **locust bean** or **locust pod**, one of the long pods of an evergreen tree (likewise called *carob*, or *carob tree*) of the Mediterranean region, containing a sweetish pulp.

carob flour, a powder extracted from the fruit of the carob tree and used as a thickener.

Carolina bean, another name for the **sieva bean**.

Carolina pompano, a certain **pompano**.

carosella or **Italian fennel**, a certain fennel, the young stems of which are used in salads.

carp [from French *carpe*], a large freshwater fish. It is a lean fish and therefore best for boiling and steaming. It is often prepared with seasoned fish stock (in French, *carpe au court-bouillon*).

carpaccio [for Vittore *Carpaccio*, 1459?-1525, Venetian painter known for his use of reds and whites], thin slices of raw beef (or other meat [e.g., buffalo] or fish [e.g., tuna]) served with a sauce.

carpincho, Spanish for **capybara**.

carrot [from French *carotte*], the long, yellow-orange or orange-red, tapering root of a certain plant (likewise called *carrot*), eaten as a vegetable.

carrot oil or **carrot-seed oil**, a light-yellow oil obtained from seeds of the carrot, having a spicy odor and used in flavors.

carte du jour [French "the day's menu"], another name for a **menu** (sense 1). In French, *manger à la carte* (compare **a la carte**) means to eat choosing freely from the menu, the opposite being *manger au menu* or *manger à prix fixe* (compare **table d'hôte**, sense 3).

casaba, or **casaba melon** [from *Kasaba*, former name of Turgutlu, city of western Turkey, whence it was introduced], a variety of **winter melon** (sense 1) having a yellow rind and sweet, whitish flesh.

cashew [from Portuguese *cajú*, *acajú*, from Tupi *acajú*], a tropical American evergreen tree bearing the **cashew apple** and the **cashew nut**.

cashew apple or **cashew** [from Portuguese *cajú*, *acajú*, from Tupi *acajú*], the pear-shaped fleshy receptacle at whose apex the **cashew nut** is borne.

cashew nut or **cashew** [from Portuguese *cajú*, *acajú*, from Tupi *acajú*], the kidney-shaped fruit of the cashew tree, rendered edible by expelling the caustic oil from the shell by roasting.

casing, a membrane used to encase processed meat.

casino ["a building used for gambling"], baked or broiled on the half shell (e.g., clams casino, oysters casino) often with a topping of green pepper and bacon.

cassareep, a flavoring (a condiment) made in the West Indies by boiling to a thick syrup the juice of grated bitter-cassava root.

cassata [Sicilian], *1.* a cake of Sicilian origin filled with ricotta cheese, candied fruit, and chocolate; *2.* an ice cream with candied fruit.

cassava or **casava** [from Spanish *cazabe* "cassava bread"] or **manioc** or **yuca**, *1.* any of various tropical American plants (also called **manioc** [French; *manioc*, Portuguese and Spanish *mandioca*], and *tapioca plants*) having large fleshy rootstocks; *2.* a starch derived from the root of any of these plants (used in **assai**, sense 2, a beverage; cassava bread and tapioca are made from this starch).

casserole [French "saucepan"], or **hot dish**, food cooked and served in a casserole (a covered, heatproof pottery or glass container, in which food may be both baked and served). A casserole dish is a mixture of foods baked together in the oven. It may consist of meat (e.g., beef, corned beef, veal, chicken, squab) with potatoes, rice, or beans; or it may contain eggs, fish or shellfish (e.g., scallops), cheese, or almost any foods (e.g., artichokes, cauliflower, noodles) which can make a main dish for a meal. Dishes prepared this way include arroz con pollo.

cassia bark or **Chinese cinnamon**, the bark of a tree (cassia, or Chinese cinnamon) of tropical Asia, used as a spice; this bark is similar to cinnamon but of inferior quality.

cassia oil or **Chinese cinnamon oil**, an oil obtained from the leaves of Chinese cinnamon (= cassia bark), used as a flavor.

cassis [French], a European black-currant bush.

cassoulet toulousain [French], a stew of goose, mutton, pork, and beans.

castana, *1.* [from Portuguese *castanha* "chestnut"], another name for the **Brazil nut**; *2.* [from American Spanish *castaña*, "chestnut"], another name for the **breadfruit** (Puerto Rico).

castor sugar, another name for **berry sugar**.

catalufa, any of various marine fishes of tropical seas.

catfish [so called from the catlike appearance of its head; Portuguese and Spanish *bagre*], any of numerous scaleless, large-headed, chiefly fresh-water fishes having long whiskerlike barbels extending from the upper jaw. It is a fat fish and therefore best for broiling, baking, planking.

catjang or **catjang pea** [from Dutch *katjang*, from Malay and Sundanese *kachang* "bean, pea"], another name for the **pigeon pea**.

catla [from Bengali *katla*], either of two large fishes of southeastern Asia.

catsup or **ketchup** [from Malay *kechap* "fish sauce"] or **red-eye**, a condiment consisting of a thick, somewhat spicy sauce usually made with tomatoes but sometimes with another foodstuff (e.g., mushrooms, wal-nuts).

cattle, live domesticated quadrupeds (as sheep, horses, swine), but espe-cially cows, bulls, steers raised for meat and dairy products.

cauchillo, a tropical American tree bearing fruits with seeds that resemble Brazil nuts and that are called *cream nuts* [probably from the rich fla-vor].

cauliflower [from Italian *cavolfiore* "cabbage-flower; flowered cab-bage,"], a plant related to the cabbage and broccoli, having a crowded whitish head of undeveloped flowers eaten as a vegetable.

cavalla [from Spanish *caballa* "horse mackerel," from Late Latin *caballa* "mare"] or **crevalle** or **king mackerel**, any of various tropical marine fishes.

caviar [from Turkish *havyar*], the roe (eggs) of a sturgeon or other large fish, salted and seasoned, and eaten (black or red) as an appetizer (40 grams per person are usually served). The finest caviar comes from the Caspian Sea (a saltwater lake between Europe and Asia [Russia, Azerbaijan, Iran, Turkmenistan, Kazakhstan]), where three varieties of sturgeon breed: beluga, ossetra, and sevruga; beluga is the best. The eggs are removed while the fish are still alive, and hand-mixed with salt (the finest of Caspian caviars are labeled *malossol* [from Russian *malosol'nyy* "with little salt"]). Caviar is best *au naturel*, but it is also served with blinis, sour cream, lightly buttered toasts. There are less expensive fish roes (salmon [orange-colored], whitefish, herring, mul-let, cod), many of them dyed with cuttlefish ink to resemble black caviar.

cavy [from obsolete Portuguese *çavía* (now *savía*), from Tupi *sawiya* "rat"], another name for **guinea pig**.

cayenne, another name for **cayenne pepper**.

Cayenne cherry [from *Cayenne*, island, city, and river in French Guiana], another name for the **Surinam cherry**.

cayenne pepper, or **cayenne** [modification of Tupi *kyinha*, influenced by *Cayenne*, island, city, and river in French Guiana], or **red pepper**, or **African pepper**, a pungent powder made by drying and grinding the whole fruits or the seeds of any of several hot peppers (e.g., the long pepper), used as a condiment.

celeriac [from *celery*] or **celery root** or **knob celery** or **turnip-rooted cel-ery**, a variety of celery grown for its thickened, turnip-like root.

celery [French *céleri*, Italian *sedano*, Spanish *apio*], a plant of the carrot family, the leafstalks of which are eaten raw or cooked; its small seeds are used as seasoning.

celery cabbage, another name for the **Chinese cabbage**.

celery root, another name for the **celeriac**.

celery salt, a seasoning made of a mixture of ground celery seed and salt.

celery seed, small seedlike fruits of a certain celery plant that are dried for use as a condiment.

celery-seed oil or **celery oil**, an oil with a celery odor and taste, obtained from celery seeds and used as a flavoring agent.

celestine [underlying idea: "in the Celestine manner," from *Celestine* "of the Celestine order (of monks)," for Pope *Celestine* V (1215-1296), its founder], garnished with shredded pancakes (e.g., consommé celestine).

cèpe or **cepe** or **cep** [from French *cèpe*], a certain edible mushroom. The best cèpes are from Bordeaux, southwestern France, and are prepared *à la bordelaise*.

cereal [from Latin *cerealis* "relating to grain or to the plants that produce it, or to agriculture," from *cerealis* "of Ceres (goddess of grain)"], *1.* an edible starchy grain or seed suitable for food (e.g., wheat, maize, rice, oats); *2.* a food (e.g., oatmeal, cornflakes) prepared from such a grain. Cereals are made from different grains left whole, cracked, rolled or ground coarse or fine.

cereza, Spanish for **cherry**.

cerise, French for **cherry**.

cero [from Spanish *sierra* "sawfish; saw"] or **cavalla**, either of two large, mackerel-like fishes of the warmer parts of the western Atlantic ocean.

cervelat [from French *cervelas*, from Italian *cervellata* "Milanese sausage, pig"s brains," from *cervello* "brain"], usually thick and short cooked sausage of several kinds made of seasoned pork and beef (often including pig"s brains), stuffed into casings and smoked. It may be served *à la vinaigrette*. Compare **saveloy**.

ceviche or **seviche** [from American Spanish *cebiche* (also *ceviche*, *seviche*), perhaps from *cebo* "bait"], a dish or appetizer made essentially of raw fish (e.g. corvina) or shellfish (e.g., shrimp, cuttlefish, periwinkle) cut in small pieces marinated in lime or lemon juice, often with onions, peppers, oil, and seasonings.

Ceylon cinnamon [from *Ceylan*, former name of Sri Lanka], the bark of a certain tree of Sri Lanka.

Ceylon tea [from *Ceylan*, former name of Sri Lanka], a pekoe tea produced in Sri Lanka.

chabacano, Mexican Spanish name for the **apricot** (in Spain, *albaricoque*).

challah or **hallah** [from Hebrew *ḥallāh*], a loaf of yeast-leavened, white egg-bread, usually braided or twisted before baking, traditionally eaten by Jews on ceremonial occasions.

chama [from Latin *chama* "cockle"], another name for **rock oyster**.

chamomile or **camomile** [ultimately from Greek *chamaimelon* "earth apple," from *chamai* "on the ground" + *melon* "apple" (from the apple-like smell of the flower)], the dried flower heads of either of two plants native to Eurasia used as a stomach tonic.

chanar [from American Spanish *chañar*], a thorny Argentine shrub that bears sweet berries.

channel bass or **red drum** or **red bass**, a large drum (fish) of the Atlantic coast of the Americas used as food when young.

channel cat or **channel catfish**, any of several large catfishes of the United States and Canada.

chanterelle [French, from New Latin *cantharella* "little cup" (from its shape), diminutive of Latin *cantharus* "drinking vessel"], an edible yellow mushroom having a fruity aroma.

Chantilly [from French *(crème) Chantilly* "(cream in the) Chantilly (manner)," from *Chantilly*, town in northern France], *1.* (of cream) whipped and often sweetened and flavored with vanilla; *2.* (of foods) prepared or garnished with whipped cream (e.g., Chantilly potatoes); a Chantilly sauce can be prepared with equal quantities of mayonnaise and whipped cream, and folded into, for instance, hot peas, asparagus, or spinach.

chaparro [Spanish "dwarf evergreen oak," from Basque *txapar* "thicket"], any of several tropical American trees which have edible fruits.

chapati [from Hindi *capati*, from Sanskrit *carpaṭī* "thin cake," from *carpaṭa* "flat"], a round, flat, unleavened bread of northern India that is usually made of wheat flour and cooked on a griddle.

chapon [French "capon"], a piece of bread rubbed with garlic (or slightly moist with broth) and placed in a salad for flavor.

¹**char** or **charr**, any of several fishes related to the trout (e.g., arctic char, brook trout).

²**char** (**to**), to burn partly, usually the surface, to scorch. Food prepared in this manner includes charred beef, pork tenderloin, salmon.

charbroil (**to**) [from *charcoal* + *broil*], to broil (e.g., beef, salmon, pork) on a rack over hot charcoal.

charcuterie [French], the cold cuts and meat dishes (mostly pork) sold in a delicatessen in France. Among such dressed meats and sausages: andouille, andouillette, bacon, boudin, *cervelas* (cervelat), *crépinette* (membrane-covered flat sausage), *fromage de tête* (headcheese), galantine, *jambon* (ham), *jambonneau* (foreleg ham), lard, *mortadelle* (mortadella), *museau* (snout), *panne* (hog's fat), pâté, *petit salé* (pickled pork), *pieds de porc* (trotters), rillettes, *saucisse* (fresh sausage), *saucisson* (dry sausage).

chard or **Swiss chard**, a variety of beet having large, yellowish green leaves and succulent stalks used as a vegetable (cooked).

charlotte [French, probably from the feminine given name *Charlotte*], a dessert, served either hot or cold, consisting of a mold of sponge cake or bread strips or ladyfingers, with a filling of fruits (e.g., apple jam, raspberry, granadilla), whipped cream, or custard.

charlotte russe [French "Russian charlotte"], a cold dessert of Bavarian cream set in a mold lined with ladyfingers or strips of sponge cake.

charqui [Spanish, from Quechua *ch'arki* "dried meat"] or **xarque**, cured or jerked meat, especially jerked beef.

charr, variant of ¹**char**.

chartreuse [from La Grande *Chartreuse*, monastery of the Carthusian order near Grenoble, city of southeastern France (with reference to the abstinence from meat by Carthusians)], *1.* a mixture of vegetables arranged and cooked in a mold; *2.* a mold of vegetables with meat (often chicken or game [e.g., partridges]) or fish in the center.

chateaubriand or **Chateaubriand** [French, for François René de *Chateaubriand*, 1768–1848, French author whose chef invented it], *1.* a thick tenderloin steak grilled slowly and served with a butter-and-lemon sauce (or a béarnaise sauce) and usually with chateau potatoes. In French, *chateaubriand* is sometimes abbreviated *château*; *2.* a steak in which a pocket is cut and stuffed with various seasonings (e.g., shallots, chives, cayenne, and salt) before grilling.

chateau potatoes, potato balls parboiled briefly and then braised in butter.

chaudfroid [French "hot-cold," from its being prepared with heat but served cold], *1.* a jellied white or brown sauce fortified with gelatin, used as an aspic for cold meats or fish; *2.* food (e.g., meat, game, chicken, or fish) covered with a chaudfroid sauce (sense 1) usually molded into shapes after cooking, and served cold.

chausson, French for **turnover**.

chayote [Spanish, from Nahuatl *chayotli*] or **huisquil** or **guisquil** [from American Spanish *huisquil*] or **mango-squash** or **tallote** or **vegetable pear**, the squashlike fruit of a certain tropical American vine (likewise called *chayote*) of the cucumber family, cooked and eaten as a vegetable. Its single seed is edible, too.

checkerberry [from *checker*, name of a certain tree, + *berry*], the red, spicy berry of a certain plant, called **wintergreen** (sense 1) and also *checkerberry*.

cheddar or **Cheddar** or **Cheddar cheese** [from *Cheddar*, village in Somerset, southwestern England, where it was first made] or **rat cheese** or **rat-trap cheese**, any of several types of smooth-textured, hard cheese with a flavor that ranges from mild (e.g., American cheese) to strong as the cheese matures.

cheese [French *fromage*, Italian *formaggio*, Spanish *queso*, Danish *ost*], a solid food prepared from the curd of milk (separated from the whey); the curd is consolidated by molding for soft cheese or subjected to pressure for hard cheese, then ripened. Cheese is made with the milk of cows, goats, sheep, or a mixture of these. It is used without cooking as an accompaniment to meals or in sandwiches. Cream, cottage, and Roquefort cheeses are employed in salads, especially with fruit (Roquefort also in soufflés). Firm cheese is often grated and used with vegetables and eggs. Cheese is added to certain bland dishes made with bread, pasta, cereals, potatoes.

Cheese is obtainable in many varieties, as American, angelot, appetitost, asiago, baker's cheese, bel paese, blue cheese, Blue Vinny, brick, Brie, Camembert, cheddar, Cheshire, chèvre, cottage, cream, Dutch (sense 1), Edam, Emmental, feta, filled, géromé, Gorgonzola, Gouda, Gruyère, Limburger, Monterey, mozzarella, Muenster, Neufchâtel, Parmesan, pecorino, Port Salut, provolone, ricotta, Roquefort, Romano, Stilton, Swiss, Tilsit.

In Spain and Latin America cheese is often eaten with quince jam after the meal; in France, Brie and Camembert are sometimes cooked in puff paste. Mozzarella is used in pizzas, Parmesan on pastas. Emmental and Gruyère are used in fondues. Cheese dishes include: balls, biscuits, cake, dips, dumplings, escalloped cheese, fondue, omelet, pie, puffs, salad, sandwiches, sauce, soufflé, soup, spread, straws (also called sticks), toast, waffles, Welsh rarebit.

cheeseburger, a hamburger (sense 3), the patty being topped with a slice of toasted (melted) cheese.

cheesecake or **cheese cake**, a dessert made by baking a mixture of cottage cheese (or cream cheese, or both), eggs, sugar, and flavorings (e.g., lemon rind and juice, vanilla), sometimes milk, in a pastry shell or a pressed-crumb shell. It can be served with a fruit sauce (e.g., blackberry, strawberry) or whipped cream.

cheese dream, a toasted or sautéed cheese sandwich. The cheese spread for it can be made with diced American cheese or with soft sharp cheese, egg, mustard, salt, and butter or cream.

cheese food, ground and seasoned cheese (e.g., cheddar) mixed with other ingredients (e.g., milk solids, cream).

cheese spread, a cheese food (e.g., cream cheese, grated American cheese) soft enough to spread (on canapés, toasts).

cheese straw or **cheese stick**, a strip of puff paste sprinkled with grated cheese before baking.

chef [French, short for *chef de cuisine* "head of the kitchen"], a skilled cook, especially the chief cook of a large kitchen staff (e.g., in a restaurant).

chef de cuisine [French "head of the kitchen"], another term for **chef**.

chef's salad, a meal-size salad (with lettuce, endive, spinach, tomatoes, celery, hard-boiled eggs), usually garnished with a chef's choice of julienne strips of meats (e.g., cooked beef, ham, tongue, chicken) and cheese (e.g., Swiss).

chenfish, a small California kingfish.

cherimoya or **chirimoya** [from Spanish *chirimoya*] or **Jamaica apple**, the round or heart-shaped fruit (with white, soft, aromatic pulp) of a certain tropical American tree (likewise called *cherimoya* or *chirimoya*). Cherimoyas were already cultivated by the ancient Peruvians, and the cherimoyas from Huánuco are famous in Peru. Compare **atemoya**.

cherry, the yellow or red, smooth-skinned, fleshy, globe-shaped or heart-shaped fruit (with a small hard stone) of any of several trees (likewise called *cherries*). Dishes made with cherries include pies, cakes (e.g., Black Forest cake), cobblers, cookies, parfaits, salads. Cherries include Bigarreau cherries, black heart, sweet cherry.

cherry pepper, the very pungent fruit of a certain tropical plant (a hot-pepper plant, likewise called *cherry pepper*).

cherry tomato, the small red or yellow fruit, of a variety of the common tomato (a plant likewise called *cherry tomato*) that resembles a cherry.

chervil, or **beaked parsley**, an aromatic plant of the carrot family, native to Eurasia, having finely divided often curled leaves used in soups and salads.

Cheshire cheese, a hard, yellow cheese similar to **cheddar** and made (from cow's milk) chiefly in Cheshire, county of northwestern England.

chess pie or **chess cake**, a dessert (pie or tart) consisting of a filling made especially of eggs, butter, and sugar and baked in individual tart shells of rich pastry. Nuts (pecans or walnuts) are often added.

Chester [from *Chester*, city of northwestern England, capital of Cheshire], another name for **Cheshire cheese**.

chestnut, the sweet nut (edible when cooked), enclosed in a prickly bur, produced by any of several trees (likewise called *chestnuts*) of the Northern Hemisphere.

chestnut bean, another name for the **chick-pea**.

chevon [from French *chèvre* "goat"], the flesh of the goat used as food. It is prepared in the same way as mutton.

chèvre or **chevrotin** or **chevret** [all three from French *(le) chèvre* "goat-milk cheese," from *(la) chèvre* "goat"; *chevrotin* is obsolete in French], a cheese made from goats' milk.

chewing gum, a sweetened, flavored preparation for chewing, usually made from **chicle** (a sapodilla gum) sometimes mixed with other plastic insoluble substances.

chia [from Spanish *chía*, from Nahuatl *chía*, *chian*, from Maya *chiháan* "strong, strengthening"], a beverage prepared from the seeds of a certain plant (likewise called *chia*) of Mexico and the southwestern United States. The seeds are seeped in water and they then let out a large amount of a gelatinous substance to which sugar and lemon juice are added.

chiccory, variant of **chicory**.

chich [from French *pois chiche* "chick-pea"], another name for the **chick-pea**.

chichituna, the edible red fruit of a tall Mexican cactus called *chichipe*.

chicken, the flesh of the common domestic fowl used as food. Chicken is prepared by many of the same methods as are meats. Some of the possibilities are: baked, barbecued, braised, broiled, fried, grilled, roast, smothered, stewed; aspic, chow mein, creamed (or chicken à la king), croquette, curry, fricassee, gumbo (sense 2), Kiev, pancakes, pie, salad, scalloped, tetrazzini, with creole sauce. Chicken stew may be accompanied by either dumplings, potatoes, rice, or noodles; a fricassee has a brown gravy made from the flour in which the chicken was first fried; roast chicken may be prepared with a savory stuffing (or it may be roasted with onions, shallots, rosemary, garlic, bay leaf, thyme, and white wine); in the South of the United States, chicken is fried, sometimes in a batter, sometimes rolled in seasoned flour or in cornmeal. Chicken dishes include arroz con pollo, beggar's chicken.

chicken cacciatore [from Italian *cacciatore* "hunter (style)"; Italian *pollo alla cacciatora* (feminine, because *maniera* "manner" is feminine)], chicken fried in olive oil, seasoned with herbs (sage, rosemary, garlic), and simmered in a tomato and vinegar (or white wine) sauce.

chicken grape or **arroyo grape**, a grape of the United States with small, black fruit.

chicken gumbo, a gumbo (sense 2) made with chicken.

chicken Kiev [from *Kiev*, Ukraine], a boneless chicken-breast stuffed with seasoned butter (with chopped chives and parsley, and white pepper) and deep fried. The butter balls are placed in the center of each pounded half breast, which is rolled so that the butter is completely enclosed.

chicken lobster, a young lobster.

chicken tetrazzini [for Luisa *Tetrazzini*, 1874–1940, Italian opera singer (coloratura soprano)], previously boiled chicken baked with pasta (macaroni or spaghetti) and a white sauce (butter, flour, chicken broth) seasoned with sherry and served au gratin, sprinkled with grated Parmesan cheese. Sautéed mushrooms are often added.

chick-pea or **garbanzo** or **cowgram** or **dwarf pea** or **garavance** or **gram**, one of the seeds of a certain bushy plant (likewise called *chick-pea*) that bears short pods (with one or two yellowish seeds in each); the seeds somewhat resemble peas in flavor. Chick-peas can be boiled and then ground and served with tahini added.

chicle [Spanish, from Nahuatl *chictli*, *tzictli*] or **zapota gum**, a gum obtained from the latex of the sapodilla tree (Yucatan [Mexico] and Central America), used as the main ingredient of chewing gum.

chico [American Spanish, short for Spanish *chicozapote* "sapodilla," probably from Nahuatl *tzicotzapotl*, from *tzicoh* "sticky" (from *tzictli* "chicle, gum") + *tzapotl* "sapodilla"], another name for the **sapodilla** (Mexico, Philippines).

chico mamey, the fruit of the marmalade tree (Philippines).

chicory or **chiccory** [from French *chicorée*] or **witloof** or **succory** or **wild succory**, *1.* a thick-rooted plant having leaves used as salad greens; *2.* the root of this plant, dried, roasted, and ground used to flavor coffee, or as a coffee substitute. Compare **endive**.

chicozapote [from Spanish *chicozapote*, probably from Nahuatl *tzicotzapotl* "sapodilla," from *tzicoh* "sticky" (from *tzictli* "chicle, gum") + *tzapotl* "sapote"], another name for the **sapodilla**.

chiffon ["light-weight fabric," from French *chiffon* "rag"], (of pies, cakes, puddings) having a light and fluffy consistency achieved usually by adding whipped egg whites or whipped gelatin. Chiffon cakes include: banana, butterscotch, cherry, chocolate chip, fruit, maple, orange, pecan, peppermint chip, spice, walnut. Chiffon pies include: chocolate, eggnog, lemon, lime, orange, pineapple, pumpkin, raspberry, strawberry.

chiffonade [French, from *chiffon* "rag," from the shredded vegetables resembling rags], shredded or finely cut vegetables (e.g., lettuce, sorrel, parsley, chervil) used in soups or salad dressings.

chilacayote [American Spanish (in Spain, it is called *cidra cayote*), from Nahuatl *tzilacayutli*, perhaps from *tzilac* "smooth" + *ayutli* "gourd"], the fruit (or its pulp) of any of several gourds (likewise called *chilacayotes*) of Mexico and the southwestern United States.

chile, variant of **chili**; it is the form used in Mexican Spanish for the meaning "hot pepper" (which in Spain is *ají* or *pimiento* or *guindilla*). A national dish of Mexico is *chile en nogada* "hot pepper in a nut sauce" (garnished with pomegranate seeds in their red pulp).

Chile. The following are among representative dishes and products of Chile: shellfish (e.g., crab [Spanish *jaiba*], lobster, shrimp, crayfish, oyster, clams; including shellfish chowder [*chupe de mariscos*]); corbina *(corvina)*, swordfish, sea urchin *(erizo)*, bouillabaisse *(paila marina);* meat, shellfish, or fish turnovers *(empanadas*, including *empanada de horno* [with a filling of minced meat, raisins, onions, olives, hard-boiled eggs]); kabob *(anticucho)*, a kind of abalone *(loco)*, conger-eel broth *(caldillo de congrio)*, mixed grill *(parrillada);* beef, chicken and vegetable casserole *(cazuela de ave)*, bean and sausage casserole *(Pancho Villa)*, avocados *(paltas)*, tamales *(humitas)*, corn with minced meat *(pastel de choclo)*, baked bananas *(plátanos en dulce)*.

Chilean guava, a shrub from Chile bearing an edible berry.

Chilean strawberry [regional Spanish (South America): *frutilla*], a certain strawberry, originally from Chile.

chili or **chile** [from Mexican Spanish *chile*, from Nahuatl *chilli*], *1.* another name for **hot pepper** (in both senses); *2.* another name for **chili con carne**.

chiliburger, a hamburger topped with chili.

chili con carne or **chili**, or **chile con carne** [from Spanish *chile con carne*, "chili (hot pepper) with meat"], a spiced stew of chopped or ground beef and minced red peppers or chili powder, usually served with beans.

chili dog, a hot dog topped with chili.

chilipepper [so called from its color], a certain rockfish that is brick-red above and pink below.

chili pepper, another name for the **chili** (sense 1).

chili powder, a condiment made from ground chilies (sense 1).

chili sauce, a condiment sauce consisting of pureed tomatoes, seasonings and spices, with sweet peppers or sometimes with hot peppers.

chili vinegar, another name for **pepper sauce**.

chill (to), to make cold, especially without freezing, to treat by cooling.

chimichurri, see under **Uruguay**.

China. The following are among the most important provinces of China from the gastronomical point of view (certain cities in the province, that are well-known for their food, are shown in parentheses [and the way some of these names used to be spelled in English]): Beijing (North; Beijing [formerly spelled Peking]), Sichuan (center; formerly spelled Szechwan), Jiangsu (Shanghai) and Fujian (East), Guangdong (South; Guangzhou [formerly written Canton]). Some representative dishes and products of these provinces are:

Beijing: duck; *Sichuan*: spicy dishes (chicken, prawn), deep-fried shredded beef, duck smoked over tea leaves and camphor; *Jiangsu* and *Fujian*: seafood; *Guangdong*: sweet-and-sour dishes (e.g., pork ribs), duck, shark's fin soup, roast suckling pig, deep-fried chicken, dim sum, spring rolls, seafood, wonton dumplings and soup.

Food found in other regions, or in several regions: white rice, fried rice, Mongolian mutton casserole, braised goose or duck. Beverage: tea (Chinese *chá*)

China orange, another name of the **calamondin**.

China tea, a tea prepared from a variety of the tea plant grown chiefly in southern China.

chinchayote [Mexican Spanish, from Nahuatl *tzinchayotli*, from *tzintli* "rear or botton part" + *chayotli* "chayote"], another name for the **chayote** (fruit of a vine).

Chinese artichoke or **crosnes** or **chorogi** or **Japanese artichoke** or **knotroot**, plant native to China and Japan, cultivated for its crisp tubers, eaten either raw or cooked, that taste somewhat like salsify.

Chinese banana, another name for the **dwarf banana**.

Chinese bean oil, another name for **soybean oil**.

Chinese cabbage or **pakchoi** or **bok choy** or **celery cabbage** or **lettuce cabbage** or **pechay** or **petsai** or **peh-tsai**, a Chinese plant related to the common cabbage, whose leaves are used as greens.

Chinese cinnamon, see **cassia bark**.

Chinese date, another name for **jujube**.

Chinese gelatin, another name for **agar**.

Chinese gooseberry, another name for the **kiwi**, the brownish, hairy fruit of a plant (likewise called *Chinese gooseberry* or *kiwi)*, eaten fresh or in preserves.

Chinese lemon, another name for the **citron** (sense 1).

Chinese mustard, any of several plants sometimes used as potherbs.

Chinese nut, another name for the **litchi**.

Chinese parsley, another name for the **cilantro**.

Chinese watermelon, another name for the **wax gourd**.

Chinese yam, another name for **cinnamon vine**.

chino [from American Spanish *china*, short for Spanish *naranja china* "Chinese orange"], another name for the **sweet orange**.

chinook salmon, or simply **chinook** [from *Chinook*, member of a certain American Indian people"], another name for the **king salmon**.

chinotto [from Italian *chinotto* (tree and fruit), from obsolete Italian *China* "China" (modern Italian *Cina*)] or **chinotto orange**, another name for the **sour orange**.

chinquapin, the nut of either of two trees (likewise called *chinquapins)* of North America.

chip, a thin slice of food (e.g., of potato or of chocolate). Chocolate chips are used in cakes, cookies, ice cream, pies.

chipolata [French, from Italian *cipollata* "with onions" (feminine), from *cipolla* "onion"], a small spicy sausage usually made of pork.

chipped beef, dried beef, smoked and sliced thin.

chip potatoes, another name for **French fries**.

chirimoya [Spanish], variant of **cherimoya**.

chito melon, another name for the **mango melon**.

chiton, an elongated marine mollusk.

chitterlings or **chitlings**, the cleaned and scraped small intestines of hogs when cooked (usually fried) and eaten as food. Compare **andouillette**.

chives [in French: *ciboule* and *ciboulette* (two related plants)], the slender, hollow leaves of a plant (called *chive*) related to the onion, used as a seasoning (e.g., in soups, omelets).

chocho [from American Spanish] or **choko**, another name for the **chayote**.

¹**chocolate** (noun) [Spanish, from Nahuatl *chocolatl (atl* = "water; drink")],
1. or **bitter chocolate**, or **cooking chocolate** or **plain chocolate**, a food prepared from husked, roasted, and ground cacao seeds. The words *chocolate* and **cocoa** are sometimes used as equivalent; when a difference is made, *chocolate* (sense 1) is a solid food, *cocoa* is chocolate freed of a portion of its fat and pulverized. A beverage can be made with either of these, and called *cocoa* when made with cocoa (powder) and *chocolate* when made with chocolate (solid); *2.* a small candy with a center (e.g., fondant, caramel custard, praline, nougat, nut, orange or grapefruit peel, raisin, shredded coconut) and a coating of chocolate (sense 1); *3.* a beverage made by cooking a portion of chocolate (sense 1) in water or milk (compare **cocoa**, sense 2). Compare **nougatine**, **truffle** (sense 2).

²**chocolate** (adjective), composed of ¹**chocolate**, flavored or coated with ¹**chocolate**. Among ²chocolate foods: Bavarian cream, blancmange, bread pudding, brownies, cake, chiffon pie, cream, cream pie, cookies, custard, éclairs, fudge, ice cream, icing, mousse, pudding, sauce, soufflé, syrup, torte. See also **chip**.

chocolate angel food, see **angel cake**.

chocolate cream, a chocolate with a creamy fondant center.

chocolate prune, a prune having the color of chocolate.

chocolate tree, another name for **cacao** tree.

choko, another name for **chayote**.

cholla [from Mexican Spanish, from Spanish *cholla* "head"], see **prickly pear**.

¹**chop**, a small slice or cut of meat often including a part of a rib. A chop may be taken from the rib but also from the shoulder or loin. Chops can be from pork, lamb, veal; pork chops can be braised or stuffed.

²**chop (to)**, to cut into fine or coarse pieces.

chopsticks, a pair of slender sticks made of wood, plastic, or ivory held between the thumb and fingers of one hand and used chiefly in China, Japan, and some other Asian countries to lift food to the mouth.

chop suey [from Cantonese *jaahp-seui* "odds and ends"], a dish of Chinese-American origin prepared chiefly from bean sprouts, bamboo shoots, water chestnuts, onions, mushrooms, and small pieces of meat (e.g., lean pork or veal), chicken, or fish and served with rice and soy sauce. Other vegetables sometimes used are celery and green pepper.

chorizo [Spanish "pork sausage"], a smoked pork sausage seasoned chiefly with cayenne pepper, pimientos, and garlic. In certain countries of South America (especially in Argentina), a *bife de chorizo* is a beefsteak.

chorogi, Japanese for **Chinese artichoke**.

chou (plural *choux*) [French "cabbage"], a round cream puff, originally made in the shape of a small cabbage. *Petits choux* are small cream puffs.

choucroute [French, from German *Sauerkraut*], *1.* another name for **sauerkraut**; *2.* or **choucroute garnie**, sauerkraut cooked and served with cold cuts and potatoes.

choux paste [translation of French *pâte à choux*], light, fluffy dough made with flour, butter, eggs, shortening, and milk or water (then baked or fried), used to make choux. Compare **chou, cream puff**.

chowchow or **chow-chow** [Chinese Pidgin English], *1.* a Chinese preserve or confection of mixed ginger, fruits, and peels in heavy syrup; *2.* a relish consisting of chopped pickles in mustard sauce (originally from southeastern Asia).

chowder [from French *chaudière* "kettle, and its contents"], *1.* a soup or stew of seafood (e.g., clams, white-fleshed fishes, lobster) usually made with milk or tomatoes and containing salt pork or bacon, onions, and other vegetables (e.g., potatoes); see also **clam chowder, Manhattan clam chowder, New England clam chowder**; *2.* any of various soups resembling chowders (e.g., corn or vegetable or chicken and corn chowder).

chow mein [from Cantonese *cháau-mihn* "fried noodles"], a Chinese-American stew of shredded or diced meat (or chicken), mushrooms, vegetables, and seasonings that is usually served over fried noodles.

chremsel [from Yiddish *chremzel*], a flat fried cake (often oblong) made with matzo meal and filled usually with prunes (or prunes and chopped nuts and raisins, or chopped cooked meat and liver, or rusell beets with honey, ginger and nuts).

Christmas pie, another name for **mince pie**.

christophine [American French *christophine*, probably from the French given name *Christophe*, corresponding to English *Christopher*], another name for the **chayote**.

chuck, *1.* a cut of beef including the neck, shoulder, and first three ribs; *2.* a similar cut from veal or lamb.

chufa [Spanish] or **edible galingale** or **ground almond** or **groundnut** or **rush nut** or **tigernut**, the small nutlike tuber of a certain European sedge (a marsh plant). In Spain, the chufas are used to make a beverage called *horchata*.

chum, or **chum salmon**, other names for **dog salmon**.

chunk honey, a mixture of extracted and comb honey.

chuño or **chuñu** [from American Spanish *chuño*, from Quechua *ch'uñu*], potatoes processed by freezing, thawing, and dehydrating prepared and eaten especially in the Andes (South America).

churrasco [Spanish], beef that has been grilled, pan-broiled, or broiled on a spit over an open fire.

chutney [from Hindi *caṭnī* "chutney," from *caṭnā* "to be licked, to be tasted," from *caṭnā* "to lick, to taste"], a pungent condiment of Indian origin that has the consistency of jam and is made with ripe acid fruit (e.g., mango, tamarind, gooseberry, apple) with added seedless raisins, dates, and onions (and other herbs) and seasoned with spices, sugar, and vinegar (or lemon juice); the ingredients are pounded and boiled together. Chutney is often served with curried dishes.

chymopapain, a papaya-latex enzyme used in meat tenderizer.

cibol or **ciboule** [from French *ciboule*], another name for **shallot**.

cicely, see **sweet cicely**.

cider [from French *cidre*], the juice pressed from apples used to produce vinegar or as a beverage. The unfermented drink is called *sweet cider*, and the fermented drink *hard cider*; in French, *cidre* always means hard cider. Pear cider is produced similarly.

cider apple, an apple grown especially to produce cider.

cider royal or **cider oil**, concentrated cider with the addition of honey.

cider vinegar, vinegar made from fermented cider (hard cider).

cilantro, or **Chinese parsley** [Spanish "coriander"], the parsleylike leaves of fresh coriander used as a flavoring or garnish.

cinnamon or **canela** (Spanish) or **canella** (Italian), or **cinnamon bark**, the yellowish-brown, aromatic bark of any of various trees (likewise called *cinnamon*) used as a spice either by powdering or by drying in small rolls. Cinnamon is used in buns, dips, fluff, kuchen, rolls; cinnamon apples are used as accompaniment for meat (e.g., sausage). Cinnamon is one of the traditional ingredients in **five-spice powder** (a seasoning). Compare [2]**canella**.

cinnamoned, (of apples, pears, buns, toast) spiced with cinnamon.

cinnamon vine, or **Chinese yam**, a Chinese vine grown in the tropics for its edible tubers.

cioppino, a dish of fish (e.g., fresh snapper) and shellfish cooked in tomato sauce and usually seasoned with wine, spices, and herbs.

ciruela, Spanish for **plum**.

cisco [short for Canadian French *ciscoette*], any of several North American (Great Lakes region) freshwater fishes resembling the whitefish, the salmon, the trout.

citrange, a hybrid citrus fruit produced by crossing the common sweet orange and the trifoliate orange.

citrangedin, a hybrid citrus fruit produced by crossing the citrange and the calamondin.

citrangequat, a hybrid citrus fruit produced by crossing the citrange and the kumquat.

citric acid, an acid that occurs in plants (e.g., citrus fruit), is extracted from lemon, lime, and pineapple juices and used as a flavoring agent in foods and carbonated beverages.

citron [French "lemon"] or **preserving melon** or **stock melon**, *1.* the fruit of a certain citrus tree (likewise called *citron*), that resembles the lemon in appearance and structure but is larger, has a thick aromatic rind and no terminal nipple; *2.* the preserved and candied rind of this fruit, used in baking (e.g., cakes, breads, puddings).

citrus fruit, any of several edible fruits having firm, usually thick, rind and pulpy flesh (e.g., grapefruit, lemon, lime, orange).

city chicken, pieces of skewered and braised veal.

cives, another name for **chives**.

civet [French], a seasoned stew of game (e.g., hare, rabbit, venison, roe deer, young wild boar) cooked with red wine, onions, and blood.

civet bean, another name for the **sieva bean**.

clabber or **loppered milk**, sour milk that has become thick or curdled.

clam, the flesh of any of various marine mollusks used as food. Compare **quahog** (a thick-shelled clam). Clams can be prepared as follows: fried, steamed in broth, stuffed and baked; as bisque, canapés, chowder (including Manhattan clam chowder and New England clam chowder), dip, pie, sauce (for pasta), soufflé.

clambake, a seashore picnic where clams, fish, corn, and other foods are baked in layers on buried heated rocks usually covered by seaweed.

clam chowder, any of various soups made of shucked clams (i.e., stripped of their shell), salt pork, potatoes, and onions (e.g., New England clam chowder, simmered in milk; Manhattan clam chowder, made with tomatoes and thyme, and no milk).

clammy sage, another name for **clary**.

clarify (to), to make a liquid (e.g., melted butter) clear or pure by freeing it from suspended matter (by heating gently).

clary or **clary sage**, any of several European aromatic herbs cultivated as a potherb.

clear plate, the layer of fat on top of a pork shoulder butt (sense 1).

clementine [from French *clémentine*], a small, nearly seedless citrus fruit similar to a tangerine.

clingstone, a fruit, especially a peach, having pulp that adheres strongly to the pit; distinguished from **freestone** (in which the flesh does not cling to the stone).

clipfish, variant of **klipfish**.

clotted cream or **Devonshire cream** [from the county of *Devonshire* or *Devon*, southwestern England], a thick cream made by slowly heating whole milk on which the cream has been allowed to rise and then skimming the cooled cream from the underlying skim milk (i.e., from the top).

cloudberry or **baked apple** or **baked apple berry**, the reddish-orange fruit of a certain creeping plant (a raspberry), of northern temperate regions.

¹**clove** [akin to *cleave* "split"], one of the small bulbs (e.g., in garlic) developed in the axils (angles) of the scales of a large bulb.

²**clove** [from French *clou (de girofle)*, "nail (of clove)"], *1.* the aromatic unopened and dried flower bud of a tropical evergreen tree (likewise called *clove)* of the myrtle family; cloves are one of the traditional ingredients in **five-spice powder** (a seasoning); *2.* a spice consisting of cloves (sense 1), whole or ground.

clove cassia or **clove cinnamon**, the bark of a Brazilian tree used for mixing with other spices.

clove pepper, another name for **allspice**.

club cheese, a processed cheese made by blending ground cheddar and other cheeses (by heating and stirring) with water and usually with added condiments and seasonings.

club sandwich, a sandwich, usually of three slices of toast with two layers of meat (e.g., turkey, chicken, bacon, ham) and lettuce, tomato, and mayonnaise.

club soda, another name for **soda water** (an effervescent water).

club steak or **Delmonico steak** or **contrefilet**, a small beefsteak cut from the end (the front section) of the short loin and containing no part of the tenderloin.

club wheat or **cluster wheat**, a wheat having short, club-shaped spikes.

cluster pepper, the pungent, bright red fruit borne by a certain hot pepper shrub.

cluster wheat, another name for the **club wheat**.

coalfish [so called from its color], any of several dark fishes (e.g., a cobia, a pollack, a sablefish).

coated ginger, another name for **black ginger** (the rootstock of ginger, dried and unscraped).

coated rice, rice covered with a layer of glucose and talc to give it a pearly appearance.

cob, another name for the **corncob** (sense 1).

¹**cobbler**, a deep-dish fruit pie (e.g., apricot, blackberry, cherry) with a thick biscuit top crust but without a bottom crust.

²**cobbler**, or **cobblerfish**, other names for the **pompano**.

cobia, or **sergeant fish** or **lemon fish** or **prodigal son**, a large bony fish of warm seas (tropical and subtropical).

cob meal, cornmeal (ground seeds of Indian corn) in which the cob is also ground.

cobnut, a large filbertlike nut yielded by a variety (likewise called *cobnut*) of the European hazel.

coca [Spanish, from Quechua *kuka*], the dried leaves (resembling tea leaves) of a certain South American shrub (likewise called *coca*) that are chewed with alkali by people of the Andean uplands.

coccagee [Irish Gaelic *cac a' gheidh*, "goose dung" (from its color)], a certain cider apple, and the cider made from it.

cochal, the edible fruit of a certain cactus (likewise called *cochal*) of Lower California (Mexico).

cochil sapota, the fruit of a large Mexican tree (likewise called *cochil sapota*), resembling the peach in flavor.

Cochin ginger [from *Cochin* China, former name for the southernmost region of Viet Nam, where it is produced], another name for the **white ginger**.

cocido, Spanish for **olla**. Compare **olla podrida**.

cock-a-leekie or **cockaleekie** or **cockieleekie**, a cream soup made with chicken and leeks.

cockle, any of various mollusks having rounded or heart-shaped, ribbed shells.

cockscomb oyster, a large tropical oyster.

cocktail, an appetizer (e.g., fruit juice, vegetable juice, fruit in a syrup, shellfish [clam, shrimp] with a sharp sauce) served as a first course at a meal.

cocktail sauce, a sauce of catsup, hot peppers, tabasco, and other seasoning, used for instance on shrimp when served as an appetizer (and on clams, mussels, oysters).

coco [Spanish, "bogeyman, goblin," from the resemblance of a coconut to a grotesque head, from Portuguese *côco* "coconut shell,"], another name for the **coconut** (both senses).

cocoa [from Spanish *cacao*, from Nahuatl *cacahuatl* "cacao bean"], *1.* a powder made from cacao seeds after they have been roasted, ground, and freed of most of their fat; the words *cocoa* and ¹**chocolate** are sometimes used as equivalent; when a difference is made, *cocoa* is this powder, *chocolate* (also called *cooking chocolate)* is a solid food; *2.* a beverage prepared by heating cocoa (sense 1, powder) with water or milk and adding sugar (compare ¹**chocolate**, sense 3).

cocoa bean, another name for the **cacao bean**.

cocoa butter or **cacao butter**, a solid with a chocolatelike odor and taste, obtained from cacao seeds and used for confections (e.g., chocolate candy [see ¹**chocolate**, sense 2]).

cocoa powder, another name for **cocoa** (sense 1, the powder).

coconut or **coco**, *1.* a large seed or nut, with a thick, hard shell, that is the fruit of the coconut palm; it contains edible white meat and, in the hollow center of the fresh fruit, a liquid called **coconut milk**; *2.* the meat of the coconut (sense 1). The following can be made with coconut: ambrosia, angel food, cake, cream pie, custard pie, drops, kisses (sense 2), sauce, tarts. Compare **coconut cream**.

coconut crab, another name for the **purse crab** (a coconut-eating land crab).

coconut cream, the white liquid obtained from the compressed meat of fresh coconuts. The following can be made with coconut cream: cake, drops, pie, sauce.

coconut milk or **coconut water**, the clear liquid in the hollow center of the fresh coconut (sense 1).

coconut oil, an oil extracted from fresh coconuts, used in making food products.

coconut palm or **coconut tree** or **coco palm**, a tropical palm bearing a large fruit called **coconut** (sense 1).

coco plum [from Spanish *icaco, hicaco,* from Arawak] or **icaco** or **hicaco** or **fat pork**, the plum-shaped fruit of a small tree of tropical America (likewise called *coco plum),* used for preserves.

cocozelle [akin to Italian *cocuzza* "squash"], an Italian vegetable marrow, a certain summer squash very similar to zucchini.

cod, any of certain marine fishes. It is a lean fish and therefore best for boiling and steaming; it is also served as broiled steaks. Compare **codfish**.

coddle (**to**), to cook (e.g., eggs) slowly in water just below the boiling point; a coddled egg resembles a soft-boiled one.

codfish or **keeling** [Scotland] or **torsk** [Scandinavia] or **Cape Cod Turkey** [Spanish *abadejo*], the flesh of the cod used as food, especially when cured or salted. It can be served as codfish balls. Compare **bacalao**.

¹**codling**, *1.* a young cod; *2.* any of several hakes.

²**codling** or **codlin**, a small unripe or inferior apple used chiefly for cooking.

coeur, [French "heart"], a word used in such expressions as *coeurs d'artichaut* "artichoke hearts," *coeur d'une lettue* "heart of lettuce," *coeur de palmier* "heart of palm."

coeur à la crème [French "heart with cream"], a dessert of cream cheese in the shape of hearts, served with cream and preserves.

coffee [from Turkish *kahve*], *1.* an aromatic beverage prepared from roasted and ground or pounded seeds or beans contained in the fruit (or berry) of a certain plant (likewise called *coffee*, and of which there are some 60 species); *2.* these seeds, green or roasted. Coffee (sense 1, the beverage) is made in a drip or percolator pot (infusion) or by boiling (decoction); in Turkey, sugar is brewed with the coffee (which is served black). The coffee berry or coffee cherry is the fruit (cherry-like in color, shape, and size) of the coffee plant, and it contains two seeds enclosed by pulp and an outer skin.

coffee bean (seed), **coffee berry** and **coffee cherry** (fruit), see **coffee.**

coffee cake, a cake to be eaten with coffee (sense 1, the beverage), especially at breakfast, made of sweetened yeast dough enriched with eggs and butter, often containing nuts or raisins, and topped with streusel, and glazed with melted sugar after baking. Coffee cakes are shaped in various forms (e.g., braids, pinwheels, rings, rolls). Coffee cakes include babka, kuchen.

coffee cherry (fruit), see **coffee.**

coffee cream, cream that contains from 18 to 30% of butterfat (compare **whipping cream,** which contains from 30 to 36%).

coffee lightener or **coffee whitener,** a nondairy product used in coffee (sense 1, the beverage) as a substitute for cream. Compare **creamer.**

coffee nib, another name for the coffee bean (see **coffee**).

coffee ring, a plain or fruited coffee cake in the shape of a ring, that is often glazed with melted sugar.

coffee roll or **sweet roll,** a coffee cake or similar sweet, raised bread shaped into rolls, often with raisins, nuts, jam, marmalade, and spices and sometimes glazed with melted sugar.

coho, another name for the **silver salmon.**

cohune oil, a semisolid fat used in cooking, obtained from fruits of a tropical American palm tree called *cohune* or *cohune palm.*

coker nut, the seed of the coquito palm of Chile, that is enclosed in a fruit like a small coconut. It is used in **sweetmeat.**

¹**cola,** a carbonated soft drink usually containing an extract prepared from kola nuts and flavored with sugar and caramel.

²**cola,** another name for **kola.**

colander, a perforated utensil for washing or draining food, for straining.

cola nut, variant of **kola nut.**

cola seed, another name for the **kola nut.**

colby or **Colby,** or **colby cheese** [probably from the name *Colby*], a soft, mild cheese similar to cheddar.

colcannon [from Irish Gaelic *cal ceannan* "white-headed cabbage," from *ceann* "head" + *fionn* "white"], a dish of Irish origin consisting of potatoes and cabbage or other greens boiled and mashed together with butter and seasoning.

cold, previously cooked or processed but served or eaten without heating (e.g., cold cereal, boiled ham, roast beef).

cold cuts, slices of assorted cooked or processed cold meats and of assorted cheese. Compare **Dutch lunch.**

cold flour, sugared, pulverized Indian corn.

coleslaw or **slaw** [from Dutch *koolsla*, from *kool* "cabbage" + *sla* "salad," short for *salade* "salad"], a salad made of finely shredded raw cabbage with a dressing (e.g., mayonnaise and vinegar). When prepared with a cooked dressing, it is called *hot slaw*.

¹**collar**, a piece of meat or fish rolled up and bound for cooking.

²**collar (to)**, to roll up and bind with a string (a piece of meat from which the bones have been removed, or a fish) for cooking, specifically to roll up and fit into a mold and cook (e.g., eels) with herbs and spices.

collards or **collard greens**, the leaves of a certain variety of kale (called *collard*), used as a vegetable. Often served with potatoes.

collop, a small portion or slice, especially of meat; also a rasher of bacon.

collyba [from Greek *kóllyba* "sweet cakes," plural of *kollybon*], small cakes of crushed wheat, raisins, nuts, almonds, and honey. Some cooks add toasted and crushed sesame seeds, grated orange rinds, and pomegranate pods.

Colombia. The following are among representative dishes and products of Colombia: ajiaco; Indian corn, potato and meat soup (Spanish *locro de choclos*), puchero; meat, cassava, and banana stew *(sancocho);* arroz con pollo, seafood (e.g., fried fish from the Caribbean), rice with coconut, fried chicken in mustard sauce *(pollo en salsa de mostaza)*, pork tamales, squash soufflé, fried cassava *(yuca frita)*, cornmeal bread *(arepas)*, fried green-banana slices *(patacones)*, figs with sweet evaporated milk *(brevas con arequipe);* a dish of several fried foods, usually including potatoes, pork or beef variety meats, pork, cracklings (sense 2), blood sausage, popcorn, banana slices *(fritanga);* beef flank with potatoes *(sobrebarriga con papas),* fried ants *(hormigas santandereanas).* Beverages: black coffee *(tinto);* masato (made with sugar and cooked Indian corn, slightly fermented).

colonial goose, a leg of mutton (boned) stuffed with herbs (Australia).

Columbia River salmon [from the *Columbia River* of western North America], another name for the **king salmon**.

colza [French, from Dutch *koolzaad*, from *kool* "cabbage" + *zaad* "seed"], the seed of rape used to make an edible oil.

comal [American Spanish, from Nahuatl *comalli*], a griddle of earthenware or metal used in Mexico and Central America to cook tortillas or toast coffee or cacao beans.

combflower, another name for the **common sunflower**.

¹**comfit** [French "prepared, preserved"], a candy consisting of a solid center (e.g., a piece of fruit) coated and preserved with sugar. In French, a *confit* can be cooked meat (duck, breast of veal) preserved in its own fat (e.g., *un confit d'oie* "a goose preparation").

²**comfit (to)**, to make into a ¹comfit, to preserve. In French, *fruits confits* are fruits coated with sugar, *cornichons confits* are gherkins preserved in vinegar.

comfiture [from French *confiture* "jam, preserve; marmalade"], a preserve.

comino, Spanish for **cumin**.

common fig, a fig not requiring caprification (artificial pollination) in order to set fruit; compare **Smyrna fig**.

common orange, another name for the **sweet orange**.

common salt, another name for **table salt**.

common sunflower or **combflower**, the annual sunflower grown for its seeds which yield an edible oil.

compote [French "stewed fruit"], a dessert of fruits stewed or cooked in syrup (sense 1) in such a way as to retain their natural shape, but they can also be cut into pieces or crushed.

concentrate, a food (e.g., orange juice) made less dilute (reduced in volume by removal of fluid).

concentrated milk, milk reduced in bulk by the removal of water. Distinguished from **condensed milk** (which is evaporated and has sugar added) and from **evaporated milk** (unsweetened, made by evaporating some of the water).

conch, the flesh of any of various tropical marine mollusks (shellfish), as an article of food. It is usually tenderized by pounding before it is cooked. Conches may be used in soups, stews, salads, and served fried.

condensed milk, evaporated cow-milk with sugar added. Distinguished from **concentrated milk** (from which water has been removed) and from **evaporated milk** (which is unsweetened).

condiment [French "seasoning," from Latin *condire* "to pickle, season"], seasoning, something used to enhance the flavor of food and make it more appetizing. It may be pungent or acid, salty or spicy; it may be of natural origin (e.g., horseradish, mustard, oregano, parsley, pepper, saffron, vanilla, vinegar) or a composition (e.g., catsup, chili powder, chutney, curry powder, pickles). See also **herb**, **spice**.

cone pepper, the pungent, conical fruit of a certain hot pepper shrub (likewise called *cone pepper*).

coney [from Latin *cuniculus* "rabbit; underground passage," akin to Basque *untxi* "rabbit"], a certain grouper (fish) of the tropical Atlantic.

confection, a sweet food, such as candy or preserves, usually a preparation of fruits, nuts, or roots with sugar.

confectioners' sugar or **icing sugar**, finely pulverized sugar (finer than powdered sugar). Sometimes, cornstarch is added.

confetti [Italian, plural of *confetto* "sweetmeat, confection, candy"], bonbons or other candies.

confiture [French], preserved or candied fruit (e.g., strawberries, oranges), jam.

conger eel, or **conger** [from French *congre*, from Latin *conger*], any of various large, scaleless marine eels.

conger pike, a large, scaleless eel with a pike-like head.

Congo (formerly *Zaire*). The following are representative dishes and products of the Democratic Republic of the Congo: rice; a dish of chicken or duck or lamb boiled in palm oil, with pilipili (red pepper), served with rice and boiled cassava leaves *(moamba);* grasshoppers, toasted caterpillars, cassava, banana, tangerine, lemon, grapefruit, orange, pineapple, papaya, avocado, mango, custard apple (French *cœur de bœuf*).

congou or **English breakfast tea**, a black tea from China.

congrio [from Spanish *congrio*, from Latin *conger*], a large Chilean eel.

conserve, a preserve prepared from a mixture of fruits (e.g., oranges, raisins) stewed in sugar, sometimes with the addition of leafstalks (e.g., rhubarb) and nuts.

consommé [French "consumed, boiled down"], a clear soup made of meat (e.g., beef, chicken, veal) or vegetable stock or both and condensed by boiling, seasoned, and strained, cleared with egg whites. Consommés include julienne, anglaise (with chopped chicken and chopped almonds), madrilene (jellied bouillon or consommé). When a distinction is made between consommé and bouillon, the main difference is that the meat for a consommé is browned before simmering with vegetables and seasonings.

Continental breakfast [from *Continental* "relating to the continent of Europe excluding the British Isles (Great Britain and Ireland)"], a light breakfast (e.g., of rolls or toast, and coffee).

contrefilet [French], another name for the **club steak**.

converted rice, rice that retains its vitamin and mineral content because of the way it has been processed.

¹**cook** [from Latin *coquus* "a cook," from *coquere* "to cook"], a person who prepares food for eating.

²**cook (to)**, to prepare food for eating by applying heat, as by boiling, frying, or baking.

cookbook, a book containing directions, recipes, and other information about the preparation of food.

cook cheese or **pot cheese,** or **cooked cheese**, an unripened cheese made from curd that has been cooked to a soft consistency and poured into hot containers. Compare **cup cheese**.

cookery, the art or practice of preparing food. Compare **cuisine**.

cookie or **cooky** [from Dutch *koekje*, diminutive of *koek* "cake"] or **tea cake**, any of various small, thin, crisp, cakes, either flat or slightly raised, cut from rolled dough (in fancy [stars, bells, trees, squares, bars] or circular shapes) before baking, or dropped from a spoon, or cut into pieces (of different shapes) after baking. Cookies are made from the same ingredients used for cake, but with less liquid (e.g., sour milk, cream), so that they will hold their shape; they may have nuts (e.g., pecans, almonds, pine nuts, hazel nuts), spices, fruit (e.g., dates, figs, prunes, plums), honey, molasses, maple, caramel, chocolate, butterscotch, vanilla, ginger, icings, glazes. Cookies include brownies, creams (sense 3), drop cookies, hermits, jumbles, kisses (sense 2), lebkuchen, macaroons, pfeffernüsse, shortbread, springerle, wafers.

cooking banana, see **plantain**.

cooler, *1.* a tall, cold, nonalcoholic, refreshing drink (e.g., lemonade); *2.* a chilled alcoholic drink with flavoring and sugar.

coon-striped shrimp [from *coon*, shortened from *raccoon*], a large Pacific Ocean shrimp.

coontie [from Seminole *kunti* "coontie flour"] or **Florida arrowroot** or **wild sago**, a plant of tropical America whose roots and half-buried stems yield an arrowroot (starch).

coppa [Italian "occiput," from *coppa* "cup," from its shape], an Italian sausage made chiefly of pork butts (in the area of Rome with flesh from the hog's head) and seasoned with cayenne pepper.

coppernosed bream or **coppernosed sunfish**, other names for the **bluegill** (a sunfish).

coq au vin [French "cock with wine"], a dish of chicken cooked in red wine, with mushrooms, salt pork, onions and a bouquet garni.

coquille [French "shell"] dish served in a shell or a scallop-shaped dish in which food is browned and served.

coquille Saint-Jacques [French "scallop; scallop shell," from *coquille* "shell" + *Saint Jacques* "Saint James the apostle," whose identifying token is a scallop shell], a dish of scallops often served in a scallop-shaped dish (called *coquille*) or a scallop shell in which it was browned.

coquito [Spanish, diminutive of *coco* "coco palm"] or **honey palm**, a Chilean palm tree whose sap is used in making palm honey (a sweet syrup), and seeds (called **coker nuts**) for sweetmeats.

coral, the cooked roe of a lobster.

coral cod, a certain fish of Australian coral reefs.

coral crab, any of various large crabs.

corbina or **corvina** [from Spanish *corvina* "ravenlike (feminine)" (from its dark color), from Latin *corvus* "raven"], any of several marine fishes.

¹**cordon bleu** (noun) [French "blue cordon, blue ribbon"], a person distinguished in his or her field, especially a cook of great skill.

²**cordon bleu** (adjective), stuffed with ham and Swiss cheese (e.g., veal cordon bleu).

coriander [from French *coriandre*] or **coriander seed**, the dried ripe seeds of an herb (called *coriander*) of the carrot family used as a condiment (e.g., to flavor pickles, curries, confections). Coriander leaves are likewise used as a condiment (see **cilantro**).

coriander oil, an oil obtained from the dried ripe fruit of coriander (herb) and used as a flavoring agent.

corm, the thick stem-base of a plant.

¹**corn**, *1.* (also called **Indian corn** [a more precise term, so there is no confusion with ¹**corn**, sense 2] or **sweet corn** or **maize**), the seeds or kernels of any of several varieties of a certain cereal plant (likewise called *corn*), borne on large ears and served as a vegetable while still soft. It has long been cultivated in the New World (some 70 centuries). Corn dishes include bread, cake, casserole, chowder, cream of corn (soup), fritters, grits, muffin, pudding, soufflé; some ways of preparing corn: creamed, popped, roasted, sautéed, scalloped; *2.* (also called **grain**) the seeds of any of several cereal plants (e.g., wheat, rye, oats, barley).

²**corn (to)**, *1.* to preserve and season with salt in grains; *2.* to salt lightly (e.g., beef [which then becomes corned beef], tongue) in brine.

corn beef, another name for **corned beef**.

corn bread, a kind of bread made from cornmeal (e.g., cornmeal mixed with shortening and water and baked or fried, or cornmeal mixed with wheat flour, eggs, milk, and leavening and baked).

corn cake, a bread made with cornmeal cooked either as small cakes on a griddle or oven-baked in a pan.

corn chip, a piece of a snack food prepared from a cornmeal batter (seasoned).

corncob or **cob**, *1.* the woody core or axis of an ear of Indian corn, on which the kernels grow; *2.* an ear of Indian corn.

corn dodger or **dogder**, a cake of corn bread fried on a griddle or baked in an oven, or broiled, or boiled as a dumpling (sense 1) with ham and cabbage or with greens.

corn dog, a frankfurter dipped in cornmeal batter, fried, and served on a stick.

corn dumpling, a boiled corn dodger.

corned beef or **corn beef**, beef cured or preserved by salting it lightly in brine, often with seasonings; corned beef dishes include casserole, ²hash.

cornflakes, toasted flakes made from the coarse meal of hulled corn by moistening and heating it, then drying and toasting the flakes, for use as a breakfast cereal, served cold.

corn flour, finely ground flour made from Indian corn.

cornichon [French "gherkin," from *corne* "horn"], a gherkin preserved in vinegar and usually flavored with tarragon.

Cornish hen, see **Rock Cornish hen**.

Cornish pasty [from *Cornish* "of Cornwall," from *Cornwall*, county of southwestern England], cooked meat and vegetables (and seasoning) encased in pastry and baked.

cornmeal or **Indian meal**, meal made from Indian corn (coarsely ground). Cornmeal dishes include ashcakes, buns, corn cakes, fried mush, tamales.

corn oil or **maizeoil**, an oil obtained from the germs of Indian corn kernels and used as a salad oil and in margarine.

corn on the cob or (Africa) **green mealie**, Indian corn cooked and eaten on the cob.

corn oyster, a fritter containing young Indian corn cut from the cob and cooked on a griddle.

corn pone, or **pone**, corn bread (see **pone**, sense 2).

corn pudding, a pudding (sense 1) made with Indian corn, eggs, and milk.

corn salad [so called from its occurrence in cornfields] or **lamb's lettuce** or **milkgrass**, a certain plant having leaves used as salad and as potherbs.

cornstarch, starch resembling a fine white flour, prepared from Indian corn and used as a thickener in cooking (e.g., in puddings and gravies) and in making corn syrup and sugars (e.g., confectioners' sugar).

corn stick, a corn bread baked in a muffin pan having cups shaped like ears of Indian corn.

corn syrup, a transparent thick syrup prepared from cornstarch and used in foods (e.g., in bakery products and candy).

Coromandel gooseberry [from the *Coromandel* Coast, the southeastern coast of India], another name for the **carambola** (fruit).

corvina, see **corbina**.

cos lettuce or **cos** [from *Cos*, Latin name of the Greek island of Kos, whence it was originally exported] or **romaine** or **romaine lettuce**, a type of lettuce used as salad greens.

cossette [French "sugar beet strip," "little pod," diminutive of *cosse* "pod"], a strip or slice (e.g., of sugar beet), a chip.

costard, any of several large English cooking apples.

Costa Rica. The following are among representative dishes and products of Costa Rica: rice and beans (Spanish *gallo pinto* "mottled rooster"), eaten with eggs or meat; heart of palm (*palmito*), posol (sense 1), tamales, mango, papaya, plantain, cassava (*yuca*), coconut, seafood (e.g., shrimp, oysters, squid, octopus, sea bass, turtle), hash (*picadillo*).

costmary [so named because it used to be regarded as sacred to *Mary*, mother of Jesus], an herb having aromatic foliage used as a potherb and salad plant.

cotechino [Italian], a smoked and dried pork sausage of Milanese origin (made with skin and lean meat).

côtelette, French for **cutlet**.

Cotherstone [from *Cotherstone*, Yorkshire, northwestern England], a Stilton-like, cow-milk, rennet cheese.

cottage cheese or **sour milk cheese** or **Dutch cheese, curd cheese** or **schmierkase** (German) or **smearcase** or **pot cheese**, a soft, uncured, white cheese made of strained and seasoned curds of skim milk.

cottage fried potatoes, another name for **home fried potatoes**.

cottage loaf, a loaf of bread consisting of two round parts of different sizes, the smaller on top of the larger.

cottage pie, a shepherd's pie made especially of beef.

cottage pudding, plain cake, without icing, covered with a hot sweet sauce.

cotton candy, another name for **spun sugar**.

cottonseed oil, an oil obtained from the cottonseed by crushing, used in cooking and as salad oil, and after hydrogenation in shortenings and margarine.

coulibiac [French, from Russian *kulebyaka*], fish (e.g., salmon) rolled in pastry dough and baked. In French, the word refers also to meat and cabbage so prepared.

coulis [French, from *couler* "to strain"], the strained product of concentrated slow cooking of food (e.g., meat, fish, shellfish [e.g., crayfish], vegetables [e.g., tomatoes, peas]). When fruits (e.g., raspberry, blackberry, orange, black currant) are so prepared, syrup is added to the resulting purée.

couma [French, from Tupi *cumá*] or **sorva**, the edible sweet fruit of a certain tropical South American tree (likewise called *couma).*

country almond, another name for the **Malabar almond**.

country sausage, fresh pork sausage (sense 1) available in bulk to be made into patties, and in links both fresh and smoked.

country-style scrambled eggs, see **scrambled eggs**.

coupe [French "stemmed glass; bowl-shaped dish"], a dessert commonly served in a stemmed glass and consisting of ice cream or a fruit-flavored ice topped with mixed fruit, nuts, or whipped cream.

course [from French *cours, course* "onward movement, ordered process or succession," from Latin *currere* "to run"], a part of a meal (e.g., "a four-course meal") served as a unit at one time with its accompaniments.

court bouillon [French "short bouillon"], a fish stock usually containing seasoning (e.g., spices, herbs), vegetables, and white wine and used to poach fish. In French, the word refers also to stock for meat.

couscous [from French *couscous, couscoussou,* from Arabic *kuskus, kuskusu,* from *kaskasa* "to pound"], *1.* a North African dish of crushed grain (wheat broken into coarse particles, semolina) steamed and served with various meats and vegetables; *2.* cracked wheat, semolina.

Coventry tartlet [from *Coventry,* city of central England], a small tart (a tartlet) containing a mixture made principally of sharp cheese (with butter, sugar, egg yolk).

cow berry, another name for **mountain cranberry**.

cowgram, another name for the **chick-pea**.

cow parsnip, a certain plant of the carrot family.

cowpea or **kaffir bean** or **lady pea** or **southern pea**, the edible seed of a plant (likewise called *cowpea*) that, despite the second part of its name, is more nearly related to the bean than to the pea.

cow tree [translation of South American Spanish *árbol de vaca*], a South American tree yielding a milky juice used as food.

coyo [from American Spanish *coyó,* from Maya], the fruit of a certain Mexican and Central American avocado tree (likewise called *coyo*).

crab or **cangrejo** [Spanish], any of various rather stocky and broadly built crustaceans. Crabmeat is extracted from the shell with difficulty; the resulting flakes may be creamed, deviled, served au gratin, made into a salad or puffs or sautéed cakes, or sandwiches, stuffed back into the shell and broiled. Crabs can also be prepared in ways similar to lobster (see **lobster**).

crab apple, the small, tart, applelike fruit of any of several trees (likewise called *crab apples*), used for making jellies and preserves.

crabmeat, the edible part of a crab.

cracked wheat [French: *blé concassé*], wheat broken into coarse particles.

cracker, a small, dry, thin, crisp bakery product (similar to a wafer or a biscuit) made of flour and water with or without leavening or shortening and salted, semisweet, or plain. It is most often made of unleavened and unsweetened dough. Crackers include saltines.

crackerjack, a candied confection of popcorn and sometimes shelled peanuts coated with syrup (as molasses).

crackling bread, Indian-corn bread made with cracklings (sense 1).

cracklings, *1.* the crisp bits that remain of pork fat after the lard has been cooked out of it; they are eaten alone or crumbled and baked into corn bread; they can also be made from whale or fish; *2.* the crisp browned pork skin (or the skin of turkey, duck, or goose), roasted or fried after the hair has been removed.

cranberry [partial translation of Low German *kraanbere* "crane berry" (because the stamens [male organs of the flowers] resemble a beak)], the red, tart berry produced by any of several plants (likewise called *cranberries*) of the heath family, often made into sauce or jelly. Dishes made with cranberries include cocktails, ices, pies, salads, sauces; pork chops and turkey can be served with it; it can be mixed with orange and used for breads, punches, relishes.

crappie [from Canadian French *crapet*], either of two North American freshwater fishes related to the sunfishes. See **black crappie, white crappie**.

crawfish, variant of **crayfish**.

crayfish or **crawfish** [from Old French *crevice, crevise* (French *écrevisse)*], *1.* any of various freshwater crustaceans resembling the lobster but usually much smaller; *2.* another name for the **spiny lobster**. Crayfish can be cooked in court bouillon, and prepared as buisson, coulis, gratin (sense 2).

¹**cream**, *1.* the yellowish, fatty part of unhomogenized milk that tends to accumulate at the surface on standing or is separated by centrifugal force; it contains from 18 to about 40% butterfat; *2.* a food containing cream (sense 1) or having a creamy consistency (e.g., Bavarian cream, bisque, mousse, oyster stew, tapioca cream, vichyssoise; cream cakes, caramels, cheese, a chocolate cream [a candy], Devonshire, dressing, filling, gravy, pies [almond, banana, butterscotch, chocolate, coconut, vanilla], puffs, sauces [e.g., white sauce], soups [cream of asparagus soup, of carrot, of celery, of chicken, of corn, of mushroom, of tomato, cream of vegetables; cheddar cheese soup], wafers).

²**cream** (**to**), *1.* to beat (e.g., butter and sugar) into a creamy consistency; *2.* to prepare or cook (e.g., a vegetable) in or with a cream sauce. Dishes so prepared include creamed asparagus, chicken, eggs, onions, potatoes, spinach, sweetbreads, mixed vegetables.

cream bun, a bun filled with cream or custard, a **cream puff**.

cream caramel, another name for **crème caramel**. See also **caramel**, sense 1.

cream Chantilly, see **Chantilly**.

cream cheese, a soft, white, unripened cheese made from whole sweet milk enriched with cream or by working cream into a skimmed-milk curd. Cream cheese is used in **coeur à la crème**.

creamer, a nondairy product used as a substitute for cream (e.g., in coffee). Compare **coffee lightener**.

cream nut [probably so called from the rich flavor] *1.* another name for **Brazil nut**; *2.* the nut of the **cauchillo**.

cream of tartar, a salt with a pleasant acid taste found in grapes and used in foods (e.g., baking powder, hard candy).

cream-of-tartar tree, a North Australian tree that produces an agreeably acid fruit.

cream puff [French: *chou à la crème*] or **cream bun**, a round shell of light pastry usually filled with whipped cream, custard, or ice, sometimes served with a frosting or sauce. Compare **chou, éclair**.

cream sauce, a white sauce made by heating a mixture of flour and butter in milk or cream.

cream soda, a carbonated soft drink, often colorless, that is flavored with vanilla and sweetened with sugar.

creamy, containing ¹cream (sense 1) or having the consistency of ¹cream (sense 1).

Crécy [French "carrot of a choice variety," from *Crécy*, a town in northeastern France where it is grown], prepared with carrots (e.g., eggs, entrées, soup).

creeping thyme, another name for **wild thyme**.

crème [French "cream"], cream or cream sauce as used in cookery. When sugar and eggs are added one gets desserts such as **crème anglaise**, **crème renversée**. In French, *crème glacée* is ice cream.

crème anglaise [French "English cream"], a vanilla-flavored custard sauce usually served with desserts.

crème brûlée [French "scorched cream"], a rich custard of creole origin (egg yolks, cream, sugar) topped with caramelized brown sugar glaze. It may be used as a filling for fruit tarts.

crème caramel or **cream caramel** [from French *crème caramel*, "caramel cream"], a custard that has been baked with caramel sauce (caramelized sugar).

crème Chantilly, see **Chantilly**.

crème fraîche [French "fresh cream"], heavy cream thickened and slightly soured with buttermilk (or a little sour cream) and often served with fruit, or it may be stirred into soup before serving.

crème renversée, in French is a molded custard cooked in a double boiler.

¹**creole** (noun) [from French *créole*] or **creolefish**, a certain tropical American fish.

²**creole** (adjective) [from Creole "descendant of early French or Spanish settlers of Louisiana and other United States Gulf states"], (typically) prepared with rice, okra, tomatoes, peppers, and seasonings (e.g., creole beignet, celery, frankfurters, jambalaya, pork cutlets, sauce; lobster creole, shrimp creole). Compare **Cajun**.

creole sauce, a form of tomato sauce cooked with vegetables and herbs; it was developed in Louisiana (a state of the southern United States) and is served on rice, pasta, seafood, omelet, or meat loaf.

crepe or **crêpe** [from French *crêpe* "pancake," from *crêpe* "a certain light fabric"], a small very thin pancake made of milk, flour (wheat or buckwheat), and eggs and fried on a metal sheet or in a skillet. Crepes may have a filling (e.g., jam, vegetables, meat) and they may be flamed.

crêpe Suzette [French, from *crêpe* "pancake" + *Suzette*, diminutive of the name *Suzanne*, corresponding to English *Susan*, possibly for French actress *Suzanne* Reichenberg (died 1924)], a small, thin, dessert pancake folded in quarters or rolled, heated in a sauce of butter, orange (or lemon or tangerine) juice, and grated rind. Often served with a flaming brandy or curaçao sauce.

cress, any of numerous plants with moderately pungent leaves used in salads and as garnishes.

crevalle, another name for **cavalla**.

crisp [from *crisp* "easily crumbled"] or **crumble**, a baked dessert of fruit with crumb toppings (e.g., apple crisp). It may be served with butterscotch sauce.

croaker [from *croak* "to make a deep harsh sound"], any of various chiefly marine fishes that make croaking or grunting noises.

croissant [French "crescent," probably translation of German *Hornchen* "little horn," a name given in Vienna to certain pastries in 1689 after the victory against the Turks; the crescent was the Turkish emblem and a symbol of Turkish or Moslem power], a flaky, rich, crescent-shaped roll of leavened dough or puff pastry.

crookneck, a squash with a long recurved neck.

croquembouche [French "it crunches in the mouth"], a cone-shaped stack of small cream puffs coated with caramelized sugar. Compare **saint-honoré**.

croquette [French, from *croquer* "to crunch"], a small cone-shaped or rounded cake consisting usually of minced fowl (e.g., chicken), meat, fish, or vegetable (e.g., potato, rice, sweet potato), often combined with a thick sauce, coated with egg and bread crumbs (or cracker crumbs or flour) and fried in deep fat.

crosnes or **crosne** [from French *crosne*, from *Crosne*, village in northern France where the plant was cultivated], another name for **Chinese artichoke**.

croustade [French], a crisp shell (e.g., of toasted or fried bread, or of puff pastry) in which to serve food.

croûte [French "crust"], a slice of toasted or fried bread cut in fancy shape and used as a foundation in serving food (e.g., cheese, mushrooms). In French it also means cooked dough (puff pastry type) wrapping food such as pâté (as in *pâté en croûte*, *jambon* ["ham"] *en croûte*; boned chicken or trout are also baked in light pastry).

crouton [from French *croûton*, diminutive of *croûte* "crust"], a small cube of toasted or crisply fried bread (sometimes with butter, or with herbs and garlic) used in soups and garnishings (e.g., on spinach or omelette).

crow [perhaps from Dutch *kroos* "intestine"], the mesentery (a certain membrane) of an animal, especially when used as food.

crowdie [from *crud* "curd"], a partially cooked Scottish cottage cheese.

crowdy, porridge (sense 1), a thick gruel of oatmeal and water or milk.

crow garlic or **crow onion**, a certain wild onion.

crown roast, a roast of lamb, veal, or pork made from the rib portions of two loins by trimming off the backbone and skewering the ends together to form a circle with the bones outside.

crow onion, another name for **crow garlic**.

crudités [French "raw foods," plural of *crudité* "rawness"], pieces of raw vegetables (e.g., carrots, cauliflower, celery) or of certain fruits, served as an hors d'oeuvre often with a dip.

cruller [from Dutch *krulle*, a kind of twisted cake, from *krullen* "to curl"], a small, sweet cake made of a rich egg batter (sweet roll dough) formed into twisted strips (or ring-shaped) and fried brown in deep fat.

crumb (**to**), to cover with crumbs.

crumble, another name for a **crisp**.

crumbs, *1.* fragments of baked bread (compare **bread crumbs**); *2.* a mixture of sugar, butter, and flour used as a topping on pastry (e.g., coffee cake).

crumpet or **pikelet**, a small, light, soft, round cake similar to a muffin, made of rich unsweetened batter baked on a griddle and usually split and toasted before serving.

crust [from Latin *crusta* "shell, crust"], *1.* the hardened outer portion or surface part of bread; *2.* a piece of bread consisting mostly of this part; *3.* the pastry cover of a pie or tart.

crustacean [from New Latin *crustacea* "the shelled ones," neuter plural of *crustaceus* "crustaceous, having a hard crust or shell," from Latin *crusta* "shell"], any of various mostly aquatic arthropods (certain invertebrate animals) including lobsters, shrimps, crabs, barnacles. See **shellfish**.

crystallize (to), to coat (e.g., grapes, cherries) with crystals especially of sugar.

crystallized, candied, coated with crystals especially of sugar (e.g., crystallized grapes, cherries).

Cuba. The following are among representative dishes and products of Cuba: arroz con pollo, roast suckling pig, beef hash (Spanish *picadillo),* beans with rice *(moros y cristianos* "Moors and Christians"), fried plantain, beef ajiaco, cassava, pineapple, coconuts, guavas, seafood (e.g., lobster, snapper, sea bream); yams and other tubers (such as malanga and *boniato* [white sweet-potato]); sweet-potato paste *(boniatillo).*

cube steak, a small, thin slice of a tough cut of beef that has been made tender by breaking the fibers, by cutting it partly through one or both surfaces in a pattern of squares. It is usually pan-broiled. Compare **minute steak**.

cube sugar or **brick sugar**, moistened, granulated sugar, molded into cubes.

cuchifrito [American Spanish, from *cuchi* "hog, pig" (from Spanish *cochino* "pig") + Spanish *frito* "fried"], a cube of pork cooked by immersing it in a deep pan of fat or oil.

cucumber or **cuke**, the usually cylindrical fruit of a vine (likewise called *cucumber*) of the gourd family, having a hard green rind and white flesh, cultivated as a garden vegetable that can be eaten raw or cooked. Compare **gherkin**.

cucumber melon or **cucumber apple**, other names for the **mango melon**.

cucumber tree, a tree of eastern Asia having edible fruit (called **bilimbi**) that resembles a small cucumber and is used for preserves.

cucurbit, any of various plants of the gourd family, which includes the squash, pumpkin, cucumber, melon, watermelon.

cuisine [French "kitchen"], a characteristic manner or style of preparing food. Kitchen operations include boiling, broiling, browning, candying, cooking, cutting, dressing, filling, flaming, frying, garnishing, grilling, larding, marinating, peeling, pickling, poaching, preserving, roasting, sautéing, seasoning, stuffing, trimming, tying, whipping.

cuisine minceur [French "slimness cooking"], a low-calorie manner of preparing French food.

cuke, another name for the **cucumber**.

culinary [from Latin *culinarius* "relating to the kitchen or to cookery," from *culina* "kitchen"], used in cooking or suited for cooking (e.g., culinary herbs).

cullis [from French *coulis* "jelly, broth, sauce," from *couler* "to strain"], a strong, clear broth of boiled meat (strained).

cultured milk or **cultured buttermilk**, the product of the souring of skimmed milk by a culture of lactic acid bacteria.

cultus, or **cultus cod**, other names for the **lingcod**.

Cumberland sauce [for *Cumberland*, a former county of northwestern England, now included in the county of Cumbria], a cold sauce flavored with orange rind, lemon, red currant jelly, port wine, and spices, that is often served with game or with cold ham; sugar may be added. Some cooks serve it hot.

cumin [from Latin *cuminum*], the aromatic seeds of a low plant (likewise called *cumin*) of the carrot family used as a condiment (spice).

cuminseed, the seed of the cumin plant.

cunner or **wharf fish**, a certain marine fish (a wrasse).

cupcake, a small cake baked in a cup-shaped mold.

cup cheese, cook cheese poured into hot china cups.

cup custard, custard baked in cup-shaped cookware (and usually served in it).

Curaçao, see **Netherlands Antilles**.

curassow [modification of *Curaçao*, island of the Netherlands Antilles, in the southern Caribbean], any of several tropical American birds related to the pheasants and to the domestic fowl.

curcuma [from Arabic *kurkum* "saffron"], any of various tropical plants, having thick, aromatic rootstocks (that yield starch [arrowroot, likewise called *curcuma*]). One of these plants is the source of turmeric.

curd (often used in plural), *1.* the thick part of coagulated milk, used to make cheese (distinguished from **whey**, which is the watery part); *2.* a food resembling milk curds (e.g., soybeans curds; *3.* the edible flower head of the cauliflower.

curd cheese, another name for **cottage cheese**.

cure (**to**), to prepare food so it keeps longer (e.g., meat or fish, by salting, smoking, or aging).

currant [from Middle English *rayson* (or *raison*) *of Coraunte* "raisin of Corinth (region of Greece)"], *1.* a small, seedless raisin, grown chiefly in the Mediterranean region and used in cookery and confectionery; *2.* the small, sour fruit of several plants (shrubs) likewise called *currants*, used chiefly for making jams and jellies (e.g., black currant, red currant, white currant). Sauces made with currants include plain currant, orange-currant (for roast duck, lamb, ham, chicken), currant mint.

¹**curry** or **currie** [from Tamil *kari*] *1.* another name for **curry powder** (a condiment); *2.* a heavily spiced sauce, dressing, or relish made with curry powder and eaten with meat, fish, rice, or other food; *3.* a dish (a stew [e.g., of chicken, fish, lamb]) cooked or seasoned with curry (sense 2, sauce) or with curry powder.

²**curry** (**to**), to season with curry. Curried dishes include chicken, eggs, lamb, pork slices, rice, shrimp.

curry powder, a blended condiment prepared from ground spices (e.g., cumin seeds, coriander seeds, turmeric; peppercorns); herbs can also be included (e.g., garlic, green ginger, hot pepper). Also called **curry**.

cush [ultimately from Arabic *kuskus* "couscous"], a dish of seasoned cornmeal dough fried, baked with meat, or boiled in pot liquor.

cushaw, a certain squash (a crookneck).

cusk, a large fish of the cod family, of North Atlantic coastal waters.

custard, a pudding-like dessert of milk, sugar, eggs (and sometimes flour), and flavoring (e.g., coffee, orange, vanilla), boiled (often in a double boiler) or baked until set. Dishes made with custard include flan, floating island, pie, pudding, puff (sense 1), sauce. Compare **caramel custard**, **parfait** (sense 1), **soft custard**.

custard apple [its pulp resembles custard] or **bullock's-heart** (Spanish: *anona;* in Cuba, *mamón*) or **Jamaica apple** or **sweetsop**, the large, heart-shaped, soft-shelled fruit of a tropical American tree (likewise called *custard apple*). See also **papaw**, sense 2.

cutlet [from French *côtelette* "small rib," from *côte* "rib"], *1.* a thin slice of meat, usually veal (also lamb, pork), cut from the leg or ribs of an animal, and suitable for broiling or frying; *2.* a food mixture of chopped meat or fish shaped to resemble a meat cutlet (a flat croquette).

cuttlefish, a marine mollusk related to the squid. Cuttlefishes secrete a dark, inky fluid, and are often served in their own "ink."

Cyprus. The following are among representative dishes of Cyprus: moussaka, shish kebab (Greek *souvlakia*), dolma (Greek *dolmades*).

Czech Republic. The following are among representative dishes and products of the Czech Republic: dumplings or quenelles (Czech *knedliky*) [which may be stuffed with fruit (e.g., plum, cherry, apple, peach, strawberries)]; roast pork *(veprová)* with sauerkraut *(zelí)* and dumplings, or goose *(husa)* with sauerkraut and dumplings; ham, mushrooms, cheese, cabbage soup, sausage, carp.

duff   dumpling   decoction   dolce   drisheen   *D*   dariole   dunderfunk

dab or **limande** [French], any of various flatfishes resembling the flounders. Dabs can be baked or served au gratin.

dacquoise [French "from Dax (feminine)," from *Dax*, a town of southwestern France], a layer cake, a dessert made of layers of baked nut meringue (egg whites, sugar, ground almonds or hazelnuts) with a filling usually of buttercream (sense 1) and with buttercream icing. It is often prepared in disc or heart shapes.

Dagwood [for *Dagwood* Bumstead, character who makes many-layered sandwiches in the 20th-century comic strip *Blondie*], a many-layered sandwich.

dahi [from Hindi *dahī*, from Sanskrit *dadhi* "sour milk"], the curd of soured curdled milk.

daikon [from Japanese "big root"] or **Japanese radish**, *1.* a large, white radish that is eaten cooked or raw, used especially in Oriental cuisine; *2.* a plant (likewise called *daikon)* whose root is this radish.

dainty, something delicious, a **delicacy**.

dairy breed, any breed of cattle developed primarily for the production of milk rather than meat (e.g., Ayrshire, Guernsey, Holstein-Friesian, Jersey).

damper, an unfermented, baking-powder bread, made of flour and water, formed into flat cakes and usually baked over a campfire on a stone or in hot ashes (Australia).

damson, or **damson plum** [from Latin *(prunum) damascenum*, "(plum) of Damascus"], the small, tart, bluish-black fruit of an Asian plum tree (likewise called *damson).* Dishes made with damsons include mousse, preserve (compare **damson cheese**).

damson cheese, a preserve made of damson plums cooked with sugar to a consistency of soft cheese.

dandelion [from French *dent-de-lion*, "lion's tooth," from its deeply indented (notched) basal leaves], a plant whose leaves are used in salads (French *salade de pissenlit* or *salade de dent-de-lion)* and as a potherb.

dandelion coffee, a beverage made from the dried roots of the dandelion.

dangleberry or **blue huckleberry** or **tangleberry**, the sweet, blue fruit of a certain huckleberry (a shrub, likewise called *dangleberry)* of eastern North America.

Danish pastry, or **Danish**, a sweet pastry (sense 3) made of dough raised with yeast with the shortening rolled in.

dao [Tagalog], a certain Philippine tree with edible fruit.

dariole [French], *1.* a small puff-pastry tart filled before cooking (in a circular mold) with cream, custard (butter and eggs), jam, macaroons or fruit, sometimes with chocolate or almonds added; *2.* a shell of pastry (in which darioles, sense 1, are cooked), shaped like a flower-pot, or a mold of aspic, filled with sweet or savory food.

Darjeeling tea, or **Darjeeling** [from *Darjeeling*, area of northeastern India], a tea of high quality from Darjeeling and other mountainous areas of northern India.

dark, *1.* of a brown shade (e.g., dark meat); *2.* made of whole wheat flour (e.g., dark bread).

dark meat, meat of those portions (e.g., thigh) of poultry (chicken, turkey) or game that are dark-colored when cooked; compare **white meat** (sense 2).

dasheen, another word for **taro**.

dashi [Japanese "broth"], a broth made from dried bonito (fish).

dassie [Afrikaans], a certain small fish of African coasts and estuaries.

date [French, from Greek *daktylos* "finger"], the sweet, oblong fruit of a certain palm (likewise called *date*, or *date palm).*

date plum, a certain Asiatic persimmon with edible fruits.

dátil, Spanish for **date** (the fruit).

dattock, a tropical African tree having pods with a sweet pulp, each with one edible seed.

daube [French], a stew of braised meat (usually beef, in red wine; also veal), vegetables, herbs, and spices, cooked in a tightly covered pot. In Seychelles creole, it is called *ladob* [from French *la daube* "the daube"] and in Seychelles it is made with coconut sauce.

dauphiné [from *Dauphiné*, region in southeastern France], (of potatoes) mashed, shaped into balls, and fried in deep fat. Bread crumbs and a grating of nutmeg may be added. In French, a *gratin dauphinois* [i.e., "from the Dauphiné"] is a dish of gratin potatoes, prepared with milk, butter, and cheese.

decapod [from New Latin *decapoda* "ten-footed ones," from Greek *deka-* "ten" + *-pod-* "feet"], *1.* a crustacean (e.g., crab, lobster, shrimp) having five pairs of locomotor (leglike) appendages; *2.* a mollusk (e.g., cuttlefish, squid) having ten armlike tentacles.

decoct (to) [from Latin *decoctus* "boiled down," past participle of *decoquere* "to boil down," from *de-* "down, away" + *coquere* "to cook"], to extract the flavor of by boiling; *2.* to steep in hot water; *3.* to concentrate by boiling.

decoction [from Latin *decoctus* "boiled down," past participle of *decoquere* "to boil down," from *de-* "down, away" + *coquere* "to cook"], *1.* a concentrated extract obtained by boiling. Distinguished from **infusion** (which is an extract obtained by steeping, without boiling); *2.* the act or process of boiling, usually in water, so as to extract the flavor.

deep-dish pie, a pie, usually with a fruit filling and no bottom crust, that is baked in a deep dish. Compare ¹**cobbler**.

deep-fry (**to**), to cook by immersing in a deep pan of fat or oil (distinguished from **sautéing** or shallow-frying). See ²**fry**.

deer, any of various mammals such as caribou, elk, moose. The edible flesh of deer (and of other game animals) is called **venison**. It is cooked like beef, well done but not overcooked, and often served with wild-plum jelly.

deerhorn cactus, a certain cactus with edible scarlet fruits.

dehydrate (**to**), to remove water from (e.g., fruits, milk, vegetables) for preservation.

delicacy, something pleasing to eat that is considered rare or luxurious, a choice food, e.g., caviar.

delicatessen [from German *Delikatessen*, "delicacies," from French *délicatesse* "delicacy"], *1.* ready-to-eat food products (e.g., cooked or processed meats [e.g., ham, sausage], caviar, salmon, foie gras, cheeses, prepared salads, preserves, relishes); *2.* a shop that sells cooked or prepared foods ready for serving.

Delicious, or **Delicious apple**, a largely red (but also yellow) apple of American origin.

Delmonico potatoes [from the *Delmonico* restaurants, New York City, so called for their founder, Lorenzo *Delmonico*, 1813–1881], chopped or sliced potatoes baked in cream sauce with butter and chives.

Delmonico steak [from the *Delmonico* restaurants, New York City, so called for their founder, Lorenzo *Delmonico*, 1813–1881], another name for **club steak**.

Demerara sugar [from *Demerara*, an area, and the principal river, of Guyana], a coarse, light-brown sugar.

demiglace [French "half glaze"], brown sauce (= espagnole) simmered down (= reduced), degreased, strained, and usually seasoned with dry wine. It may be served with filet mignon.

demitasse [French "half cup"], a small cup of black coffee usually served after dinner.

Denmark. The following are among representative dishes and products of Denmark: open-faced sandwiches (Danish *smørrebrød*, "butter bread") with a variety of fish, meat, or cheese fillings (often on rye bread [*rugbrød*]), cheeses, milk, fish (including fried eel [*stegt ål*], smoked salmon, smoked herring, trout, boiled cod), shellfish (including lobster, crayfish, shrimp, oysters), soup made of rye bread and beer; cold meats, roasts, ham, pastries (*kage* or *vienerbrød*), a dessert called *rødgrød*, "red mush (or porridge)."

dent, or **dent corn**, the kernels of a variety of Indian corn (likewise called *dent corn*) that become indented at the tip at maturity.

Denver omelet [from *Denver*, western United States city], another name for the **western omelet**.

Denver sandwich [from *Denver*, western United States city], another name for the **western sandwich**.

Derby, or **Derby cheese**, a hard-pressed mild-flavored English cheese that is prepared from whole cow's milk and resembles cheddar.

desiccate [from Latin *desiccare* "to dry up," from *siccare* "to dry," from *siccus* "dry"], to dehydrate, preserve by drying (e.g., desiccated coconut).

dessert [French, from *desservir* "to clear the table," from *des-* "reversal" + *servir* "to serve"], *1.* a usually sweet course or dish served at the end of a meal (e.g., fruit, pastry, pudding, ice cream, or cheese); *2.* a fresh fruit served after a sweet. Desserts (sense 1) include angel food, baked Alaskas, baklava, bananas Foster, banana split, Banbury tarts, barley sugar, Betties, biscuit tortoni, blancmange (cornstarch pudding), bombes, brown Betties, cakes (sense 1; some with fruit [apple, peach, apricot] baked on the top), ¹candy (sense 2), caramel (sense 1), charlotte russe, ¹cobblers, cooked fruit, cookies, cottage (or castle) puddings, coupes, cream (Bavarian, Spanish, tapioca), cream puffs (including choux, éclairs), crème brûlée, crêpes Suzette, custard (soft or baked), duff, dumplings (sense 2), fondant (sense 2), ¹frappés, fritters (that enclose pieces of fruit), fudge, gelatin (sense 3), gingerbread (both senses), ¹ice (sense 1), ice cream, jellies (gelatin [senses 1 and 2] with fruit juice; may contain fruit, nuts, marshmallows), layer cakes, macaroons, marshmallow, meringues (sense 2), mousse (sense 1), nougatine, parfait (both senses), pastries (sense 3), pear Helene, pies (sense 2), puddings (sense 1; plum, rice, steamed, tapioca), sherbets (sense 1), shortcakes (sense 2), snow, sorbets, ¹soufflés, steamed puddings, sundaes, taffy, tarts, tortes, tortoni, upside-down cakes, zabaglione.

Many desserts are served with whipped cream (which is also used as a garnish or a cake filling); dessert sauces (made of apple, cherry, peach, pear, plum) are served, hot or cold, on desserts. Many cakes have icing (frosting).

dessert raisin, raisin dried in the cluster for eating out of hand.

dessert wine, a sweet wine served with dessert. Compare **table wine**.

¹**devil** [from Greek *diábolos* "the spirit of evil" (from the notion of heat), "slanderer"], any of various highly seasoned dishes, especially one of broiled or fried meat (e.g., chops, crabmeat, ham, meaty bones), a grill with cayenne pepper.

²**devil (to)**, to prepare (usually to chop fine) with pungent seasoning or sauce, such as mustard or cayenne pepper, usually after cooking (e.g., deviled crabmeat, eggs, ham).

devil's fig, another name for the **prickly pear** (fruit).

devil's food cake [so called from the contrast in color (dark) with angel food cake (which is light)], or simply **devil's food**, a dark chocolate cake. Compare **angel cake**.

devils on horseback [so called from the similarity to **angels on horseback**, which are likewise oysters wrapped in bacon], or **pigs in blanket**, a dish consisting of broiled or fried, bacon-wrapped, oysters or pieces of chicken liver.

devil's-tongue, a certain prickly pear.

Devon, any of a breed of cattle developed in the county of *Devon* or Devonshire, southwestern England, and raised primarily for beef.

Devonshire cream, another name for **clotted cream**.

dewberry or **lowbush blackberry** or **low blackberry**, the sweet berry (resembling a blackberry) of any of several trailing forms of the black-berry.

dextrose, another name for **glucose** (sense 1).

diamondback terrapin or simply **diamondback**, an edible North American terrapin.

dibs [Arabic], a sweet syrup of Syrian origin, made from grape juice (concentrated) or from dates or figs.

diet, *1.* habitual nourishment, the usual food and drink of a person; *2.* a regulated selection of foods (kind and amount) prescribed for a person for a special reason.

dietetic, adapted (e.g., by elimination of sugar or salt) for use in restrictive diets.

dietetics, the science or art of applying to the diet the principles of nutrition in relation to health and hygiene.

diet loaf, another name for **sponge cake** (a cake made without shortening).

digestive, a substance that aids digestion (making food absorbable in the alimentary canal).

dika, *1.* or **dika nut**, the fruit or seed of the African **wild mango**; *2.* another name for **dika bread**.

dika bread or **Gaboon chocolate**, a paste (an oily, chocolate-like substance) prepared (West Africa) by grinding and heating the seeds of the African **wild mango** usually together with pepper and other spices.

dill, *1.* the leaves or seeds of a certain aromatic herb (likewise called *dill)* of the carrot family used in flavoring foods and especially pickles; *2.* another name for the **dill pickle**.

dill oil, an oil obtained from the dill plant and used as a flavoring agent.

dill pickle, a pickle (sense 2, cucumber) seasoned with fresh dill or dill juice.

dillseed, the seed of the dill plant used for flavoring pickles. It can also be used, as well as the dill leaf, in sour cream, fish, bean, cucumber, and cabbage dishes, as well as in potato salad, or on new potatoes.

dilly [from *sapodilla*], *1.* another name for **sapodilla** (tree); *2.* or **wild sapodilla**, a small tree of the West Indies and Florida having small, edible fruits.

dim sum [Cantonese *dím sām* "small center," from *dím* "dot, speck" + *sām* "heart"], traditional Chinese food consisting of a variety of items (as steamed or fried dumplings with a savory filling [small casings of dough filled variously with minced meat or vegetables], pieces of chicken, and rice balls) served in small portions as a light meal.

dingleberry, the round red berry of a shrub of the southeastern United States (likewise called *dingleberry).*

dip, a sauce or soft mixture (e.g., guacamole) into which solid food (e.g., crackers, potato chips, corn chips, cheese chips, raw carrots and celery) may be dipped. Some cheese dips add one of the following: deviled ham, garlic, minced clam. "Bowls" for holding dips (and spreads) can be avocado, grapefruit, and melon shells, pepper halves, scooped-out tomatoes, sea shells.

dish, *1.* an open container (usually of china or pottery) for holding and serving food; *2.* the food served or contained in such a vessel; *3.* food prepared for the table in a particular way.

dish gravy, meat juice served as gravy.

ditali [Italian "thimbles," from *dito* "finger"] or **ditalini** [Italian "small thimbles"], macaroni cut in short lengths. When ditalini are distinguished from ditali, they are cut in very short lengths. Both are often somewhat elbow-shaped.

divinity [from *divine* "of a god"], *1.* or **divinity fudge**, fudge made from whipped egg whites, white or brown sugar, and nuts (a soft, creamy kind of candy); *2.* a frosting made of egg whites, corn syrup, white or brown sugar, and flavoring (broken nut meats, or raisins, or crushed peppermint candy may be added).

Dobos torte, or **Dobos** [for a Hungarian pastry chef, Jozef *Dobós*, who died in 1928], a torte made of multiple layers of sponge cake, often with ground hazelnuts, put together with a mocha-chocolate filling, and glazed with caramel.

dock, any of certain plants of the buckwheat family, sometimes used as potherbs. Compare **alpine dock**.

dodger, another name for **corn dodger**.

dog, another name for a **hot dog**.

dog cabbage, a certain fleshy herb often eaten as a potherb.

dogfish or **grayfish**, any of various small sharks.

dog mint, another name for **wild basil**.

dog salmon or **keta** [Russian] or **lekai salmon** or **calico salmon**, any of various salmons.

dolce [Italian "a sweet," from *dolce* "sweet (adjective)"], a sweet dessert.

dolma [Turkish "something stuffed," from *dolma* "stuffed"], a vegetable shell (e.g., of eggplant, green pepper, tomato, zucchini) or a grape or cabbage leaf stuffed with a mixture of rice, meat, herbs, and seasonings (allspice, cinnamon, black pepper) and boiled; the word *dolma* is used more often for a stuffed grape leaf. Chopped onions, raisins, pine nuts may be added.

dolphin or **dolphinfish**, either of two marine fishes. Not to be confused with the small whale also called *dolphin*.

dom or **dom palm**, other names for the **doom palm** (that has a fruit used to make a beverage).

Dominica. Callaloo, crapaud ([from French *crapaud* "toad"] a large frog), and salt codfish are among representative dishes of Dominica.

Dominican Republic. The following are among representative dishes and products of the Dominican Republic: a stew of meat (e.g., pork, oxtail), yam, cassava, pumpkin, and sausage (Spanish *sancocho)* [there is a *sancocho de siete carnes*, "seven-meat sancocho," that includes beef, pork, chicken, pigeon, goat, sheep, and hen], arroz con pollo, cassava baked with cheese and boiled eggs; rice and beans or peas *(moro)*, vegetable broth with chicken or smoked pork, roast suckling pig, shrimp, fish, tripe *(mondongo)*, heart of palm *(palmito)*, papaya drink *(refresco de lechosa;* with coconut milk).

done, cooked or roasted to the desired degree.

doneness, the condition of being cooked sufficiently.

donut, a variant spelling of **doughnut**.

doodskop [from Afrikaans *doods* "of death" (genitive of *dood* "death") +

kop "head"], a southern African, shallow-water marine fish (a chimaera).

doom palm or **doum** [from French *doum* "doom palm," from Arabic *dawm*] or **dom palm** or **gingerbread palm**, an African palm tree that has a fruit (whose pulp tastes like gingerbread) whose rind is used in making a beverage.

dorado [Spanish "golden," from *dorar* "to gild"], a large, golden, South American fish that resembles the salmon.

Dorset [from *Dorset*, county of southern England where it was first made], another name for **Blue Vinny**.

dormouse, a small rodent.

dotterel, any of various plovers.

double boiler or **water bath** or **bain-marie** [from French *bain-marie* "the lower pan", from Medieval Latin *balneum Mariae* "bath of Maria" (mistranslation of Medieval Greek *káminos Marias* "furnace of Maria"), from *Maria* (Hebrew *Miriam*), sister of Moses in the Bible (Exodus 15.20) to whom was attributed a treatise on alchemy], a cooking utensil consisting of two pans, the upper fitting into the lower, designed to allow slow, even cooking or warming of food in the upper (smaller) pan by the action of water boiling in the lower (larger) pan.

Double Gloucester [from *Gloucester*, town and county of southwestern England], a firm English cheese similar to cheddar.

dough, a soft, thick mixture that consists essentially of flour or meal and a liquid (e.g., milk or water) and is stiff enough to knead or roll, after which it is baked as bread, pastry, or the like. Various dry ingredients can be added. Compare **batter** (that has egg, and is thin enough to pour or drop from a spoon).

doughball, a lump of dough cooked with meat or vegetables.

doughboy, *1.* bread dough that is rolled thin and cut into various shapes, fried in deep fat and served as a hot bread; *2.* a small, flattish, Australian ¹**scallop** (sense 1).

dough god, a fried biscuit.

doughnut or **donut** or **nutcake** or **olykoek** (Dutch) or **sinker** (slang), a small, usually ring-shaped cake made of light dough that is fried in deep fat. It is made of a mixture similar to that of pancakes but stiffer. It can also be shaped in braids. Compare **bismarck**, **French doughnut**, **jelly doughnut**.

doum or **doum palm**, other names for the **doom palm** (that has a fruit used to make a beverage).

downy myrtle, a certain evergreen shrub having berrylike fruits.

dragée [French "sugar-coated almond or hazelnut," from Latin *tragemata* "sweetmeats, fruits eaten as dessert," from Greek *tragemata* "sweetmeats, dried fruits," from *trogein* "to gnaw, eat fruits"], *1.* a small candy in the form of a sugar-coated nut (e.g., almond, hazelnut); *2.* a small, round, usually silver-colored confection often used for decorating cakes.

drawn butter, the clarified butter that separates from the salt and curds after melting, often used with chopped herbs or other seasoning as a sauce (e.g., on cooked celery, green and wax beans, shredded carrots or beets).

dredge (**to**) [from French *dragée* "sugar-coated almond or hazelnut," from Latin *tragemata* "sweetmeats, fruits eaten as dessert," from Greek *tragemata* "sweetmeats, dried fruits," from *trogein* "to gnaw, eat fruits"], to coat food by sprinkling it with a powder, such as flour or sugar.

drepane, a certain fish.

dress (**to**), to prepare for cooking or for the table, to clean fish or fowl.

dressing [from to *dress* "to prepare for the table or for cooking"], *1.* a sauce or similar mixture (e.g., mayonnaise) for certain dishes (e.g., salads, meat). Compare **salad dressing**; *2.* a seasoned mixture (e.g., of bread, potato, nuts, oysters) usually used as a stuffing (e.g., for poultry, fish, meat [e.g., pig]), or baked separately.

dried beef, beef pickled in brine and smoked (to preserve it). It may be used in sandwiches with American cheese and mayonnaise.

dried milk, see **powdered milk**.

drink, *1.* a beverage, a liquid swallowed to quench thirst or to provide nourishment; *2.* an alcoholic beverage, intoxicating liquor.

drip coffee or **French drip**, coffee (sense 1, the beverage) made by pouring boiling water over finely ground coffee (sense 2, the seeds or beans) and letting it drip slowly.

drippings, fat and juices let out from meat during roasting especially when used as a shortening or a spread. Often used in making gravy.

drisheen [Irish Gaelic *drisín*], a kind of sausage made from sheep's blood (chiefly in the vicinity of Cork, southwestern Ireland), with milk and seasonings.

drop, a small, round candy or cookie.

drop batter, a batter of such consistency (thick) as to drop from a bowl or spoon without running. Drop batter is usually made in a proportion of two parts flour to one part liquid. Distinguished from **pour batter** (made from equal parts of flour and liquid).

dropped egg, another name for a **poached egg**.

drop scone, another name for **pancake**.

drum, any of various fishes that make a drumming noise.

drumhead, or **drumhead cabbage** [from being similar to a *drumhead* (the membrane stretched over the open end of a drum)], a flat-topped variety of cabbage.

drupe, a fleshy fruit, such as the cherry, plum, and peach, usually having a single hard stone that encloses a seed.

dry (**to**), to preserve meat or other foods by extracting the moisture (by exposure to heat or air). Compare **dehydrate, evaporate**.

dryland blueberry, the sweet blue berry borne by a certain low shrub (likewise called *dryland blueberry*) of eastern North America.

dry-salt (**to**), to treat with salt, to preserve meat by salting and drying.

dry sausage, another name for **summer sausage**.

Du Barry [for Jeanne Bécu, Comtesse *du Barry*, 1746?-1793, mistress of King Louis XV of France], (of a soup or sauce) made with cauliflower.

duchesse [French "duchess"], a small puff with sweet or savory filling.

duchesse potato [from French *duchesse* "duchess"], potato mashed or riced and mixed with beaten raw egg, butter, and cream, used as a garnish (for borders of planks or baking dishes and for other decorations; e.g., around boeuf bourguignonne or coq au vin) or made into patties (or mounds, or rosettes) and oven-browned. In French (plural), *pommes duchesse*.

duck, the flesh of any of certain wild or domesticated aquatic birds (generally smaller than geese and than swans). Frequent ways of serving duck: with orange sauce, with olives, with turnips (in French, respectively, *canard à l'orange, aux olives, aux navets)*, roasted. For stuffed wild duck, a mixture of equal parts of chopped carrots, celery, and onion can be used. Or diced orange and grated orange rind can be added; some chefs also add dried marjoram, sage, or thyme.

duck potato, another name for **wapatoo** (that has edible tubers).

duff, a stiff flour pudding (sense 1) often containing raisins and currants (or plums) and boiled in a cloth bag or steamed. Compare **plum duff, plum pudding**.

du jour [French "of the day"], (of an item not specified on the regular menu) cooked or prepared for a particular day.

duke, or **duke cherry**, a type of cherry intermediate between a sweet and a sour cherry.

duku [Malay] or **lanseh**, a lanseh tree having a round edible berry (called *lanseh).*

dulce [Spanish "sweetmeat," from *dulce* (adjective) "sweet"], sweetmeat, candy (in the southwest of the United States).

dulse, any of several reddish-brown seaweeds used as a food condiment or eaten as a vegetable.

dum palm, another name for the **doom palm** (that has a fruit used to make a beverage).

dumpling, *1.* a small ball of leavened dough cooked by boiling or steaming (e.g., with the soup or the stew with which it is to be served; cheese, chives, egg, herbs, parsley, may be added); *2.* a dessert made by wrapping fruit (e.g., peach, a whole apple) in biscuit dough (sweetened) and baking. For other dumplings, see **dim sum**.

dunderfunk, broken sea biscuits or crackers mixed with molasses and baked.

dunfish, fish (e.g., cod) cured by dunning (i.e., salting, laying in a pile in a dark place, and covering [e.g., with salt grass]).

Dungeness crab [from *Dungeness*, village in the northwest of the state of Washington], a large crab of the Pacific coast of North America.

durian [Malay, from *duri* "thorn"] or **jackfruit**, the large, oval, tasty but foul-smelling fruit of a certain southeast Asian tree (likewise called *durian)* of the silk-cotton family. The fruit has a hard, prickly rind, a soft cream-colored pulp, and seeds that are roasted and eaten like chestnuts.

durum wheat, or **durum** [Latin, neuter of *durus* "hard"] or **macaroni wheat**, a wheat that yields a glutenous flour used especially in making pasta and similar products (e.g., semolina, macaroni, spaghetti, noodles).

Dutch cheese, *1.* a small, round, firm cheese made from skim milk, produced in the Netherlands; *2.* another name for **cottage cheese**.

Dutch lunch, an individual serving of assorted, sliced cold meats and cheeses. Compare **cold cuts**.

duxelles or **d'Uxelles** [for the Marquis Louis Chalon du Blé *d'Uxelles*, 17th-century French nobleman, patron of the chef Sieur de la Varenne], a garnish or stuffing whose chief ingredients are minced sautéed mushrooms and tomato puree.

dwarf banana or **Canary banana**, a low-growing banana plant of the West Indies.

dwarf pea, another name for the **chick-pea** (seed).

early winter cress, or **early cress**, a cress used for a salad plant or potherb.

earth apple, another name for both the **potato** and the **Jerusalem artichoke**.

earth bread, *1*. another name for any of the manna lichens of African and Arabian deserts; *2*. a food prepared from one of these lichens.

earthnut or **pignut**, the edible nutlike tuber or other underground parts of any of various plants.

earthnut oil, another name for **peanut oil**.

earth plum, the plum-like pods (edible when unripe) of any of various leguminous plants (likewise called *earth plums*) of northern Mexico and the southwestern United States.

Easter egg, *1*. a dyed or painted hard-boiled egg used as an Easter gift; *2*. a symbolic representation of an egg (e.g., in confectionery) also used as an Easter present.

éclair [French "lightning"], an often chocolate-frosted (or mocha-frosted) tubular cream puff with whipped cream or custard filling. The custard filling may be coffee- or chocolate- flavored.

Ecuador. The following are among representative dishes and products of Ecuador: a thick soup (Spanish *locro*) made from potatoes (or from corn kernels) and cheese; ceviche (from crayfish, corbina, shrimp, crab, conch); a meat (or fish), cassava *(yuca)*, and banana stew *(sancocho);* empanadas, fish, shellfish, cassava, roast suckling pig *(hornado)*, sheep, rabbit, fried mashed potatoes with cheese *(llapingachos)*, fried pork *(fritada)*, corn *(mote)*, corn on the cob *(choclo)*, avocado, chicken in hot-pepper sauce *(ají de pollo)*, tamales *(humitas)*, tamal with raisins *(quimbolito)*, fried plantain, a purple-corn dessert *(mazamorra morada)*, naranjilla, cookie sandwich filled with jam *(alfajor)*. Beverage: naranjilla juice.

Edam, or **Edam cheese** [from *Edam*, town in northwestern Netherlands], a mild, yellow cheese of Dutch origin, similar to Gouda (which contains more fat), pressed into flattened balls and usually covered with dark red wax.

eddo, another name for **taro** (the rootstock).

edible bird's nest, another name for **bird's nest**.

edible canna, an Asiatic herb cultivated for its starchy rootstocks. The starch from its rootstocks is called *tous-les-mois*.

edible dormouse, any of various dormice of the Mediterranean region.

edible frog, a certain European frog.

edible galingale, another name for the **chufa**.

edible-podded pea, or **edible pod pea** or **sugar pea**, a pea of a variety with pods which are eaten with the seeds they contain (e.g., snow pea).

edible snail, a snail of any of several European varieties used as food.

eel [French *anguille*, Italian *anguilla*, Spanish *anguila*], any of various long, snakelike fishes. Eels can be cooked matelote.

eelpout, another name for the **muttonfish** (sense 1).

¹**egg**, the oval, hard-shelled reproductive body produced by a bird; especially that produced by the common chicken and used as food. Eggs can be soft or hard cooked (boiled) in the shell, poached out of the shell in salted water, baked, coddled, creamed, curried, deviled, pan-fried (shallow fried, in butter, margarine, bacon, fat), scrambled, shirred. They may be used in custards (and other desserts like cakes, cookies, meringues), omelets (e.g., French, puffy, western), salads, soufflés. When fried on one side, they are known in the United States as "sunny-side up," when turned and fried on both sides they are known as "over" or "once over lightly." They can be served with bacon or ham, or be baked on corned beef hash. Dishes using eggs include eggs Benedict, Mornay, stuffed. Scrambled eggs or puffy omelets may be combined with a sauce, such as cheese, mushroom, or tomato sauce, or creamed asparagus, chicken, ham.

²**egg** (**to**), to mix or cover with beaten egg. For instance, once slices of meat are egged, they are crumbed and fried.

egg apple, another name for an **eggplant**.

egg bird, any of several seabirds whose eggs are used for food (e.g., in the West Indies, the sooty tern).

egg cream, a drink of milk, a flavoring syrup (often chocolate), and soda water.

eggfruit, *1.* or **lucuma**, any of several edible fruits (e.g., **canistel**) of certain plants; *2.* another name for an **eggplant**.

eggnog, or **nog**, a thick drink composed of eggs beaten with sugar, milk or cream (and often a distilled liquor [e.g., rum, brandy]), usually served cold and flavored with grated nutmeg. A dessert sauce can be prepared with eggnog.

eggplant or **egg apple** or **eggfruit** or **garden egg** or **guinea squash** or **mad apple** or **melongene** or **vegetable egg** or **aubergine** [from French *aubergine*; Italian *melanzana*, Spanish *berenjena*], the usually smooth, ovoid fruit of a certain plant, having glossy, dark-purple skin, and cooked and eaten as a vegetable. It can be fried, grilled, pickled, roasted, stuffed; cooked in a casserole, used in canapés, in sweets (e.g., jam).

egg powder, a powder made from dried eggs.

egg roll, a dish of Chinese-American origin consisting of a thin egg-dough casing filled with minced vegetables and often bits of meat (e.g., chicken, shrimp) and usually fried in deep fat. Compare **spring roll**.

93

egg sauce, any of various sauces containing eggs. For instance, a sauce made of fish or meat stock (with flour) and beaten eggs, or a drawn butter sauce with beaten egg yolks or minced hard-boiled eggs (and lemon juice). Egg yolks not only thicken but also enrich a sauce.

eggs Benedict, poached eggs and slices of broiled ham placed on toasted halves of English muffin and topped with hollandaise sauce.

eggs Florentine, see **poached egg**.

eggs foo yong, see **foo yong**.

eggs Mornay, see **Mornay sauce**.

egg white, see **white**.

egg yolk, see **yolk**.

Egypt. The following are among representative dishes and products of Egypt: lamb kabob (ground or in chunks), couscous; assorted hors d'oeuvre (Arabic *mazza*), including tahini dip, stuffed grape-leaves, salad, grilled mutton, pistachios; moussaka, giant shrimps from the Red Sea *(jambari*, pronounced *gambari* in Egypt), roast pigeon, grilled lamb's head; boiled beans with lemon, parsley, garlic, caraway seeds *(ful mudammas);* baked meat-croquettes *(kufta)*, chick peas *(ḥummuṣ)*, falafel (sense 1, in Arabic also called *ta'miyya*), dates, baklava; a chopped walnut or pistachio dessert *(kunafa*, called *kadaif* in Greece and Turkey), shaped like vermicelli. Beverage: Turkish coffee.

Egyptian ginger, the root of the **taro**.

elderberry, the small, red or blackish, berrylike fruit of any of various shrubs called *elder*, that is eaten raw or used to make preserves.

election cake, a fruit cake (yeast raised) usually made of bread dough, raisins, figs, candied fruit (e.g., citron), sugar, egg, and butter and baked in a bread pan.

elk, a certain large deer of northern regions, often called *moose* in North America. See **venison**.

El Salvador. The following are among representative dishes and products of El Salvador: chicken marinated in *chicha* (Spanish *gallo en chicha*), chicha being a kind of cider made with corn and pineapple peel fermented in vinegar and sugar; cornmeal tortillas filled with cheese, ground chitterlings, or refried beans *(pupusas)*; seafood, tropical fruits.

embolo, the fruit of the Cape ebony (a certain African tree).

Emmental or **Emmentaler** [from German *emmentaler (Käse)*, "Emmental (cheese)," from *Emmental*, valley of Switzerland, from *Emme* river], another name for **Swiss cheese**.

empanada [Spanish "breaded," feminine past participle of *empanar* "to bread, put a crust of dough around," from *pan* "bread"], a roundish, baked pastry-turnover stuffed with a sweet or savory filling (e.g., ground meat, fish, vegetable).

emperor fish, a large fish of the Japanese seas.

en brochette [French "on a skewer"], broiled on a skewer (e.g., fish, kidney, liver).

en casserole [French "in a casserole, in a saucepan"], cooked and served in a casserole. Said for instance, of veal, chicken, ham, fish, vegetables.

enchilada [American Spanish "seasoned with chili (= hot pepper)," feminine past participle of *enchilar* "to put chili in, season with chili," from *chile* "chili, hot pepper"], a dish of Mexican origin consisting of a tortilla (large, thin, cornmeal pancake) spread with chili-flavored tomato sauce, rolled up, stuffed with a mixture containing meat (usually chicken) or cheese, fried, and served with more of the sauce on top.

en coquille [French "in the shell"], in the shell. When oysters are baked in their shells, they are said to be "en coquille."

en croûte, in French, it means "wrapped in cooked dough"; see **croûte**.

encurtido, Spanish for **pickle** (sense 2).

Endeavor River pear [from *Endeavor* river, Queensland, northeastern Australia], an Australian plant whose fruits are used in jams.

endive or **escarole** or **winter lettuce**, *1.* a plant cultivated for its crown of crisp, succulent, broad leaves used in salads (also called *broad-leaved endive;* in French, *scarole); 2.* another form of the same plant, that has curled leaves (also called *curly-leaved endive;* in French, *chicorée frisée); 3.* a variety of the common chicory (sense 1) when cultivated to produce a cluster of whitish leaves (blanched by growing in darkness or semidarkness) for use as a vegetable (e.g., braised) or in salads (also called *French endive* or *witloof;* in regional French [Belgium], *chicon).*

English breakfast, a substantial breakfast (e.g., of eggs, toast, cereal, and ham or bacon).

English breakfast tea, or simply **English breakfast**, another name for **congou** (a black tea from China).

English chop, a lamb or mutton chop cut across the undivided loin, boneless and with the kidney rolled in.

English muffin, bread dough (yeast dough) rolled and cut into rounds, baked on a griddle, and split and toasted.

English sole, a certain flatfish.

English walnut or **European walnut** or **French walnut** or **Italian walnut** or **Turkish walnut**, the large edible nut of a certain tree (likewise called *English walnut).*

en papillote, see **papillote**.

enrich (**to**), to improve the nutritive value of a food by adding nutrients (e.g., vitamins, minerals).

ensete [from Amharic *ensat*], another name for the **Abyssinian banana**, a banana plant that has edible young flower stalks (but inedible fruit).

entire wheat flour, another name for **whole-wheat flour**.

entrecote or **entrecôte** [French "between the ribs"], a cut of steak taken from between the ribs.

entrée or **entree** [from French *entrée* "entry, entrance"], *1.* the main course of an ordinary meal (United States); *2.* a made dish served before the roast (England, France). In sense 1, an entrée can be made from meat, poultry, fish (e.g., chicken, mixed grill, pork chops, risotto); in sense 2 it can be made from these or from eggs, cheese, vegetables. Entrées may be hot (e.g., crab cakes, croquettes, loaves, patties, soufflés, timbales [sense 1]) or cold; they may be prepared au gratin, or a la king.

entremets [French "between dishes"], *1.* a side dish served in addition to the main course of a meal; *2.* a dessert. In French, the word used to mean a' dish served between the roast and the dessert; it now means dessert (e.g., cake, compote, custard, sherbet) served after the cheese and before the fruits.

epaulet fish, a fish of the southern Queensland coast (northeastern Australia).

epazote [Mexican Spanish, from Nahuatl *epazotl*], an herb used as seasoning.

épinard, French for **spinach**.

Equatorial Guinea. The staple foods of Equatorial Guinea are millet, rice, yams, and bananas.

Eritrea. The following are representative dishes of Eritrea: bread (Tigre *enjerá*) similar to a pancake; raw meat *(berundó)*, a stew *(zighní)*, roast (all meat with red peppers [*berberé*]); a flour polenta mixed with chick-peas and peas, with oil, garlic, onion *(shiró)*. Beverage: a drink *(miés* or *tej)* prepared with honey and water fermented with aromatic leaves *(gheshó)*.

erizo [Spanish "hedgehog"], any of several porcupine fishes.

erizo de mar ["hedgehog of the sea"], Spanish for **sea urchin**.

escabeche [Spanish], fish or chicken fried in oil, then marinated in a spicy sauce (with wine or vinegar, bay leaf) and served cold. In Spanish, the word also means the sauce itself; in Portuguese, it means only this sauce.

escallop (**to**), variant of ²**scallop**.

escallopine, variant of **scallopini**.

escalope [French], another name for **scallopini**.

escargot [French "snail"], a snail, especially when cooked for use as food. The kinds of escargots preferred are called in French *escargot de Bourgogne* and *escargot chagriné*. Escargots are often prepared with butter, garlic, and parsley, or à la **bourguignonne**.

escarole [from French *scarole*], another name for **endive** in either of its first two meanings.

eschalot [from French *échalotte*], another name for a **shallot**.

escolar [Spanish "scholar," from the fish having rings like spectacles around the eyes] or **oilfish** or **tapioca fish**, a large fish that resembles a mackerel.

Eskimo pie, a chocolate shell filled with ice cream. In French, it is called *esquimau* or *chocolat glacé*.

Eskimo potato, a plant of western North America that has a starchy edible root.

espagnole [French "the Spanish one (feminine)"] or **espagnole sauce**, other names for **brown sauce**.

espárrago, Spanish for **asparagus**.

espinaca, Spanish for **spinach**.

espresso [Italian "pressed out" or "for the express purpose, on request"], or **caffè espresso** or **espresso coffee**, coffee (sense 1, the beverage) that is brewed by forcing steam under pressure through long-roasted, powdered coffee beans.

essence, *1.* a substance obtained from a food (e.g., from lemon [a solution of lemon in alcohol]) used as flavoring in cooking; *2.* the concentrated juices of foods obtained in the process of cooking.

estragon, French for **tarragon**.

Ethiopia. The following are among representative dishes and products of Ethiopia: millet bread (Amharic *injera)* similar to a sourdough pancake; a highly seasoned (with hot peppers) stew *(wat)* of lamb or chicken or beef. Beverage: an alcoholic honey-drink *(tej).*

European chestnut, another name for **Spanish chestnut**.

European walnut, another name for **English walnut**.

evaporate (**to**), to draw moisture from.

evaporated milk, concentrated, unsweetened milk made by evaporating (by heat) some of the water from whole milk (to reach one half or less of its bulk). Distinguished from **condensed milk** (that has sugar added), and from **concentrated milk** (from which water has been removed).

extract, a concentrated preparation of the essential constituents (flavor and odor) of a food (e.g., meat) or flavoring (e.g., lemon, maple, vanilla).

eye, *1.* anything suggestive of an eye (the organ of sight) in appearance, as a hole in cheese; *2.* an undeveloped bud on a twig or tuber (e.g., on a potato); *3.* see also **rib eye**.

faba, variant of **fava** (**broad bean**).

fadge, *1.* a round loaf of bread (Scotland); *2.* potato cake or bread (Ireland).

fagot cinnamon or **Batavia cassia,** a cinnamon bark from an Asiatic tree.

fairies'-table, another name for **meadow mushroom.**

fajitas [American Spanish, "little belts," diminutive plural of Spanish *faja* "sash, belt"], marinated strips of beef or chicken grilled or broiled and served with a flour tortilla and various fillings.

falafel [from Arabic *falāfil* (in Arabic, it is also called *ta'amia)*], *1.* a mixture of Egyptian origin of dried chick-peas or fava beans and spices (e.g., ground cumin and coriander), formed into patties with onion, garlic, parsley, and fried (deep-fried in oil); *2.* a sandwich of pita bread filled with falafel (sense 1).

false banana, another name for **papaw** (sense 2, custard apple).

Fameuse [French "famous, superior (feminine)"] or **snow apple,** a North American variety of apple having deep-red stripes and crisp white flesh.

family flour, another name for **all-purpose flour.**

famine bread, an arctic lichen.

fanchonette [French, from *franchonette,* diminutive of *Franchon,* nickname of *Françoise,* a feminine given name corresponding to English *Frances*], a tart covered with meringue or whipped cream.

fancy bread, bread in a form other than a loaf (e.g., a raised bread enriched with eggs or nuts and baked in a shape like a braid or twist).

fancy meat, another name for **variety meat.**

farce [French], another name for **forcemeat.**

farci (masculine) and **farcie** (feminine), French for **stuffed.**

fard [from Arabic *farḍ*], a shiny, dark-brown date.

farfel [from Yiddish *farfl* (plural), from Middle High German *varveln* "noodles, noodle soup"], noodles in the form of small pellets.

¹**farina** [Latin "meal, flour," from *far* "spelt"], fine meal prepared from cereal grain and other plant products (e.g., nuts, sea moss) used as a cooked cereal, in puddings, and to prepare pasta.

²**farina**, Italian for **flour**.

¹**farine** [from Portuguese *farinha* "flour, cassava meal"], farina (a fine meal), especially one made from cassava root, which in Portuguese can also be called *farinha de mandioca*, "cassava flour."

²**farine**, French for **flour**.

farinha [Portuguese "flour; cassava meal"], cassava meal.

farl or **farle** [from Scottish *fardel*, "fourth part," from *ferde* "fourth" + *del* "part"], a small cake or biscuit made with oatmeal or wheat flour (Scotland).

farmer cheese, a pressed, unripened cheese of whole milk or partly skimmed milk made on farms; it is drier and firmer than cottage cheese.

farofa, Portuguese for cassava flour, see **feijoada**.

fast-food, (of a business, e.g. a hamburger stand) offering food (e.g., hamburgers, fried chicken) prepared and served quickly.

fastnacht [from German *Fastnacht* "Shrove Tuesday, the Tuesday before Ash Wednesday"], a diamond-shaped, yeast-raised potato pastry deep-fried like a doughnut, traditionally eaten on Shrove Tuesday.

fat, *1.* a part of the tissues of an animal that consists of cells swollen with greasy or oily matter; *2.* the oily or greasy matter that makes up the adipose (fatty) tissue of animals or plants, often abundant in seeds, nuts, fruits; *3.* a solidified animal or vegetable oil. Saturated fat comes from red meat, butter, cream, cheese, palm oil; two kinds of unsaturated fat: monounsaturated, that comes from olive and canola (rapeseed) oils, and polyunsaturated, that comes from safflower, sunflower, corn, and soybean oils. Compare **oil**.

fat-choy [from Cantonese *faàt ts'oì*, "hair vegetable"], an edible blue-green alga.

fat mouse [so called from the accumulation of fat before its hibernation], any of several silky, furred, African short-tailed mice.

fat pork, another name for **coco plum**.

fava [Italian "broad bean"] or **fava bean** or **faba** [Latin "bean"], other names for the **broad bean**.

fei [Tahitian] or **mountain banana**, a wild Polynesian banana with fruits that are edible only when cooked.

feijão, Portuguese for **bean** (sense 1).

feijoa [from João da Silva *Feijó*, 19th-century Brazilian naturalist], the greenish red fruit of an originally South American shrub of the myrtle family.

feijoada [Portuguese, from *feijão* "bean"], a thick stew of Brazilian origin made of black beans and fatty meat (e.g., sausage, salt pork) with vegetables (e.g., kale, rice), served with cassava flour (in Portuguese, *farofa*). Jerked beef, spices, herbs, orange slices, may be added.

fennel, the aromatic seeds (also called **fennel seeds**) or the stalks of a plant (likewise called *fennel*) of the carrot family. Fennel (seeds) is one of the traditional ingredients in **five-spice powder** (a seasoning). Compare Florence fennel.

fennel oil, an oil obtained from fennel seeds and used as a flavoring.

fenugreek [from Latin *fenum Graecum*, "Greek hay," from the use of the dry plant as fodder], the pungent, aromatic seeds of a cloverlike plant

(likewise called *fenugreek),* used as a flavoring (e.g., in making curry, chutney, imitation vanilla flavoring).

ferment [from Latin *fermentum* "yeast"], a living organism (e.g., a yeast) that causes fermentation by virtue of its enzymes.

fermentation, *1.* a chemical change (the breakdown of complex molecules in organic compounds) with effervescence (e.g., the formation of alcohol from sugars, of vinegar from cider, the souring of milk). Alcoholic fermentation takes place when a saccharine solution is exposed to the action of yeasts (grape-sugar is decomposed into alcohol and carbon dioxide by the action of yeast); lactic fermentation, when the sugar of the milk is converted into lactic acid; *2.* any of various industrial processes for improving the flavor or the aroma (e.g., of cheese, tea) by means of such a chemical change (fermentation, sense 1).

feta or **feta cheese** [from Modern Greek *(tyri) pheta,* from *tyri* "cheese" + *pheta* "slice," from Italian *fetta* "slice"], a white cheese of Greek origin made of the milk of sheep or goats and cured in brine.

fettuccelle [Italian, plural diminutive of *fettuccia* "small slice, ribbon," diminutive of *fetta* "slice"], pasta in ribbon shape.

fettuccine or **fettuccini** [from Italian *fettuccine,* plural of *fettuccina* "very small slice," diminutive of *fettuccia* "small slice, ribbon," diminutive of *fetta* "slice"], *1.* pasta in narrow strips, noodles; *fettuccine* is the word used in the area of Rome for what elsewhere in Italy is called *tagliatelle*; *2.* a dish of which fettuccine (sense 1) forms the base.

fettuccine Alfredo or **fettuccine all'Alfredo** [from *Alfredo* all'Augusteo, restaurant in Rome, where the dish originated], a dish consisting of fettuccine, with butter, Parmesan cheese, cream, and seasonings.

feuilleté, French for a puff-pastry cake, see **puff pastry.**

ficin [from Latin *ficus* "fig"], a proteinase (a certain enzyme) obtained from the latex of certain species of fig trees and used as a protein digestant (e.g., for curdling milk).

fiddlehead, the young fronds of certain ferns (e.g., the cinnamon fern, and the ostrich fern), that are often cooked and eaten as greens.

field bean, another name for the **broad bean.**

field mushroom, another name for both the **meadow mushroom** and the **horse mushroom.**

field pea, a certain small-seeded pea.

fig, the sweet, fleshy, pear-shaped, many-seeded fruit of any of several trees (likewise called *figs,* or *fig trees).*

figaro sauce [for *Figaro,* the hero of French dramatist Pierre-Augustin Caron de Beaumarchais' comedies *Le barbier de Séville* (1775) and *Le mariage de Figaro* (1784)], hollandaise sauce with tomato puree and chopped parsley added.

fig banana, a tropical American banana whose flavor may recall that of a fig.

fig bar, *1.* a bar-shaped form of pressed figs; *2.* a cookie shaped like a bar and having a fig filling.

fig newton, another name for the second sense of **fig bar.**

Fiji, the following are among the most representative dishes and products of Fiji: fish and shellfish cooked in coconut milk; marinated fish (Fijian *ika vakalolo); yams, taro *(dalo),* rice, tapioca, Indian curries, tropical fruits (e.g., pineapple, banana, papaya, mango). Beverage: *yakona* (non-alcoholic, made from the pounded root of *kava*, a species of pepper plant).

filbert [for Saint *Philibert*, 7th-century Frankish abbot (c.608—c.685) whose feast day (20 August) falls in the nutting season] or **avellana** (Spanish), the rounded, thick-shelled, sweet nut of a certain Eurasian shrub (likewise called *filbert*), a species of hazel.

filé [French "twisted, spinned"] or **gumbo filé**, powdered (in a mortar), very young leaves of sassafras used to thicken soups or stews (especially gumbos, sense 2). Dried okra, allspice, coriander and sage may be added. Compare **gumbo** (sense 2), **gumbo filé** (sense 1).

filet, see **fillet**.

filet mignon [French "small fillet, dainty fillet"], a small, round, tender fillet of beef cut from the thick end of the loin. Compare **chateaubriand**, **tournedos**.

filled cheese, a product made from milk to which fatty material is added.

filled milk, skim milk with vegetable oils added to substitute for butterfat.

¹**fillet** or **filet** [from French *filet*, diminutive of *fil* "thread"], a strip or compact piece of boneless meat or fish. Beef fillet can be roasted, panbroiled (though not if very thick), oven-broiled, charcoal grilled (**chateaubriand**, **tournedos**); fish fillet can be baked, broiled, panfried, served amandine. There can be a fillet of roe-deer, pork, of sole, cod, smoked herring.

²**fillet (to)**, to cut into ¹**fillets**.

filling, a food mixture used to fill pastry, cake, or sandwiches. When sweet (e.g., for a pie), it can be custard, with different flavors added, such as chocolate, lemon, orange, pineapple.

filo, see **phyllo**.

financière [French "financial (feminine)," with the underlying idea of "in the manner of a financier"], being a garnish or a sauce the principal ingredients of which are truffles, mushrooms, olives, and sometimes sweetbread or quenelles. In French, the sauce is called *sauce financière* or simply *financière*. The sauce is used, for instance, with vol-au-vent.

fine herbs [translation of French *fines herbes*], another name for **fines herbes**.

fines herbes [French "fine herbs"], a mixture of finely chopped herbs (e.g., basil, chervil, chives, coriander, fennel, laurel, oregano [= wild marjoram], parsley, tarragon, thyme). Dishes using such mixture include cream cheese, cream soup, omelette, tartar sauce, or it can be used as a garnish (e.g., veal fines herbes). Compare **bouquet garni** (which is a mixture of herbs tied together).

fingered citron, or **fingered lemon**, or **Buddha's-hand**, an Asian citron tree with a fragrant fruit.

finger food, a food that is to be held with the fingers for eating (e.g., a carrot, a radish, a sandwich).

finger roll, *1.* bread shaped in slender rolls; *2.* an Italian breadstick.

Finland. Representative dishes include smorgasbord or hors d'oeuvre (Finnish *voileipäpöytä* ["butter bread table"]; including smoked fish, meats, cheeses, sausages); pasties *(piirakka*, from Karelia, in the south-

finnan haddie

five-spice powder

east); pork and herring baked in a pastry loaf *(kalakukko,* "fish cock"), reindeer (especially the ribs), crayfish, salmon, herring, trout. Beverage: *mehua,* made with forest berries.

finnan haddie, or **finnan haddock** [from *Findon haddock,* from *Findhorn haddock* "smoked haddock", from *Findhorn,* fishing port in Scotland confused with *Findon,* village near Aberdeen, northeastern Scotland], smoked haddock.

finnock or **finnoc** [from Scottish Gaelic *fionnag* "whiting," from *fionn* "white"], a whitish sea trout.

finocchio or **finochio** [Italian], see **Florence fennel**.

fiorentina, Italian for Florence-style (e.g., cannelloni).

fire bean, another name for the **scarlet runner**.

firepot or **hot pot,** the food cooked at the table, in broth, in a vessel (likewise called *firepot*) used in Oriental cuisine.

first run, the earliest and richest sap flow in the sugar maple.

fish, the flesh of fish (aquatic vertebrate animal) used as food. The ending -*fish* is used in English in the names of certain unrelated aquatic animals (e.g., *crayfish, cuttlefish, jellyfish, starfish* [all four are invertebrates, as are shellfish]). Fish can be baked, boiled (often wrapped in a square of cheesecloth), broiled (buffalofish steaks, cod, gar, salmon, shad steaks), fried (flounder, pike, smelt), planked, poached, steamed, and served creamed (haddock, hake, halibut steaks), en papillote, as zarzuela; and as fish balls (e.g., codfish) and fish hash (mixed with cooked and mashed potatoes); it can be made into a soup (bouillabaisse, chowder). Fat fish are generally best for broiling, baking, planking (e.g., barracuda, catfish, herring, lake trout, mackerel, pompano, rosefish, salmon, shad, sturgeon, tuna, whitefish); lean fish are generally best for boiling and steaming (e.g., bass, buffalofish, carp, cod, croaker, flounder, haddock, halibut, perch, pike, red snapper, whiting). Small fish, fillets, or steaks can be broiled, baked (in brown sauce, milk, tomato, cheese sauce), sautéed, or deep-fried. Large fish may be baked whole. A sauce is served with boiled or steamed fish; fish sauce is made like white sauce, using fish stock or hot water for the liquid called for. Fillets can be served amandine (pike, sole, whitefish), fillet of sole (French *filet de sole)* can be served bonne femme. Fish loaf can be made with salmon. Fish is at its best when very fresh, served free of skin and bones, and with lemon. Compare **roe** (sense 1), **seafood, shellfish**.

fish-and-chips or **fish and chips,** fried fillets of fish (e.g., haddock) and French-fried potatoes.

fish ball, a patty or globular cake made of fish (e.g., salted codfish) shredded or minced, often mixed with mashed potato (or with rice), and fried. Normally used as a synonym of **fish cake**.

fish cake, a fried cake, patty, or flattened ball of chopped fish, often mixed with potato or rice. Normally used as a synonym of **fish ball**.

fish flour, a flour made of dried and powdered fish.

fish fry, fried fish.

five-spice powder, a blend of ground spices (a powder of Chinese origin), typically including pepper (Chinese cooks prefer Sichuan [formerly spelled *Szechwan*] pepper), fennel (seeds), cloves, star anise, and cinnamon. It is used in Chinese cooking and is excellent on vegetables, seafood, and meat.

flake, a dogfish (small shark) when used as food.

¹**flambé** or **flambée** [from French *flambé* (masculine), *flambée* (feminine) "singed, passed through a flame"], served covered with flaming liquor (e.g., brandy, cognac, rum). An omelette, bananas, or crêpes may be served flambées.

²**flambé (to)**, to douse with a liquor (e.g., brandy, cognac, rum) and ignite.

flame (to), to dress food with flaming liquor (e.g., brandy, rum).

flan [French], *1.* a tart with a filling (e.g., of custard, fruit, cheese, jam) and often glazed with fruit syrup; *2.* a molded custard baked with a burnt-caramel glaze.

flank, a cut of meat from the fleshy part of the side between the last rib and the hip of an animal.

flanken [Yiddish "flanks," plural of *flank* "flank"], beef flank boiled in stock with spices and vegetables.

flannel cake, a pancake, especially of wheat flour.

flapjack, another name for **pancake**.

flatbread or **flatbrod** [from Norwegian *flatbrød*, "flat bread"], a thin dry wafer of Scandinavian origin made of rye flour dough.

flatfish, any of numerous fishes distinguished as adults by having both eyes on one side of their slim body (in an early stage of their development, one eye moves to the same side as the other); they swim with the eyeless side downward. They include brills, flounders, halibuts, soles, turbots, whiffs.

flathead, any of various fishes with more or less flat heads.

flathead catfish, a large catfish of the United States.

flat peach, another name for **peen-to** (a peach).

flavor or **flavoring**, a seasoning, a substance (e.g., cinnamon, vanilla) that imparts a blend of taste and smell sensations.

flesh, *1.* the parts of a mammal or fowl eaten as food; *2.* the pulpy part of a fruit or vegetable.

flesh-meat, another name for the first sense of **flesh**.

flint corn or **flint maize**, a variety of Indian corn (¹**corn**) having small, hard, horny, usually rounded kernels (= seeds).

flitch, *1.* a salted and cured side of bacon; *2.* a strip or steak of fish (e.g., halibut) prepared by smoking.

floating island, a dessert consisting of soft custard with masses of whipped egg whites or of whipped cream floating on its surface.

Florence fennel or **finocchio**, the blanched stalks of a plant (likewise called *Florence fennel*) of the carrot family, eaten as a vegetable. This plant is a variety of **fennel**.

Florida arrowroot, *1.* an arrowroot obtained in Florida from the coontie (a plant); *2.* another name for **coontie**.

Florida cherry, another name for the **Surinam cherry** (sense 2, fruit of a Brazilian tree).

flounder, a certain **flatfish** resembling the sole. It can be fried; because it is a lean fish, it is best for boiling and steaming.

flour, *1.* a soft, powdery substance obtained by grinding and sifting the meal of a cereal grain (or of other edible seeds), especially wheat, but

also barley, buckwheat, Indian corn, rice, rye (and bean); 2. any similar soft powder obtained from dried food products other than cereals or seeds (e.g., banana, cassava, dried processed fish, potato).

flour corn, another name for **soft corn**.

flour gravy, gravy thickened with flour, made of milk, water, or stock as well as fat and seasoning.

flour tortilla, a tortilla of northern Mexican origin made with wheat flour instead of cornmeal. Flour tortillas are best when eaten freshly made.

flower, the part of a seed plant that normally has the reproductive organs (which are enclosed in an outer envelope of petals and sepals). Among flowers used as food: artichoke, broccoli, cauliflower, chrysanthemum, mallow, pumpkin flower, rose, spikenard, violet. Compare ¹**spice**.

flowering raspberry, the red fruit of a shrubby bramble (likewise called *flowering raspberry*) of eastern North America.

fluff, a food rendered light and soft by incorporating air through beating. Often this texture depends, as in whips and soufflés, on beaten egg whites; e.g., cinnamon fluff.

flummery [from Welsh *llymru*], 1. a soft jelly or porridge made by straining boiled, slightly fermented oatmeal or flour. Compare **sowens**; 2. any of several sweet, light dishes (e.g., custard, blancmange).

flute, something shaped like a flute (the musical instrument), i.e. long and slender (e.g., a long French breakfast roll or a baguette).

focaccia [Italian, from Latin *focus* "hearth"], a flat Italian bread seasoned with herbs and olive oil.

fogas [Hungarian], a perch-like eastern European fish; especially, one from Lake Balaton in western Hungary.

foie gras [French, "fat liver"], the fatted liver of an animal, especially of a goose or a duck usually served in the form of a pâté (see **pâté de foie gras**), puree, or terrine. Foie gras is obtained by overfeeding geese and ducks by force.

fold in (**to**) or **fold into** (**to**), to incorporate (an ingredient [e.g., raisins or beaten egg whites]) into a mixture (usually a batter) by repeated gentle overturnings without stirring or beating; it is usually done with the edge of a spoon or spatula.

fondant [French, "melting"], 1. a soft, creamy preparation of cooked or uncooked sugar with water and flavorings used as a basis for the centers and coatings of many candies (e.g., chocolates), for mints, for icings (compare **icing**); 2. a candy containing such a preparation.

fondante potatoes [from French *fondante* "melting (feminine)"], potato balls that are half cooked in water and then braised in butter.

fondue [French "melted (feminine)"], 1. a hot dish of Swiss origin made of melted cheese (usually Swiss cheese or Gruyère) and white wine and eaten with small pieces of bread that each person dips into it at the table; 2. the same melted-cheese preparation, with eggs, butter, and milk; 3. a dish that consists of small pieces of food (e.g., meat, fruit, cake) cooked in or dipped into a hot liquid at the table. When beef is cooked in boiling oil in this manner by each person at the table, the dish is called *fondue bourguignonne* ("Burgundy fondue") and sauces are served on the side; 4. a soufflé made with cheese and bread crumbs.

fonduta [Piedmontese, from French *fondue* "melted (feminine)"], a preparation of Piedmontese origin (from Piedmont, region of northwestern Italy) consisting of melted cheese (e.g., fontina) usually with milk or cream, egg yolks, and sliced white truffles; it may also contain butter.

fonio, a certain crabgrass of northern Africa with seeds that are used as a cereal.

fontina, a soft cheese of creamy texture, typical of Val d'Aosta, region of northwestern Italy (to the northwest of Piedmont).

food processor, an appliance that can chop, shred, or slice food.

foo-foo [African], a kind of dough made from boiled and mashed plantains.

foo yong [from Chinese *fú yóng* "hibiscus," from the fancied resemblance between the omelet and the flower] or **eggs foo yong** [part translation of Chinese *fú yóng dàn* "hibiscus egg"], in Chinese cooking, an omelet made with green peppers, bean sprouts, and onion and fried in deep fat.

forcemeat or **farce** [from French *farce*], finely ground and seasoned meat, poultry, or fish, used in stuffing (e.g., for poultry, roasts, fish, tomatoes, eggplants) or as a garnish. Herbs and vegetables are often added.

forequarter, the front part of the lateral half of a carcass (e.g., of beef, veal, lamb, mutton) usually divided between the twelfth and thirteenth ribs.

foreribs, the prime ribs, a roasting cut of beef including the ribs immediately in front of the loin.

foresaddle, a cut of veal, lamb, or mutton consisting of the undivided forequarters. Compare **hindsaddle**.

foresey, a cut of beef including the foreribs (Scotland). Compare **backsey**.

forktail perch, either of two fishes of the Pacific coast of North America.

formaggio, Italian for **cheese**.

fortune cookie, a cookie of Oriental origin made from a thin layer of dough folded and baked around a slip of paper bearing a prediction of fortune or a maxim (usually printed).

fowl, the meat of any of various birds, especially of the common domestic chicken.

France. The following are among the most important regions of France from the gastronomical point of view (certain cities in the region that are outstanding for their food are shown in parentheses): Alsace (Strasbourg), Bourgogne (Dijon), Ile-de-France (Paris), Loire valley (Nantes, Orléans, Tours), Normandy (Caen, Rouen), Provence (Marseille, Nice).

Some representative dishes and products of these regions are:

Alsace. Sauerkraut (French *choucroute*), goose-liver pie (*pâté de foie gras*), quiche, hare civet with noodles (*civet de lièvre aux nouilles*), stuffed goose (*oie farcie*), Munster cheese, pheasant on sauerkraut (*faisan sur choucroute*).

Bourgogne. Snails (*escargots*) baked in their shells, in hot butter, with parsley and garlic; beef bourguignon (*boeuf bourguignon*), pike dumplings (*quenelles de brochet*).

Ile-de-France. Onion soup (*soupe à l'oignon*), duck with blood sauce, duck with oranges, pressed duckling (*canard à la presse*), chicken in red wine (*coq au vin*), sirloin steak with red-wine sauce (*entrecôte*

**Franconia
potatoes**

frangipane

marchand de vin), pike dumplings (quenelles de brochet), snails (escargots) baked in their shells, in hot butter, with parsley and garlic, fruit tarts, saint-honoré cake, goat-milk cheese (fromage de chèvre, or simply chèvre), Brie cheese.

Loire valley. Pike with white butter (brochet au beurre blanc), stuffed shad (alose farcie), andouille, pheasant (faisan), rillettes, eel matelote (matelote d'anguilles), duck (canard), Pithiviers almond cake (gâteau aux amandes de Pithiviers), Tatin tart (tarte à la Tatin), goat-milk cheese (fromage de chèvre, or chèvre).

Normandy. Tripe in the Caen fashion (tripes à la mode de Caen), duck in the Rouen fashion (canard à la rouennaise), fluffy omelet (omelette du Mont-Saint-Michel), mussels in a white court bouillon (moules marinières), andouille, matelote, oysters (huîtres), mussels (moules), lobster (homard), sole, Camembert cheese.

Provence. Bouillabaisse; frogs' legs fried with garlic (cuisses de grenouilles), salad in the Nice fashion (salade niçoise, a combination of calery, olives, peppers, tomatoes, and tunafish, seasoned with olive oil and pissala [crushed anchovies]), vegetable soup with basil (Provençal lou pistou), a dish between bouillabaisse and aioli (bourride), a cooked onion tart with a puree of anchovies and black olives (pissaladière), ratatouille, beet-leaf tart with pine nuts and raisins (Provençal tourta de bléa, French tourte de blette); garlic mayonnaise (aïoli); bread impregnated with olive oil, with tomatoes, sweet peppers, radishes, onions, black olives, hard-boiled eggs (Provençal pan bagnat), candied fruits (fruits confits).

Food found in other regions, or in several regions: onion soup (soupe à l'oignon), goose livers ground to a fine paste (pâté de foie gras; Alsace, Périgord, Landes); chestnuts cooked with celery, spices, and chicken consommé (purée de marrons); sweetened chestnut cream (crème de marrons), snails in garlic sauce (escargots); stew of goose, mutton, pork, and beans (cassoulet toulousain, Languedoc); frogs' legs (cuisses de grenouilles), chicken in red wine (coq au vin; Bordeaux, Bourgogne), dish of boiled beef or pork with vegetables (especially cabbage and potatoes; potée lorraine), lobster in cream sauce (homard à l'armoricaine; Brittany), duck (canard), trout (truite), salmon (saumon), other fish (sea-perch [loup], pike [brochet]), shellfish (Norway lobster [langoustines], oysters [huîtres], mussels [moules], lobster [homard]), pâtés, terrines, soufflés; tiny dumplings (quenelles) with fish (e.g., pike [brochet]), liver, bone marrow (moelle); quiche, matelote, ham wrapped in cooked dough (jambon en croûte), hare civet (civet de lièvre), turkey with chestnuts (dinde aux marrons), duck with olives (caneton aux olives), omelets (omelettes; with mushrooms, herbs, asparagus tips, or ham), pot-au-feu, goat cheese (chèvre), pastries (pâtisserie), fruit tarts (tartes aux fruits), mousses (e.g., chocolate), croissants, tiny wild strawberries (fraises des bois).

Franconia potatoes [from Franconia, former duchy of southern Germany (German Franken)], potatoes cooked (browned) with a roast and basted with the drippings.

frangipane [Italian, frangipani, a kind of perfume (that imitates the odor of the flower of a certain shrub likewise called *frangipane* or *frangipani*), for Muzio *Frangipane*, 16th-century Italian nobleman], *1.* a dessert of almond cream flavored with frangipani-flower or jasmine perfume; *2.* a creamy tart filling flavored with almonds.

frank, another name for a **frankfurter**.

frankfurter or **frankfurt** [from German *frankfurter* "of Frankfurt," from *Frankfurt* am Main, city of western Germany] or **weenie** or **wiener-wurst**, a cured cooked sausage (e.g., of beef or beef and pork, or smoked pork) that may be skinless or stuffed in a casing. It is often made in long, reddish links. Compare **hot dog** (a frankfurter in a long roll), **Vienna sausage**.

¹**frappé** [French "struck; chilled"], a partly frozen drink (e.g., of diluted, sweetened fruit juice) similar to sherbet and served in a glass as a dessert or appetizer.

²**frappé**, chilled (e.g., champagne, white wine, coffee) or partly frozen.

³**frappé** or **frappe**, a thick milk shake containing ice cream.

frawn, another name for a **whortleberry**.

freestone, a fruit (e.g., certain varieties of cherry, peach, plum) having a stone to which the flesh does not cling; distinguished from **clingstone** (in which the pulp adheres to the pit).

French (**to**) [from the idea of "to prepare in a French manner"], *1.* to cut green beans in lengthwise strips before cooking; *2.* to trim the meat from the end of the bone (e.g., from a chop) leaving the bone bare so as to fit it for convenient handling; *3.* to cut a tenderloin into slices and pound the slices flat before cooking.

French bean, a bean (e.g., a green bean) of which the whole pod is eaten (when young).

French bread, *1.* a crusty white bread made with water, flour, and yeast and baked in long loaves, often in a traditional wood-fired stone hearth; *2.* any of various fancy shaped breads (e.g., French rolls [round, oval] and crescents, round loaves, long thin loaves).

French chestnut, another name for **Spanish chestnut**.

French chop, a rib chop with the meat and fat trimmed from the end of the rib.

French doughnut, a doughnut of cream-puff dough, fried in deep fat.

French dressing, *1.* a salad dressing (French *sauce vinaigrette)* made with oil and preferably wine vinegar or lemon juice, seasoned with salt, pepper, mustard, or other condiments (e.g., fresh green herbs in season, chutney, spices, sweet and sour cream, garlic); the classic proportions are three parts of oil to one part lemon juice or vinegar; *2.* a tomato-flavored, creamy salad dressing. Compare **salad dressing**.

French drip, another name for **drip coffee**.

French endive, another name for the third sense of **endive**.

French-fried potatoes, another name for **French fries**.

French fries, or **fries**, or **French-fried potatoes**, or **chip potatoes**, thin strips of potatoes fried in deep fat until brown.

French fry (**to**), *1.* to fry strips of potato in deep fat (e.g., cooking oil, rendered beef-kidney fat) until golden brown; *2.* to cook (e.g., onion rings, shrimp or other seafood, bread) by frying in deep fat until light brown. Compare ²**fry**.

French Guiana. The following are among representative dishes and products of French Guiana: smoked and marinated (French *boucané*) chicken or fish cooked under banana leaves; a dish of curried fish, pork, or chicken with vegetables (e.g., cucumbers, beans, and potatoes) *(colombo*, not to be confused with French *colombo*, an African root); fricasseed game; codfish or shrimp fritters *(accras)*, stuffed crab *(crabe farci)*, avocado with shrimp; a dish of meat and fish in *awara* (fruit of a palm tree)-paste broth; ^{2}callaloo *(callalou); tripe in tomato sauce, fish in coconut milk or in tomato sauce, fish or shrimp court bouillon *(blaff)*, mango, papaya, banana, guava, coconut, fried bananas, fried breadfruit slices, cream turnover *(oeuf mulet)*.

French ice cream, an ice cream made with cream and egg yolks.

French omelet, an omelet of lightly beaten eggs stirred gently until set, often with a filling.

French pastry, any of a variety of pastries, of different shapes, made of puff paste (sense 1), baked in individual portions and variously filled (e.g., with custard or preserved fruit). Compare **petit four**.

French peas, another name for **petits pois** (very small green peas).

French Polynesia. Some representative dishes and products of French Polynesia are: marinated raw fish; roast suckling pig (French *cochon de lait rôti)*, cooked in an underground oven (also so cooked: potatoes, bananas, fish); yams, shellfish, fish, wild pigeons; a dish of seafood and coconut *(taioro);* grapefruit, papaya, mango; coconut cream dessert.

French roast, coffee of a darker roast than is usual in the United States but less dark than Italian roast.

French tea or **green tea**, an infusion made from a southern French sage.

French toast, sliced bread soaked in a milk and egg batter and lightly fried. It is often served with maple syrup, honey, jelly, or sprinkling of confectioners' sugar.

French walnut, another name for the **English walnut**.

fresh, recently produced, gathered, or made; not spoiled or stale; not stored, cured, or preserved (e.g., by pickling in salt or vinegar, or by canning, drying, smoking, or freezing).

freshwater clam, or **freshwater mussel**, a freshwater **mussel**.

freshwater herring, any of several fishes likened to the herring in food qualities.

fricandeau [French, from *fricasser* "to cook as a fricassee (a stew of meat in gravy)"], a cut of veal, usually rump or shoulder, that has been larded and braised or roasted with vegetables, and glazed in its own juices. When small, it is called **grenadin**.

^{1}**fricassee** or **fricassée** [from French *fricassée*], a dish of cut-up pieces of meat (e.g., chicken, rabbit, young turkey, veal) stewed (simmered) in stock and served in a thick white sauce. The sauce may be a gravy made by adding flour and water to the fat and browned juices in the pan.

^{2}**fricassee (to)**, to cook as a fricassee (a stew of meat in gravy). Fricasseing is a combination of shallow-frying and simmering.

fried, cooked by frying (see ^{2}**fry**).

friedcake or **fried cake**, a small pastry or cake, fried in deep fat (e.g., doughnut, cruller). The shape may be that of a twist, ring, strip, or ball.

fries, another name for **French fries**.

frijol [Mexican Spanish "kidney bean"] or **frijole** [from *frijoles*, plural of Mexican Spanish *frijol* "kidney bean"], bean used in Mexican-style cooking.

frijoles refritos [Mexican Spanish "refried beans"] or **refried beans**, frijoles (beans) cooked with seasonings (e.g., onion, garlic), fried, then mashed and fried again.

fritos [Spanish, plural of *frito* "anything fried,"], tortillas fried in deep fat.

frittata [Italian *frittata*, from *fritto* "fried"], an unfolded omelet (turned when the bottom has set firm) often containing chopped vegetables (e.g., herbs [for instance, basil], garlic, tomato, zucchini, celery, artichokes) or meats (e.g., tongue, ham) usually mixed into the stirred eggs before they are cooked. Other fillings: cheese, mushrooms, seafood (anchovy, tunafish).

fritter [from French *friture* "action of frying; fried food," from *frit* "fried"] or **beignet**, a small mass of fried or sautéed batter, often containing fruit (e.g., apple, banana, pineapple), vegetables (e.g., Indian corn), meat, or fish.

fritto misto [Italian "mixed fried (food)"], small pieces of seafood, meat, or vegetables dipped in batter and deep-fried.

frizzle (to), to pan-fry (e.g., bacon, beef) until crisp and curled.

frog [in French, *grenouille*], any of various largely aquatic amphibians. Their long hind legs, adapted for leaping, are the main part that is eaten.

fromage, French for **cheese**.

frost (to), to cover with icing.

frosting, another name for **icing**. Some people use the word *icing* when it is uncooked, *frosting* when prepared by cooking.

frozen food, food preserved by freezing.

frozen pudding, a frozen custard containing nuts and candied fruit.

fruit, the edible reproductive body (having sweet pulp) of a seed plant, used as a dessert or in a sweet course. Fruits include apples, apricots, bananas, berries (blackberries, blueberries, raspberries, strawberries), cantaloupe, cherries, figs, grapefruit, grapes, mangoes, melon, orange, peaches, pears, pineapple, plums, quince. Many kinds are served without cooking; many fruits are stewed (e.g., plums, prunes) or canned in a syrup of sugar and water (e.g., apricots, pineapple). Apples, bananas, pears, and quinces can be baked with sugar and little or no water; prunes, apricots and other dried fruits are usually soaked in water to cover before being boiled or simmered. Fruits can be broiled and used as garnishes around meats.

fruit cake or **fruitcake**, a heavy and often spiced cake containing a variety of nuts and dried or candied fruits (e.g., citron, raisins). Among nuts used: almonds, hazels, pine nuts, walnuts; among fruits used: cherries, dates, figs, prunes.

fruit cocktail, a mixture of usually tart and sweet fruits cut in pieces, chilled, and served in a small stemmed glass as a first course. Compare **fruit cup**.

fruit cup, a mixture of fresh or preserved fruits cut in pieces and served in

fruited

fusilli

a medium-sized stemmed glass as an appetizer or dessert, sometimes topped with a small ball of fruit ice. Compare **fruit cocktail**.

fruited, having fruit added (e.g., cereal, Jell-O).

fruit leather [Mexican Spanish: *cueritos*, "little leathers" *(cuero* = "leather")], a sheet of dried, pureed fruit. In Mexico, and especially in the area of Morelia, the most popular fruits for this dessert are quince, guava, mango, and papaya with pineapple.

fruity, tasting and smelling of ripe fruit.

frumenty [from obsolete French *frument* "grain, wheat"], a dish of hulled wheat boiled in milk and usually flavored with sugar, spices, and raisins.

frutilla [regional Spanish (South America) "little fruit," diminutive of Spanish *fruta* "fruit"], another name for the **Chilean strawberry**.

¹fry, a dish of any fried food.

²fry (to), to cook in a pan or on a griddle over direct heat (on top of the range), especially with the use of fat or hot oil; distinguished from panbroiling (which uses little or no fat). There are two main kinds of frying: shallow-frying (in a small amount of fat; this is really sautéing—sometimes called *pan-frying)* and deep-frying (in fat or oil deep enough to cover the food to be fried; this is also called *French frying);* most food (except potatoes) that is fried in deep fat contains egg or is coated with egg (e.g., doughnuts, fritters, croquettes, breaded chops, fish and fish fillets). Shallow-frying is usually done in a skillet of iron or heavy aluminum; food may be covered with flour before frying (which gives it a thin brown crust) or it may be breaded (first dipped in beaten egg, then in bread crumbs; e.g., veal, scallops); compare **²fricassee**. Deep-frying is done in a rather deep, heavy pan containing enough oil to float the food during the cooking process. Fish that is often fried include flounder, pike, smelt; shellfish that is often fried include clam, oyster, scallops, shrimp. Beefsteak can be fried. Vegetables that can be fried include eggplant, zucchini.

fry bread, quick bread cooked (e.g., by American Indians) by deep frying.

fry-up, an easily prepared and quickly cooked dish or meal of fried food, especially of cold food heated up in a frying pan.

fudge, a soft creamy candy made typically of white, brown, or maple sugar, with milk, butter, and flavoring (e.g., chocolate) cooked together.

full-cream cheese, cheese made from unskimmed milk.

fulmar, or **fulmar petrel**, or **malduck**, a gull-like seabird of Arctic regions, closely related to the petrels, whose eggs are used for food.

fumet [French "pleasant aroma of meat cooking," from *fumer* "to give off smoke or steam"], reduced and seasoned (with herbs, spices, truffles, mushrooms) fish, meat (including game), or vegetable stock.

fungus, any of a group of organisms that includes mushrooms and yeasts.

funnel cake, a small spiral-shaped cake made by dough poured through a funnel, then fried in a skillet.

fusilli [from regional Italian (South) *fusilli*, diminutive plural of Italian *fuso* "spindle"], spiral-shaped pasta.

ghee grissino gaufrette gigot ganache gazpacho G gingerbread

Gabon. Chicken in ground palm-nut sauce *(nyembwè)*, stuffed crab, fish broiled in banana leaves are among representative dishes of Gabon.

Gaboon chocolate [from *Gaboon*, variant of *Gabon*, river in Gabon, country of western Africa], another name for **dika bread**.

galantine [French], a cold dish of boned, stuffed meat (e.g., sucking pig, veal, poultry) or fish, cooked and coated with aspic or with its own jelly.

galette [French, from *galet* "pebble"], a flat, round cake of pastry (flour, butter, eggs) sprinkled with sugar before baking. Fruit (e.g., pear) may be added. In French, the *galette des Rois* ("twelfth-cake," "galette of the Kings [Wise Men, Magi]") is prepared on occasion of Twelfth-day and contains a broad bean; lots are drawn for slices and he or she who gets the bean acts as master (or mistress) of ceremonies. Compare **twelfth-cake**.

galjoen [Afrikaans "galjoen; galleon"], a fish of the coasts of southern Africa.

Gambia. Grain sorghum, rice, and kola nuts are among representative products of Gambia.

game, the flesh of wild animals taken in hunting and eaten as food. Game includes partridge, pheasant, plover, prairie chicken, quail, ruffed grouse, wild duck; deer, elk, moose, reindeer; rabbit, squirrel.

ganache [French, "jowl"], a sweet, creamy chocolate mixture (with cream, coconut, liquor) used as a filling or frosting.

gar or **garfish,** any of several fishes of North and Central America. It is often served in the form of a broiled steak.

garambulla or **garambullo** [from Mexican Spanish *garambullo*], the small, oblong, red fruit of a certain cactus of western Mexico (likewise called *garambulla).*

garam masala [Hindi, "hot spices"], a pungent and aromatic mixture of ground spices used in Indian cooking. It is often a mixture of black pepper and cardamom with some of the following: cloves, cinnamon, nutmeg, coriander, cumin, turmeric.

garavance [from Spanish *garbanzo*] or **garbanzo,** other names for **chick-pea**.

garden balm, another name for **lemon balm**.

garden burnet, another name for **salad burnet**.

garden egg, another name for **eggplant**.

garden mint, another name for **spearmint**.

garden orache or **mountain spinach**, an Asiatic potherb resembling spinach.

garden rocket, another name for **arugula**.

garlic [French *ail*, Italian *aglio*, Spanish *ajo*], the bulb of a plant (likewise called *garlic*) of the lily family that has a strong odor and taste and is used as a condiment; it is divisible into cloves. Garlic may be used to flavor salad dressing and dips and many other dishes. In Spain, it is used in several soups *(sopas de ajo)*.

garlic bread, slices of French or Italian bread spread with evenly distributed garlic-seasoned butter (garlic pounded with butter in a mortar) and heated in the oven until the bread is light brown.

garlic oil, an oil obtained from garlic and used in flavoring.

garlic salt, a seasoning of ground dried garlic and salt.

garlion [from *garlic* + *onion*], a vegetable that is a cross between garlic and onion.

garni [French "garnished"], the French way of saying *garnished*. *Choucroute garnie* (French feminine form) is sauerkraut cooked and served with cold cuts and potatoes.

[1]**garnish (to)** [from French *garnir* "to garnish"], to add decorative or savory touches to food or drink. A baked fish, for example, may be surrounded by small bouquets of parsley or radishes and sliced cucumber, which offers a contrast in color, shape, flavor, texture.

[2]**garnish**, a decorative or flavorful adjunct to a dish prepared for the table or to a drink. Usually garnishes are as good to eat as to see, and they add contrast in color, shape, flavor, texture. Broiled fruits may be added to meats, orange slices to duck, pear halves to lamb, bunches of grapes to chicken, peach halves and watercress to ham; lemon wedges sprinkled with parsley, or orange slices, to fish; sieved hard-cooked eggs to vegetables; cherries or berries to desserts.

gastronomy [from Greek *gastronomía*, "belly law"], *1.* the art of good eating; *2.* cooking customs or style of a particular region or country.

gâteau or **gateau** [from French *gâteau* "cake"], *1.* a fancy cake filled with custard (or apple puree, or apricot jam, or chocolate butter cream, or coffee butter cream, or whipped cream) and chopped nuts and crystallized fruit; it may be covered with icing, frosting, or other topping (e.g., apricot jam, butter cream, chantilly, meringue, strawberries, sugar and roasted almonds); *2.* food (e.g., eggplant) baked or served in the form of a cake. In French, a gâteau is any cake, so that the word includes babas, *barquettes* (light puff-biscuits), *bûches* ("Yule logs"), *chaussons* (turnovers), *clafoutis* (cherry cakes), éclairs, *feuilletés* (puff-paste cakes), *friands* (small almond-paste cakes); *kouglofs* (gugelhupfs), meringues, mille-feuilles, *moka* (mocha cakes), petits fours, *pithiviers* (almond-paste cake), *polonaise* (cake enclosed in a meringue shell, with candied fruits), puddings, *quatre-quarts* ("four fourths"] a cake with equal parts, by weight, of flour, eggs, sugar, butter), *religieuses* (custard-filled pastry, in the shape of a small ball on top of a bigger one), *saint-honorés* (cakes of frosted choux), savarins, ²tarts, *vacherins* (whipped-cream meringues). Also in French, *gâteaux secs* are those that keep long without spoiling (e.g., biscuits, cookies, galettes, gaufres, *gaufrettes* [cream-filled wafer biscuits], *macarons* [macaroons], madeleines, marzipans, *nonnettes* [small iced-gingerbread cakes], *palmiers* [small, flat, puff-paste cakes], *petit-beurre* [rectangular butter-cookie], *sablés* [shortbread]).

gaufre [French "honeycomb; waffle"], a thin, light, crisp wafer baked with a wafer iron (that impresses a design upon the batter on either side, hollow and in relief, that makes it look like a honeycomb). In French, when filled with cream or jam, it is called *gaufrette*.

gaufrette [French "small gaufre"], a fried potato wafer, cut with the design described under **gaufre**.

gazpacho [Spanish], a vegetable soup made of chopped raw tomatoes, cucumbers (peeled and seeded), sweet peppers (green or red), onions, garlic (with vinegar or lemon juice, oil, condiments), often thickened with bread crumbs, and served cold. In Spain, gazpacho is typical of the Andulusian region; in Portugal, it is spelled *gaspacho* and is typical of the Alentejo area. The following mixed herbs may be added: chives, parsley, basil, chervil, tarragon.

gefilte fish [Yiddish] "filled fish"], chopped fish mixed [or stuffed] with bread crumbs, eggs, and seasonings, cooked in a broth (fish stock) and served cold in the form of balls or of oval cakes.

geiger tree, a small, tropical-American evergreen tree with a small white fruit called **sebesten** (sense 2).

gel (to), to set, become more solid, change into a jelly. Compare **agar**.

gelatin or **gelatine** [from French *gélatine*], *1.* a glutinous substance obtained from animal tissues (skins, tendons, ligaments, bones) by prolonged boiling in water, used as a food (e.g., fish gelatin); *2.* any of various substances (e.g., agar) resembling gelatin (sense 1); *3.* a jelly made with gelatin (sense 2), often used as a dessert or salad base. Compare **aspic**.

gelatinize (to), to convert to gelatin or jelly.

genip or **ginep** [from Spanish *genipa*], the sweet, yellow fruit of a certain tropical-American (West Indies) tree (likewise called *genip*).

genipap or **genipapo** [from Portuguese *genipapo*, from Tupi], the reddish-brown, orange-sized fruit of a certain evergreen tree (likewise called *genipapo*) of the West Indies.

genoise or **génoise** [from French *génoise* "of Genoa (feminine)," from *Gênes* "Genoa, city in northwestern Italy"], a sponge cake of butter, sugar, and flour, leavened by stiffly beaten eggs. Almonds are often added.

geoduck [American Indian], a very large clam of the Pacific coast of northwestern North America.

Georgia. The following are among representative dishes and products of Georgia: lamb soup (Georgian *kharcho),* mutton or fowl soup with saffron and other spices *(chikhirtma),* pilaf *(plov),* boiled fish from the Kura river *(loko),* kabob *(shashlik),* beef kabob *(basturma),* chicken or fish on a spit *(chakhakbili).*

German fried potatoes, raw or cooked potatoes sliced and fried in a skillet.

German pancake, a pancake cooked in a skillet in the oven until brown and puffy.

Germany. The following are important regions of Germany from the gastronomical point of view (certain cities in the region that are outstanding for their food are shown in parentheses): Bavaria (Munich, Nuremberg), Berlin (Berlin); Hamburg, Bremen, and Saxony (Hamburg, Bremen, Hanover), Hesse (Frankfort on the Main), North Rhine-Westphalia (Düsseldorf, Cologne).

Some representative dishes and products of these regions are:

Bavaria. Spaetzle (German *Spätzle*), dumplings *(Knödel)*, sausages *(Würste)*, cold meats *(Schlachtplatte)*, apple strudel *(Apfelstrudel)*.

Berlin. Carp, doughnuts *(Pfannkuchen)*, pig's knuckles with sauerkraut *(Eisbein mit Sauerkraut)*.

Hamburg, Bremen, and Saxony. Fish (e.g., salmon, plaice, turbot, herring) and shellfish (e.g., lobster, crayfish); a dish of beans, pears, and bacon *(Bohnen und Birnen);* a dish of boiled potatoes, meat, herring, and cucumbers *(Labskaus);* eel soup *(Aalsuppe)*, pea soup, tender chicken *(Stubenküken,* "parlor chicken, room chicken").

Hesse. Little frankfurters *(Würstchen)*, pork rib with sauerkraut, dumplings *(Knödel)*, boiled beef, sausages, onion cake *(Zwiebelkuchen)*, strudel.

North Rhine-Westphalia. Rhine eel *(Rheinaal)*, potato pancakes *(Reibekuchen)*, Westphalian ham *(Westfälischer Schinken)*, open cheese-sandwich *(halve Hahn)*.

Food found in other regions, or in several regions: frankfurters *(Frankfurter Würstchen)*, cheeses, St. Martin's goose, spaetzle *(Spätzle)*, schnitzel, sausages *(Würste)*, veal knuckles, carp, pig's knuckles with sauerkraut *(Eisbein mit Sauerkraut)*, pork with sauerkraut, beef roast, potato pancakes *(Kartoffelpuffer* or *Reibekuchen)*, sauerbraten, Lake Constance trout *(Bodensee Felchen)*.

géromé [French, from the regional pronunciation of *Gérardmer*, a town in the Vosges, northeastern France], a soft cheese from the Gérardmer area (with cumin and anise).

gervais [French, from the family name of cheese manufacturer Jules *Gervais*], French cream cheese made from whole milk and cream.

ghee or **ghi** [from Hindi *ghī*], clarified butter made from the butterfat of buffalo milk (or sometimes other milk) especially in India and neighboring countries. Compare **butter oil**.

gherkin or **gerkin** [from Dutch *gurken* "cucumbers," plural of *gurk*] or **Jamaica cucumber**, *1.* the prickly fruit of a certain tropical American vine (likewise called *gherkin)* of the gourd family; *2.* a small immature cucumber, especially one used for pickling.

giant bass or **black sea bass**, a very large fish of California and Lower (Baja) California, that is dark above and lighter below.

giant clam or **pahua**, a very large clam of the Indian and Pacific oceans that sometimes weighs more than 200 kilograms (440 pounds).

giant crab or **Japanese (spider) crab**, *1.* a Japanese spider crab; *2.* an Australian sea crab.

giant perch, another name for **begti**.

giant puffball, an edible **puffball** (globose fungus).

giant salamander, a large salamander of Japan and China.

giant scallop or **sea scallop**, a very large scallop of the Atlantic coast of North America.

giant sunflower, a North American sunflower with edible tuberous roots.

gibelotte, [French] a rabbit fricassee stewed in white wine.

giblet or **jiblet**, the viscera (heart, liver, gizzard) of a fowl (chicken, duck, goose, turkey). Compare **umbles** (that are the viscera of an animal).

gigot [French], a leg of meat (e.g., of lamb, mutton, veal, roe deer) especially when cooked. It may be roasted and served with kidney beans.

gilthead, any of several European marine fishes.

gingelly or **jinjili** [from Hindi and Marathi *jinjalī*, from Arabic *juljuān* "sesame"], another name for the **sesame** seed.

gingelly oil, another name for **sesame oil**.

ginger, the pungent, aromatic rootstock of a plant (likewise called *ginger)* of tropical Asia, often dried and ground and used as flavoring, or, in sugared form, as a sweetmeat. The undried ginger is called *green ginger*.

gingerade, a beverage flavored with ginger.

ginger ale or **ginger pop**, a sweetened, effervescent, nonalcoholic beverage flavored mainly with ginger extract.

gingerbread, *1*. or **pfefferkuchen**, a dark molasses cake flavored with ginger; *2*. a soft molasses and ginger cookie cut in fancy shapes, sometimes frosted. Also called **ginger cake**.

gingerbread palm [so called from the flavor of the fruit], another name for the **doom palm**.

gingerbread plum, the fruit of a West African tree (likewise called *gingerbread plum)*, having a soft mealy pulp.

ginger cake, another name for **gingerbread** (sense 2).

ginger nut, another name for **gingersnap** (a cookie spiced with ginger).

ginger oil, an oil obtained from ginger and used as a flavoring material.

ginger pop, another name for **ginger ale**.

gingerroot or **race ginger**, the unpulverized ginger rootstock.

gingersnap or **gingernut**, a flat, brittle cookie (with a crinkled surface) flavored with ginger and sweetened with molasses. Cinnamon and cloves may be added. Some cooks add a topping of marshmallow, and icing.

ginseng [from Chinese *rénshēn*], a Chinese plant having an aromatic root.

gjetost or **gjedost** [from Norwegian *gjetost* "goat cheese"], a hard, darkbrown, goat-milk cheese (sometimes made of a combination of cow's and goat's milk).

¹**glacé** (adjective) [French "frozen, iced, glazed," from *glace* "ice"], candied, glazed, coated with a transparent sugar-glaze. This is done, for instance, to chestnuts (then called *marrons glacés*), cherries, mille-feuilles.

²**glacé (to)**, to candy, glaze, coat with a glaze (e.g., fruits, nuts).

³**glace** (noun), *1*. a frozen dessert (e.g., ice cream, sherbet); *2*. a coating of glaze (e.g., on candied nuts or fruits).

¹**glaze (to)**, to apply a ²**glaze** (syrup, jelly) to (e.g., doughnuts, fruits, vegetables). Ham can be glazed with a sauce in which sugar is combined with spices. Meat, fowl, game, and fish can be glazed by covering with

a gelatinous sauce made by the long boiling of meat and bones. Compare **candied**. Foods that are glazed include babkas.

²**glaze**, a liquid preparation (e.g., sugar syrup, stock cooked down to a thin paste, gelatine dissolved in meat stock) brushed over, spread on, or otherwise applied to the surface of food (e.g., meat, fish, pastry) on which it becomes firm and adds flavor and a smooth, glossy appearance. Compare **icing**.

globe artichoke, another name for the **artichoke**.

glucose, *1.* a certain sugar, also called **dextrose**; *2.* a light-colored syrup made from cornstarch.

glue plant [this alga is also used for making *glue*], an alga eaten chiefly in Japan and China.

gluside, another name for **saccharin**.

gluten, a substance of wheat (also of Indian corn) flour that gives cohesiveness to dough.

gluten bread, bread made of wheat flour with a high gluten content and low starch content.

gnocchi [Italian "lumps," plural of *gnocco*], soft dumplings made of flour, semolina, or riced potatoes, boiled or baked and served with grated cheese or with a sauce (e.g., **Bolognese**). In Italian, those made with semolina are called *gnocchi alla romana* "in the Roman fashion."

Goa bean [from *Goa*, state of western India] or **asparagus pea**, the edible seed of a tropical vine likewise called *Goa bean*.

Goa butter [from *Goa*, state of western India], another name for **kokum butter**.

goat, any of various ruminant mammals related to the sheep.

goat cheese, any of various cheeses made from goat's milk.

goatfish or **red mullet**, any of various fishes.

goat pepper, any of various hot peppers with small fruit.

¹**gobo** [from Japanese *gobō*], a burdock (an herb) cultivated in Japan as a vegetable.

²**gobo** or **gobbo**, another name for **okra** (sense 1, a pod).

gold apple, another name for a **tomato**.

gold cake, a butter cake in which egg yolks but not the whites are used (e.g., Lord Baltimore cake). Distinguished from **white cake** (in which the whites but not the yolks are used).

golden apple, another name for a **tomato**.

golden buck, Welsh rabbit (a dish made of melted cheese poured over toasted bread) topped with a poached egg.

golden perch, another name for a **callop** (Australian fish).

golden spoon, a tropical American tree sometimes cultivated for its sweet yellow fruits called **nance**s or **nanches**.

golden syrup, another name for **treacle** (sense 2).

goldeye, a small North American fish.

gombo, variant of **gumbo**.

goober or **goober pea** [African (Bantu)], another name for a **peanut**.

goose, any of numerous long-necked, web-footed waterfowl that are in many respects intermediate between the swans and ducks and whose flesh is used for food. It can be roasted.

gooseberry, the acid, green fruit of any of several shrubs (likewise called *gooseberries*). Dishes using gooseberries include Barleduc-preserve pies.

goosefoot, see **lamb's quarters**, sense *1*.

gopher, *1*. any of several land tortoises of the southern United States whose eggs and flesh are used as food; *2*. any of several ground squirrels; *3*. or pocket gopher, any of a certain family of rodents.

gopher tortoise or **gopher turtle**, another name for a **gopher** (in the first sense).

Gorgonzola or **Gorgonzola cheese** [Italian, from *Gorgonzola*, village near Milan, northern Italy, where it was first made], a pungent, blue-green-veined cheese usually made of cow's milk.

gorp, a snack of high-energy food (e.g., raisins and nuts).

gosling, a young goose.

Gouda or **Gouda cheese** [from *Gouda*, town in southwestern Netherlands, where it was originally made], a mild, whole-milk (or partially skimmed milk) cheese similar to Edam (but it contains more fat), shaped in flattened spheres and covered with a protective coating of red wax. Onion soup may be topped with melted Gouda cheese.

goulash or **gulash** or **Hungarian goulash** [from Hungarian *gulyás*, "herdsman," short for *gulyáshús* "herdsman's meat"], a stew of beef or veal and vegetables, seasoned mainly with paprika (sometimes with caraway).

gourami [from Javanese *graméh*], a large freshwater fish of southeastern Asia.

gourd or **calabaza** (Spanish), the fruit of any of certain plants (likewise called *gourds*); gourds include cucumber, melon, pumpkin, squash.

gourmet [French], a connoisseur of food and drink.

government bream [so called because its markings suggest the broad arrow placed on government materials by the British Board of Ordnance], a fish of tropical Australian seas marked when young by scarlet bands that together resemble a broad arrow.

graham (adjective), made from graham flour (whole-wheat flour), as certain bread and certain rolls.

graham cracker [from *graham (flour)*], a dry, slightly sweet, rectangular or square cracker made of whole-wheat flour.

graham flour [for Sylvester *Graham*, 1794-1851, United States vegetarian and dietary reformer], another name for **whole-wheat flour**.

grain, *1*. the hard seed or fruit resembling seed of any cereal grass (e.g., wheat, barley, buckwheat, millet, oats, rice, rye); *2*. the seeds of such plants collectively, especially after having been harvested; *3*. a small hard particle (e.g., of sugar or salt).

grain amaranth, any of several amaranths cultivated, especially in South America, for their seed.

grains of paradise, *1*. or **guinea grains**, the pungent, aromatic seeds of a tropical West African plant, used as a spice; *2*. the seeds of cardamom.

gram [Portuguese, former spelling of *grão* "grain, seed, chick-pea," from Latin *granum* "grain"], another name for **chick-pea**.

grana or **grana cheese** [from Italian *grana* or *(formaggio di) grana*

117

"parmesan," "granular (cheese)," from *grana* "grain"], another name for **Parmesan**.

granadilla or **grenadilla** [from Spanish *granadilla* "little pomegranate," diminutive of *granada* "pomegranate"; Portuguese *maracujá*], the fleshy, oblong fruit of various passionflowers (plants likewise called *granadillas*), used as a dessert and for flavoring.

granita or **granite** [from Italian *granita* "grained, granulated (feminine)," from *grano* "grain"], a coarse-grained sherbet made from fruit (e.g., tangerine).

granjeno [from Mexican Spanish *granjeno*], a shrub with edible berries, occurring in Mexico and the adjacent United States.

granola, a mixture of rolled oats and other ingredients (e.g., brown sugar, raisins, coconut, nuts) that is eaten as a breakfast food or as a snack.

granulated sugar, sugar processed so that the crystals are dried and separated.

grape, a smooth-skinned, juicy berry ranging in color from greenish white to deep red or purple eaten both dried and fresh; it is fermented to produce wine. Grapes are used in pies and salads, and their juice is used as a beverage.

grapefruit [so called because, like *grape*s, it grows in clusters] or **pomelo**, a large, round citrus fruit with a yellow rind and a somewhat acid, juicy pulp varying in color from yellow to pink.

grape juice, the diluted juice of grapes used as a beverage.

grape-seed oil or **raisin-seed oil**, an oil obtained from grape seeds and used in foods.

grass egg, an egg with a greenish yolk due to the hen having fed on green food (e.g., grass).

grasser, a calf brought up on grass as distinguished from one fed on prepared food or with supplementary feeding.

grassnut, *1*. another name for **peanut**; *2*. or **Ithuriel's spear**, a California plant with edible corm (underground stem base).

grass pea or **Indian pea** or **lang**, the white, wedge-shaped seed of a plant (likewise called *grass pea)* used as food in India.

grass pike, another name for the **pike** (fish).

grate (to), to reduce to small particles or fragments by rubbing on something having a rough surface.

gratin [French, from Old French *grater* (French *gratter)* "to scratch, scrape" (because a part of the crust had to be scraped from the bottom and sides of the pot)], *1*. a crust consisting of browned crumbs and butter, often with grated cheese; *2*. a dish (e.g., crayfish, macaroni, potatoes, whiting, zucchini) with such a crust. Compare **au gratin**.

gratinate (to) [from French *gratiner*, from *gratin* "crust"], to cook (in the oven) with a covering of buttered crumbs or grated cheese until a golden crust or crisp surface forms.

gratiné [from French *gratiné* "gratinated"], having (e.g., artichoke heart, brains, chopped broccoli, chicken, eggplant, gnocchi, mussels) a browned (under hot grill) covering or crust (e.g., of buttered crumbs or grated cheese).

gravied, covered with gravy (e.g., beef, potatoes).

gravlax or **gravlaks** [from Swedish *gravlax* or Norwegian *gravlaks*, from *grav* "buried" + Swedish *lax*, Norwegian *laks* "salmon"; this salmon is called "buried" because it is packed in salt], salmon usually cured with salt, pepper, dill, and aquavit (a Scandinavian liquor). Compare **lax**, **lox**.

gravy, a sauce made by thickening (e.g., with flour, cornstarch) and seasoning the juices that drip from cooking meat (e.g., steaks, chops, fried chicken, roasts) in the roasting pan. Flour is browned in the fat and liquid (e.g., milk) added. Mushrooms may be added to the gravy for beef, veal, chicken; cream, for chicken, pork, ham. Distinguished from **pan gravy** (which is made from non-thickened juices).

grayfish, *1.* another name for a **dogfish** (small shark); *2.* another name for a **pollack** (fish of the cod family), especially a young pollack.

grayling, any of several freshwater salmonoid fishes.

gray pike, another name for both a **sauger** and a **walleye** (fishes).

gray snapper or **mangrove snapper**, a snapper (fish) of the tropical western Atlantic.

gray squeteague, another name for a **gray trout**.

gray trout, a weakfish of the Atlantic coast of the United States.

gray walnut, another name for a **butternut**.

great barracuda or **saltwater muskellunge**, a grayish brown barracuda.

Great Lake trout or **Great Lakes trout** [from the *Great Lakes*, chain of five lakes in central North America (Canada and United States)], another name for the **lake trout** (fish).

great northern pike, another name for **pike** (a fish).

great pompano, another name for **permit** (a fish).

Greece. The following are some representative dishes and products of Greece: moussaka, shish kebab (Greek *souvlákia*), meat on small spits *(kokkoretsi);* appetizers *(mezedes* = Arabic *mazza)* may include black olives, outsize shrimps, fried sardines, cheese, radishes, fish-roe pâté *(taramosaláta);* olive oil, pita, avgolemono, cheese, dolma *(dolmadakia* or *dolmádes)*, fish and shellfish, grilled octopus *(oktapódi)* in olive oil, grilled fish, fried fish *(marida)*, fried squid *(kalamarákia)*, fish soup *(kakkaviá* "pot"), lamb and suckling pig spit-roasted over charcoal, lamb casserole, stuffed lamb baked whole, braised veal with tomato sauce *(pastitsada);* veal with vinegar, first fried then baked *(sofrito);* tomato sauce with cinnamon and allspice, baklava, pastry rolls *(katáifi)*, a kind of soft nougat *(mandole or mandolato).*

In ancient Greece, they ate mainly olives, lentils, wild bulbs; stuffed fig and grape leaves; berries; fish baked with wine and marjoram.

green almond, another name for **pistachio** (green seed).

greenback mackerel, another name for the **Pacific mackerel**.

green bean, another name of the **snap bean** (= **string bean**), any kidney bean used as a snap bean when the color of the pods is still green. Compare **wax bean**.

green cheese, *1.* cheese (e.g., sapsago, which is colored by leaves of sweet clover) having a green color (which may be due to having added sage); *2.* cheese made of whey or skim milk.

green corn, the young (unripe) tender ears of Indian corn (sweet corn) suitable for cooking as a table vegetable. Compare **sweet corn**.

green crab

greyskin

green crab or **joe rocker**, a certain edible crab.

greenfish or **opaleye**, any of several greenish or bluish fishes (e.g., pollack, coalfish; bluefish, horse mackerel).

greengage [introduced into England from France by English botanist Sir William *Gage*, 1777–1864], a variety of plum having greenish skin and sweet flesh, cultivated for its superior dessert quality.

greengill, or **green oyster**, an oyster with parts tinged with a green pigment that results from its feeding on green marine algae.

green ginger, another name for undried **ginger**.

green goddess dressing [from *The Green Goddess*, a play (1921) by Scottish author William Archer, 1856–1924], a green salad-dressing consisting of mayonnaise, sour cream, anchovy fillets, minced chives, minced parsley, tarragon vinegar, and seasonings. It may also be used on fish or shellfish. Lemon juice may be added.

green gram, another name for **mung bean** (sense 1).

greening, any of several green-skinned apples used chiefly in cooking.

Greenland. The following are some representative products of Greenland: salmon, whale, seal, shrimp, lamb.

greenling or **rock trout**, any of various fishes of the northern Pacific.

green mealie, another name for **corn on the cob** (Africa).

green onion or **scallion**, a young onion used in salads.

green oyster, another name for the **greengill**.

green pepper, another name for the **sweet pepper**, especially for the unripened green fruit (which turns red at maturity). Often served stuffed.

greens, another name for both **potherbs** and **green vegetable**s.

green shrimp, a shrimp of the Atlantic coast of North America, having the telson (the middle lobe of the tail) edged with green.

green sloke, another name for **sea lettuce**.

green squash, another name for **zucchini**.

green tea, tea that is light in color because it is made from leaves that are not fermented before drying. Compare **black tea** (that is fermented).

green turtle, a large sea turtle having a greenish or olive-colored shell and greenish flesh. Compare **mock turtle soup**.

green vegetables, or **greens**, vegetables whose foliage or foliage-bearing stalks are the chief edible parts. These are rich in chlorophyll and form an important source of vitamins and micronutrients. Green vegetables include beet leaves, Boston lettuce, cabbage, chicory, cos lettuce, curly endive, escarole, French endive, head lettuce, mint, mustard greens, nasturtium leaves, turnip greens, watercress. Compare **potherbs**.

Grenada. Soup of breadfruit and cream, and a cornmeal dish *(coo-coo;* with coconut milk) are representative dishes of Grenada.

grenadilla, variant of **granadilla**.

grenadin or **grenadine** [from French *grenadin*, from *grenade* "pomegranate"], a small **fricandeau**.

grenadine [French, from *grenade* "pomegranate"], a red syrup originally flavored with pomegranates (now sometimes with red currants or with raspberries).

greyskin, a small marine fish found from eastern Africa to Australia.

griddle cake, another name for **pancake**.

grieben [German "cracklings," plural of *Griebe*], cracklings (sense 2) from goose fat.

¹**grill** (**to**) [from French *griller* "to grill"], *1.* to broil (e.g., meat, fish, sausages) on an open grill or gridiron; *2.* to fry or toast (e.g., bread, chestnuts) on a grill.

²**grill**, *1.* gridiron, a cooking utensil of parallel metal bars on which food (e.g., meat, fish) is exposed to red heat (e.g., from charcoal or electricity); *2.* food cooked by broiling (usually on a grill) or grilling. Compare ²**broil, mixed grill**.

grillade [from French *griller* "to grill"], *1.* broiled meat, or another broiled food; *2.* a dish of veal cooked and served in a brown gravy (Louisiana).

grinder, another name for a **hero** (sandwich).

griskin, a pork chop or other broiled meat.

grissino [Italian], a long, slender, crisp breadstick of Italian (especially Piedmont, northwestern Italy) origin.

grits [French *gruau*, *grosse farine*, Spanish *sémola*, *farro*] or **hominy grits**, *1.* hulled and coarsely ground Indian corn or other grain (e.g., rice, wheat; especially ground hominy with the germ removed); *2.* coarsely ground soybean oil cake.

groats, hulled grain broken in fragments larger than grits.

groom's cake, a light fruit cake served at a wedding.

groper [like English *grouper*, from Portuguese *garoupa*], either of two fishes of southern seas.

Gros Michel [from French *gros* "big, fat" + *Michel*, a given name corresponding to English *Michael*], another name for **Jamaica banana** (a large banana).

ground almond, another name for **chufa**.

ground-cherry, another name for **strawberry tomato**.

groundfish, a fish keeping to the bottom of the water (e.g., cod, flounder, haddock, pollack).

groundhog, another name for **woodchuck**.

groundnut, *1.* another name for **peanut**; *2.* another name for **chufa**; *3.* the edible tuberous root of any of several plants (likewise called *groundnuts).*

groundnut oil, another name for **peanut oil**.

ground pea, another name for **peanut**.

ground pistachio, another name for **peanut**.

grouper [from Portuguese *garoupa*], any of various fishes that are typically bottom-dwelling and of warm seas.

grouse, any of several game birds.

grub, the soft, thick, wormlike larva of certain beetles and other insects. Compare **grugru, witchetty**.

gruel, a thin, watery porridge made by boiling a cereal (e.g., cornmeal, oatmeal, wheat flour) in water or milk.

grugru [from Puerto Rican Spanish *grugrú*] or **grugru grub** or **grugru worm**, a large edible grub that is the larva of certain tropical American insects (weevils) and that feeds on the pith of coconut and other palm trees, and on the sugarcane.

¹**grunt**, a dessert made by dropping biscuit dough on top of boiling berries

(e.g., blackberries, blueberries) or other fruit and steaming. Compare **apple grunt**.

²**grunt**, any of various marine fishes that make grunting noises.

gruntling, a young pig.

Gruyère cheese, or **Gruyère** [from *Gruyère*, district in Fribourg canton, western Switzerland, where it was originally made], a pressed, cow-milk cheese with small holes (that form during ripening) and a nutty flavor, often used in cooking. Compare **Swiss** (which has large holes).

guacamole [Mexican Spanish, from Nahuatl *ahuacamolli* "avocado sauce"], a mixture or spread of pureed or mashed avocado, often with tomato and onion, and seasoned with condiments.

Guadalupe palm [from *Guadalupe*, island of northwestern Mexico], a palm of Guadalupe Island with edible buds, and with sweet fruit called *Guadalupe plum*.

Guadalupe plum [from *Guadalupe*, island of northwestern Mexico], the sweet, pulpy fruit of the Guadalupe palm.

Guadeloupe. The following are among representative dishes and products of Guadeloupe: ²callaloo (regional French *calalou*), fish soup, stuffed crabs *(crabes farcis)*, fish stew *(daube de poisson)*, poached fish *(poisson en blaff);* curry *(colombo)* with chicken or pork (or kid or lamb or fish or shellfish); duckling *(caneton);* fritters *(accras)* filled with codfish or shrimp (or eggplant or hearts of palm); cucumber ratatouille *(ratatouille créole)*, green-mango chutney or relish *(rougail de mangues vertes)*.

guamuchil [from Mexican Spanish *guamúchil*], variant of *huamuchil*, another name for **camachile** (tree and fruit).

guan [American Spanish], any of several tropical American birds that somewhat resemble turkeys.

guana, variant of **iguana**.

guanabana [from Spanish *guanábana* "fruit of the soursop"], another name for **soursop**.

Guatemala. The following are some representative dishes and products of Guatemala: chicken marinated in pineapple cider (Spanish *gallo en chicha)*, tamales, enchiladas (but, unlike Mexican enchiladas, the tortilla is not rolled), stuffed peppers *(chiles rellenos)*, fried bananas with black beans *(rellenitos de plátano)*, a rice and milk dessert *(arroz con leche)*.

guava or **guayaba** [Spanish] or **bay plum**, the globose, sweet, yellow fruit of a tropical American tree (likewise called *guava*), having pink flesh, eaten fresh and used for jellies and preserves.

guayaba, another name for **guava**.

gudgeon, a small Eurasian freshwater fish related to the carp.

gugelhupf [German "hood yeast"] or **kugelhof**, a cake of yeast-leavened dough, baked in a fluted pan. It usually contains raisins, citron, and nuts.

Guiana, see **French Guiana**.

Guinea corn [from *Guinea*, region of western Africa], a variegated Indian corn.

Guinea duck [from *Guinea*, region of western Africa], another name for **Muscovy duck** (a tropical American duck).

guinea fowl or **guinea hen** [from *Guinea*, region of western Africa], an African bird related to the pheasants. It is often broiled.

guinea grains [from *Guinea*, region of western Africa], another name for **grains of paradise** (in sense 1).

guinea hen [from *Guinea*, region of western Africa], *1.* a female guinea fowl; *2.* any guinea fowl.

Guinea pepper [from *Guinea*, region of western Africa], the pungent, aromatic fruit of a tropical African tree (likewise called *Guinea pepper*), that is used as a condiment.

guinea pig [probably from a confusion of Guyana (South America) with Guinea (western Africa)] or **cavy**, a small, domesticated, South American rodent. The ancient Incas bred it for food.

guinea plum [from *Guinea*, region of western Africa], a West African tree with a plum-like brown fruit.

guinea squash [from *Guinea*, region of western Africa], another name for **eggplant**.

guisquil [from American Spanish *güisquil*], variant of **huisquil** (another name for **chayote**).

gulash, variant of **goulash**.

gulfweed [from *Gulf* of Mexico + *weed*], a tropical American seaweed.

gumbo or **gombo** [from Louisiana French *gombo*], *1.* the mucilaginous pods of okra (often used to flavor or thicken); *2.* or **okra**, a soup or stew thickened with okra (sense 1, pods of a plant) or with filé and containing a variety of vegetables (e.g., tomatoes, onions) with meat (e.g., chicken, beef) or seafood (e.g., shrimp, or shrimp and crab and oysters); *3.* a thick conserve of one or more fruits.

gumbo filé [from Louisiana French *gombo filé*, from *gombo* "gumbo" + *filé* "powdered young leaves of sassafras"], *1.* gumbo (sense 2) prepared with filé; *2.* another name for **filé**.

gumdrop, a small candy made of gum arabic, gelatin, or cornstarch, and coated with coarse granulated sugar.

gummy shark, any of several small Indo-Pacific sharks.

gunpowder tea, a type of green tea of which the leaves are rolled into pellets or small balls.

gur or **goor** [from Hindi *gur* "coarse sugar, molasses"], another name for **jaggery** (brown sugar).

gurnard [from obsolete French *grognard* "grunter," from *grogner* "to grunt, grumble"], any of various European marine fishes.

Guyana. The following are some representative dishes and products of Guyana: noodles, curries, ¹pepper pot, coconuts, *callaloo* (a vegetable) soup (see ²**callaloo**), crabs, taro leaves, breadnut soup, fish, guava, soursop, pineapples.

gyro [pronounced /year-o/] [modern Greek "turn"; from the rotation of the meat on a spit], a sandwich especially of lamb and beef, tomato, and onion on warm pita bread. Often also with peppers, lettuce, and a dressing.

haba [Spanish], another name for the **broad bean**.

hackberry or **pompion berry**, the small, often edible, dark-purple fruit of any of various trees (likewise called *hackberries*) of the elm family.

haddie, another name for **haddock** (Scotland).

haddock, a fish of northern Atlantic waters related to the cod. It is a lean fish and therefore best for boiling and steaming. Haddock steak can be served creamed.

haggis, a dish of Scottish origin consisting of the minced heart, lungs, and liver of a sheep (preferably lamb) or a calf mixed with suet, onions, oatmeal, and seasonings, and boiled in the stomach of the animal.

Haiti. The following are among representative dishes and products of Haiti: rice and beans (or peas), salt codfish salad (regional French *chiquetaille de morue)*, pickled oysters *(huîtres marinées)*, spiny lobster *(langouste)*, fritters *(marinades)*, smoked herring pâté *(pâté de harengs saurs);* glazed pork pieces *(griots de porc)*, served with hot-pepper sauce *(sauce ti-malice);* fried plantain slices *(banane pesé)*, curried chicken *(poulet à la créole)*, stuffed chicken *(poulet farci)*, rice with tiny black mushrooms *(riz au djon-djon)*, avocados, coconut, bananas *(figues* or *figues bananes)*, plantain *(banane)*, stuffed bananas *(figues bananes fourrées)*, mango pie, sweet potato cake *(gâteau de patates)*, sweet potato bread *(pain de patates)*.

hake, any of various marine fishes related to the cod. Hake steak can be served creamed.

halal (to) [from Arabic *ḥalāl* "that which is lawful"], to slaughter for food according to Moslem law.

half-baked, only partly baked.

halibut, any of several large marine flatfishes. It is a lean fish and therefore best for boiling and steaming. Halibut steak can be served creamed.

hallah, see **challah**.

halvah or **halva** [from Yiddish *halva*, from Romanian *halva*, from Turkish *helva* "halvah," from Arabic *ḥalwā* "sweetmeat"], a flaky confection of

Turkish origin consisting of crushed sesame seeds in a binder of syrup (e.g., of honey).

ham or **jambon** [French] or **jamón** [Spanish], a cut of meat consisting of a hind leg, especially one from a hog (but also from a deer or elk), either fresh or cured by salting and smoking or drying. Some of the areas renowned for their hams are Auvergne and Bayonne in southern France, Westphalia (Westfalen) in western Germany, Parma in northern Italy, York in northern England, Virginia in the eastern United States. Ham may be baked; ham slices may be baked, broiled, pan-broiled.

hamburg, another name for **hamburger**.

hamburger [from *Hamburger* "of Hamburg (city of northern Germany)," from *Hamburg*] or **beefburger** or **hamburg steak**, *1.* ground beef; *2.* a patty of ground beef cooked by frying, grilling, broiling, or baking; compare **Salisbury steak**; *3.* a sandwich made of a hamburger patty in a split round bun (or in a roll).

Hamburg parsley, a parsley grown primarily for its enlarged taproot which resembles a small parsnip.

hamburg steak or **hamburger steak**, other names for **hamburger**.

hand, or **hand cheese**, any of several soft, sharp cheeses of a kind originally molded by hand.

hand apple, an apple suitable for eating without cooking.

hand cheese, see **hand**.

hand of pork, a shoulder of pork without the blade bone.

hangi [Maori], a Maori underground oven consisting of a pit in which stones are heated and wrapped food is then placed on stones and branches (wet sacks and earth are used to cover the stones and foods). Compare **imu**.

Hangtown Fry [from *Hangtown*, nickname of Placerville, California], a scrambled egg dish or omelet containing fried oysters.

hardbake, a sweetmeat of boiled brown sugar or molasses with blanched almonds.

hard-boil (to) [from *hard-boiled*], to cook an egg in the shell by boiling until white and yolk have solidified.

hard-boiled, (of eggs) cooked in the shell by boiling in water until both white and yolk have solidified.

hard candy, a fruit-flavored candy made of sugar and corn syrup.

hard crab, another name for **hard-shell crab**.

hardhead, another name for **Atlantic croaker**.

hard maple, another name for **sugar maple**.

hard sauce, a creamed mixture of butter, powdered sugar, and flavoring (e.g., vanilla, rum). It is served chilled with plum pudding, fruit cakes, or gingerbread.

hard-shell, another name for **hard-shell crab**.

hard-shell clam, another name for the **quahog**.

hard-shell crab or **hard-shelled crab** or **hard crab**, a marine crab that has not recently shed its shell and therefore has the shell rigid (fully hardened). Distinguished from **soft-shell crab** (that has recently shed its shell and has a very soft new one).

hardtack or **sea biscuit** or **ship biscuit** or **pantile** or **pilot bread** or **sea**

bread or **ship bread**, a saltless hard biscuit, bread, or cracker (or loaf bread), made of flour and water, prepared for use on shipboard (formerly eaten by sailors).

hard wheat, a wheat with hard kernels that yields a strong flour especially suited for bread and pasta (these kernels are high in gluten). Distinguished from **soft wheat** (which is suitable for pastry and breakfast foods).

hare, any of various swift mammals related to the rabbit. Hare dishes include **civet**.

¹**haricot** [French "lamb stew," probably from Old French *harigoter* "to cut in pieces"], a highly seasoned mutton or lamb stew with vegetables (usually potatoes, or turnip). In 1611, Randle Cotgrave *(A dictionarie of the French and English tongue)* described it as "mutton sod with little turneps, some wine, and tosts of bred crumbled among."

²**haricot** [French "bean" (influenced in form by French *haricot* [stew]), from Nahuatl *ayacotli, ayecotli*] or **haricot bean**, the ripe seed (dried and shelled) or unripe pod of any of several beans (especially the string bean and the common kidney bean) used as a vegetable. Compare *cassoulet toulousain* under **France**.

harlequin quail, a small African quail.

Harvard beets [from *Harvard* University, Cambridge, Massachusetts, United States], cooked beets (sense 2), diced or sliced, served in a vinegar and sugar sauce thickened with cornstarch.

hasenpfeffer [from German *Hasenpfeffer*, from "hare pepper"], a highly seasoned stew made of rabbit meat that has been soaked for two days in vinegar and pickling spices (juniper berries, bay leaves, garlic, onion), often served with sour cream or with noodles. Compare **civet**.

¹**hash (to)** [from French *hacher*, from *hache* "ax"], to chop (meat or vegetables) into small pieces, mince.

²**hash**, a dish of chopped meat (e.g., corned beef), potatoes, and sometimes vegetables, usually browned by baking or frying.

hashed brown potatoes or **hashbrowns** or **American fried potatoes**, boiled potatoes that have been diced, mixed with chopped onions and shortening, packed into a skillet and fried brown on both sides.

haslet, *1.* the heart, liver, lungs, and other edible viscera of a butchered hog or other animal; *2.* a braised dish made of viscera.

hasty pudding, *1.* a porridge or pudding made of oatmeal or flour stirred into boiling water or milk and quickly cooked (England); *2.* cornmeal mush usually served hot with milk and maple syrup, brown sugar, or other sweetening (United States).

hautbois or **hautboy** [from French *hautbois* "oboe," from *haut* "high" + *bois* "wood"], a European strawberry.

haute cuisine [from French *haute cuisine* "high (superior) cooking"], *1.* a refined or elaborate style of cooking, especially of French cooking; *2.* food prepared in this style.

Havarti [from *Havarti*, place name in Denmark], a semisoft Danish cheese.

Hawaiian crab, a large Pacific crab.

Hawaiian duck, a small duck of Hawaii.

hazel, a shrub of the birch family bearing nuts called *hazelnuts*. Filberts are the nuts of a shrub (likewise called *filbert)* that is a species of hazel.

hazelnut or **avellana** [Spanish], the nut of a hazel.

head cabbage or **heading cabbage**, another name for **cabbage** (sense 1).

headcheese or **mock brawn**, a preparation of parts of the head, feet, and sometimes the tongue and heart of an animal, usually a pig, chopped up fine, seasoned, and, after being boiled and jellied, pressed into the form of a cheese, a loaf, or a sausage.

heading broccoli, another name for **broccoli**.

head lettuce or **cabbage lettuce**, any of various lettuces whose leaves develop into a compact head suggesting that of cabbage; distinguished from **leaf lettuce** (whose leaves do not form a compact head).

health food, a food advertised as assisting health.

heart, a certain organ of animals. It is one of the variety meats (from beef, lamb, pork, veal).

heart cherry, any of several sweet cherries with heart-shaped fruits.

heart of palm (Spanish *palmito)*, the young terminal bud (tender and ivory-colored) of various palms (e.g., a cabbage palmetto) usually served raw and dressed as a salad.

heath pea, a leguminous European plant bearing small tubers eaten as a vegetable.

heavy, not easily or quickly digested.

heavy cream, a noticeably thick cream.

Hélène, see **pear Helene**.

helzel [Yiddish "little neck," diminutive of *hals* "neck"], a skin of the neck of poultry (e.g., goose, chicken), one end sewn or tied together to keep in the stuffing, filled with seasoned fat and flour, usually roasted in the pan with the bird. The stuffing may also have matza meal and onion.

hen clam, another name for **surf clam**.

herb, a savory or aromatic plant used as seasoning. Culinary herbs include anise, bergamot, caraway, chervil, chives, coriander, dill, epazote, fennel, lovage, marjoram (= sweet marjoram), oregano (= wild marjoram), parsley, rosemary, sage, sweet basil, tarragon, thyme. See also **bouquet garni**, **fines herbes**, **sweet herbs**. Herbs are added to salads, meat, fish, mustards, vinegars. Herbs are seed-producing plants and their seeds, too, are used to flavor food (e.g., poppy, sesame). For herb tea, see **infusion** (sense 2).

hermit, a spiced molasses cookie (e.g., with cinnamon, cloves) often containing chopped, seeded raisins and broken nuts (e.g., hickory). Coconut may be added.

hero or **submarine** or **grinder**, a large sandwich made with a small loaf of crusty bread cut lengthwise, often buttered, and containing lettuce, condiments, and a variety of meats (e.g., ham, salami, meatballs) and cheeses.

herring, any of various fishes of northern Atlantic and Pacific waters. The herring is a fat fish and therefore best for broiling, baking, planking. Compare **alewife**. Herring dishes include Bismarck herring.

hicaco, another name for **coco plum**.

hickory, any of several North American trees having nuts with an edible kernel.

hickory nut, the sweet nut of the hickory.

high blueberry, another name for the **highbush blueberry**.

highbush blueberry or **swamp blueberry** or **tall blueberry**, the fruit of a certain shrub (likewise called *highbush blueberry)* that is the source of most cultivated blueberries.

highdried, another name for a **red herring**.

high tea, a substantial (meat, salad, stewed fruit, cakes, cookies, bread and butter) late afternoon meal at which tea is served.

hinalea [from Hawaiian *hinalea*], a certain fish of Hawaii.

hindquarter, the back half of a side of beef, lamb, veal, mutton, including a leg and one or two ribs. Compare **beefsteak, forequarter**.

hindsaddle or **saddle**, a cut of veal, lamb, or mutton consisting of the undivided hindquarters and including one pair of ribs. Compare **foresaddle**.

hind shank, a cut of mutton, beef, or veal from the upper part of a hind leg.

hiwihiwi [from Maori *hiwihiwi*], a small marine fish of New Zealand.

hock, a cut of meat from the leg, just above the foot.

hoecake [from its being sometimes baked on the blade of a *hoe*], *1.* a small, thin, coarse bread or cake made of cornmeal, water, and salt usually cooked before an open fire; *2.* a hoecake (sense 1) to which shortening has been added and which is usually baked on a griddle or in an oven.

hog, see **swine**. Wild hogs are called *boars*.

hog banana, a large, red-skinned banana usually eaten cooked.

hogfish or **pig fish** [some feel it resembles a hog], a large West Indian and Florida wrasse, the adult male having a long snout.

hog peanut [from its seed being relished by hogs] or **wild peanut**, a twining North American vine having basal or subterranean, fleshy, one-seeded fruits, each containing a single edible seed which resembles a peanut.

hog sucker, a certain North American fish.

hoisin sauce [from Cantonese *hoisin* "seafood," from *hoi* "sea" + *sin* "fresh"], a thick, jam-like, reddish sauce of soybeans, spices, and garlic used in Oriental cookery. It is often served as a dip for pork. In Northern Chinese, it is called *haixian jiang*.

hojaldre, hojaldra, Spanish for puff pastry; see **puff pastry**.

hokey-pokey, a cheap kind of ice cream packaged in small portions (e.g., between sweet wafers or in a paper cup) and sold by street vendors.

holishkes [from Yiddish *holishkes*], stuffed cabbage.

hollandaise sauce, or simply **hollandaise** [part translation of French *sauce hollandaise* "Dutch sauce"], a creamy sauce made basically of melted butter, egg yolks, and lemon juice or vinegar (and seasonings), used with seafood and vegetables such as asparagus, broccoli, cauliflower. Hollandaise is different from other sauces in that it is not thickened with flour. Compare **béarnaise, ¹mousseline**.

holy herb [translation of Late Greek *hierobotane*], another name for **yerba santa** (which in Spanish literally means "holy herb").

home fried potatoes, cottage fried potatoes, or **home fries**, potatoes that have usually been parboiled, sliced, and fried in a heavy skillet.

hominy [from an Algonquian word], kernels of hulled Indian corn (e.g., white flint corn) with the germ removed and either whole or coarsely ground and prepared for use as food by boiling.

hominy grits, another name for **grits** (sense 1).

hommos, see **hummus**.

Honduras. The following are among representative dishes and products of Honduras: tamales stuffed with rice, potatoes, pork, or chicken, with raisins and olives added (Spanish *nacatamales);* tripe *(mondongo)* with vegetables; fried tamale slices; conch soup *(sopa de caracol)* with plantain and coconut milk; sun-dried, salted meat *(tapado de carne salada)* with plantain, cassava *(yuca)* and potatoes, served in broth; cheese, tortillas, beans, rice, shellfish, enchiladas, avocados, mangoes, papaya, pineapple, bananas.

honey, a sweet, viscid, syrupy, yellowish or brownish substance that is elaborated out of the nectar collected from flowers in the honey sac of various kinds of bees and that the bees deposit in cells of the comb in hives (they store it as food). The flavor and color of honey depend largely on the plants from which the nectar is gathered, with that of clover being especially esteemed. The word *honey* is used also for certain syrups. Compare **apple honey**.

honey agaric, another name for **honey mushroom**.

honeyberry, a sweetish berry (from either of two trees).

honeycomb, a mass of hexagonal wax cells (built by honeybees in their nest) containing honey, used as an article of food.

honeydew, *1.* a sweet, sticky substance (a saccharine deposit) found on the leaves of many plants that is secreted usually by aphids or scale insects or sometimes by a fungus; *2.* a honeydew melon.

honeydew melon, a smooth-skinned, greenish white, winter melon having very sweet, green pulp.

honey locust or **sweet bean** or **three thorn acacia** or **thorn locust**, a tall thorny tree of eastern North America, having long, twisted pods containing seeds resembling beans and separated by a sweet pulp.

honey mushroom or **honey fungus** or **honey agaric**, an edible agaric.

honey palm, another name for **coquito** (a palm tree).

honeysuckle apple, another name for **swamp apple**.

hoopid salmon, or simply **hoopid**, another name for the **silver salmon**.

horchata, see **chufa**.

hors d'oeuvre [French "outside of the work," i.e. of the ordinary meal, side dish] or **relish**, an appetizer or canapé, usually one of an assortment, served before a meal, with crackers or toast bits on the side. In addition to the kinds mentioned under **antipasto** and **canapé**, fish, eggs, vegetables (e.g., radish), fruit, salami, miniature hamburgers, pizzas, or sausages, as well as flattened meat balls and slices of turkey or baked ham, cheese in various shapes and combinations, are also used as appetizers or hors d'oeuvres. Compare **zakuska**.

horse mackerel, any of several large marine fishes.

horse mushroom or **field mushroom**, a coarse edible mushroom with a broad white cap.

horseradish, a condiment made of the shredded or grated (thick, whitish,

129

pungent) root of a tall, coarse plant (likewise called *horseradish*) of the mustard family, often moistened with vinegar or a similar substance. Horseradish sauce can be used on ham loaf or tongue. In Japanese cooking, a similar condiment is called **wasabi**.

horseradish tree [from its root's pungent odor and taste resembling that of horseradish], a tree of southeastern Asia and of Africa that has a horse-radish-flavored root and is grown throughout the tropics for its fruit which when young is pickled or cooked as a vegetable and for its seeds which yield ben oil.

horsetail agaric or **horsetail fungus**, another name for the **shaggymane**.

horsetail corn, another name for **Indian corn**.

¹**hot** (adjective), *1.* having a high temperature; *2.* pungent, peppery, suggestive of heat.

²**hot** (noun), another name for a **hot dog**.

hot bread, bread, biscuits, or the like served still hot from baking.

hotcake or **hot cake**, other names for a **pancake**.

hotchpotch, a thick soup or stew of various young vegetables (e.g., barley, peas, and potatoes) and often also meat (e.g., mutton).

hot cross bun [it was served in England in the pre-Christian era in honor of the Goddess of Spring; later, the cross was placed on the bun in a missionary spirit], a sweet bun (a yeast bread) made with raisins and marked with a cross of sugar frosting on top, traditionally eaten on Good Friday and during the whole of Lent.

hot dish, another name for a **casserole** dish.

hot dog [perhaps so called from the fancied resemblance of a frankfurter to a dachshund] or simply **dog** or ²**hot**, a hot, cooked frankfurter (sausage) enclosed as a sandwich in a long, split, soft, bread roll and garnished with mustard, catsup, onion, or other savory substance.

hotel rack, the rib section (unsplit) of a foresaddle of lamb (used for chops or for roasts).

hot pepper or **chile** or **chili** or **spur pepper**, *1.* the pungent fruit (usually thin-walled) of any of several small varieties of capsicum shrubs (likewise called *hot peppers)* of the nightshade family; distinguished from **sweet pepper** (which is mild); *2.* a condiment made from such fruit (usually dried).

hot pot, *1.* another name for **firepot**; *2.* a stew of meat and vegetables.

hot slaw, coleslaw with a cooked dressing.

Hottentot bread or **Hottentot's bread**, the rootstock of elephant's-foot (a southern African vine likewise called *Hottentot bread).*

huamuchil, another name for **camachile**.

huarache [Mexican Spanish "sandal," from Tarascan *kwaráchi* "low-heeled sandal"], a bean-filled long tortilla with the edges folded up (Mexico).

Hubbard squash or simply **Hubbard**, any of various often large winter squashes.

huckleberry, the glossy, blackish berry, with 10 nutlets, of any of several New World shrubs (likewise called *huckleberries)* of the heath family.

huisquil, another name for **chayote**.

humble pie or **umble pie** [from *humbles* or *umbles* "entrails of an animal"], a meat pie made from the edible organs of a deer or a hog.

humbles [from *umbles* "entrails of an animal"], the heart, liver, kidneys, and other small pieces of a deer or of a hog.

hummus or **hommos** [from Arabic *ḥummuṣ* "chick-peas"], a paste of smoothly pureed chick-peas mixed with sesame oil or sesame paste and eaten as a dip or sandwich spread. It can be used as a base for a tahini cream. Hummus with tahini (with lemon juice, garlic, parsley, mint) may be an appetizer served as a dip (traditionally with a decorative pattern of whole chick-peas on top).

humpback salmon or **pink salmon**, or **pink**, a small Pacific salmon.

Hungarian goulash, another name for **goulash**.

Hungarian paprika or **Hungarian pepper**, a paprika (sense 1, a condiment) produced in Hungary from peppers (sense 3, a pod-like fruit) of slight pungency, especially from the fruit with seeds and stalk removed. Compare **king's paprika**.

Hungary. The following are among representative dishes and products of Hungary: goulash (Hungarian *gulyás*), fish (best: *fogas* [a pike-perch]) from Lake Balaton; mixed grill *(fatányéros)* with salad and fried potatoes, served on a wooden platter; fish soup *(halászlé);* cabbage soup *(kaposztaleves)*, stuffed cabbage *(töltött káposzta)*, chicken paprika *(paprikás csirke)* with sour cream; carp, sausages; pastries *(retes* [a strudel]), fritters with apricot jam *(csoroge)*, cake *(vargabéles)*.

hush puppy or **hushpuppy** [from its occasional use as food for dogs], a cornmeal dough shaped into small balls and fried in deep fat, commonly eaten in the South of the United States.

husk corn, another name for **pod corn**.

hyacinth bean or **labbab** [Arabic], a large, twining, tropical vine grown for its edible pods and seeds.

icaco, another name for **coco plum**.

¹**ice**, *1.* a frozen dessert containing a flavoring (e.g., fruit juice), especially one containing no milk or cream; *2.* cake frosting, icing; *3.* a serving of ice cream.

²**ice (to)**, *1.* to cover or decorate a cake with a sugar coating; *2.* to chill by setting in ice.

iceberg lettuce or simply **iceberg**, any of various lettuces that grow in compact heads (head lettuces), with large, crisp, curling leaves.

ice cream, a smooth frozen food containing cream (sense 1, the fatty part of milk) or butter fat, sugar, flavoring, and often eggs. It may also contain milk thickened with flour, tapioca, eggs or gelatin. Some of the many popular flavors are: banana, chocolate, coffee, mocha (sense 1, a flavoring made of a coffee infusion), peach, peppermint, pineapple, pistachio, raspberry, strawberry, vanilla, walnut. Compare **French ice cream**, **mousse** (sense 1, chilled dessert), **parfait** (both senses).

ice-cream cone, a conical wafer holding ice cream.

ice-cream soda or **soda**, a sweet drink of soda water, ice cream scoops, and flavoring syrup.

ice cube, a block of ice formed in a small mold and used for icing drinks. It may be decorative (e.g., with a maraschino cherry or a preserved strawberry or a piece of lemon or pineapple, or a sprig of mint).

Iceland. The following are among representative dishes and products of Iceland: smoked mutton (Icelandic *hangikjöt*), dried fish *(hardhfiskur)*, smorgasbord, seafood (e.g., herring, salmon, trout, shrimps), lamb, salted cod *(saltfiskur)*, small lobster *(humar* or *smáhumar);* a dish of boiled sheep's head *(svidh)*, served cold with mashed rutabaga; blood sausage *(blodmor)*, liver sausage *(lifrarpylsa);* a kind of yogurt *(skyr)*, eaten with cream and sugar; pickled whale blubber; shark that has been buried in the sand for five or six months *(hákarl);* mushrooms; an assortment of pickled meats *(thorramatur)*, such as whale, shark, and seal, served cold; ptarmigan *(rjúpa)*.

Iceland moss or **Iceland lichen**, a brittle, edible lichen of northern regions.

ice lolly, a confection of frozen, flavored water on the end of a stick.

ice milk, frozen custard, a sweetened, skim-milk, frozen food.

ice tea or **iced tea**, tea that is chilled with ice.

icing or **frosting**, a sweet, flavored, usually creamy mixture used to coat or decorate baked goods (e.g., cakes, cookies, cupcakes). Icing is usually made from sugar and butter combined with water, milk, or egg white; it may be flavored with chocolate, coffee, fruit, vanilla. Compare ²**glaze**, **fondant**. Some people use the word *icing* when the mixture is uncooked, *frosting* when prepared by cooking.

icing sugar, another name for **confectioners' sugar**.

Idaho, an elongated potato of a variety grown especially in the state of Idaho (United States) and suited for baking.

ide [from Swedish *id*], a certain European freshwater fish.

iguana [Spanish, from Arawak and Carib *iwana*], any of several large, herbivorous, tropical American lizards, usually living in trees.

illupi, a tree of southeastern Asia whose sweet flowers are eaten dried or cooked with other foods. Compare **mahua**.

imperial tea [from *imperial* "of outstanding quality"], a high-grade Chinese green tea.

imu [Hawaiian], a Hawaiian cooking pit used for baking meat or vegetables by means of heated stones. Compare **hangi**, **laulau**.

inconnu or **sheefish**, a large fish related to the whitefish.

India. The areas centered on the following cities are among the most important regions of India from the gastronomical point of view (regional languages in parentheses): Calcutta (Bengali), Chennai (formerly Madras; Tamil), Delhi (Hindi), Mumbai (formerly Bombay; Marathi).

Some representative dishes and products of these regions are:

Calcutta. River fish (e.g., bhekti [pomfret], hilsa) from the Ganges delta (e.g., fish curry and rice, or fried or grilled or steamed fish); other curries (e.g., mutton, egg, or prawn); kabobs, meat or vegetable patties *(shinghara);* pomfret in coconut milk; seafood from the Bay of Bengal; potato curry *(alu dom);* balls of cream cheese in syrup *(rossogolla).*

Chennai. Tandoori, curries, coconut rice, pickles, prawns, frog legs, fish; rice and coconut pancake *(appam);* rice cake or cookie *(iddli),* eaten with lentils and coconut chutney; vegetable fritters *(pakoras);* a semolina dish *(uppama);* fried lentil-paste *(vadas);* pilafs; a dish of spiced peas with mango chutney *(pattani sundal);* guavas, mangoes, pomegranates.

Delhi. Tandoori chicken with nan, tandoori fish, pilaf with meat or vegetables (one pilaf with many ingredients is called *navratan* "nine-jeweled"), biryani, chicken *(murgh)* curry, other curries (e.g., partridge, mutton, peas), kabobs (e.g., mutton), meat balls *(kofta),* stuffed sheep or goat; mutton curry cooked in yogurt *(rogham josh),* rice pudding *(firnee),* rice cake *(kheer)* with almonds, halvah. Beverages: lemon-juice water *(nimbu pani),* a yogurt or buttermilk drink *(lassi).*

Mumbai. Tandoori chicken, pilafs, biryani, meat balls *(kofta)*, puri, fish (e.g., "Bombay duck"; fried, curried or tandoori pomfret), lobster, prawns, mangoes; curds or yogurt with nuts *(shrikhand).*

Food found in other regions, or in several regions: chapati; several vegetarian courses in bowls in a round tray *(thali);* curried lentils *(dal),* biryani, pilaf, samosas, tandoori chicken, milk curd *(dahi),* pickles, chutney, fudge *(barfi),* halvah, pan (sense 2, a preparation of betel nut used for chewing), lemon-juice water *(nimbu pani).*

Indian almond [from *Indian* "of India"], another name for **Malabar almond**.

[1]**Indian arrowroot** [from *Indian* "of American Indians"], starch from a tropical American arrowroot (a plant likewise called *Indian arrowroot).*

[2]**Indian arrowroot** [from *Indian* "of India"], starch from the tuberous rootstock of an herb (likewise called *Indian arrowroot)* cultivated in the tropics.

Indian bread, see **tuckahoe**.

Indian breadroot [from *Indian* "of American Indians"], another name for **breadroot**.

Indian buffalo [from *Indian* "of India"], a buffalo of eastern Asia kept for milk production.

Indian butter [from *Indian* "of India"] or **phulwa butter**, a substance similar to butter derived from the seeds of the Himalayan butter tree.

Indian cherry [from *Indian* "of American Indians"], another name for the **Juneberry**.

Indian corn or **Indian maize** or **Indian wheat** [from *Indian* "of American Indians"] or **Turkey wheat** or simply **maize** or **corn**, or **sweet corn** or **horsetail corn**, the kernels (seeds) of a tall cereal grass (likewise called *Indian corn*) or grain native to the New World, that bears them on large elongated ears. More information under [1]**corn** (sense 1).

Indian fig [from *Indian* "of American Indians"], the edible acid fruit of either of two American prickly pears (likewise called *Indian figs)* —a tropical one and an eastern North American one.

Indian kale [from *Indian* "of American Indians"], any of several arums (plants; e.g., taro, yautia) having rootstocks rich in starch.

Indian maize, another name for **Indian corn**.

Indian meal [from *Indian* "of American Indians"], another name for **cornmeal**.

Indian mustard [from *Indian* "of India"] or **leaf mustard** or **Japanese mustard** or **brown mustard** or **mustard spinach** or **Oriental mustard**, an Asiatic mustard that is used as a potherb.

[1]**Indian nut** [from *Indian* "of American Indians"], another name for **pine nut**.

[2]**Indian nut** [from *Indian* "of India"], another name for **betel nut**.

Indian pea [from *Indian* "of India"], another name for both the **pigeon pea** and the **grass pea**.

Indian pear [from *Indian* "of American Indians"], another name for the **Juneberry**.

Indian plum [from *Indian* "of India"], the edible plum-shaped fruit of any of several tropical trees (likewise called *Indian plums).*

Indian potato [from *Indian* "of American Indians"], any of various American plants with edible tuberous roots.

Indian pudding [from *Indian* "of American Indians"], a pudding (sense 1, sweet dessert) usually made of cornmeal, molasses, milk, sugar, butter, and spices and baked (or steamed) and served as a dessert (an old New England dish).

Indian rhubarb [from *Indian* "of American Indians"], a plant of western North America with leaves that have edible petioles (leafstalks).

Indian rice [from *Indian* "of American Indians"], another name for **wild rice**.

Indian Runner [from *Indian* "of India"], a breed of small domestic ducks (having several varieties) noted for their egg production.

Indian wheat [from *Indian* "of American Indians"], another name for **Indian corn**.

indienne [French "Indian, of India (feminine)"], seasoned in Indian ("of India") style (e.g., with curry). For instance, *rice indienne* is curried rice.

Indonesia. The following are among representative dishes and products of Indonesia: rijsttafel; steamed rice fried in coconut oil (Indonesian *nasi goréng*, "rice fried"), cooked vegetables with peanut-butter sauce *(gado gado)*, meat grilled on bamboo spits *(sate)*, rice with curried meat and vegetable dishes *(nasi padang* "rice field"), fried prawns *(udang goréng)*, hot-pepper condiment *(sambal)*, white rice *(nasi putih)*, chicken soup *(soto ayam; soto* "soup, broth"), minced fish baked in coconut leaves *(otak otak)*, prawn paste *(belacan)*, rice, mangoes, mangosteens, papaya, bananas, pineapples, passion fruit, rambutan, durian.

infusion, *1.* the liquid extract obtained by steeping or soaking a substance (e.g., boldo, chamomile, cinnamon, manzanilla, mint), usually in water, without boiling. Distinguished from **decoction** (which is an extract obtained by boiling); *2.* the process described in sense 1.

instant, (of a food or beverage) that can be prepared quickly.

instantize (to), to make a food product instant (e.g., an instant pudding), by premixing or precooking for easy final preparation (e.g., instantized coffee, milk).

Iran. The following are among representative dishes and products of Iran: grilled (marinated) spitted lamb (Persian *chelow kebab)* served with rice; pilaf; chicken kabob; caviar from the Caspian sea; grilled sturgeon; rice (e.g., with almonds [*polo*]); duck or lamb cooked with pomegranate juice and walnuts *(fesenjan);* sheep broth *(kaleh pacheh,* "head [sheep]trotters"), melon, grapes, watermelon, puff-paste cakes with rose aroma.

Iraq. The following are among representative dishes and products of Iraq: stuffed (with rice and minced meat) roasted lamb (Arabic *quzi);* Tigris salmon grilled on wooden pegs, with tomatoes and onions *(masquf);* kabobs; stuffed (with rice and minced meat) vegetables (dolmas, e.g. grape or cabbage leaves, eggplant, squash, peppers); okra (sense 1, the pods), tomatoes, dates, pomegranates, apricots, peaches, figs, sweet pastries.

135

Ireland. The following are among representative dishes and products of Ireland: roast beef, Irish stew, corned beef and cabbage, steak, ham, bacon, fish (e.g., salmon), fish soup, prawns, oysters, kippers, pheasant, grouse, wild duck, potatoes.

Irish potato, another name for **potato**.

Irish stew, a stew of vegetables (potatoes, onions) and meat (e.g., lamb, beef) cut into small pieces, in a thick gravy.

isinglass, a gelatin prepared from the swim bladders of such fishes as sturgeons, and used in jellies.

Israel. The following are among representative dishes and products of Israel: kabobs, herring, hummus, pita, falafel (sense 2, pita bread filled with chick-peas), gefilte fish, kasha, tahini, dolma, oysters, carp, dates, mutton, lamb; puff paste filled with spinach or cheese *(borekas);* assorted hors d'oeuvre (Arabic *mazza)*, including olives, pickles, eggplant, marinated fish.

Italian corn salad, a southern European plant used as a salad vegetable.

Italian dressing, a salad dressing (oil, vinegar, salt, pepper) flavored especially with garlic and oregano and often a little tomato purée.

Italian fennel, another name for **carosella**.

Italian kale, another name for **seven-top turnip**.

Italian paste or **Italian pasta**, another name for **pasta**.

Italian roast, coffee of a very dark roast. Compare **French roast**, which is less dark.

Italian sandwich, another name for **hero**.

Italian turnip or **Italian turnip broccoli**, or **broccoli rab**, a plant whose tops and flower shoots are used as greens.

Italian vegetable marrow, another name for **cocozelle**.

Italian walnut, another name for **English walnut**.

Italy. Among the most important regions of Italy from the gastronomical point of view are (certain cities in the region that are outstanding for their food are shown in parentheses): Campania (Naples), Latium (Rome), Lombardy (Milan), Tuscany (Florence), Veneto (Venice).

Some representative dishes and products of these regions are:

Campania: pasta (e.g., macaroni with tomato sauce, spaghetti, thin pasta with mussels [Italian *vermicelli alle vongole*]), pizza, fish stew *(zuppa di pesce)*, fried mozzarella between two slices of bread *(mozzarella in carrozza* "in a carriage"), fish, shellfish, cheeses.

Latium: pizza; pasta (e.g., spaghetti all'amatriciana or alla carbonara, fettuccine [elsewhere in Italy called **tagliatelle**], macaroni) with meat sauce *(al sugo)*, with tomato sauce *(al pomodoro)*, with butter *(al burro);* lamb *(abbacchio)* seasoned with bacon and rosemary; saltimbocca; artichokes *(carciofi* [e.g. *alla giudia* (whole, cooked in oil)]); gnocchi alla romana, antipasto, minestrone, sliced veal simmered in Marsala wine *(scaloppine al marsala)*, cheeses, roast sucking pig *(porchetta)*.

Lombardy: risotto, osso buco, veal cutlet *(cotoletta)*, prosciutto (served with melon or figs), minestrone, lake trout, panettone.

Tuscany: lasagna, tagliatelle, minestrone, artichokes *(carciofi)*, peas *(piselli)*, fish, veal cutlet; many fried dishes (e.g., brains, shrimp, fish); lamb, pigeon, panforte.

Veneto: polenta; polenta with tiny birds (Venetian *polenta e osei),* rice with peas *(risi e bisi),* other rice dishes *(risi e lugánega* [= "and sausage"], *risi e peoci* [= "and clams"]), fish and shellfish, cod *(baccalà),* almond tart (Italian *torta di mandorle),* zabaglione.

Food found in other regions, or in several regions: pasta asciutta (e.g., spaghetti, ravioli, tagliatelle, lasagna), tagliatelle with meat sauce *(tagliatelle alla bolognese),* tortellini (Modena), antipasto, risotto, mashed-potato balls (gnocchi), veal scaloppine, fish, shellfish, sausages, prosciutto; loaf stuffed with sardines, cheese, and sausages *(pasta imbottita);* stuffed vegetables (e.g., eggplant, artichokes, peppers, mushrooms), panforte (Siena), zabaglione, cheeses. Beverages: espresso, cappuccino.

ita palm or **eta palm** [of Arawakan origin], another name for the **miriti palm** (that has edible fruit).

Ithuriel's spear [from the phrase *Ithuriel with his spear,* in *Paradise Lost* (4:810) by English poet John Milton, 1608–1674], another name for **grassnut** (sense 2).

ita palm

Ithuriel's spear

jowl   julienne

jambalaya   jambo

jackfruit   juniper

jaboticaba

jabalí [American Spanish "peccary," from Spanish *jabalí* "wild boar"], another name for **peccary**.

jaboticaba [Portuguese, modern *jabuticaba*, from Tupi], the purplish fruit (that resembles grapes in appearance and flavor) of a tree (likewise called *jaboticaba*) of Brazilian origin, of the myrtle family.

¹**jack**, another name for the **jackfruit**.

²**jack**, any of several fishes.

Jack cheese or simply **Jack**, other names for **Monterey cheese** (= **Monterey Jack**).

jack mackerel or **saurel**, a California fish.

jacket, an outer covering or casing, especially the skin of cooked potatoes (e.g., potatoes in their jackets).

jackfruit or **jack** or **jak** [from Portuguese *jaca* "jackfruit," from Malayalam *cakka*] or **jakfruit** or **kathal** or **sourjack**, *1.* the large, edible fruit of a tree (likewise called *jackfruit*) of tropical Asia; its seeds are eaten roasted; *2.* another name for **durian** (whose seeds are eaten roasted, too).

jack mackerel, a California fish.

jaggery [from Portuguese *jágara*, probably from Malayalam *chakkara* "sugar"] or **gur** or **goor**, an unrefined brown sugar made from the sap of palm trees (southeastern Asia).

jaggery palm or **toddy palm**, a palm of southeastern Asia whose sap is a chief source of jaggery (brown sugar).

jak and **jakfruit**, other names for **jackfruit**.

jalapeño or **jalapeño pepper** [Mexican Spanish, "of Jalapa," from *Jalapa*, city of eastern Mexico], a small green Mexican hot pepper.

¹**jam**, a food made by boiling fruit (e.g., apple, apricot, blueberry, cherry, elderberry, loganberry, peach, pear, quince, raspberry, rose-hip, strawberry) or a plant such as rhubarb, and sugar (or honey) to a thick consistency (to a pulp), without preserving the shape of the fruit. A typical proportion is 60% fruit to 40% sugar. Jams include Barleduc. Compare **jelly**, ¹**preserve**.

138

²**jam (to)**, *1.* to spread (e.g., bread) with jam; *2.* to make into jam.

Jamaica. The following are among representative dishes and products of Jamaica: codfish and akee (also called *salt fish and akee*), boiled green bananas, yam, plantain, ¹**callaloo**, stuffed breadfruit (filled with salt fish and akee); a soup with beef, kale, ¹**callaloo**, and okra *(pepper pot,* not the same as ¹**pepper pot**); bean soup *(red pea soup),* roast suckling pig, baked black crab, turtle (soup, stew), chayote with beef stuffing *(stuffed cho-cho);* a puff-pastry turnover filled with ground beef or vegetables *(Jamaican patty);* jerked chicken, cassava, arrowroot, black-eyed peas fritters *(akkras or accras),* mackerel with tomatoes *(run down),* codfish cakes *(stamp and go),* curried goat *(curried kid),* lamb cutlets, papaya *(papaw),* baked papaw, stuffed papaw (filled with minced beef and tomatoes); cornmeal *(coo-coo)* and codfish; coconut, mango, pineapple, oranges, grapefruit, guinep (a fruit), ortanique (a fruit), sweetsop, soursop, Otaheite apples, mango chutney, coconut soufflé. Beverages: mangoade, tamarinade (made from tamarind).

Jamaica apple, another name for both **cherimoya** and **custard apple**.

Jamaica banana or **Gros Michel**, the large banana of the Caribbean region.

Jamaica cherry, a West Indian fig (tree) having round fruits the size of a cherry.

Jamaica cucumber, another name for **gherkin**.

Jamaica ginger, a high grade of ginger grown in Jamaica.

Jamaica honeysuckle or **yellow granadilla**, a West Indian passionflower having yellow fruit.

Jamaica pepper, another name for **allspice**.

jambalaya [Louisiana French, from Provençal *jambalaia* "stew of rice and fowl"], rice cooked usually with diced cooked ham, sausage, chicken, shrimp, or oysters (each of these alone or in combination), and tomato, and seasoned with herbs (thyme, bay leaf, parsley). It can be prepared ²**creole** style. It may be vegetarian (with sweet peppers, celery) or it can also be prepared with meat or fish (with tongue, crab).

jambo [from Hindi *jambū, jambu,* from Sanskrit] or **jambos** or **jambosa** or **jamrosade** [from English *jambo* + *rose*], another name for **rose apple**.

jambon, French for **ham**.

jamón, Spanish for **ham**.

Japan. The following are among representative dishes and products of Japan: rice, sukiyaki, tempura, sushi, dried bonito, tofu, broiled eels (Japanese *kabayaki*), yakitori, sashimi, noodles *(udon);* thin slices of beef cooked in broth *(shabu shabu);* grilled beef *(teppanyaki);* boiled beef, chicken or seafood *(mizutaki);* soup made from a fermented malt *(miso shiru).* The various dishes with a Japanese name ending in *-mono* "thing" are *agemono* ("fried food," e.g., tempura), *mushimono* ("steamed food," e.g., eggs), *nabemono* ("open saucepan food [one-pot meal]," e.g., sukiyaki), *nimono* ("boiled food," e.g., chicken), *suimono* (clear soup), *yakimono* ("broiled food," e.g., eels). Beverage: green tea *(cha).* In Japan, as in China, 5 is traditionally considered a lucky number. There are therefore 5 cooking methods: deep-fry, broil, boil, steam

139

and stir-fry; 5 flavors: sweet, salty, sour, pungent, and bitter; 5 colors that should be present in dishes: white, black, red, green, and yellow.

Japanese artichoke, another name for **Chinese artichoke**.

Japanese chestnut, the fruit of a certain Japanese nut tree (likewise called *Japanese chestnut).*

Japanese crab, another name for **giant crab** (sense 1).

Japanese gelatin, another name for **agar**.

Japanese ginger, a commercial gingerroot prepared from a certain Japanese ginger plant.

Japanese hazel, a Japanese shrub with edible nuts.

Japanese millet, a coarse grass cultivated especially in Asia for its edible seeds.

Japanese mint or **Japanese peppermint**, a Japanese mint that is a variety of the common mint of Europe.

Japanese mustard, another name for **Indian mustard**.

Japanese nutmeg, a Japanese tree with edible seeds.

Japanese oyster, a certain large oyster (sense 1, mollusk).

Japanese persimmon, or **kaki**, the fruit of an Asiatic persimmon tree (likewise called *Japanese persimmon).*

Japanese radish, another name for **daikon** (sense 2, plant).

Japanese raisin tree, a shrub or small tree of eastern Asia having reddish, edible fruit stalks.

Japanese spider crab, another name for **giant crab** (sense 1).

jardiniere or **jardinière** [from French *jardinière* "gardener (feminine)," from *jardin* "garden"], a garnish for meat consisting of several vegetables (especially carrots and peas) cooked separately or together, and cut into pieces. It is sometimes prepared with mayonnaise.

jasmine tea or **scented tea**, tea having a jasmine scent or odor because it was packed with or fired with jasmine flowers (from jasmine, a shrub of the olive family).

jaudie [from archaic English *chawdron* "entrails of an animal used as a food"], (Scotland) *1.* a pig's stomach; *2.* a pudding made of pig's stomach.

jell (**to**), to set, come to the consistency of jelly. Compare **aspic**.

jello [from *Jell-O*, a trademark for a gelatin dessert] or **table jelly**, a gelatin dessert often given the flavor of fruit and shaped in molds.

jelly, a food product made usually with gelatin (senses 1 and 2) or pectin; it may be an aspic (beef or chicken broth that sets when cooling) or a dessert made by boiling sugar and the juice of fruit (e.g., apple, currant) with pectin. Agar may be used as a gelling and thickening agent. Compare **jam**, **preserve**.

jelly bean, a small, sugar-glazed, bean-shaped candy with a gum or jelly center.

jellybread, a piece of bread and jelly.

jelly doughnut, a raised doughnut (rounded cake of deep-fried dough) with a jelly center.

jellyfish, any of various free-swimming marine coelenterates (certain invertebrate animals) that have a gelatinous, nearly transparent, saucer-shaped or bell-shaped body.

jelly plant, *1.* an Australian seaweed used for making jelly; *2.* another name for the **Kei apple.**

jelly powder, gelatin (sense 1) mixed with sugar and flavoring, used in jelled desserts.

jelly roll or **Swiss roll,** a thin sheet of sponge cake spread with jelly and rolled up while hot so as to form layers. Many fillings other than jelly are possible, such as chocolate, lemon, orange, pineapple (these are spread after the sheet has cooled).

jemmy, a baked sheep's head.

jenoar, a certain snapper (fish resembling bass) of the Indian Ocean.

jerk (to), to preserve meat in long, sun-dried slices.

jerky [from Spanish *charqui,* from Quechua *ch'arki* "dried meat"], meat (especially beef) that has been preserved in long, sun-dried slices or that has been cured by exposing it to smoke. Compare **charqui.**

Jerusalem artichoke [by folk etymology, from Italian *girasole* "sun-flower" (underlying idea: the flower or stem turns toward the sun), from *gira* "it turns" + *sole* "sun"] or **earth apple** or **topinambour,** the tuber of a North American sunflower (likewise called *Jerusalem artichoke*) eaten as a vegetable (it resembles a potato). It can be served creamed, fried, mashed, scalloped, or sliced cold in salad.

Jerusalem pea, an Indian ("from India") bean closely related to the **urd bean** and to the **mung bean.**

Jesuits' nut, another name for **water chestnut** (sense 1, fruit).

Jesuits' tea or **Jesuit tea,** other names for **maté.**

Jesuits' waternut, another name for **water chestnut** (sense 1, fruit).

Jew plum, another name for **Otaheite apple.**

jicama [from Mexican Spanish *jícama,* from Nahuatl *xicamatl*], *1.* a starchy tuberous root of a leguminous, tropical twining plant. It may be eaten raw (as a salad) seasoned with salt and lemon, or cooked; *2.* another name for **yam bean** (whose roots are eaten).

jikungu [Tanzania], a tropical African plant of the gourd family grown for its edible seeds.

jimmies, another name for **sprinkles.**

joe rocker, another name for **green crab.**

John Brown, a small, plump fish of southern Africa.

John Dory, either of two fishes of the Atlantic.

johnnycake, a corn bread, made of cornmeal and water and milk.

jojoba [Mexican Spanish], a shrub or small tree of the box family of southwestern North America, with edible seeds.

Jordan. The following are among representative dishes and products of Jordan: rice; vine leaves (or cucumbers or zucchini or eggplant) stuffed with a mixture of rice, chopped meat, and ground nuts (Arabic *mahshi);* lamb, hummus; whole stewed lamb with rice and *laban* (sour milk), called *mensaf;* chicken in olive oil *(musakhan),* meat-and-vegetable stew *(maqluba)* with steamed rice; camel, black carrots, pine nuts, dates, citrus fruit, thin pastries stuffed with nuts and honey.

Jordan almond [by folk etymology from French *jardin* "garden" + English *almond*], a large variety of almond from Málaga, southern

Spain, especially when salted or covered with a hard sugar coating of various colors.

Josephine [for *Josephine*, Napoleon I's first wife], a tart, a small napoleon.

¹**jowl**, the boneless cheek meat of a hog.

²**jowl**, a cut or dish of fish (e.g., salmon, sturgeon) consisting of the head and adjacent parts.

¹**juice**, the extractable fluid contents of plant or animal cells or tissues.

²**juice (to)**, to extract juice from.

juice pear or **juicy pear**, another name for **Juneberry**.

jujube, or **Chinese date**, *1.* the fleshy red fruit of any of several trees (likewise called *jujubes)* of the buckthorn family; *2.* a fruit-flavored, usually chewy gumdrop or lozenge.

¹**julienne** (noun), consommé or broth containing vegetables (e.g., cabbage, carrots, celery, leeks, potatoes, turnips) cut in long, thin strips. In French, a *julienne* is a soup containing vegetables that have been diced or cut in small pieces.

²**julienne** (adjective), cut in long, thin strips. This adjective is normally used of vegetables but may be used of fruit.

³**julienne (to)**, to cut in long thin strips.

jumble, a small, thin, sugared cookie or cake usually shaped like a ring.

jumbo, as in *jumbo shrimp*, means "very large."

Juneberry or **serviceberry** or **Indian cherry** or **Indian pear** or **juice pear** or **sugar pear**, the usually purple or red fruit of any of various North American trees and shrubs (likewise called *Juneberries*; also *shadbushes)*.

juniper, any of various evergreen shrubs or trees of the cypress family having aromatic, berry-like fruit (see **juniper berry**).

juniper berry, the bluish-gray, berry-like fruit of the juniper. The berries can be toasted just before adding to a dish, left whole for marinades but crushed for sauces and stuffings; they complement game, lamb, and duck and are an ingredient of **choucroute** (sense 2).

junket, *1.* a dessert of sweetened, flavored milk (or cream) that is coagulated (thickened into curd) in a smooth jelly by rennin (produced from rennet, sense 1); *2.* a cream cheese or a dish of curds and cream.

junk food, food considered worthless because it is high in calories but low in nutritional value.

kaawi yam, a yam (plant) with sweet tubers (southern Asia, Polynesia).

kabeljou or **kabeljauw** [from Afrikaans *kabeljou*, from Dutch *kabeljauw* "cod"], a large South African food fish.

kabob or **kabab** or **kebab** or **cabob** [from Persian and Hindi *kabab*, from Arabic *kabab*, from Turkish *kebap* "roast meat"] or **shashlik** [from Russian *shashlyk*, of Turkic origin], a dish of Oriental origin consisting of small pieces of meat (e.g., lamb, beef, veal; often neck or loin of mutton) marinated and cooked (grilled or roasted) with vegetables (e.g., slices of onions, tomatoes, eggplant, green peppers) especially on a skewer. Compare **shish kebab** (which is always broiled on skewers).

Kaffir, in the following four entries, can also be spelled **Kafir**.

Kaffir bean [from archaic English *Kaffir*, a member of a certain group of southern African peoples, from Arabic *kāfir* "infidel"], another name for **cowpea** (Africa).

Kaffir bread, the starchy pith of the fruit of a plant (likewise called *Kaffir bread*), used as food in southern Africa.

Kaffir orange, the dark green, round, aromatic fruit of an East African tree (likewise called *Kaffir orange*).

Kaffir plum or **Kaffir date**, the fruit of a certain African tree (likewise called *Kaffir plum* or *Kaffir date*).

kahawai [Maori], another name for the **Australian salmon**.

kahika tea [Maori], a New Zealand evergreen tree having a sweet edible aril (= "outer covering").

kaki [Japanese], another name for **Japanese persimmon**.

kale or **borecole**, *1.* a cabbage with curled leaves that do not form a dense head; *2.* broth, soup, especially soup made with kale or other greens (Scotland).

kalumpit or **calumpit** [from Tagalog *kalumpit*], a Philippine tree that yields dark red fruits used for preserves.

kamani [Hawaiian], another name for **Malabar almond**.

Kamloops trout or **Kamloops** [from Kamloops, city in southern British

143

Columbia (western Canada)], a large, black-spotted, rainbow trout of western North America.

kangaroo [Queensland (northeastern Australia)], any of various leaping marsupial (= animal whose female has a pouch on the abdomen) mammals of Australia, New Guinea, and adjacent areas.

kangaroo apple or **poroporo**, a yellow, egg-shaped fruit of Australia and New Zealand borne by a shrubby plant (likewise called *kangaroo apple*).

kanya butter, another name for **shea butter**.

kaoliang [from Chinese *gaoliang* "tall grain"], any of various sorghums (sense 1, the grass) grown chiefly in China for their grain.

kapok oil, oil obtained from the seeds of the kapok tree (also called *silk-cotton tree*).

karaka [Maori] or **kopi**, a New Zealand tree having orange-colored fruit with edible pulp and poisonous seeds which, however, may be eaten after being roasted and dried.

karite [from French *karité*, from a West African language], another name for **shea tree**.

karite butter or **karite oil**, other names for **shea butter**.

kasha [Russian], a mush or porridge made usually from coarse cracked buckwheat (buckwheat groats) but also from coarse cracked barley, millet, or wheat.

kasher, see **kosher**.

kathal [from Hindi *kaṭ-hal*, from Sanskrit *kaṇtakaphala* "thorn fruit"], another name for the **jackfruit** tree.

kebab or **kebob**, variants of **kabob**.

kedgeree or **kegeree** [from Hindi *khicaṛī*, from Sanskrit *khiccā*], *1.* an Indian dish of seasoned rice and lentils and sometimes onions, eggs, smoked fish; *2.* an English dish of cooked flaked fish, rice, and eggs, served hot, sometimes heated in cream.

kedlock, another name for **white mustard**.

keeling, another name for **codfish** (Scotland).

Kei apple [from Great *Kei* river, Cape Province, southern South Africa] or **jelly plant**, the fruit of a southern African shrub (likewise called *Kei apple*), used for pickles and preserves; it is shaped like a small apple.

kelp, any of various large brown seaweeds.

Kenya. The following are representative dishes and products of Kenya: meat roasted over an open fire; a maize-meal (sometimes made not of maize but of cassava flour) porridge (Swahili *ugali;* also called *posho,* that literally means "rations, daily supply" in Swahili); a dish of beans, maize, and peas (sometimes also potatoes, chickpeas) mashed together (Kikuyu *irio);* another corn and bean dish (Kikuyu *githeri); irio* balls dipped into meat or vegetable stews; fresh and dried fish, rice, curries, samosas; a dish of greens (Swahili *sukuma wiki;* underlying idea: "sees you through," literally = "push the week"); a dish of different cuts of goat or sheep *(mutura),* grilled leg of raised wild animals (e.g., impala); *muteta* soup; a cooked mixture of grains (Swahili *mseto);* tropical fruits.

keta [Russian], another name for the **dog salmon** of the northern Pacific.

ketchup, variant of **catsup**.

ketembilla or **kitambilla** [from Sinhalese *kätämbilla*], the hairy, purple fruit of a small tropical tree (likewise called *ketembilla)*, that is used especially for preserves and is related to the Kei apple.

khoa [from Hindi *khoā*], (India) a whole milk product.

kibbe or **kibbeh** [from Arabic *kubbah*], a Middle Eastern dish of ground lamb and bulgur (parched cracked wheat) that may be eaten cooked (baked as a cake) or raw.

kichel [from Yiddish *kikhel* "small cake," diminutive of *kukhen* "cake"], a food (a kind of puffy wafer or cookie) made of eggs, flour, and sugar, usually rolled and cut in diamond (or square) shape and baked until puffed. Some cooks add poppy seeds.

kid, the flesh of a young goat or of a young individual of a similar animal, such as an antelope or a deer.

kid-glove orange, another name for **tangerine**.

kidney, one of a pair of organs of a vertebrate animal, situated near the spinal column, eaten as a food. It is a variety meat; beef, lamb, pork, veal kidneys can be eaten broiled or breaded.

kidney bean or **bon** or **calico bean**, a dark red, kidney-shaped bean seed.

kidney chop, a loin chop (e.g., of lamb or veal) containing a kidney.

kiekie [Maori], a New Zealand climbing shrub of the screw pine family, with edible berries.

kielbasa [from Polish *kiełbasa* "sausage"], an uncooked, smoked sausage of Polish origin.

Kiev, see **chicken Kiev**.

kimchi or **kimchee** [from Korean *kimch'i*], a raw, strongly-flavored vegetable (e.g., cabbage or turnips) pickle seasoned with garlic, red pepper, and ginger that is usually a fiery hot relish and is the national dish of Korea.

king crab or **pan fish**, a large crab of the northern Pacific Ocean that is the largest of the edible crabs.

kingfish, any of several fishes.

king mackerel or **cavalla** or **cero**, a fish of warm Atlantic Ocean waters.

king salmon or **chinook salmon** or **spring salmon** or **Columbia River salmon** or **quinnat salmon** or **Sacramento salmon**, a large salmon of the northern Pacific Ocean.

king's-fruit, another name for **mangosteen**.

king's paprika [translation of German *Königspaprika*], Hungarian paprika made from whole peppers including seeds and stalks (in regular Hungarian paprika, the fruit is freed from seeds and stalks).

kipfel [German, diminutive of *Kipf* "kipfel; wagon post"], a crescent-shaped cookie or yeast-pastry with a filling of chopped nuts and brown sugar; the cookie may also have a jam filling instead.

kipper, a herring that has been split, cleaned, salted, and smoked.

kipper (**to**), to cure fish (e.g., herring, salmon) by splitting, cleaning, salting, and drying in the air or in smoke.

kiss, *1.* a small piece of candy, especially of chocolate; *2.* a baked drop-cookie made of meringue, sometimes with shredded coconut added.

kiwi or **kiwifruit**, the brownish, hairy fruit of the Chinese gooseberry (a vine native to Asia), eaten fresh or in preserve.

klipfish or **clipfish**, a fish (e.g., cod) split open, boned, salted, and dried.

knäckebröd [Swedish "to break bread"], a crisp and brittle unleavened rye bread.

knackwurst or **knockwurst** [from German *Knackwurst*, from *knacken* "to crackle" (the skin cracks open when the sausage is bitten)], a short, thick, heavily seasoned sausage.

knead (**to**), to work dough into a well-blended mass by repeatedly drawing out (stretching), folding, and pressing together, especially with the hands.

knee-high blackberry, another name for **sand blackberry**.

knish [Yiddish, from Polish *knysz*], a small round or square of baking-powder dough folded over a filling (e.g., potato, meat, or cheese) and baked or fried.

knob celery, another name for **celeriac**.

knockwurst, see **knackwurst**.

knotroot, another name for the **Chinese artichoke**.

knuckle, a cut of meat consisting of the tarsal (= of the foot) or carpal (= of the part that corresponds to the wrist in humans) joint with the adjoining flesh in a quadruped (e.g., a pig).

kohlrabi [German *Kohlrabi*, from Italian *cavolo rapa* "cabbage turnip"] or **turnip cabbage** [the stem is turnip-shaped] or **noll-kholl** (India), a cabbage having a thickened, fleshy stem that is eaten as a vegetable.

koko [West African], any of several tropical plants, including the taro, grown in western Africa for their starchy roots.

kokum butter [Marathi "mangosteen"] or **Goa butter**, an oil obtained from the seeds of a small Indian tree and used for food (India).

kola or **cola**, either of two African trees bearing kola nuts.

kolacky or **kolach** [from Czech *koláč* "wheel-shaped cake," from Old Slavonic *kolo* "wheel"], a bun of eastern European origin made of sweet yeast-leavened dough filled with poppyseed, jam, or fruit pulp.

kola nut or simply **kola**, or **cola nut**, the bitter seed of a kola tree, yielding an extract used in the manufacture of certain carbonated beverages.

kola tree or **cola tree**, a tree cultivated in various tropical areas for its kola nuts.

koorka, a plant native to Africa cultivated in India for its edible tubers.

kopi [New Zealand], another name for **karaka**.

Korea. The following are representative dishes and products of Korea (both North and South): rice, fish, shellfish, pickled vegetables (e.g., cabbage or turnips; Korean *kimch'i*), roasted meat strips *(bulgogi)*.

korhaan or **knorhaan**, any of several fishes of southern Africa.

kosher [Yiddish, from Hebrew *kasher* "fit, proper"] or **kasher**, ritually fit or prepared in accordance with Jewish dietary laws. Opposite of **tref**.

kraut [German "sauerkraut; cabbage; plant"], *1.* another name for **sauerkraut**; *2.* turnips cured in the same way as cabbage **kraut** (sense 1).

kreef [Afrikaans, from Dutch *kreeft* "lobster, crayfish"], another name for **Cape crayfish**.

kromeski [from Russian *kromochki* "slices of bread," plural diminutive of *kroma* "slice of bread"], a croquette made of meat or fish minced, wrapped in bacon or calf's udder, dipped in batter, and fried.

kuchen [German "cake"), any of various coffee cakes made from sweet yeast dough containing fruits and nuts, and frosted (with sugar and spices).

kugel [from Yiddish *kugl* "ball"], a baked suet-pudding made of noodles, sliced or grated potatoes, or bread, sometimes with raisins added, usually served as a side dish. The basis may also be: flaked fish, pearl barley (with chopped mushrooms), rice, shredded cabbage (with potato flour).

kugelhof, another name for **gugelhupf**.

kulich [from Greek *kóllix*, a kind of bread], a Russian Easter cake, a sweet loaf made of wheat flour.

kumara [Maori], another name for **sweet potato** (New Zealand).

kumquat [from Cantonese *gām-gwāt* "gold citrus fruit"], any of several small citrus fruit with thin, edible rind, of the rue family, that are used chiefly candied or in preserves. Compare **marumi kumquat** (that has round fruit), **nagami kumquat** (that has oval fruit).

kuchen

kumquat

langouste

limu

lutefisk

lovage

lobster

lemon oil

*L*eberwurst

lablab [from Arabic *lāblab*], another name for the **hyacinth bean**.

Labrador tea [from *Labrador*, peninsula of eastern Canada], a North American shrub with leaves sometimes used for making a tea.

lachsschinken [German "salmon ham"; probably from its color], a boned double loin of pork that is rolled, cured, and pressed into a casing.

Lady Baltimore cake [probably for Lady *Baltimore*, wife of Lord Baltimore 1580?–1632, English colonizer of Maryland, United States], an egg-white cake (with egg whites, flour, sugar, butter, milk, vanilla, baking powder, salt) with boiled frosting and filling of chopped raisins, figs, and nuts. Once upon a time, five layers were considered none too many. Compare **Lord Baltimore cake** (which is a gold butter-cake).

ladyfinger or **savoy finger** or **savoy biscuit** or **sponge finger**, a small, oval, sponge cake, with a shape suggestive of a finger.

ladyfish, any of several marine fishes.

lady pea, another name for the **cowpea**.

lady's-finger, another name for **okra** (sense 1, a pod).

lafayette [for Marquis de *Lafayette*, 1757–1834, French statesman], any of various fishes.

lake salmon, another name for both the **landlocked salmon** (sense 1) and the **lake trout**.

lake shrimp or **white shrimp**, a certain salt-water shrimp.

lake trout or **lake salmon** or **longe** or **lunge** or **mackinaw trout** or **namaycush** (Algonquin), any of several trout and salmon found in lakes. They are fat fishes, and therefore best for broiling, baking, planking.

lamb, the flesh of a young sheep used for food (the flesh of an older sheep is called *mutton*). Lamb may be roasted or broiled. Common favorites are leg of lamb and lamb chops. It is also eaten as stuffed shoulder (with apple or bread stuffing), baked breast, baked shoulder, roast shank, curry, kabobs, Irish stew, patties, Scotch stew. The variety meats include heart, kidney, liver, tongue.

lamb mint or **lamb's-mint**, another name for both **spearmint** and **peppermint** (sense 1).

lamb's lettuce, another name for the plant called **corn salad**.

lamb's-quarters or **lamb's-quarter**, *1.* a goosefoot (a certain plant whose leaves are used as a potherb); *2.* any of several oraches, especially garden orache (potherb).

lamprey, an eel-shaped fish.

Lancashire or **Lancashire cheese**, a moist, crumbly, white, English cheese made from finely cut curds of different ages, that is used especially in cooking.

land crab, any of various crabs that live mostly upon land but breed in the sea.

land cress, another name for both **winter cress** and **bitter cress**.

landlocked salmon [from *landlocked* "confined to inland waters"], *1.* certain salmon of lakes of eastern North America; *2.* another name for **lake trout**.

lane cake, an egg-white butter cake with the layers separated by a filling of pecans, raisins, candied fruit, coconut, and often whiskey or wine.

lang [India], another name for **grass pea**.

langosta [Spanish "European lobster; locust, grasshopper"], a South or Central American spiny lobster.

langouste [French "spiny lobster"], another name for the **spiny lobster**. Some French names of spiny lobster dishes include *langouste à l'américaine, langouste au court-bouillon, langouste au gratin.*

langoustine [French, diminutive of *langouste* "spiny lobster"] or **langostino** [Spanish, diminutive of *langosta* "spiny lobster; locust, grasshopper"], any of several small lobsters. Some French names of langoustine dishes include *langoustines à la mayonnaise, langoustines en beignets.*

lanseh or **lansa** or **lansat** [Indonesian] or **duku** [Malay], the yellow berry of a southeastern Asian tree likewise called *lanseh* (and also *duku*).

Lao Republic. The following are representative products and dishes of the Lao Republic: rice, poultry, pork, green peas, corn, soya-bean curd, yams, potatoes, sweet potatoes, fish, stuffed frogs, freshwater shrimp and crabs, coconut, carp, eel. Beverage: tea.

Lapsang souchong, a fine grade of souchong tea with a pronounced smoky flavor and aroma.

¹**lard** [French "hog fat"], a soft fat obtained by rendering (melting) fatty tissue of a hog (especially the internal fat of the abdomen). Compare **leaf lard**.

²**lard (to)**, to insert (e.g., strips of bacon) in lean meat (e.g., beef, veal) or poultry before roasting for flavor and moisture.

lardoon or **lardon** [from French *lardon* "piece of fat pork," from *lard* "hog fat"], a strip of fat (e.g., of salt pork) for insertion into meat in larding.

lasagna [Italian], *1.* broad, flat (sometimes ruffled) noodles; *2.* a baked dish of layers of boiled lasagna (sense 1) and of ground meat, tomato sauce, and cheese.

lassi, see under **India** (*Delhi*).

laughing frog, an edible European frog.

laulau [Hawaiian, reduplicated form of *lau* "leaf"], a portion of a dish of meat and fish (e.g., pork and salmon) wrapped in leaves (often, first taro leaves and then ti leaves) and baked or steamed in an imu (Hawaii).

laurel or **bay** or **bay laurel** or **bay tree** or **sweet bay**, a shrub or tree having aromatic leaves called *bay leaves* (see **bay leaf**).

laver, see **amanori** (a seaweed).

lax [from Norwegian *laks* "salmon"], another name for **salmon**.

layer cake, a cake of two or more layers separated by a sweet filling (e.g., of jelly or cream) and usually covered with frosting.

leaf fat, the fat built up in layers around the kidneys of a hog and that is used in making leaf lard.

leaf lard, high-grade lard made from the leaf fat of a hog. Compare ¹**lard**.

leaf lettuce, any of various lettuces with leaves having curled or crisped margins and forming a loose cluster. Distinguished from **head lettuce** (whose leaves form a compact head).

leaf mustard, another name for **Indian mustard**.

leaping tuna, another name for the **bluefin tuna**.

¹**leaven** or **leavening**, *1.* a substance (e.g., sourdough, yeast, cream of tartar) used as an ingredient in batters or doughs to produce fermentation; *2.* a portion of fermented dough used to produce fermentation in a new batch of dough; *3.* a substance (e.g., baking powder, or sour milk and soda) used to produce a gas that lightens dough or batter while it is baking.

²**leaven** (**to**), *1.* to add yeast or other fermenting agent; *2.* to raise, produce fermentation. Usually, breads, rolls, coffee cake are yeast-leavened; biscuits, cookies, crackers, pretzels, most cakes are chemically leavened.

Lebanon. The following are representative dishes and products of Lebanon: rice, lamb, ground eggplant, pumpkin, hummus, assorted hors d'oeuvre (Arabic *mazza*), tahini dip, meat balls *(kubbah)*, falafel (sense 1, chick-pea patties), roast mutton *(mashwi* "roast"), roast chicken *(farruj mashwi)*, minced meat patties *(kufta);* salad with tomatoes, ground wheat, mint, and parsley *(tabule);* grape leaves stuffed with rice and minced mutton *(mahshi);* lamb roasted on a vertical spit *(shawarma);* puff paste and nut desserts, such as baklava; sour milk *(laban* "milk"), cream cheese *(labna).*

leben or **leban** [from Arabic *laban*], a liquid or semisolid food made from curdled milk (Middle East and North Africa). Compare **yogurt**.

leberwurst [German *Leberwurst* "liver sausage"], another name for **liver sausage**.

lebkuchen [German], a Christmas cookie made with honey, candied fruit peel, spices (e.g., allspice, cinnamon, clove, and nutmeg), brown sugar, and almonds (or other chopped nuts).

lechosa [Spanish "milky (feminine)," from *leche* "milk"], another name for **papaya**.

leechee, variant of **litchi**.

leek or **scallion**, a plant of the lily family, related to onion and garlic, grown for its pungent leaves and especially for its thick stalk consisting of blanched leafstalks and small onionlike bulb.

lefse [Norwegian], a potato pancake served buttered and folded.

leg, *1.* the back part of the hindquarter of a food animal (lamb, mutton, veal); *2.* the drumstick of a fowl.

legume [from French *légume*], *1.* a pod or a seed, such as that of a bean, lentil, or pea, used for food. The pods split into two valves with the seeds attached to the lower edge of one of the valves; *2.* (in menus) any vegetable. In French, *légume* means any vegetable used as food; in Spanish, *legumbre* means legume (seeds that grow in pods, used as food), but by extension, it also means any vegetable.

Leicester or **Leicester cheese** [from *Leicester*, central England], a hard, usually orange-colored cheese made of whole cow's milk, resembling cheddar and Cheshire cheese.

lekach [Yiddish], a leavened cake made with honey.

lekai salmon, another name for the **dog salmon** of the northern Pacific Ocean.

lekvar [from Hungarian *lekvár* "jam"], a prune butter used as a pastry filling.

lemon, the fruit of a spiny tree, having an aromatic rind (that is often candied or preserved) and acid, juicy pulp. Dishes made with lemon include barbecue sauce, dressings, sauces; avgolemono, Bavarian cream, cake pudding, chiffon pie, cookies, fillings, frostings, ice, meringue pie, pie, punches, sherbet, torte.

lemonade, a beverage of lemon juice mixed with plain or soda water and with sugar. The rind of lemons can be added (cut into pieces and strained). The ingredients may be combined in a saucepan over low heat.

lemonade bush, another name for **squawberry**.

lemon balm or **garden balm** or **sweet balm**, a mint cultivated for its fragrant lemon-flavored leaves. It can be used in salads and marinades, with fish or fruit, and as an infusion.

lemon cucumber, another name for **mango melon** (a melon used for pickles and preserves).

lemon curd, a mixture of lemon juice and rind, eggs, sugar, and butter, cooked until thick and used as a spread or tart filling.

lemon fish, another name for **cobia** (fish).

lemongrass, any of several tropical grasses used as an herb and that yield an aromatic oil used as flavoring. The leaves are discarded, leaving the white portion of the base for cooking.

lemon oil, a fragrant oil obtained from the peel of lemons, used as a flavoring agent.

lemon sole, any of several flatfishes, especially a flounder of the northeastern Atlantic.

lemon verbena, an aromatic plant cultivated for its fragrant foliage used as a green.

lemon vine, another name for the **Barbados gooseberry**.

lemon walnut, another name for **butternut**.

lentil [from French *lentille*, from Latin *lenticula* "lentil," diminutive of *lens* "lentil," from *lent-*, base of *lens*], the round, flattened seed of a plant (likewise called *lentil*), cooked like beans or peas; it is often used for soup.

lettuce, the leaves of a vegetable (likewise called *lettuce*) eaten as salad. The hearts of lettuce can be eaten braised. Lettuces include asparagus lettuce, Bibb lettuce, cos lettuce, head lettuce, leaf lettuce.

lettuce cabbage, another name for **Chinese cabbage**.

Libya. The following are representative dishes and products of Libya: minced meat patties (Arabic *kufta*), mutton kabobs, couscous, dates, figs.

lichee and **lichi**, variants of **litchi**.

lichen, any plant made up of an alga and a fungus.

licorice [ultimately from Greek *glykyrrhiza*, from *glykys* "sweet" + *rhiza* "root"] or **sweet root** or **sweet wood**, *1.* the long, thick, sweet root of a plant (likewise called *licorice*), that is the source of extracts (prepared in the form of a gummy or rubbery paste) used to impart flavor to confections; *2.* one of these extracts; *3.* a confection made from this root.

liederkranz [from German *Liederkranz*, a trademark, "song garland"], a soft cheese with a pungent flavor and odor, resembling a mild Limburger.

light bread, spongy or well-leavened bread, wheat bread in loaves made from white flour leavened with yeast.

light meat, meat that is light in color (e.g., veal).

lights [from *light* (in weight)], the lungs of a slaughtered animal.

lima bean or **lima** [from *Lima*, capital of Peru], the large, flat, light-green seed of a tropical American plant (likewise called *lima bean).*

limande, French for **dab** (fish). Some dishes are *limande au four, limande au gratin.*

Limburger or **Limburger cheese** [from Flemish "one from Limburg," from *Limburg*, province in northeast Belgium], a pungent, semisoft, surface-ripened, white cheese with a strong odor and flavor, originally produced in Limburg.

lime, the small, egg-shaped fruit of a spiny, tropical, citrus tree (likewise called *lime)*, having a green rind and juice used as flavoring. Dishes prepared with lime include: Bavarian cream, cake pudding, chiffon pie, meringue pie; dressings.

limeade, a beverage of lime juice mixed with plain or soda water and with sugar. The rind of limes can be added (cut into pieces and strained).

limeberry or **lime myrtle** or **limoncito** (Philippines), the fruit (a red berry) of a spiny Malayan shrub (likewise called *limeberry).*

lime myrtle, another name for **limeberry**.

limequat [from English *lime* + *kumquat*], the fruit of a tree (likewise called *limequat)* that is produced by crossing a lime and a kumquat.

limon [from English *lime* + *lemon*], a citrus fruit that is a hybrid between the lime and the lemon.

limoncito [Philippine Spanish, from Spanish, diminutive of *limón* "lemon"], another name for **limeberry** (Philippines).

Limousin [French, from *Limousin*, region of France, "of Limoges," from *Limoges*, city of southwestern France], an animal (cattle) of a French breed (likewise called *Limousin*) bred especially for meat.

limpa [Swedish], rye bread (a yeast bread) made with molasses or brown sugar.

limpet, a marine mollusk.

limu [Hawaiian], any of many edible seaweeds (Hawaii).

limu-eleele [from Hawaiian *limu-'ele 'ele*], an edible marine green alga (Hawaii).

limu-kohu [Hawaiian], an edible brown alga (Hawaii).

¹**ling** , any of various marine fishes of the cod family (e.g., a burbot or a hake).

²**ling** or **ling ko** [from Chinese *líng*], another name for **water chestnut** (sense 1, fruit).

lingcod or **cultus** or **cultus cod** or **Pacific cultus**, a large greenish-fleshed fish of the eastern coast of the North Pacific, related to the greenlings.

lingonberry or **lingon** [Swedish "mountain cranberry"] or **mountain cranberry**, the fruit of the mountain cranberry.

linguine or **linguini** [from Italian *linguine*, plural of *linguina* "small tongue," diminutive of *lingua* "tongue"], narrow, flat pasta in long solid strands. One way of serving them: linguine carbonara.

link ["loop making up a chain"], *1.* any of the segments in a chainlike arrangement of sausages; *2.* a small sausage resembling one of these segments.

links, sausages in a chain-like arrangement.

Linzer torte [German "torte from Linz," from *Linz*, city of northern Austria], a baked torte (an open jam pie) made of a pastry dough composed of chopped unblanched almonds, butter, flour, cocoa, sugar, eggs, and spices (cinnamon, cloves), filled with jam or preserves (often raspberry), and topped with a lattice. Grated lemon rind may be added. Compare **Sacher torte**.

Liptauer [from *Liptau*, German name of a formerly Austro-Hungarian area, now in Slovakia (Liptov)], *1.* a soft Hungarian cheese, usually colored and flavored with paprika and other seasonings; *2.* a cheese spread of Liptauer (sense 1) and seasonings (e.g., caraway seeds, chopped capers and chives, mustard, anchovy paste, paprika); *3.* an imitation of this cheese spread made with cream cheese or cottage cheese.

liquid sugar, a solution of cane or beet sucrose.

liquor, *1.* broth, the liquid (usually water) in which meat or vegetables have been boiled; *2.* gravy, the juice of meat given off during cooking and often combined with a thickening agent and spices and served with the meat (also the fat in which bacon or fish have been fried); *3.* a dressing or sauce served with foods; *4.* the liquid contained in oysters or clams; *5.* sugarcane sap that has not been crystallized to sugar; *6.* an alcoholic beverage (= drink) produced by distillation (e.g., brandy, rum, tequila, whiskey) rather than by fermentation (e.g., beer, ale, wine).

litchi [from Cantonese *lai zhi* or from Chinese *lìzī*] or **lichi** or **lychee** or **leechee** or **lichee**, or **litchi nut**, or **Chinese nut**, the oval fruit of a Chinese tree (likewise called *litchi*) of the soapberry family, having a hard, scaly, reddish outer covering and sweet whitish flesh that surrounds a single large seed; on drying, it becomes firm and black.

littleneck or **littleneck clam** [from *Littleneck* Bay, inlet of Long Island

153

Sound, New York], a young quahog when small, but large enough to be eaten raw.

liver, a large organ of vertebrates (e.g., of a calf, chicken, cow, lamb, or pig), used as food. It can be braised, fried, prepared as a loaf, as liver suprême. It is a variety meat.

liver sausage or **liver pudding** or **leberwurst**, a sausage containing cooked chopped liver and lean pork trimmings, seasoned with condiments and herbs, and stuffed into casings and boiled or smoked. Mixed to a paste with cream (and chopped watercress), or with tomato paste, it may be used for canapés (spread on rye bread or toast). Combined with eggs, cracker crumbs, and chopped parsley and simmered in soup stock it makes good dumplings.

liverwurst [from German *Leberwurst* "liver sausage"], another name for **liver sausage**.

loaf, *1.* a shaped or molded mass of bread baked in one piece; *2.* any shaped or molded mass of food (e.g., a sugar loaf, a loaf of cheese); *3.* a baked dish consisting of ground meat or fish (e.g., beef, jellied chicken, salmon, veal) held together with soft crumbs or eggs and liquid (e.g., tomato sauce, or milk). Compare **meat loaf**.

loaf cake, a cake (e.g., a pound cake) that acquired the shape of a loaf because it was baked in a loaf pan.

loaf cheese, process cheese molded in the form of a rectangular loaf (sense 2).

loaf sugar, refined sugar molded into loaves (usually small and in the form of a cone) or into small cubes.

lobscouse or simply **scouse**, a seaman's dish consisting of bits of meat (often salt meat) stewed or baked with vegetables (e.g., potatoes, onions), hardtack, and other ingredients.

lobster, *1.* the flesh of any of several large marine crustaceans (likewise called *lobsters)* having a pair of large claws or pincers, used as food; *2.* another name for the **spiny lobster** (that has unenlarged claws). Lobster dishes include baked (often stuffed), bisque, broiled, *homard à l'américaine* (literally = "American-style lobster") or *homard à l'armoricaine* (literally = "Brittany-style lobster" [from French *armoricaine* "of *Armorique*," from *Armorique* "Brittany," from *Armor*, in Breton, "Sea Country, the coast of Brittany" (*Arcoat* being "Woods Country, inland Brittany")]), lobster Newburg, salad, Thermidor. In the American or Armorican style, lobster is prepared by browning it in oil and then cooking it in gravy with condiments and wine. In Spain, a *bogavante* is a big lobster with large claws; it may be prepared as a salad, or in puff paste with tarragon.

lobster Newburg or **lobster Newburgh**, pieces of cooked lobster meat heated in a sauce of cream, sherry, and egg yolk (compare **Newburg**).

lobster roll, lobster salad (with shredded apples and mayonnaise) in a long roll.

lobster Thermidor [from French *Thermidor*, 1891 drama by Victorien Sardou (1831–1908), from thermidor, month of the French revolutionary calendar beginning 19 July], a dish consisting of cooked lobster meat, mushrooms, cream, egg yolks, and sherry stuffed into a lobster shell often sprinkled with Parmesan cheese, and oven-browned. In French, *homard Thermidor.*

Loch Leven trout [from Loch "lake; bay, inlet" Leven, eastern Scotland, south of Perth], a brown trout native to Loch Leven and other lakes in that area (southern Scotland, northern England).

locust bean, another name for **carob**.

locust berry, the drupe (one-seeded fruit) of any of several nances of southern Florida and the West Indies.

locust lobster, a large crustacean of the Mediterranean sea that somewhat resembles a lobster.

locust pod, another name for **carob**.

loganberry [for James H. *Logan*, American holticulturist who died in 1928], the red berry borne by a certain dewberry (likewise called *loganberry*). It is used for pies.

loin, a cut of meat comprising the part of the side and back between the ribs and the hipbone on each side of the spinal column. Compare **beefsteak**.

lokshen [Yiddish "noodles," plural of *loksh*], another name for **noodles**.

lollipop or **lollypop**, a lump of hard candy on the end of a stick.

lolly, a piece of candy, especially hard candy. Often = lollipop.

lo mein [from Cantonese *lòu-mihn* "stirred noodles"], a dish of Chinese origin consisting of sliced vegetables, soft noodles, and usually meat (often pork) or shrimp in bite-size pieces stir-fried in a seasoned sauce. It is composed of approximately the same amounts of noodles and sauce served in one bowl. The sauce is usually thickened first with cornflour or water chestnut flour.

lomilomi salmon [from Hawaiian *lomilomi* "vigorous massage," reduplication of *lomi* "to rub with the hand"], a dish consisting of salmon worked with the fingers, mixed with onions, and seasoned (Hawaii).

London broil [from *London*, England], a broiled boneless cut of beef (e.g., from the shoulder or flank) usually served sliced diagonally across (or against) the grain (to make it more tender).

longan or **lungan** [from Chinese *lóng yǎn*, "dragon's eye"], a pulpy fruit related to the litchi and produced by a southeastern Asian evergreen tree (likewise called *longan*).

long clam, another name for both **soft-shell clam** and **razor clam**.

long-clawed prawn, another name for **river prawn**.

longe [from English *muskellunge* "a large pike," of Ojibwa origin], another name for **lake trout**.

long-finned tuna, another name for **albacore**.

longfin pompano, a pompano of the western Atlantic having long fins.

longhorn or **longhorn cheese**, a firm-textured, mild, cheddar cheese.

long-neck clam, another name for **soft-shell clam**.

loppered milk, another name for **clabber**.

loquat [from Cantonese *làuh-gwat*] or **nispero**, the pear-shaped, yellow fruit of an Asiatic evergreen tree (likewise called *loquat)* of the rose family, used for preserves, jams, and jellies.

Lord Baltimore cake [probably for Lord *Baltimore*, 1580?–1632, English colonizer of Maryland, United States], a gold butter-cake with a filling

Loch Leven trout

Lord Baltimore cake

155

of macaroons, nuts (e.g., pecans, almonds), and cherries (maraschino) and a boiled frosting (often fruity: lemon, orange, strawberry). Compare **Lady Baltimore cake** (which is an egg-white cake).

lote, *1.* or **lotebush**, a shrub of Mexico and southern Texas having edible fruit; *2.* a fruit-flavored gum drop.

lotus, any of various water lilies.

lovage, an aromatic herb of the carrot family; its stalks and foliage are used as a flavoring agent and as a potherb, its aromatic seeds are used as a seasoning, and its root and flowering tops yield an oil used in flavoring.

lovage oil, an oil used in flavoring, obtained from the root of lovage.

love apple [probably translation of French *pomme d'amour* "tomato," "love apple," from the belief that tomatoes are aphrodisiac], an archaic name for the **tomato**.

low blueberry, another name for **lowbush blueberry**.

lowbush blackberry or **low blackberry**, other names for **dewberry**.

lowbush blueberry, the sweet fruit of any of several low-growing North American blueberries likewise called *lowbush blueberries*.

lox [from Yiddish *laks*], smoked salmon (often eaten on a bagel).

luau [from Hawaiian *lu'au*], *1.* an elaborate Hawaiian feast with Hawaiian food and usually with entertainment; *2.* cooked young taro leaves usually with coconut cream and chicken or octopus.

lucerne, another name for **alfalfa**.

lucuma [from Spanish *lúcuma* "eggfruit," from Quechua], another name for **eggfruit** (sense 1).

luderick [Australian] or **black bream** or **blackfish**, an Australian fish.

luncheon, a light meal at midday.

luncheon meat, packaged ready-to-eat meat.

lunge [from English *muskellunge* "a large pike"], another name for both **lake trout** and **muskellunge** (a large pike).

lutefisk [from Norwegian *lutefisk*, from *lute* "to wash in lye solution" + *fisk* "fish"], dried codfish that has been soaked in a water and lye solution, skinned, boned and cooked (usually boiled).

Luxembourg. The following are representative dishes and products of Luxembourg: ham, jellied suckling pig, crayfish, trout, pike, smoked pork and broad beans, black pudding and sausages, wild game, calf's liver quenelles with sauerkraut, potatoes, fried fish, civet of hare and thrushes, pastries, cakes, cooked cheese.

lychee, variant of **litchi**.

lyonnaise [from French *(à la) lyonnaise* "(in the manner of) Lyons," from *lyonnaise* "of Lyons (feminine)," from *Lyon* "Lyons," city of southeastern France], cooked with onions (and usually parsley). The term often refers to potatoes: potatoes lyonnaise or lyonnaise potatoes.

mako   marjoram   muesli   mirabelle   mandlen   mahimahi   marguerite

maasbanker, a horse mackerel of southern Africa.

mabi [from Caribbean Spanish *mabí*], a beverage prepared from the bark of a nakedwood (small tree) likewise called *mabi*.

mabolo [from Philippine Spanish *mabolo*], another name for **camagon**.

macadamia nut or **bush nut** or **Queensland nut** or **bauple nut**, the hard-shelled, white-fleshed, nutlike seeds of the macadamia tree (native to Australia), eaten raw or roasted.

macaroni [from Italian *maccheroni* (plural), from dialectal Italian (Naples) *maccarone* "dumpling, small cake, macaroni"], a pasta made from semolina dried in the form of tubes and prepared for eating (like noodles and spaghetti) by boiling. The word is often used as a generic for all pasta (see **pasta**). It can be served with a sauce, or prepared sauté, or as a loaf, or a casserole.

macaroni wheat, another name for **durum wheat**.

macaroon [from French *macaron*, from dialectal Italian (Naples) *maccarone* "dumpling, small cake, macaroni"], a chewy cookie composed chiefly of egg whites, sugar, and almond paste, or ground almonds, or coconut (or other chopped nuts), or corn flakes or other cereal.

mace, a fragrant and aromatic spice consisting of the dried covering that partly encloses the kernel of the nutmeg.

macédoine [French, from *Macédoine* "Macedonia" (perhaps in allusion to the mixture of ethnic groups in Macedonia], a mixture of fruits or vegetables cut in pieces and dressed and served as a salad or cocktail, sometimes in jelly.

mackerel, a fish of the North Atlantic. It is a fat fish and therefore best for broiling, baking, and planking.

mackinaw trout, another name for the **lake trout**.

macquarie perch, [for Lachlan *Macquarie*, died 1824, British governor of New South Wales, southeastern Australia], a fish of Australia.

macupa [Spanish, from Tagalog], another name for **Otaheite apple** (Philippines).

Madagascar. The following are among representative dishes and products of Madagascar: pork and rice, fish and rice, arrowroot, cassava, *romazava.*

mad apple, another name for **eggplant**.

made dish, a dish of food prepared from several ingredients, usually with a special seasoning, sauce, or garnish.

madeleine [French], a small cake made with flour, eggs, butter and sugar, baked in a shell-shaped mold.

madrilene [from French *(consommé) madrilène* "Madrid (consommé)," from Spanish *madrileño* "of Madrid"], a consommé (or bouillon) flavored with tomato and served hot or cold, often jellied (by chilling).

madrona [from Spanish *madroño*] or **manzanita**, *1.* an evergreen tree of the heath family, of the Pacific coast of North America, that bears red-orange berries, called *madrona apples; 2.* another name for **strawberry tree**.

madrona apple, one of the berries of the madrona (sense 1).

maguey [Spanish, from Taino], any of various plants native to tropical America (e.g., the century plant) used as a source of certain alcoholic beverages (e.g., mezcal, pulque).

maguey worm, another name for **agave worm**.

mahimahi [Hawaiian], the flesh of a dolphin used for food (Hawaii).

mahseer or **mahsir** or **mahasir** [from Hindi *mahāsir*], a large Indian fish.

mahua [from Hindi *mahūā*, from Sanskrit *madhūka*, from *madhu* "sweet, honey, mead"], any of various southeastern Asia trees with honey-filled flowers that are used for food. Compare **illupi**.

maigre [French] or **sciène**, a large European marine fish.

maître d'hôtel or **maître d'hôtel butter** [from French *(sauce) maître d'hôtel* "head steward (sauce)," "master of house (sauce)"], a sauce of melted butter, minced parsley, a little lemon juice (or vinegar), salt, and pepper. It is spread on steak or fish before serving.

maize [from Spanish *maíz*, from Taino *mahiz*], another name for **Indian corn** (a grain native to the New World, also called simply **corn**).

maize oil, another name for **corn oil**.

mako [from Maori *mako*] or **mako shark** or **bonito shark**, any of several sharks whose steaks are eaten (e.g., au poivre).

Malabar almond [from *Malabar*, area of western India] or **tropical almond** or **Indian almond** or **kamami**, the edible, almond-shaped kernel of the seed of the fruit of a tropical Asian evergreen tree (likewise called *Malabar almond).*

Malabar nightshade or **Malabar spinach**, an Asiatic climbing plant with fleshy leaves, cultivated in the tropics as a potherb.

Malawi. The following are among representative dishes and products of Malawi: fish (e.g., chambo), cornmeal porridge (Chichewa *nsima* = Swahili *ugali* [compare **Kenya**]). Beverage: tea.

Malay apple or **mountain apple** or **pomarrosa**, the edible fruit of a certain tree of Asia and Polynesia.

Malaysia. The following are among representative dishes and products of Malaysia: fish cooked with sweet-and-sour sauce; meat (e.g., beef, chicken) and vegetable curries; rice; meat (e.g., beef, chicken, pork, goat) grilled on bamboo spits (Malay *sate*), served with peanut sauce; grilled turtle meat; pork, noodles in a bowl of soup, fried rice *(nasi goréng);* minced fish or meat cakes baked in coconut leaves *(otak otak)*, side dishes *(sambal)*, stewed food rolled in banana leaves; a prawn paste *(belacan)* used as a spice; rice with curried meat and vegetable dishes *(nasi padang)*, cooked vegetables with peanut-butter sauce *(gado gado)*, chicken soup *(soto ayam; soto* = "soup, broth"), bamboo shoots, guava, rambutan, mangosteen, starfruit, desserts with coconut or banana.

malduck, another name for **fulmar**.

Mali. The following are among representative products of Mali: maize, beans, yams, cassava, sweet potatoes.

mallard, a wild duck of the northern hemisphere that is the ancestor of most domestic ducks.

¹**malt**, grain, usually barley (also oats), softened by steeping in water, allowed to sprout, used especially in brewing and distilling and as a nutrient.

²**malt (to)**, to convert (e.g., barley) into malt.

Malta. The following are among representative dishes and products of Malta: tuna, swordfish, shellfish (e.g., crabs, lobster, crayfish, mussels, octopus), chicken casserole, meat and macaroni pie (Maltese *timpana*) dried-pumpkin dishes, painted frog, pork.

Malta orange or **Maltese orange** [from *Malta*, island of the Mediterranean], another name for **blood orange**.

malted milk, *1.* a soluble powder made of dried milk, malted barley, and wheat flour; *2.* a beverage made by dissolving malted milk (sense 1) in milk or other liquid and adding ice cream and flavoring.

malt extract, *1.* a syrup prepared by infusing malt with water and evaporating; *2.* a powder made by drying this syrup.

maltose or **malt sugar**, a crystalline sugar formed especially from starch.

mamamu (from Hawaiian *mamamo*] or **mu**, a large eyed Indo-Pacific porgy.

mamey, variant of **mammee**.

mammee or **mamey** [from Spanish *mamey*, from Taino] or **tropical apricot**, the large, ovoid fruit, with reddish juicy flesh, of a tropical American tree likewise called *mammee* or *mamey*.

manatee or **manati**, any of several aquatic, herbivorous mammals of Atlantic coastal waters of the tropical Americas and Africa.

Manchu cherry, another name for **Nanking cherry**.

mandarin, or **mandarin orange** [from French *mandarine*, from Spanish *mandarina*, probably from *mandarín* "mandarin (Chinese public official)," from Portuguese *mandarim*; probably from the orange color of a mandarin's robes], another name for **tangerine**.

mandarin oil, an oil expressed from the peel of mandarin oranges (tangerines) and used in flavoring.

mandioc or **mandioca** [from Portuguese or Spanish *mandioca*], variant of **manioc** (a tropical plant also called **cassava**).

mandlen [from Yiddish "almonds," plural of *mandel*], fragments of fried or baked dough; they are used in soups.

mange-tout [French "eat everything"], see **snow pea**.

mango [from Portuguese *manga*], *1.* a yellowish, oblong tropical fruit having a smooth rind, cultivated for its juicy, aromatic pulp; it is borne by a large evergreen tree (likewise called *mango*) of the cashew family; *2.* a pickled, stuffed (e.g., with cabbage) sweet pepper.

mango melon or **lemon cucumber**, **cucumber melon**, **cucumber apple** or **melon apple** or **pomegranate melon** or **vine peach** or **orange melon** or **vegetable orange**, a muskmelon vine that bears orange-like fruit, used for pickles and preserves.

mango-squash, another name for **chayote**.

mangosteen [from Malay *mangisutan*] or **king's-fruit**, the dark, reddish brown fruit of a southeast Asian tree (likewise called *mangosteen*), with a thick rind and segmented, sweet, juicy pulp having a flavor suggestive of both peach and pineapple.

mangrove snapper, another name for **gray snapper**.

Manhattan clam chowder [from *Manhattan*, borough of New York City], a chowder made of minced clams, salt pork, vegetables (especially tomatoes), with water and seasoned with herbs; compare **New England clam chowder** (which is made with milk).

manicotti [Italian "muffs," from *manica* "sleeve"], an Italian dish consisting of tubular pasta shells filled with ricotta cheese (sometimes also with chopped ham), usually served hot with a tomato sauce.

Manila tamarind, the edible pods of camachile.

manioc or **manioca** or **mandioca** [from French *manioc* and Portuguese and Spanish *mandioca*], another name for **cassava** (a tropical plant).

manna lichen, *1.* any of several lichens that are blown about over the African and Arabian deserts and are used there for food; *2.* a lichen used in Japan for food.

manzanilla [Spanish, diminutive of *manzana* "apple"], the flower (with yellow center and white circumference) of a plant (likewise named *manzanilla*) with which an infusion (likewise called *manzanilla*) is made.

manzanita [American Spanish, diminutive of Spanish *manzana* "apple"], another name for **madrona**.

maori, an Australian marine fish.

maple, *1.* a certain tree found in the North Temperate Zone; *2.* the flavor of maple sap or its products (e.g., maple syrup or sugar).

maple cream or **maple butter**, maple syrup boiled, then cooled, and stirred to the density of cream.

maple honey, maple syrup boiled to the consistency of strained honey.

maple sugar, a sugar made by evaporating (by boiling down) maple syrup.

maple syrup, *1.* a sweet, finely flavored syrup made by concentrating (by evaporation, by boiling down) the sap of maple trees and especially the sugar maple; *2.* syrup made from other sugars and flavored with maple syrup or artificial maple flavoring.

maracujá, Portuguese for **granadilla**.

marang [Tagalog], the fruit of a Philippine tree (likewise called *marang*), consisting (somewhat like granadilla) of a mass of small seeds embedded in a sweetish white pulp.

marasca or **marasca cherry** [Italian, from *amarasca* "bitter wild cherry," from *amaro* "bitter"], a bitter wild cherry from the fermented juice of which maraschino liqueur is made.

maraschino [from Italian *marasca*, from *amarasca* "bitter wild cherry," from *amaro* "bitter"], *1.* a sweet liqueur distilled from the fermented juice and crushed pits of the marasca; *2.* or **maraschino cherry**, a cherry grown in Dalmatia (Croatia), and especially about Zadar, preserved in real or imitation maraschino (sense 1; liqueur).

marble cake, a cake made with light (from egg white or butter) and dark (from chocolate or egg yolks) batter so as to have a streaked or mottled appearance suggestive of marble (the stone).

margarine [French, ultimately from Greek *margaron* "pearl"] or **oleo**, a food product (a fatty substance) that is used like butter and is made from a blend of refined oils especially vegetable oils (e.g., cottonseed, soybean, peanut, sesame, soya, coconut oils) to which other ingredients (e.g., salt, emulsifiers, vitamins A and D) are added and that is churned with ripened skim milk to a smooth emulsion so as to have a consistency that permits ready spreading (the consistency of butter).

margate, or **market fish**, any of several grunts.

marguerite [French "daisy; pearl," ultimately from Greek *margaron* "pearl"], a salty cracker covered with a mixture of whipped egg white and boiled sugar syrup, and nuts or coconut, baked in the oven until browned.

mariculture, the cultivation of marine organisms in their natural environment.

¹**marinade (to)**, variant of **marinate**.

²**marinade** [French, from *mariner* "to pickle, marinate"], a savory pickling liquid of vinegar or wine and oil, with various spices and herbs (e.g., bay leaf, celery seed, garlic, onion, pepper, thyme), in which a food (e.g., meat, fish, a vegetable) is soaked, often before cooking to enrich its flavor or to tenderize it.

marinara [from Italian *(alla) marinara* "in sailor style," from *marinara* "of sailors" (femenine), from *marino* "marine, of the sea," from *mare* "sea"] (adjective), *1.* made (e.g., a sauce) with tomatoes, onions, garlic, and spices. The sauce, of Neapolitan origin, is often made also with olive oil, anchovies, oregano, chopped parsley, grated cheese; sometimes with chopped artichoke hearts; *2.* served with marinara (sense 1) sauce. Spaghetti (meatless) and other pasta and seafood (also green beans) are often served with marinara sauce.

marinate (to) [probably from Italian *marinato*, past participle of *marinare* "to marinate"], to season (e.g., meat [beef], fish [herring, macquerel], vegetables [salad materials]) by steeping in a ²marinade. Dishes such as beef Provençale (a French stew in red wine) begin with marinating before further cooking. Marinated dishes include beggar's chicken.

marjolaine, French for **marjoram**.

marjoram [French *marjolaine*, Spanish *mejorana, orégano*], any of various usually fragrant mints whose leaves are often used in cookery and in infusion.

market fish, see **margate**.

marmalade [from Portuguese *marmelada* "quince conserve," from *marmelo* "quince"], a soft, clear, sweetened, translucent jelly (a preserve) holding in suspension pieces or slices of fruit and fruit rind (especially citrus fruit; e.g., sour orange).

marmalade tree or **marmalade plum**, a tropical American tree (also found in the Philippines) that has an egg-shaped, single-seeded, edible fruit (called *vegetable egg*, sense 2).

marmite [French], *1.* a large, covered soup kettle; *2.* a small, covered individual casserole used especially for soups (in this sense, called also *petite marmite); 3.* the broth made in such a kettle (marmite, sense 1) or served in such a casserole (marmite, sense 2); *4.* a yeast product (made with fresh brewer's yeast) used in preparations for flavoring soups and meats and as a dietary supplement.

maror or **moror** [from Hebrew *mārōr*], the bitter herbs (e.g, horseradish root) eaten by Jews as part of the Passover seder to symbolize, on account of their pungent taste, the bitterness of the ancient Egyptian oppression of the Israelites (compare Exodus 12.8).

marron [French], another name for **Spanish chestnut**; French *dinde au marrons* "turkey with chestnuts," *crème de marrons* "chestnut cream," *purée de marrons* "mashed chestnuts."

marrons, also **marrons glacés** [French], chestnuts preserved in syrup (sense 1) flavored with vanilla.

marrow, *1.* the soft material that fills bone cavities; *2.* **marrow** or **marrow squash**, another name for the **vegetable marrow** (a squash).

marrow bone, a bone (e.g., a shinbone) containing marrow in sufficient quantity to be used in cookery (e.g., for flavoring soup).

marrowfat, *1.* a tallowy product obtained by rendering bone marrows; *2.* or **marrowfat pea**, any of several varieties of pea that produce large, wrinkled seeds.

marsh cress, a cress that grows in moderately wet places; it has leaves used in salads or as a potherb.

marsh fleabane or **marsh groundsel**, a plant (an herb) of northern regions that has leaves sometimes used as a potherb.

marsh hare, the flesh of the muskrat (an aquatic rodent of Canada and the United States).

marsh mallow or **mortification root**, a plant having a mucilagenous root sometimes used in confectionery.

marshmallow, a confection of sweetened paste, formerly made from the root of the marsh mallow, now from corn syrup, sugar, albumen, and gelatin beaten to a light, spongy consistency and usually dusted with powdered sugar when partly dry.

mart, *1.* a cow or ox fattened for slaughter (Scotland); *2.* meat salted and stored for winter provision (Scotland).

Martinique. The following are among representative dishes and products of Martinique: [2]callaloo (regional French *calalou*), fish soup (e.g., bream, bass; French *soupe au poisson*), stuffed crabs *(crabes farcis)*, fish stew *(daube de poisson)*, poached fish *(poisson en blaff);* curry *(colombo)* with chicken or pork (or pumpkin [*giraumont*] or beef or kid or lamb or fish or shellfish), eaten with rice; freshwater-crayfish bisque (regional French *bisque de cribiches* [from French *écrevisses*]); fritters *(accras)* filled with codfish or shrimp (or eggplant or hearts of palm); fried codfish; gumbos eaten with rice, chayote *(christophine)* with cheese stuffing, yam baked with cheese and butter, pumpkin sauté *(daube de giraumont)*, stewed cucumbers *(concombres en daube)*, salad of palm hearts, lamb curry, pork stew; green-mango chutney or relish *(rougail de mangues vertes)*, banana sauté with cream cheese *(banane céleste)*, banana fritters *(beignets de banane)*, banana pudding *(daube de banane)*, sweet potato cake *(gâteau patate* or *gâteau martiniquais)*, pineapple mousse *(mousse à l'ananas)*, breadfruit pudding *(pudding au fruit à pain)*.

marula or **maroola** or **marula plum** [from a language of southern Africa], the fruit of a tree of southern Africa, resembling a plum, which contains an edible seed and can be used to prepare an intoxicating beverage.

marumi kumquat or **marumi**, any of several round-fruited kumquats. Distinguished from **nagami kumquat** (that has oval fruit).

marzipan [German, from Italian *marzapane* "marzipan; box for confections (originally a box containing a tenth of a load)," from Venetian *matapan*, coin bearing a seated Christ figure (originally a 10% tax), from Arabic *mawthabān*, a coin of the Middle Ages "seated king"], a confection of almond paste or crushed almonds, sugar, and egg whites that is often molded into various forms (e.g., animals, fruits).

masa [Spanish "mash; dough; mass"], a moist mash resulting from the grinding of Indian corn (boiled, dried corn) soaked in a lime and water solution (the limed kernels are called *nixtamal*) and used in preparing tortillas, tamales, and similar food of Mexican origin. Compare **nixtamal**.

masala [Hindi "spice"], see **garam masala**.

mascarpone [Italian, from regional Italian (Lombardy) *mascarpón* "large cream-cheese," augmentative of *mascarpa* "cream cheese"], an Italian cream cheese.

¹**mash (to)**, to convert (e.g., apples, potatoes) into a soft, pulpy mixture by beating or pressure.

²**mash**, another name for mashed potatoes.

maté or **mate** or **yerba maté** [from American Spanish *mate* "maté (beverage, and vessel for drinking it)", from Quechua *mati* "vessel, gourd"] or **Paraguay tea** or **Jesuits' tea**, an aromatic beverage popular in South America made by steeping (in hot water) the dried and ground leaves (likewise called *maté* or *yerba maté*) of the maté tree (of the holly family). In French it is called *maté* or *thé des Jésuites* or *thé du Paraguay*.

matelote [French, from *(à la) matelote* "in sailor fashion," from *matelot* "sailor"], *1*. fish (often eel) stewed in a sauce made of red wine, onions, and seasonings; *2*. this sauce. In France, burbot is also prepared in this fashion, perhaps partly because of the rhyming name *(lotte à la matelote)*.

matriciana, see **amatriciana**.

matzo [from Yiddish *matse*, from Hebrew *maṣṣāh*], a wafer or a brittle flat piece of unleavened bread eaten during the Passover.

163

matzo ball, a ball-shaped dumpling made from matzo meal.

matzoon or **madzoon** [from Armenian *madzun*], a fermented milk food similar to yogurt.

mayberry, a bramble having yellow, edible fruits.

mayhaw, a hawthorn of the southern United States that bears a scarlet, juicy, acid fruit that ripens in May and is used for making jellies and preserves.

mayonnaise [French, from obsolete French *mahonnaise*, perhaps from Spanish *Mahón*, city of Minorca, in commemoration of its capture in 1756 by the Duke of Richelieu], a dressing made of beaten, raw egg yolks, vegetable oils (often olive oil), and lemon juice or vinegar, together with salt and condiments. Mayonnaise is often served with salads, lobster, shrimp. For a garlic mayonnaise, see **aioli**.

mazagran [French, from *Mazagran*, village in northwestern Algeria], sweetened and usually cold and diluted (in water) black coffee served in a glass.

meadow mushroom or **fairies'-table** or **field mushroom**, a common edible agaric that is often cultivated.

meal, *1.* the coarsely ground seeds of a cereal grass or pulse, especially cornmeal; also oatmeal (sense 1); *2.* a granular product resembling seed meal, especially in particle size or texture, obtained by grinding any of various dried food products (e.g., fish or meat).

measure, *1.* a unit of measurement; *2.* the quantity or capacity of something (in the case of this dictionary, of ingredients for food or beverages). Mass (or weight) and volume (or capacity) are basic measures for cooking.

The system of measurement units (units for measuring, for ascertaining quantity, weight, or capacity) that has the widest use in the world is the International (Metric) System; another is the United States Customary System (which has its origins in the British Imperial System but is not identical).

Eight tables follow showing (often approximate) equivalences within each of the International and the United States System and between these two systems. In certain countries, another system is also used in cookery, with units of measure such as cups, tablespoons, teaspoons; these are also shown.

Note: in the United States system, the words *dram* and *ounce* are used both for weight and for capacity; when they refer to capacity, it is important to call them *fluid dram* and *fluid ounce*, as they are not equivalent (for instance, 1 fluid ounce = 8 fluid drams, but 1 ounce [avoirdupois] = 16 drams). The words *pint* and *quart* are used for capacity both for liquid and for dry measure; when they refer to liquid measure, one pint = 28.875 cubic inches (= 0.473 liter), one quart = 57.75 cubic inches (= 0.946 liter), but when they refer to dry measure, one pint = 33.6 cubic inches (= 0.551 liter), one quart = 67.201 cubic inches (= 1.101 liters).

WEIGHT

from the United States system – avoirdupois

			metric equivalent
one grain (gr)	= 0.037 dram	= 0.002286 ounce	= 0.0648 gram
one dram (dr)	= 27.344 grains	= 0.0625 ounce	= 1.772 grams
one ounce (oz)	= 16 drams	= 437.5 grains= 0.0625 pound	= 28.35 grams
one pound (lb)	= 16 ounces	= 7,000 grains	= 0.454 kilogram

from the International System

		United States equivalent
one gram (g)	= 1 gram	= 0.035 ounce
one dekagram (dag)	= 10 grams	= 0.353 ounce
one hectogram (hg)	= 100 grams	= 3.527 ounces
one kilogram (kg)	= 1,000 grams	= 2.2046 pounds

CAPACITY

from the United States system – liquid measure

			metric equivalent
one fluid dram (fl dr)		= 0.226 cubic inches	= 3.697 milliliters
one fluid ounce (fl oz)	= 8 fluid drams = $^1/_{16}$ pint	= 1.805 cubic inches	= 29.573 milliliters
one gill (gi)	= 4 fluid ounces = $^1/_2$ cup	= 7.219 cubic inches	= 118.294 milliliters
half a pint	= 8 fluid ounces = 1 cup	= 14.438 cubic inches	= 0.24 liter
one pint (pt)	= $^1/_2$ quart = 16 fluid ounces = 4 gills = 2 cups	= 28.875 cubic inches	= 0.473 liter
one quart (qt)	= 2 pints = 32 fluid ounces = 4 cups	= 57.75 cubic inches	= 0.946 liter
one gallon (gal)	= 4 quarts = 16 cups	= 231 cubic inches	= 3.785 liters

from the International System – liquid measure

			United States equivalent
one milliliter (ml)	= 0.001 liter	= 0.061 cubic inch	= 0.27 fluid dram
one centiliter (cl)	= 0.01 liter	= 0.61 cubic inch	= 0.338 fluid ounce
one deciliter (dl)	= 0.10 liter	= 6.1 cubic inches	= 0.21 pint
one cubic decimeter (dm^3)	= 1 liter	= 61.02 cubic inches	= 1.057 quart

				metric equivalent
one teaspoon (tsp)	= $^1/_3$ of a tablespoon	= $1^1/_3$ fluid drams	= 60 drops	= 4.928 milliliter
			= $^1/_6$ fluid ounce	
two teaspoons	= $^2/_3$ of a tablespoon	= $2^2/_3$ fluid drams	= 120 drops	= 9.8 milliliters
three teaspoons	= 1 tablespoon	= 4 fluid drams	= 180 drops	= 14.784 milliliters
one tablespoon (tbsp)	= $^1/_{16}$ of a cup	= 3 teaspoons	= 4 fluid drams	= 14.784 milliliter
			= $^1/_2$ fluid ounce	
two tablespoons	= $^1/_8$ of a cup	= 1 fluid ounce		= 29.573 milliliters
three tablespoons		= $1^1/_2$ fluid ounces		= 44.373 milliliters
four tablespoons	= $^1/_4$ of a cup	= 2 fluid ounces		= 59.146 milliliters
$^1/_2$ cup	= 1 gill = 8 tablespoons	= 4 fluid ounces		= 0.118 liter
one cup	= 16 tablespoons	= 8 fluid ounces	= $^1/_2$ pint	= 0.236 liter
two cups		= 16 fluid ounces	= 1 pint	= 0.473 liter
three cups		= 24 fluid ounces		= 0.708 liter
four cups		= 32 fluid ounces	= 1 quart	= 0.946 liter

From the United States system – dry measure

			metric equivalent
one pint (pt)	= $^1/_2$ quart	= 33.6 cubic inches	= 0.551 liter
one quart (qt)	= 2 pints	= 67.201 cubic inches	= 1.101 liter

From the International System – dry measure

		United States equivalent
one deciliter (dl)	= 6.1 cubic inches	= 0.18 pint
one cubic decimeter (dm³) = one liter (l)	= 61.02 cubic inches	= 0.908 quart

OVEN TEMPERATURES – Equivalences (°F to °C)
(Some ovens use a system of numbers or marks. These too are shown)

250–300°F	low	120–150°C	$^1/_2$–2
325–375°F	moderate	165–190°C	3–5
400°F	moderately hot	200°C	6
425–450°F	hot	220–230°C	7–8
475–500°F	very hot	245–260°C	9–10

meat, *1.* animal tissue used as food, especially the edible flesh of mammals, as distinguished from that of fish or poultry (chicken, duck, goose, turkey), and even more specifically the flesh of domesticated cattle, swine, sheep, and goats; *2.* the edible parts of any animal (e.g., crab); *3.* the edible portions of eggs, fruits, or nuts.

For roast meat: tender cuts of beef, veal, pork, lamb are placed in the roasting pan without a cover in the oven.

For broiled meat: beef steaks and lamb chops, 1 to 2 inches thick, are best. Those that are less than 1 inch thick (e.g., cube and minute steaks) may be pan-broiled, like hamburgers.

Braising or stewing (low heat on top of the stove or in a slow oven) is used for meats that are not tender enough for roasting or broiling, as well as for pork and veal steaks and chops. As with roast meats the time depends on the size, shape, and desired doneness of the meat. Pot roast is a large piece of meat that is braised. Stews are small uniform pieces in a heavy covered kettle, with or without vegetables.

Cuts that are even less tender (e.g., corned beef and cured hams, shoulders, spare ribs, neck and shank of veal, tongues, hearts) are cooked in water, in small or in large pieces, simmered until tender. Of course they can also be done in a pressure cooker.

Variety meats include brains, hearts, kidneys, liver, sweetbreads, tongue, tripe, oxtails, pigs' feet. Most of these are first simmered in water and then served with a sauce. Calf's liver is often pan-fried or broiled.

Sausages made of fresh pork are cooked slowly. Smoked sausages are only reheated. Bologna and dry or summer sausages need no cooking, they are ready to serve. See also **game** (which includes rabbit, squirrel, venison [deer, elk, moose], pheasant, prairie chicken, quail, ruffed grouse, wild duck). Dishes made with meat include casserole, croquettes, chili con carne, goulash, meat loaf, meat pies, stuffed green peppers.

meatball, a small ball of chopped or ground meat often mixed with bread crumbs and spices (sometimes also vegetables) and browned in a skillet; Swedish meatballs, for instance, may contain ground beef and pork, bread crumbs, minced onion, parsley, and pepper. Spaghettis can be served with meatballs.

meat loaf, a baked dish of ground meat held together with soft crumbs or eggs.

meat pie, see **pie** (sense 1).

meat tenderizer, see **tenderizer**.

medallion [from French *médaillon*, from Italian *medaglione* "large medal," augmentative of *medaglia* "medal"], a small round or oval serving (e.g., of meat: tenderloin of beef, lamb, veal, deer).

medlar, the fruit of a small Eurasian tree (likewise called *medlar*), resembling a crab apple, used as a base for preserves.

mejillón, Spanish for **mussel**.

mejorana, Spanish for **marjoram**.

melada [American Spanish, from Spanish *mel-*, base of *miel* "honey"], crude cane sugar (in the form of a syrup) as it comes mixed with molasses from the boiling of cane juice.

mélange or **melange** [from French *mélange* "mixture"], a blended mixture

167

(e.g., coffee mixed with cream, served in a tall glass, topped with whipped cream).

melba [created by French cook Escoffier in honor of Dame Nellie *Melba* (originally Helen Porter Mitchell), 1861–1931, Australian soprano, whose stage name she adopted from Melbourne, city of southeastern Australia], fruit (e.g., peach, pear, strawberries) served on ice cream (often vanilla), with raspberry sauce and whipped cream (sometimes also with grilled almonds). Compare **pêche melba**.

melba sauce [for Dame Nellie *Melba* (see **melba**)] a bright-red, sweet sauce made essentially of sieved raspberries and sugar (often with currant jelly and corn starch), in the top of a double boiler, and served often with ice cream and whipped cream on fruit or on fruit sundaes, pêche melba, and similar desserts. Compare **pêche melba**.

melba toast [for Dame Nellie *Melba* (see **melba**)], very thinly sliced crisp toast (dried and browned in a slow oven). Served with consommé, foie gras, caviar.

melocoton [from Spanish *melocotón* "melocoton; peach"], a peach grafted on a quince rootstock.

melon, any of various gourds (e.g., cantaloupe, honeydew melon, muskmelon, watermelon) usually eaten raw as fruits and characteristically having a hard rind and juicy flesh.

melon apple, another name for **mango melon**.

melon fruit, another name for **papaya**.

melongena [from Italian *melanzana* "an eggplant"], *1.* another name for **eggplant**; *2.* a large Caribbean mollusk that resembles a whelk.

melongene [from archaic French *mélongène* "an eggplant" (French *aubergine)*, from Italian *melanzana*], another name for **eggplant**.

melon pear, another name for **pepino**.

Melton Mowbray [from *Melton Mowbray*, town in Leicestershire, central England], an English meat pie.

menhaden, a marine fish of the herring family.

menta, Italian and Spanish for **mint**.

menthe, French for **mint**.

menu [French "list of dishes," from *menu* "detailed, slender, small"], *1.* or **menu card**, bill of fare, printed or written list of the dishes that may be ordered (e.g., in a restaurant) or of specially prepared dishes that are to be served (e.g., at a banquet); *2.* the dishes available for or served at a meal; *3.* the meal itself. In French *menu* is also short for *menu à prix fixe* (see **table d'hôte** [sense 3], **prix fixe**); the opposite is *repas à la carte* (see **a la carte**).

meringue [French], *1.* a dessert topping (e.g., for pies [lime, orange, pineapple], bread puddings) baked (at low temperature) from a mixture of beaten egg whites and sugar; *2.* a small, light, pastry shell or cake made of meringue (sense 1) often containing fruit or cream or ice cream or nutmeats. A large one can be called a meringue torte.

mero [Spanish], any of several large groupers of warm seas.

mesquite or **mezquite** [from Spanish *mezquite*, from Nahuatl *mizquitl*], a spiny tree of Mexico and the southwestern United States that bears pods called *mesquite beans*.

mesquite bean or **algarroba**, the pulpy pod of a mesquite (or its seed), which is rich in sugar.

meunière [from French *(à la) meunière* "in the manner of a miller," from *meunier* "miller"], rolled lightly in flour and sautéed in butter; lemon juice or coriander may be added. Scallops, sole, trout may be cooked in this way.

Mexico. The following are among representative dishes and products of Mexico: turkey with mole (regional Spanish *mole de guajolote); mole poblano* and *mole negro* (either of them with beef, or chicken, or pork), tacos, guacamole, tortillas, enchiladas, stuffed hot peppers *(chiles rellenos)*, stuffed hot peppers covered with nut sauce *(chiles en nogada)*, tamales, posol (sense 1, corn and pork soup; *pozole);* tostadas topped with frijoles refritos, lettuce, onion, tomato, meat; [1]barbecue (sense 3, pit-roasted goat or sheep; *barbacoa)*, frijoles, frijoles refritos; red snapper (sense 1, a reddish marine fish), Veracruz style *(huachinango a la veracruzana)*, i.e., sautéed with tomatoes, onions, olives, capers, hot peppers; pork in orange juice and vinegar (from Yucatán; *cochinita pibil)*, roast cabrito (from the North), avocados, bananas, pineapple, guavas, mangos, [1]tuna (fruit of a prickly pear), mammee *(mamey)*.

meze, see under **Turkey**.

mickey [probably from *Mickey*, nickname from *Michael*, a common given name in Ireland], an Irish potato (= white potato, the tuber) roasted at an outdoor fire.

microwave (to), to cook or heat food in a microwave oven.

microwave oven, an oven in which food is heated or cooked by the heat produced by the absorption of the energy of a short electromagnetic wave by water molecules in the food.

middle, *1.* the part of the side of an animal between the shoulder and rump or ham; *2.* the large intestine of beef used as casing for bologna.

midshipman's-butter [from *midshipman* "student in a naval academy"], another name for **avocado**.

midshipman's-nuts [from *midshipman* "student in a naval academy"], pieces of broken hardtack.

mignon [French "dainty"], short for **filet mignon**.

milanaise [from French *milanaise* "of Milan (feminine)," from *Milan*, city of northern Italy], garnished (e.g., a veal cutlet) with spaghetti or macaroni; the pasta is served in a tomato sauce (containing truffles and mushrooms) topped with Parmesan cheese. In French, *à la milanaise* (of a meat) means, like **milanese**, coated with bread crumbs (and egg and grated Parmesan) and fried in oil or butter.

milan cabbage, another name for **Savoy cabbage** (see **savoy**, sense 1).

milanese [Italian "of Milan," from *Milano* "Milan," city of northern Italy], coated with bread crumbs or flour, fried in oil or butter, often seasoned with cheese (e.g., veal cutlet milanese). In Spanish, a *milanesa* is a breaded cut of meat.

milk, *1.* a whitish liquid secreted by the mammary glands of female mammals; *2.* the milk (sense 1) of cows, goats, or other animals, used as a food by humans; *3.* a liquid similar to milk in appearance, such as the juice of a coconut.

milk chocolate, sweetened chocolate (sense 1) made with milk solids.

milkfish or **sabalo**, a large herbivorous fish of warm parts of the Pacific and Indian oceans.

milkgrass, another name for **corn salad**.

milk gravy, gravy made with milk, flour, and pork fat.

milk shake, a beverage made of milk, shaken or whipped until foamy, with a flavoring syrup, and often ice cream (may be topped with whipped cream and sprinkled with nutmeg).

milk toast, hot, usually buttered, toast, which is softened in hot milk and sweetened with sugar or seasoned with salt and pepper.

mille-feuille [from French *mille-feuilles, millefeuille*, from *mille feuilles* "a thousand leaves"], a dish composed of puff pastry (sense 1, pastry dough) layered with a filling (e.g., salmon or cream), especially another name for **napoleon**.

millet, the small, white seeds of a cereal grass likewise called *millet*.

mince (**to**), to chop or cut into very small pieces. Several dishes are made with minced meat or seafood.

mincemeat, *1.* a finely chopped and usually cooked mixture of raisins, apples, spices, and other ingredients, sometimes with meat and suet, often used as a pie filling; *2.* (obsolete) finely chopped meat.

mince pie or **minced pie** or **Christmas pie**, a pie filled with minced meat.

minestra [Italian "soup," from *minestrare* "to serve soup, dish up"], Italian vegetable soup (with pasta or rice, and with much [Italian *minestra in brodo*] or very little [Italian *minestra asciutta*] broth).

minestrone [Italian "big soup," augmentative of *minestra* "soup"], a thick vegetable soup of Italian origin usually with dried beans and pasta (e.g., vermicelli, macaroni) and herbs, sometimes topped with grated cheese.

mint or **menta** (Italian and Spanish) or **menthe** (French) or **nana** (Arabic), *1.* any of various aromatic plants (peppermint, spearmint) cultivated for flavoring (their foliage is used in cookery, e.g. in vegetable dishes and desserts) and for their aromatic oil; mint sauce is often used with roast lamb; *2.* a soft or hard confection (a piece of candy or chewing gum) flavored with mint (peppermint or spearmint) and often served after dinner.

minute pudding [from *minute* "60-seconds, unit of time"], a pudding (sweet dessert) made with flour stirred into boiling milk.

minute steak [from *minute* "60-seconds, unit of time"], a small, thin steak, often scored or cubed, that can be cooked quickly (usually panbroiled). Compare **cube steak**.

mirabelle [French], the round, yellow fruit of a small European plum tree (likewise called *mirabelle*), used especially for preserves and for making a liqueur (likewise called *mirabelle*).

miracle fruit or **miraculous fruit** or **miraculous berry**, either of two tropical African fruits that have a lingering sweetish aftertaste, due to a glycoprotein that also causes sour foods eaten after one of these fruits to taste sweet.

mirepoix [French, probably for the duc de *Mirepoix*, 18th-century French diplomat], a foundation of diced ham or bacon, vegetables (e.g., onions, carrots, celery hearts), herbs (crushed bay leaf, thyme), and seasonings used chiefly under meat (also fowl, shellfish) in braising. It is used in brown sauce.

mirgil or **mirga** or **mirgal** [from Bengali *mirgala* and Oriya *mirgā*], a large Indian fish.

miriti palm [from Portuguese *muriti* "muriti palm; miriti palm," from Tupi *muriti, buriti*] or **ita palm** or **moriche (palm)**, a South American palm having edible fruits and buds; the plant also yields a sago (a starch used in foods) from the stem and wine from the sap.

miso [Japanese], a food paste used in preparing soups and other foods, that is made by grinding a mixture of steamed rice (or barley), cooked soybeans, and salt and fermenting it in brine, and ranging in taste from very salty to very sweet.

mixed grill, a dish consisting of a variety of broiled meats and vegetables typically including a lamb chop, perhaps also kidney, bacon, mushroom, tomato. It may also include breast of chicken, pork, sausage.

moano or **moana** [Polynesian or Maori], either of two Hawaiian fishes.

mocha or **moka** [from *Mocha*, southwestern Yemen (Arabic *Mukhā*), Red Sea port near which the coffee was originally grown and from which it was originally exported], *1.* a flavoring made of a coffee infusion or of a mixture of cocoa or chocolate with coffee; *2.* coffee grown in Arabia that produces a superior beverage. Compare **Arabica coffee**.

mock brawn, another name for **headcheese**.

mock chicken, meat other than chicken (e.g., veal) cooked to resemble chicken.

mock duck, a boned shoulder of lamb shaped to resemble a duck (the foreshank forms the head and neck).

mock turtle soup, a soup made of meat (e.g., calf's head or veal) and wine and spiced to taste like green turtle soup.

moharra, variant of **mojarra**.

mohnseed [part translation of German *Mohnsame*, from *Mohn* "poppy" + *Same* "seed"], another name for **poppy seed**.

mojarra or **moharra** [from American Spanish *mojarra*, a tropical American fish, from Spanish *mojarra*, a small European flat fish], any of several tropical American fishes.

moka, variant of **mocha**.

molasses [from Portuguese *melaço*], *1.* any of various thick, brown syrups drained off from raw sugar during the process of sugar manufacture (compare **treacle**); *2.* a syrup made by boiling down sweet vegetable (e.g., sorghum) or fruit juice or sap.

mole [Mexican Spanish, from Nahuatl *molli* "sauce"], any of many Mexican hot sauces of chili, other spices and sometimes a very little chocolate. It is served with various meats (e.g., turkey, chicken, pork, beef). In Mexico, some well-known moles are *mole poblano* (= "from Puebla") and *mole negro* ("black").

mollusk or **mollusc** [from French *mollusque*, from Latin *mollis* "soft"], another name for certain shellfish (e.g., clams, cuttlefish, mussels, octopuses, oysters, scallops, squids, whelks). Shellfish that are not mollusks are crustaceans.

mombin, the purplish fruit of a tropical American shrub (likewise called *mombin*).

Monaco. The following are among representative dishes and products of Monaco: fish (e.g., mostelle), grilled sardines (French *sardines grillées*), shellfish, pasta (e.g., ravioli), stuffed vegetables *(farcis;* may be tomatoes or peppers or onions), pizza, vegetable soup with basil (Provençal *lou pistou)*, a cooked onion tart with a puree of anchovies and black olives (Provençal *pissaladière)*.

monkey apple, a tropical Old World tree having a fruit resembling a plum.

monkey bread, the gourdlike fruit of the baobab (a certain tropical tree) having edible pulp.

monkey-nut, another name for **peanut**.

monkey orange, the fruit of either of two African shrubs (likewise called *monkey oranges)*, having edible pulp.

monosodium glutamate or **sodium glutamate**, a white crystalline compound having a meatlike taste, used in cooking to enhance the natural flavor of foods (e.g. meat, soup).

Monterey cheese or **Monterey Jack** [from *Monterey* county, California] or **Jack cheese**, a semisoft, whole milk cheese.

moo goo gai pan [Cantonese from Chinese *mógu jī piàn* "mushroom chicken slice"], a Cantonese dish of chicken, mushroom, vegetables, and spices, steamed together.

moon cake, a small, round pastry filled with a mixture of meat and other ingredients traditionally eaten during the Chinese harvest festival (mid-Autumn).

moonfish, another name for **opah**.

moose [Algonquian], a ruminant mammal found in forests of North America, the largest existing member of the deer family; it is also found in Eurasia, where in English it is usually called *elk*. See **deer**.

moray eel or simply **moray** [from Portuguese *moréia*, from Latin *muraena*], any of various eels of chiefly tropical coastal waters.

morel [from French *morille*] or **sponge mushroom**, any of various edible mushrooms. They may be used with chicken (French *poulet aux morilles*).

morello, a variety of the sour cherry.

moriche or **moriche palm** [from Spanish *moriche,* from Tupi *muriti*], another name for the **miriti palm**.

Mornay sauce or **Mornay** [perhaps for Philippe de *Mornay*, 1549–1623, French Huguenot leader], a white sauce (a cream sauce) flavored with grated Swiss or Parmesan cheese. Eggs Mornay are served with this sauce.

Morocco. The following are among representative dishes and products of Morocco: couscous; roast mutton (Arabic *mashwi* "roast"); pastilla; chicken stuffed with almonds and raisins; minced meat patties *(kufta, kefta);* spiced stew of meat, poultry, or fish *(tajin);* olives. Beverage: sweet mint-tea.

moro crab [part translation of Spanish *cangrejo moro* "Moorish crab"], another name for **stone crab**.

moror, see **maror**.

mortadella [Italian, from Latin *murtatum* "sausage seasoned with myrtle berries," from *murtus* "myrtle"], a large, cooked, smoked sausage made of chopped pork and pork fat (and sometimes beef), seasoned with pepper and garlic; finocchio is often added.

mortification root, another name for **marsh mallow**.

morwong or **sea carp**, any of several Australian fishes.

mostaccioli [Italian "little mustaches," from Old Italian *mostaccio* "moustache"], a short tube of pasta with oblique ends. Mostaccioli are often served with a sauce of ground beef, tomatoes, onion, garlic, olive oil. In Italian, a *mostacciolo* [perhaps from *mosto* "must, grape juice"] is a cookie made of flour, sugar, and raisins, with the addition of candied fruit, dry figs, or almonds.

moth bean, the small, yellowish brown seed of a bean plant (likewise called *moth bean*) cultivated in India.

mother cloves, the dried fruits of the clove tree (a tropical evergreen) that resemble true cloves (which are the unopened flower buds) but are less aromatic.

mountain apple, another name for **Malay apple** (Hawaii).

mountain balm, either of two yerba santas.

mountain banana, another name for **fei**.

mountain cabbage, a certain cabbage palm.

mountain crab, another name for **black crab**.

mountain cranberry or **cowberry** or **lingonberry** or **windberry**, an evergreen shrub of north temperate uplands having dark red berries.

mountain oyster or **Rocky Mountain oyster**, the testis of a bull calf (in this sense, also called *prairie oyster)*, sheep, boar, or other animal cooked and served as food.

mountain spinach, another name for **garden orache**.

mountain tea, *1.* another name for **wintergreen** (sense 1, a shrub); *2.* an infusion of wintergreen leaves.

moussaka [from modern Greek *mousakas*, from Turkish *musakka*], a Middle Eastern, oven-baked dish of ground meat (e.g., lamb, beef) and sliced eggplant or potatoes often topped with a seasoned sauce. Tomatoes and eggs may be added.

mousse [French "froth, foam; moss"], *1.* a molded, chilled dessert made with sweetened and flavored (e.g., with chocolate, coffee, apricot, fruit juice, orange, peppermint, raspberry, strawberry) whipped cream or egg whites and gelatin; *2.* a molded dish made from a purée of meat (e.g., chicken, chicken liver, foie gras, ham), fish (e.g., salmon), or shellfish; *3.* or ²**mousseline**, a food (e.g., broccoli, potatoes) so prepared as to be light or creamy in texture and usually containing gelatin, cream, or egg whites (compare ¹**soufflé**); a trout mousse may be used as stuffing for a skinned and boned trout.

¹**mousseline** or **mousseline sauce** [French "muslin"], a sauce or purée often consisting of mayonnaise or of hollandaise sauce made frothy by the addition of whipped cream or beaten egg whites. It can be used on artichokes, asparagus, boiled fish, broccoli, cauliflower, eggs, soufflé, spinach.

²**mousseline**, another name for **mousse** (in sense 3).

mozzarella [Italian, diminutive of *mozza*, a kind of cheese, from *mozzare* "to cut off"], a moist, white, unsalted, unripened, often round Italian cheese, made from buffalo milk, often melted in cookery. In Italian, a *mozzarella in carrozza* "mozzarella in a carriage" is fried mozzarella between two bread toasts.

mu [Hawaiian], another name for **mamamu**.

mucket, any of various freshwater mussels.

Muenster or **Muenster cheese** or **Munster** [from *Münster, Munster*, city of northeastern France], a semisoft, creamy, yellow, fermented, Alsatian cheese made with cow milk in the Vosges mountains. It may have cumin.

muesli [from Swiss German *Müsli*, diminutive of German *Mus* "soft food, mush"], a breakfast cereal of Swiss origin consisting of rolled oats, nuts, and fruit (e.g., grated apples) to which milk is usually added, and sometimes lemon juice.

muffin, *1.* a small, round cake (quick bread) prepared with batter (made with wheat flour or cornmeal) containing egg, baked in a small cup-shaped mold, often sweetened, frequently eaten with butter, and usually served hot; *2.* a similarly shaped biscuit made from dough leavened with yeast (see **English muffin**).

muktuk [from Inuit *maktak*], whale skin used for food.

mulberry, the usually dark purple, berry-like fruit of a tree (likewise called *mulberry)*, that is an aggregate of juicy, one-seeded drupes.

mullagatawny, variant of **mulligatawny**.

mullet, any of various chiefly marine fishes.

mulligan stew or simply **mulligan** [probably from the name *Mulligan*], a stew of various meats and vegetables. It may also be made with fish.

mulligatawny or **mullagatawny** [from Tamil *mịlakutaṇṇi* "pepper water"], a southeast Asian soup usually of chicken stock (or other meat stock) seasoned with curry powder.

mulloway, a large Australian marine fish.

multiplier onion or **potato onion**, any of several onions cultivated for salad onions, that are propagated by offsets (small bulbs arising from the base of the primary bulb).

mummy apple [from *mammee*], another name for **papaya**.

munchies [from *munch* "to chew with a crunching sound; to eat with relish; to snack on"], light snack foods.

mung bean or simply **mung** [from Hindi *mũng*], *1.* or **urd bean** or **green gram**, a bean widely cultivated in warm regions for its seeds, and that is the chief source of the bean sprouts used in Oriental cookery; *2.* the green or yellow seed of the mung bean (sense 1).

Munster, variant of **Muenster**.

muriti palm or **buriti** [from Portuguese *muriti, buriti* "muriti palm; miriti palm," from Tupi], a Brazilian palm yielding edible nuts.

murphy [from *Murphy*, a common Irish surname; from the potato's being regarded as a staple Irish food], a slang name for **potato**.

Murray cod [from the *Murray* River, southeastern Australia], a large freshwater fish of Australia.

Murray crayfish or **Murray lobster** [from the *Murray* River, southeastern Australia], a large Australian crayfish.

muscadine or **muscadine grape**, the fruit (a purple grape) of a vine (called *muscadine*) of the southeastern United States.

muscat or **muskat** or **muscatel**, any of various white grapes used for making wine or raisins.

muscatel, a raisin produced from muscat grapes.

muscovado or **muscavado** [from Spanish *(azúcar) mascabado*, from Portuguese *(açúcar) mascavado*, from *açúcar* "sugar" + *mascavado*, past participle of *mascavar* "to separate raw sugar (from molasses)"], raw, dark, or unrefined, sugar extracted from the juice of the sugarcane by evaporation and draining off the molasses.

Muscovy duck [from *Muscovy* "Principality of Moscow, Russia"] or **Guinea duck**, a large duck of tropical America.

mush, a thick porridge made by boiling meal (especially cornmeal) in water or milk until it forms a soft mass. It may be eaten hot as a cereal or pudding, fried as cakes, or molded until cold and then sliced and fried. Compare **hasty pudding** (sense 2, cornmeal mush).

mushroom, any of various enlarged, fleshy, fruiting bodies of fungi. Edible mushrooms can be served creamed, sautéed, stuffed, in soups, sauces, as garnishes. Dishes using mushrooms include a la king dishes, beef Stroganoff.

muskat, variant of **muscat**.

muskellunge or **lunge** [Ojibwa], a large pike.

muskmelon, a sweet, juicy, musky-odored melon (e.g., cantaloupe, mango melon) with superficially netted or ribbed skin.

muskrat, an aquatic rodent (see **marsh hare**).

muskrat potato, another name for **wapatoo**.

muslin kail, broth of barley and greens (Scotland).

mussel [French *moule*, Italian *vongola*, Spanish *mejillón*], any of several bivalve mollusks. Mussels are often served steamed in white wine.

must or **stum**, *1.* the unfermented juice pressed from grapes (or other fruit) being processed for wine (before and during fermentation); *2.* this unfermented juice in combination with the pulp and skins of the crushed fruit.

mustard, *1.* a pungent yellow powder made from the seeds of any of several common mustards (plants) used as a condiment; compare **black mustard**, **white mustard**; *2.* a condiment consisting of a paste made from powdered mustard seeds mixed with wine, vinegar, or water, and various spices, such as turmeric; *3.* any of several plants cultivated for their seed (see sense 1) or for their foliage; mustard greens are used in salads (they are called *mizuna* in Japanese, *bok choy* or *tat soi* in certain southern Chinese dialects); mustard seed is also called *senvy*. Arugula is an herb of the mustard family.

mustard oil, an oil obtained from mustard seeds and used in salads.

mustard spinach, another name for **Indian mustard**.

mutton, the flesh of a mature sheep used for food (the flesh of a young sheep is called *lamb*); mutton may be used for broth.

mutton chop, a thick chop cut from the loin section of mutton.

mutton corn, roasting ears (of Indian corn), sweet corn that is just ripe enough to be eaten.

muttonfish

---

myrtle

muttonfish or **eelpout** or **mutton snapper** [so called from its flavor], *1.* a species of eelpout of the coastal waters of northeastern North America; *2.* a snapper from the warmer parts of the western Atlantic.

mutton ham, a leg of mutton cured in the same fashion as ham (Scotland).

mutton snapper, another name for **muttonfish**.

Myanmar. The following are among representative dishes and products of Myanmar: rice and curry dishes (Burmese *hin;* many curries include coconut), fish *(nga)* fried in peanut oil, salted fish; dried-fish paste *(ngapi)* used as a sauce; noodles *(kauswe)*, noodles and chicken *(panthay kauswe)*, vermicelli *(mohinga)*, boiled rice *(tamin)*, rice cooked with coconut *(ohn tamin)*.

mycophile, a person whose hobby is picking wild mushrooms for food.

myrtle, an evergreen aromatic shrub having blue-black berries.

nacho [from American Spanish *nacho*, perhaps from Spanish *nacho* "flat-nosed"], a tortilla chip topped with melted cheese and often additional savory toppings (as chili peppers or refried beans) and broiled.

nagami kumquat, or simply **nagami**, a kumquat having oval fruit. Distinguished from **marumi kumquat** (that has round fruit).

namaycush [of Algonquian origin], another name for **lake trout**.

nan [from Hindi *nān*], a round, flat, leavened bread of the Indian subcontinent, usually cooked in a tandoor, sometimes dotted with poppy seeds.

¹**nana** [from Portuguese *naná*], another name for **pineapple**.

²**nana** [from Arabic *n'nā'*], another name for **mint** (sense 1, a plant).

nance or **nanche** [American Spanish, from Nahuatl *nantzi*], the fruit of a tree (likewise called *nance*) and especially of the **golden spoon**. Compare **locust berry**.

nangca or **nangka** [from Tagalog], the jackfruit tree or its fruit (Philippines).

Nanking cherry or **Manchu cherry**, the round, light red fruit of a shrub likewise called *Nanking cherry*.

nannygai, a red Australian fish.

nannyberry, another name for **sheepberry** (a blue-black fruit).

Nantua sauce [from *Nantua*, town of eastern France, on Lake Nantua *(lac de Nantua)*], a cream sauce flavored with shellfish (e.g., crayfish, lobster, shrimp). It may be served on sole fillets or used in sandwich spreads or canapés.

nap (to) [from French *napper* "to cover meat in a sauce," from *nappe* "tablecloth, cover"], to pour or spread a sauce (or gelatin, jam) over a prepared dish (e.g., a meat, a cake).

napoleon or **mille-feuille** [for *Napoleon* I, 1769–1821, French emperor], a rectangular piece of pastry consisting of several layers of puff paste, iced on top, with a filling of custard, cream, or jelly. Compare **Josephine** (a small napoleon).

naranja, Spanish for **orange**.

naranjilla [Spanish "little orange"], *1.* the bright orange fruit of a shrubby herb

cultivated in the uplands of northern South America (especially in Ecuador); *2.* a beverage made from this fruit.

naras, a southern African shrub with a fruit resembling a melon and with edible seeds.

nargil [from Persian *nārgīl* "coconut"], the Indian coconut.

nasturtium [Latin, a kind of cress (underlying idea: "nose twister"), so called because when eaten it causes burning sensations in the nose, from *nasus* "nose" + *tort-*, past stem of *torquere* "to twist"], any of various plants of Central and South America whose pungent leaves and seeds are used as seasoning. Nasturtium leaves are used as greens in salads.

Natal orange [from *Natal*, province of eastern South Africa], the greenish yellow berry of a spiny shrub (likewise called *Natal orange)* of tropical and southern Africa.

Natal plum [from *Natal*, province of eastern South Africa], the scarlet berry of either of two shrubs (likewise called *Natal plum)* of southern Africa.

native, as an adjective referring to indigenous plants or animals.

native cherry, the bright red, edible pedicel (= fruit stalk) of a low Australian tree (likewise called *native cherry).*

native currant, any of several Australian trees bearing berries resembling currants.

native guava, the edible fruit of an Australian tree likewise called *native guava.*

native mulberry, an Australian tree having edible white berries.

native peach, another name for **quandong**.

native pomegranate, the fruit (resembling pomegranate) of any of several Australian plants (likewise called *native pomegranates).*

navarin [from French *navarin* "turnip," joking alteration of *navet* "turnip," based on *Navarin* "Navarino; Pylos," Greek town that became famous for the naval battle of 20 October 1827], a mutton stew prepared with vegetables (e.g., small onions, carrots, turnips, potatoes).

navel orange, or **navel** or **seedless orange** or **California orange**, a sweet, seedless orange having a navellike formation (that can be seen from the outside) at the apex where the fruit encloses a very small secondary fruit.

navy bean [from being, formerly, a standard provision of the United States Navy], another name for **pea bean**.

neapolitan ice cream, or simply **neapolitan** [from *Neapolitan* "of Naples"], a brick of ice cream of from two to four flavors (and colors) in layers, usually including lemon ice or orange ice, and often chocolate, strawberry, vanilla.

nectar, *1.* a beverage of fruit juice and pulp (e.g., apricot) or of blended fruit juices; *2.* the sweetish liquid that is secreted by the nectaries of a plant and that is the chief raw material used by bees for the making of honey.

nectarine, a variety of peach having a smooth skin.

neoza pine [Bhutanese], a Himalayan pine with edible nuts.

Nepal. The following are among representative products of Nepal: meat, such as buffalo, goat, sheep, fowl (including ducks); duck eggs.

neroli oil or **orange-flower oil**, a fragrant oil distilled from orange flowers (especially of the sour orange) and used as a flavoring.

nessberry, a hybrid bramble with fruit of superior flavor produced by crossing a dewberry and a raspberry.

Nesselrode [for Count Karl *Nesselrode*, 1780–1862, Russian diplomat], a mixture of candied fruits (e.g., preserved oranges, cherries), nuts (e.g., chestnuts), and dried fruits, used in puddings, ice cream, or pies.

Nesselrode pie [for Count Karl *Nesselrode*, 1780–1862, Russian diplomat; this pie was invented by his chef], a cream pie filled with mixed preserved fruits (e.g., chopped raisins and cherries, with flour, milk, and whipping cream) and topped with shaved chocolate.

Nesselrode pudding [for Count Karl *Nesselrode*, 1780–1862, Russian diplomat], a frozen pudding (e.g., cabinet pudding) containing chestnuts (sweetened chestnut purée and crumbled glazed chestnuts) and maraschino. It is often garnished with Chantilly.

Netherlands. The following are among representative dishes and products of the Netherlands: pea soup (Dutch *erwtensoep)* with pieces of sausage or pig's knuckle; herring, smoked eel, oysters, small fritters *(poffertjes)*, cheeses (e.g., Edam, Gouda); minced beef *(rolpens)*, usually served with fried apples; asparagus; Indonesian rice table *(rijsttafel*, some fifteen varieties of food served with rice); a dish of vegetables and sausage *(boerenkool met worst); stew (hutspot);* openfaced sandwich *(uitsmijter* "bouncer") of ham or roast beef topped with fried eggs; sandwiches *(broodje)* on rolls; pancakes *(flensjes)*, fruit juice *(vruchtensap)*.

Netherlands Antilles. The following are among representative dishes and products of the Netherlands Antilles (especially Curaçao): conch; kid or lamb and cucumber soup (Papiamento *stobá di concomber);* a soup of fish, corned beef, and coconut cream *(sopito)*, tripe soup *(sopi mondongo)*, cornmeal pudding *(funchi)*, goat stew with papaya chunks *(papaya stobá)*, iguana, fish, stuffed cheese *(keshi yená;* if stuffed with chicken, *keshi yená coe galinja;* if with minced beef, *keshi yená coe carni*; if with shrimp, *keshi yená coe cabaron)*, fried plantain; a mixture of beans and cornmeal *(tutu);* coconut patties *(kokadas; kokada pretu* "black coconut-pattie," because it includes the dark skin of the coconut; *kokada blanku* "white coconut-pattie"); green papaya mixed with anise seeds *(konserbe);* sweet-potato balls *(dushi di batata dushi* "sweet-potato sweets").

netted melon or **nutmeg melon**, a variety of the muskmelon having a rind with a network of lines, and green flesh.

Neufchâtel, or **Neufchâtel cheese** [French, from *Neufchâtel*, France (not the Neuchâtel of western Switzerland)], a white, soft, unripened cheese similar to cream cheese, made from skimmed or whole cow-milk, often with condiments added.

Newburg or **a la Newburg**, served with a sauce made of cream, butter, sherry or Madeira, and egg yolks, and often nutmeg (e.g., seafood, shrimp, lobster Newburg).

New Caledonia. The following are among representative products of New Caledonia: coconuts, yams, taro, bananas, cassava.

New England boiled dinner, another name for **boiled dinner**.

New England clam chowder, a chowder made of minced clams, salt pork (or slices of bacon), minced onions, diced potatoes, and hot milk; butter may be added. It is often served with large crackers. Compare **Manhattan clam chowder** (which is made with water and no milk, and with tomatoes).

New Mexican piñon, a certain nut pine.

New Orleans molasses, a light-colored molasses (sense 1, sugar syrup).

New York cut, (of beef sirloin) cut with the hipbone included.

New Zealand. The following are among representative dishes and products of New Zealand: fish (e.g., whitebait [the young of smelt], trout), shellfish (e.g., oysters, clams, crayfish, scallops, mussels), lamb, beef, pork, venison, duck, dairy products, toheroa soup, mutton bird, sweet potatoes (Maori *kumara*), pork with tree tomatoes *(pork with tamarillos)*, stewed fruit (plums, peaches, apples), rice pudding, sago pudding.

New Zealand blue cod, smoked Australian freshwater catfish.

New Zealand spinach, a coarse herb used as a potherb.

ngaio [Maori], a small evergreen tree of the New Zealand coast, with edible fruit.

ngege, an African food fish.

nib, *1.* a roasted and crushed cacao seed, with germ removed; *2.* a coffee bean.

Nicaragua. The following are among representative dishes and products of Nicaragua: corn, rice, beans, cassava (Spanish *yuca);* tripe *(mondongo)*, tripe soup *(sopa de mondongo);* corn, pork, and rice wrapped in banana leaves *(nacatamal);* rice and beans, fried *(gallo pinto* "mottled rooster"); salted and sun-dried beef with plantain, cassava, and vegetables wrapped in banana leaves and steamed *(bajo);* tropical fruits; a dessert of firm bananas *(maduro en gloria* "heavenly bananas"). Beverage: *tiste* (nonalcoholic, made with corn).

Niçoise [French "of Nice"], prepared with oil, garlic, and onion. See also *salade niçoise* under **France** *(Provence)*.

Nigeria. The following are among representative dishes and products of Nigeria: West African curries, peanuts, palm oil; rice with onions and red peppers *(jollof rice);* vegetable stew with meat and dry fish *(efo);* fried bean cakes *(akara);* steamed bean cakes stuffed with fish and eggs *(moin moin);* greens and dried fish with spices *(ewedu).*

Niger seed [probably from the *Niger* river, West Africa], the seed of the African plant ramtil, that yields an oil used in food.

Niger-seed oil, an oil obtained from the seeds of ramtil and used in food.

nightshade, any of a genus of plants that includes the potato and the eggplant.

Nile perch or **capitaine**, a large fish of the rivers and lakes of northern and central Africa.

nipper, *1.* a certain marine fish (a wrasse); *2.* the large claw of a crustacean; *3.* any of various crabs, shrimps, and prawns.

nispero [from American Spanish *níspero*, from Spanish *níspero* "medlar"], another name for both **sapodilla** and **loquat**.

nixtamal [Mexican Spanish, from Nahuatl, from *nextli* "ashes" + *tamalli* "tamale"], limed kernels of Indian corn (boiled dried corn) that is ready to be ground into masa (mash used in preparing tortillas and tamales).

njave or **djave**, a tropical African tree having an edible fruit and a seed with fat similar to shea butter.

noble cane, any of various sugarcanes with juicy stalks, considered the best of the species.

nocake [Algonquian], a food formerly used by North American Indians, made of Indian corn parched and pounded into a powder.

nockerl [Austrian German, diminutive of *Nock* "a kind of mountain; dumpling"], a rich, light dumpling (a souffléed pancake, a fluffy puff) of Austrian origin (butter, eggs, sugar). It is often served with fruit sauce or fruit.

noekkelost or **nokkelost** [from Norwegian *nøkkelost* "key cheese"; modeled after cheese from Leiden, Netherlands, that was marked with the crossed keys of Leiden's coat of arms], a dark cheese spiced with caraway, cloves, or cumin, or all three.

nog, *1.* another name for **eggnog**; *2.* any of several mixed drinks containing beaten egg and milk, and often spirits.

nogada, Spanish for a sauce made with nuts and spices (used in Spain with certain fishes, in Mexico with stuffed hot peppers). Compare **chile**.

¹**noisette** (noun) [French "hazelnut," by comparison of size], a small rounded morsel of food (e.g., a potato ball browned in butter [when more than one potato ball is served, the dish is called in French *pommes noisette*], a piece of butter the size of a hazelnut, a dish prepared with a small piece of beef or mutton [for instance, a small slice of tenderloin, of lamb, of mutton, of kid, of veal, the eye of a chop]). In French, *noisettes d'agneau* might be lamb roasted with garlic, rosemary, butter.

²**noisette** (adjective), (of meat or of a sauce) prepared with brown butter.

nokkelost, variant of **noekkelost**.

noll-kholl [from Dutch *knolkool* "turnip cabbage"], another name for **kohlrabi** (India).

nombles, variant of **numbles** (which is another name for **umbles**).

nonda or **nonda plum**, an edible plumlike fruit of an Australian tree likewise called *nonda* or *nonda plum*.

nondairy, containing no milk or milk products.

nondo, an tall plant found in eastern North America, having an aromatic root.

nonfat, having fat removed or lacking it from the first.

nonpareil [French "(having) no equal, peerless"], *1.* small sugar pellets of various colors used in decorating cookies or cakes or in covering candy; *2.* a disk or drop of chocolate covered with white sugar-pellets.

¹**noodle** [from German *Nudel*] or **lokshen** (Yiddish), a thin ribbonlike strip of pasta made with eggs and flour. Noodles and spaghettis are cooked in the same way as macaroni (i.e., they are boiled). Noodles can be served boiled, and as casserole, lasagne, ring, or with poppy seeds or veal steak; they are also used in lo mein; noodles Romanoff are made with cottage cheese and sour cream, and minced onion and garlic.

²**noodle** (**to**), to feed geese forcibly with a long roll of fattening mixture.

nopal [Spanish, from Nahuatl *nohpalli*], a cactus of Mexico and Central America, similar to the prickly pear. Its fruit is called *tuna* and in Spain *higo chumbo*. The leaves, with thorns removed, are cooked in Mexico and eaten as a salad called *nopalitos* (literally = "little nopals"); when served in their own broth, they are called *nopales navegantes* "sailing nopals."

nori, see **amanori**.

normal honey, honey produced from flower nectars (distinguished from honey produced from honeydew [saccharine deposit on the leaves of plants]).

normand, see **trou normand**.

normande [French "from Normandy (region of northwestern France)" (feminine)], prepared with any of various foods associated with Normandy (e.g., cream, apple, cider, oysters, mushrooms, crayfish).

Normande sauce or **Normandy sauce** [from French *normande* "from Normandy (region of northwestern France)" (feminine)], a white sauce made of fish stock (and butter, flour), flavored with wine (or lemon juice) and enriched with cream and egg yolks. May also have mushroom juice, mussels, shrimp. Used especially with fish.

northern anchovy, an anchovy of the Pacific coast of North America.

northern black currant, the edible black fruit of a shrub (likewise called *northern black currant)* of northern North America.

Northern Spy, a large, yellowish-red, apple.

northern sucker, a sucker (fish) of northern North America.

Norway. The following are among representative dishes and products of Norway: open-faced sandwiches (Norwegian *smørbrød* "butter bread"), salmon *(laks;* e.g., smoked or poached), halibut *(kveite)*, herring *(sild)*, fish soup *(fiskesuppe)*, trout (e.g., fried in sour cream), lobster, crayfish, shrimp, venison (e.g., reindeer steak [*rensdyrstek*]), game birds (e.g., grouse, woodcock, wild duck, ptarmigan [*fjellrype*]), cured leg of mutton *(fenalår);* a combination of meat, potatoes, and other vegetables *(lapskaus)*, cured ham *(spekespinke)*, a stew of lamb and cabbage *(får i kål)*, cheese *(ost)*.

Norway lobster, a lobster of European seas.

nougat [French, Provençal "nutty, having nuts"], a confection made by mixing nuts (e.g., almonds, walnuts, hazelnuts, pistachios) or sometimes fruit pieces in a sugar or honey paste whose composition is varied to give either a chewy (French *nougat mou)* or a brittle (French *nougat dur)* consistency. Egg whites are also used. The Spanish equivalent is *turrón (de Jijona* when soft, *de Alicante* when hard).

nougatine, a chocolate with a nougat center.

nouvelle cuisine [French "new cooking"], a form of usually French cuisine that stresses lightness (uses light sauces and little flour or fat) and freshness (uses seasonal produce).

numbles or **nombles**, another name for **umbles**. Compare **giblet**.

nut, *1*. a hard-shelled dry fruit or seed with a separable rind or shell and interior kernel or meat; note: botanically, some edible tree capsules and herb seeds that in English have the element *nut* in their name (e.g., Brazil nuts, peanuts) are not considered true nuts; *2*. or **nutmeat**, the kernel of a nut (sense 1); *3.* a dry one-seeded fruit (e.g., chestnut, hazelnut) with a woody pericarp; *4.* a rounded cake or biscuit (e.g., doughnut, spice nut). Nuts (in a wider sense) include almonds, cashew nuts, coconuts, filberts, pecans, pistachios, walnuts; they can be roasted and salted, ground, grated, used in salads, cakes, cookies, candy, toppings, breads (loaves, rolls), ice cream, parfaits, waffles.

nut brittle, see **brittle**.

nutburger, a patty containing ground nuts.

nutcake, *1.* a cake containing nuts; *2.* another name for a **doughnut**.

nut grass, a sedge that has slender rootstocks bearing small, edible, nutlike tubers.

nut margarine, margarine made from nut oils (chiefly from coconut and peanut oils) churned with sour milk and often salt.

nutmeat, the edible kernel of a nut.

nutmeg, the hard, aromatic seed of an evergreen tree (likewise called *nutmeg*), used as a spice when grated or ground (e.g., on eggnog). Compare **mace**.

nutmeg melon, another name for **netted melon**.

nutmeg oil, an oil distilled from nutmegs and used in flavoring.

nut oil, an oil obtained from nuts (e.g., peanut oil, walnut oil).

nut palm, a palmlike Australian plant having edible seeds.

nut pine, a pine with edible seeds (e.g., any of several piñons).

olla   origanum

obley

opakapaka

osoberry

orangelo

oyster nut

oarweed, any of several large brown algae.

oat, see **oats**.

oatcake, a thin flattened cake made of oatmeal mixed with water, milk, or buttermilk and cooked on a griddle or in an oven (i.e., baked).

oaten, made (said, for instance, of bread) of oat grain or of oatmeal.

oatmeal, *1.* meal made by grinding oats from which the husks have been removed; *2.* rolled oats or ground oats; *3.* a porridge made from rolled or ground oats.

oats or **oat** [French *avoine*, Italian, Latin, and Spanish *avena*], the edible seeds of a certain plant (a cereal grass likewise called *oats*).

obley, a small flat cake or wafer.

O'Brien potatoes, diced potatoes sautéed in butter and dressed with chopped sweet pepper.

oca or **oka** [from Spanish *oca*, from Quechua *oqa*], the edible tuber of either of two South American wood sorrels (likewise called *ocas* or *okas*).

ocean perch, any of several marine fishes.

ocean whitefish, a large fish of the Americas found along the warmer parts of the Pacific coast.

octopus [from Greek *oktōpous* "eight-footed"; French *poulpe, pieuvre*, Spanish *pulpo*], any of numerous marine mollusks that have eight tentacles (muscular arms), each bearing two rows of suckers. They secrete a dark, inky fluid and are often served in their own "ink." Compare **squid** (that has 10 arms).

oenomel [from Greek *oinomeli* "wine honey"], a beverage of ancient Greece, consisting of wine and honey.

offal, the viscera (e.g., brain, heart, liver, sweetbreads) and trimmings (e.g., blood, head meat, tail, skin) of a butchered animal that are removed in dressing and that are used as edible products.

oil or **olio** (Italian), any of various unctuous, liquid substances of vegetable origin used in cooking and flavoring. A classification of some vegetable oils, according to the type of fat:

saturated fat: palm oil (people also get such fat from butter, cheese, cream, red meat)

unsaturated fat (two kinds):

• monounsaturated fat (olive oil, canola [rapeseed] oil);

• polyunsaturated fat (safflower, sunflower, corn, and soybean oils).

Compare **fat** (sense 3).

oilfish, another name for **escolar**.

oil nut, another name for **butternut**, especially for this nut with its husks pickled.

oilseed, any of various seeds that yield oil (e.g., sesame, cottonseed).

oily bean or **oily grain**, another name for **sesame**.

o'io [Hawaiian], another name for **bonefish** (Hawaii).

Oka [from Canadian French *oka*, from *Oka*, village in Quebec, province of eastern Canada, where this cheese is made], a cheese made by Trappist monks in Quebec.

okra [West African] or **gobo** or **lady's finger**, *1.* the mucilaginous, green pods of a tropical and semitropical plant (likewise called *okra*), used as the basis of soups and stews and as a vegetable. The pods can also be pickled; *2.* another name for **gumbo** (sense 2, a dish prepared with okra pods).

old Ned, home-cured salt pork or bacon.

oldwife, any of several marine fishes (e.g., an alewife, a triggerfish).

oleo, short for *oleomargarine*, which is another name for **margarine**.

oleo oil, *1.* a butter-like oil obtained from edible tallow (e.g., beef fat) and used in making margarine; *2.* any of various other oils (e.g., a hydrogenated vegetable oil) so used.

¹**olio**, Italian for **oil**.

²**olio**, another name for **olla podrida**.

olive, the small ovoid fruit of an evergreen tree (likewise called *olive*), eaten as a pickle or relish either when unripe and green or when bluish black and ripe; it is also a source of oil.

olive oil, oil pressed from the pulp of olives (see **olive**) used in salad dressings and in cooking.

olives, small slices of meat (e.g., of veal) seasoned, rolled up, and cooked.

olla [Spanish "pot"], another name for **olla podrida**.

olla podrida [Spanish "rotten pot"] or **pote**, a seasoned stew or soup made of one or more meats (e.g., beef, bacon) and several vegetables usually including chick-peas and potatoes. In Spain, an *olla podrida* is slightly different from an *olla* in that the former includes, in addition, ham, fowl, and sausages. In Spanish, both an *olla* and an *olla podrida* are also called *cocido* "cooked". The French term *pot pourri* (see **potpourri**) is a translation of Spanish *olla podrida*.

olykoek [from Dutch *ollekoek*, from *olle* "oil cake"], another name for **doughnut**.

Olympia oyster or **Olympia** [from *Olympia*, capital of the state of Washington, United States, on Puget Sound], a flavorful oyster of the Puget Sound area (North America).

omelet or **omelette** [from French *omelette*], a dish consisting of eggs beaten to a froth, cooked without stirring until set, and served folded in half, often around a filling (e.g., cheese, mushrooms, fines herbes, spinach, ham, shredded fish, chopped parsley, salami, chopped cooked spinach, jelly, asparagus, oysters, crab, shrimp). Compare **French omelet** (which has lightly beaten eggs), **frittata** (which is unfolded), **Spanish omelet** (which has a sauce made of tomato, onion, and green pepper folded in or poured over the top), **Western omelet** (which has chopped onion and ham mingled with the egg yolks). In French, an *omelette norvégienne* is a kind of baked Alaska —a dessert consisting of ice cream completely covered with a hot soufflé.

onion [from French *oignon*], the rounded, pungent bulb of a plant (likewise called *onion)* of the lily family, made up of concentric layers, that has a strong, sharp smell and taste and that is widely used as a vegetable. Compare **chives, garlic, leek, shallot**. Onions can be served creamed, escalloped, fried, French fried, glazed, sautéed, stuffed baked, in the form of rings, of soup au gratin.

onion ring, a ring of sliced onion coated with batter or crumbs and fried.

onion soup is made with thinly sliced onions, and bouillon (= beef stock), in baking dishes, with dried (in a heated oven; not toasted) slices of bread on top, sprinkled with grated Swiss cheese.

oolong [from Chinese *wūlóng* "black dragon"], a dark Chinese tea made from leaves that have been partially fermented before firing. Compare **black tea**.

opah or **moonfish** or **San Pedro Fish**, a large marine fish having edible red flesh.

opakapaka [Hawaiian], any of several Hawaiian snappers (fishes).

opaleye or **greenfish**, a small, green [it feeds chiefly on seaweeds] shore fish of the California coast.

open sandwich, one slice of bread covered with food.

opihi [Hawaiian], any of several edible limpets (mollusks).

opium poppy, a poppy (plant) cultivated since antiquity as the source of opium (obtained from the juice of its unripe pods) and for its edible oily seeds (that are used as a food; see **poppy seed**).

opossum, any of various marsupials (mammals whose female has a pouch on the abdomen) of the Western Hemisphere.

opuntia, any of various cacti (desert plants) with pulpy edible fruits, including the prickly pears.

orache, any of various herbs, some of which are used as potherbs, especially the **garden orache**.

orange [French] or **naranja** [Spanish], a round, tropical or subtropical fruit that is technically a berry, with a reddish yellow rind used in confectionery, preserves, and cookery and with a pulp having a sweetish, acid juice.

orangeade, a beverage of orange juice mixed with plain or soda water and with sugar.

orangeado [from French *orangeat*], an archaic word for finely chopped candied orange peel.

orange drink, a beverage produced by distillation of orange oils and citric acid with sugar and water.

orange-flower oil, another name for **neroli oil**.

orangelo [from *orang*e + pom*elo*], a citrus fruit that is a cross of an orange and a pomelo.

orange melon, another name for **mango melon**.

orange oil or **sweet orange oil**, oil from the peel of the sweet orange, used as a flavor.

orange peel, the peel of an orange.

orange pekoe, tea made from the smallest and youngest leaves of the shoot.

orange rockfish, a rockfish found from Puget Sound to southern California (western United States).

oregano [from Spanish *orégano* "wild marjoram," from Latin *origanum*] or **sweet marjoram**, *1*. a bushy mint used as a seasoning; *2*. an herb seasoning made from the dried leaves of a species of marjoram called in Spanish *orégano*.

Oregon grape, the small, bluish-black berry of an evergreen shrub likewise called *Oregon grape*.

organ meat, an edible part of a slaughter animal that consists of an internal organ or forms part of one (e.g., the brain, heart, kidney, liver).

¹**orgeat** or **sirop d'orgeat** [from French *orgeat*, from *orge* "barley" (the syrup used to be prepared from barley)], a sweet, nonalcoholic syrup of almond and orange used as a flavor in drinks and food.

²**orgeat,** a nonalcoholic beverage prepared from the sweetened juice of almonds (originally from barley) and other flavorings (e.g., orange blossom essence, rose water) with water added and usually served cold.

Oriental mustard, another name for **Indian mustard**.

origan [from Latin *origanum* "wild marjoram"], any of several aromatic mints (e.g., wild marjoram).

origanum [Latin "wild marjoram"], any of several fragrant aromatic mints, especially oregano, used as seasonings in cookery.

ortolan [French, or Italian *ortolano* "of gardens," from Latin *hortolus* "small garden," diminutive of *hortus* "garden"], an Old World bunting (bird) commonly netted and fattened for a table delicacy.

orzo [Italian "barley"], rice-shaped pasta.

osoberry, the blue-black fruit resembling a cherry of a shrub (likewise called *osoberry)* of the rose family (California and Oregon, United States).

osso buco [from Italian *ossobuco* "marrowbone, veal shank," literally = "pierced bone"], a dish of Milanese origin, of veal shanks (served with the bone) braised with vegetables (tomato, parsley, garlic, grated lemon peel), white wine, and seasoned stock. It may be garnished with risotto or with fried chipolata (a sausage).

ost, Danish for **cheese**.

ostrich, a swift-footed, flightless African bird that is the largest of existing birds and often attains a weight of 140 kilograms (308 pounds).

Otaheite apple or **Jew plum** or **viapple** [from *Otaheite* (now Tahiti), island in the southern Pacific] or **macupa**, the fruit of a Polynesian tree likewise called *Otaheite apple*.

Otaheite gooseberry [from *Otaheite* (now Tahiti), island in the southern Pacific], the fruit of a tropical African and Asiatic tree likewise called *Otaheite gooseberry*.

ouricury or **aricuri** or **ouricuri** (from Portuguese *aricuri*, *ouricuri*, from Tupi), either of two Brazilian palms.

ouricury oil, an edible oil obtained from the kernels of the fruit of an ouricury palm.

over, (of eggs) fried on both sides.

overcooked, cooked too much.

overdo (to), to cook too much or too long.

ox, a domestic bovine mammal especially an adult castrated male. Compare **steer**.

oxcheek, an ox's cheek especially when cut for meat.

¹**oxheart**, any of various large, juicy cherries shaped somewhat like a heart.

²**oxheart** or **oxheart cabbage**, any of various cabbages with oval or conical head.

oxtail, the tail of a beef animal, especially the skinned tail used for food (e.g., in soup or stew).

oyster, *1.* any of various marine mollusks, chiefly of shallow waters. It can be eaten fresh on the half shell, or can be prepared au gratin, creamed, fried, French fried, scalloped, as a bisque, soup, or stew, or used in stuffings (compare **angels on horseback**, **devils on horseback**). In New Orleans, an *oyster loaf* is a small loaf of French bread, split open, rubbed with butter and garlic and filled with fried oysters; *2.* a small mass of muscle, regarded as a delicacy, found in the hollow of the pelvic bone on each side of the back of a fowl.

oyster agaric, another name for **oyster mushroom**.

oyster cracker, a small, salted, usually round cracker for serving with oyster stew and soups.

oyster mushroom or **oyster fungus** or **oyster agaric**, a certain edible agaric.

oyster nut, an East African climbing plant having large, edible, nutlike seeds; these seeds yield an oil similar to olive oil.

oyster plant, another name for **salsify**.

oysters Rockefeller [for John Davison *Rockefeller*, 1839–1937, American oil magnate], a dish of oysters on the half shell baked with various toppings typically including chopped spinach and a seasoned sauce.

oyster stew, see ¹**stew**.

pepo

pancetta

pekoe

provolette

pahutan

palometa

perciatelli

pablum [from *Pablum*, a trademark for an infant cereal, based on Latin *pabulum* "food"], food for infants.

pabulum [from Latin *pabulum* "food"], food, nutrient.

paca [Portuguese and Spanish, from Tupi *páka*], a rodent of northern South America.

pacay [Spanish, from Quechua *pa'qay*], a small tropical American tree cultivated in Bolivia, Ecuador, and Peru for the white edible pulp of its large pods.

pacaya [from American Spanish *pacaya*], any of various Central American palms having spadices (floral spikes) eaten as vegetables.

Pacific cultus, another name for **lingcod**.

Pacific mackerel or **greenback mackerel**, a fish of the Pacific coast of North America resembling the mackerel of the Atlantic.

Pacific sardine, a fish of the Pacific coast of North America used for canning and for production of fish meals and fish oils.

paddlefish or **shovelfish**, a large fish of the Mississipi River basin having a long, paddle-shaped snout, flesh which though coarse is used as food, and roe that is made into caviar.

paella [Catalan "pot, frying pan"], a Spanish dish (originally from the area of Valencia, and often called in Spanish *paella valenciana*) containing saffron-flavored rice with varying combinations of seafood, chicken, meat, and vegetables.

pahua [Marquesan], another name for the **giant clam**.

pahutan or **paho** [from Tagalog *pahútan, páho*], a Philippine mango tree bearing fruit that is often pickled.

paillard [French, from *Paillard*, late 19th-century French restaurateur], a slice of beef or veal pounded thin and quickly grilled or sautéed.

pain, French for **bread**.

pakchoi or **bok choy** [from Cantonese *baahk-choi* "white vegetable" corresponding to Chinese *bái cài*], other names for **Chinese cabbage**.

189

Pakistan. The following are representative dishes and products of Pakistan: curries, pilafs, kabobs, meat balls (Urdu *kofta*), biryani; chicken *(murgh)* masala; mutton, seafood; sweetbreads cooked in milk and honey *(shahi tukra)*, melon, coconut, raisins. Beverage: tea.

palatable, agreeable to the palate or taste, of sufficiently pleasant flavor to be eaten.

palm, any of various chiefly tropical evergreen trees. Compare **betel palm, cabbage palm, coconut palm, palmyra, sugar palm**.

palm crab, another name for **purse crab**.

palm honey, a sweet table syrup used as a substitute for sugar (Chile); it is the boiled sap of the coquito.

palmito, Spanish for **cabbage palm** and for **heart of palm**.

palm oil, an edible fatty oil obtained from the flesh of the crushed nuts of any of several palms, used in the manufacture of chocolates (sense 2, small candies).

palm sugar, a brown sugar made from the sap of any of various palm trees.

palmyra or **palmyra palm** [from Portuguese *palmeira* "palm tree," from *palma* "palm tree"], a tall palm of tropical Asia widely cultivated in India for its sugar-rich sap and large edible fruits.

palolo [Samoan or Tongan], a worm that burrows in the coral reefs of various Pacific islands (especially the Samoas and Fiji) and swarms (only the posterior body portions) at the surface of the water for breeding annually in October and November when these palolo end portions are gathered (fished for, using baskets) and used as food.

paloma, any of various sharks used as food (Southwest of the United States).

palometa [Spanish, diminutive of *paloma* "dove"], *1.* any of several pompanos; *2.* any of various butterfishes.

palta [South American Spanish, from Quechua], another name for **avocado**.

pampelmoes [from Afrikaans *pompelmoosje*], a large butterfish of the West coast of Africa and the Mediterranean.

¹**pan** [from Hindi *pān*, from Sanskrit *parṇa* "wing; feather; leaf"], *1.* the leaf of the betel palm, used to enclose the preparation described in sense 2; *2.* a preparation of betel nut that is sliced and rolled in betel leaf mixed with a little shell lime and is used for chewing in the Orient.

²**pan**, Spanish for **bread**.

panaché [French "variegated"], comprised of several foods (e.g., mixed vegetables or fruits). In French, a *glace panachée* is ice cream of several flavors.

panada [from Spanish *pan* "bread"], *1.* a paste or gruel made of flour or bread crumbs or toast combined with milk or stock or water and used for soups, as a base for sauce, or for a binder for forcemeat or stuffing; *2.* a dish made of bread boiled to a pulp in milk, broth, or water, often variously seasoned or flavored.

Panama. The following are representative dishes and products of Panama: arroz con pollo; chicken (or other meat) and yam (Spanish *ñame)* stew *(sancocho);* tamales, rice with shellfish, marinated fish, fried plantain slices *(patacones de plátano verde)*, rice and beans *(gallo pinto* "mottled rooster"); shredded meat and tomato stew *(ropa vieja* "old clothes").

panatela [from Spanish *pan* "bread"], American Spanish for a long, thin biscuit, and for bread pudding.

pan-broil (**to**), to cook (usually meat) uncovered over direct heat (on top of the range) on a hot metal surface (e.g., in a heated, heavy frying pan) with no fat or only enough fat to prevent sticking, pouring off grease as it accumulates. Distinguished from frying (which uses more fat). See also **broil**.

pancake or **drop scone** or **flapjack** or **slapjack** or **griddle cake** or **hotcake** or **battercake**, a flat cake made of thin batter (the flour may be of wheat or buckwheat) enriched with eggs, milk, or cream and cooked (e.g., on a griddle or in a pan) on both sides until brown, sometimes rolled up with a sweet or savory filling (e.g., blueberry, cheese, corn, nuts, potato, prunes, raisins); cinnamon and other spices, cardamom and caraway seeds, buttermilk or sour milk may be added. Compare **crêpe Suzette**.

pancetta [Italian "little belly," diminutive of *pancia* "belly, paunch"], unsmoked bacon used especially in Italian cuisine. It is a specialty of the Parma area.

pancreas, a large gland of vertebrates (compare **beef bread**, **sweetbread**).

pandowdy or **apple pandowdy**, a deep-dish apple dessert (sliced apples) that is spiced, usually sweetened with molasses, but also with sugar or maple syrup, and covered with a biscuit crust (it has a top crust only) and baked, and that is served warm with a sauce or cold with the crust cut into the apples.

pan dulce [American Spanish "sweet bread"], a raisin bun or other sweet bread.

pane, Italian for **bread**.

pané, [French], "breaded."

panela [Mexican Spanish, diminutive of Spanish *pan* "bread; loaf"], brown sugar in round loaves.

panettone [Italian, from *panetto* "small loaf," diminutive of *pane* "bread"], a holiday bread or cake (originally from Milan, Italy), made with eggs, sugar, flour, leavening, butter, containing raisins and candied fruit peels.

[1]**panfish**, any fish small enough to be fried whole in a pan (e.g., a sunfish, bluegill, white crappie).

[2]**panfish**, another name for **king crab**.

panforte [Italian "strong bread," from *pane* "bread" + *forte* "strong"], a holiday bread (originally from Siena, Italy) that is hard in texture and is made with honey (or sugar), nuts (typically almonds), candied fruit peels, and flour.

panfry (**to**), to cook in a frying pan (a skillet) with a small amount of fat, to sauté. Distinguished from **deep-fry** (which is cooking by *immersing* in fat). Compare [2]**fry**.

panga [Afrikaans], a small fish of southern Africa.

pan gravy, gravy consisting of juices extracted from meat in cooking (not thickened). Distinguished from **gravy** (which is made by thickening the juices).

panic, *1.* another name for **panic grass**; *2.* the edible grain of many panic grasses.

panic grass, any of various grasses grown for grain.

panocha [Mexican Spanish "raw sugar," from Spanish *panocha* "ear of maize"] or **penuche**, a coarse grade of Mexican sugar. See also **penuche**.

pansit [Tagalog], a Chinese noodle dish (Philippines).

pantile, another name for **hardtack**.

pap, a soft or semiliquid food (e.g., of bread boiled or softened in milk or water) as for infants or invalids.

¹**papa**, variant of **papaw** (sense 2, custard apple).

²**papa** [American Spanish "potato," from Quechua], another name for **potato**.

papagallo [from Spanish *papagayo* "parrot," from its many colors] or **roosterfish**, a large fish of tropical waters of the eastern Pacific Ocean, having bright colors.

papaia, variant of **papaya**.

papain or **papayotin**, an enzyme capable of digesting protein obtained, usually as a brownish powder, from the juice of the unripe fruit of the papaya and used as a tenderizer for meat.

papaw or **pawpaw** [probably from Spanish *papaya*], *1.* other names for **papaya**; *2.* also **papa**, **custard apple**, **false banana**, the yellow, fleshy fruit of a tree of central North America (likewise called *papaw* or *custard apple*).

papaya or **papaia** [from Spanish *papaya*] or **lechosa** or **melonfruit** or **mummy apple** or **papaw**, the large, oblong, yellow fruit of an evergreen tropical American tree (likewise called *papaya*), that has a pulpy flesh and is eaten raw, boiled as a vegetable, pickled, or preserved.

papayotin [from *papaya*], another name for **papain**.

papelon [from American Spanish *papelón*, from Spanish *papelón* "thin cardboard," augmentative of *papel* "paper" (this sugar is hardened in cardboard molds)], brown sugar produced in northern South America.

papillote [French, from *papillon* "butterfly"], *1.* a greased (with oil or butter) wrapper or oiled parchment, usually paper, in which certain foods (e.g., meat, fish) are baked and served. *En papillote* (French *en papillotes*) is the phrase used after the name of the food so cooked, which can be, for instance, cutlet, lamb chop, pompano, quail, red mullet.

paprika [Hungarian, ultimately from Latin *piper* "pepper"], *1.* a usually mild red condiment, less pungent than ordinary red pepper, consisting of the dried, ground pods of various cultivated sweet red peppers. Goulash is seasoned mainly with paprika; *2.* a sweet pepper used for making this condiment.

paradise nut, another name for **sapucaia nut**.

Paraguay. The following are representative dishes and products of Paraguay: chicken or beef puchero; broth with corn flour balls (Guarani *borí borí);* baked corn-cake with cheese and onion (Spanish *sopa paraguaya);* charqui; pickled and fried spareribs (Spanish *costil-*

las de cerdo en vinagre); pasta; cornmeal rolls stuffed with cheese (Guarani *chipa),* beef on spit (Spanish *asado),* rice, cassava, sweet potatoes, peanuts.

Paraguay tea, another name for **maté.**

Para nut [from *Pará,* state of northern Brazil], another name for **Brazil nut.**

parasol mushroom, a certain long-stalked, white, edible mushroom.

parboil (to) or **to parcook,** to cook partially by boiling briefly. This is done in water or, for shellfish, in their own juices. The cooking is usually completed by another method. Meat, such as kidneys or game, may be parboiled to remove some of the strong flavor before the cooking is completed by braising, broiling, fricasséeing, or frying. Compare **scald.**

parboiled rice, rice that has been soaked, steamed, and dried before milling (to retain certain vitamins and improve the cooking quality).

parch (to), to toast or brown (e.g., corn, peas) with dry heat, to roast superficially.

parfait [French "perfect"], *1.* a flavored custard containing whipped cream and syrup frozen together without stirring (examples of flavors: cherry, vanilla, even poppy); *2.* a cold dessert made of layers of fruit, syrup, different flavors of ice cream or ices, and whipped cream.

pargo [Portuguese or Spanish], *1.* the European porgy (fish); *2.* any of various snappers (fishes).

parkin, a kind of gingerbread or cake made of rolled oats, butter, molasses, flour, milk, and ginger (leavened with baking powder), especially popular in Scotland and northern England. Compare **tharfcake.**

parliament cake, a ginger cookie.

Parmentier or **Parmentière** [from French *parmentier* (feminine *parmentière*), from Antoine *Parmentier,* French horticulturist (1737–1813) who popularized the cultivation of potatoes in France], made with or accompanied by potatoes.

Parmesan or **grana** or **grana cheese** or **Parmesan cheese** [from *Parmesan* "of Parma (city of northern Italy)," from Italian *parmigiano,* from *Parma*], a hard, dry Italian cheese with a sharp flavor, made with skim milk, typically used grated to season other foods (e.g., pasta, asparagus, sauces); also grated it can be used to coat other foods (e.g., veal cutlets).

parmigiana or **parmigiano** [from Italian *(alla) parmigiana* "(in) Parma (fashion)," from *parmigiano* "Parmesan," from *Parma,* city of northern Italy], made or covered with Parmesan cheese. In Italian *parmigiana* is a baked dish of eggplant, tomato sauce, and Parmesan; *alla parmigiana* is used of any food cooked with butter and Parmesan cheese.

parmigiano, another name for **Parmesan.**

parr, a young salmon during the first two years of its life when it has parr marks (dark traverse bands) on its sides and feeds in fresh water.

¹**parsley** (noun), an herb of the carrot family, cultivated for its leaves that are used as a garnish and for seasoning.

²**parsley** (adjective) or **parsleyed** or **parslied,** dressed or flavored with parsley (e.g., of butter, onions, potatoes).

parsnip, the long, white, tapered, edible root of a strong-scented herb (likewise called *parsnip*) of the carrot family.

partan, a certain European crab.

partridge or **perdiz** [Spanish] or **perdue** [French], any of various game birds; they may be served pan-broiled, baked, stewed with olives.

Pascal celery or **pascal celery**, any of several types of cultivated celeries having long, firm, green, unblanched stalks.

passionflower [16th-century Spanish missionaries in the New World tropics fancied a resemblance between parts of the flower of this vine and certain particulars of the *Passion* "the sufferings of Jesus between the night of the Last Supper and his Crucifixion and death": the curling tendrils stood for the whips with which the Roman soldiers scourged Jesus; the five-parted leaves represented the clutching hands of the soldiers; the corona corresponded to the crown of thorns; the five stamens symbolized the five wounds; the three-part, knoblike stigma was a reminder of the nails; and the five sepals and five petals signified the ten faithful apostles. These resemblances can best be seen in some of the many species, e.g. in *Passiflora caerulea* (native of southern Brazil)], any of various climbing vines bearing edible fruit called *passion fruit*. Compare **Jamaica honeysuckle**.

passion fruit, the edible fruit (a pulpy berry) of a passionflower. Certain passion fruits are also called *granadillas*.

pasta [Italian "dough, paste"], *1.* or **paste** or **alimentary paste** or **Italian paste**, a shaped dough made of semolina, farina, or wheat flour, or a mixture of these, with water, usually dried, as in spaghetti, macaroni, fettuccine (which is the word used in the area of Rome for what elsewhere in Italy is called *tagliatelle*), vermicelli, and noodles, or in the form of fresh dough, as in ravioli; *2.* a prepared dish of cooked pasta (sense 1).

Sometimes soybean flour is added to the wheat flour; the finest pasta products are made from durum semolina. Smaller pasta is often served in broth (in Italian, *pasta in brodo*), the other is prepared with a sauce and no broth (and called in Italian *pasta asciutta*). Compare **al dente**. The sauce can be made with one of the following main ingredients: hot melted butter (in Italian, *al burro*), garlic and oil, tomato, mussels or other seafood, meat, mushrooms, cream, or the sauce can be Bolognese, marinara, carbonara, amatriciana, and pasta may also be served with meatballs; grated cheese (e.g., Parmesan, Romano, American) may be sprinkled on it. Pasta may be baked, boiled, creamed, sautéed.

Some pasta forms include angel-hair pasta, cappelletti, fettuccine, fusilli, lasagna, linguine, macaroni, noodles, pastina, perciatelli, ravioli, spaghetti, spaghettini, tagliarini, tagliatelle, tortellini, vermicelli.

pasta filata cheese [from Italian *pasta filata* "spun paste"], a cheese distinguished by plasticity of the curd while it is being stretched and shaped by hand (e.g., caciocavallo, mozzarella, provolone).

paste [from Late Latin *pasta* "dough, paste"], *1.* a smooth dough of water and flour, containing fat (butter or other shortening) and used in making pastry crust and fancy rolls (e.g., brioches); *2.* a food that has been pounded until it is reduced to a smooth, creamy mass (e.g., almond, anchovy, sardine, tomato pastes); *3.* a sweet, jelly-like, doughy candy or confection made by evaporating fruit (e.g., figs) with sugar or by flavoring a gelatin, starch, or gum arabic preparation; *4.* [translation of Italian *pasta*], another name for **pasta** (sense 1, alimentary paste).

pasteurization [from the process having been invented by French chemist Louis *Pasteur*, 1822–1895], the process of destroying most disease-producing microorganisms in milk and other liquids by partial or complete sterilization, or, for other perishable food products (e.g., fish, fruit), by radiation (e.g., gamma rays).

pastilla or **bstilla**, a Moroccan dish perhaps of Andalusian origin; it is a large pigeon-pie (that may be made instead with small broilers or larger chickens). Eggs and pigeon (or chicken) constitute the filling of the pie; they are placed, with spices, between puff-paste sheets.

pastille [French], an aromatic lozenge, a flavored tablet.

pastina [Italian "tiny pasta" or "tiny dough"], very small pasta used in soup or as baby food.

pastrami [from Yiddish *pastrame*, from Romanian *pastramă* "pressed and cured meat," from *păstra* "to preserve"], a highly seasoned, smoked cut of beef, usually from the shoulder or the breast.

pastry, *1.* a baked paste of flour, water, salt, and shortening (e.g., lard, vegetable shortening, butter), used for the crusts of pies, tarts, and the like); chilling before baking is desirable, especially for puff paste; *2.* sweet baked goods made of dough having a high fat content (paste dough), as cakes, Danish pastry, dumplings, French pastry, Josephines, pies, tartlets, tarts, turnovers; *3.* a piece of pastry (baked goods) made of the dough described in sense 2.

pastry flour, a flour made with soft wheat (which is low in gluten content) milled very fine; this flour is especially suitable for making pastry (sense 2) and cake (sense 1, sweet baked food).

pastry shell, a shell (covering, outer case) of puff pastry made to hold a creamed filling.

pasty, *1.* a pie consisting of a seasoned meat (or fish) and vegetable mixture or fruit filling wholly surrounded with a crust made of a sheet of paste dough and often baked without a dish. Compare **Cornish pasty**; *2.* another name for **turnover**.

patashte [from American Spanish *pataxte*, *pataste*, from Maya], the cocoa (a chocolate substitute) obtained from a tropical American tree (likewise called *patashte*) resembling cacao.

patauá oil [from Portuguese *patauá*, a Brazilian palm], an oil obtained from the fruit of a Brazilian palm. It is similar to olive oil.

pâté [French], *1.* a pie, patty, or pasty containing meat (e.g., duck, veal, fish [for instance, salmon, shellfish (e.g., oysters)], game [for instance, hare, sweetbreads]), poultry, vegetables, or a mixture. In French, a *pâté en croûte* is one covered with a crust (flour, butter, egg, salt, water) and baked; without a crust, it is often served cold in a terrine (sense 1). A *pâté de campagne* is often made with pork, spices, herbs, onions; *2.* a spread (a paste) of mashed spiced meat (e.g., chicken or goose liver).

pâté de foie gras [French "pâté (or paste) of fat liver"], a paste of fat goose

195

or duck liver (compare **foie gras**) and truffles sometimes with added fat pork. The liver is obtained by overfeeding geese and ducks by force (the ancient Romans used to fatten them with figs). Dishes using pâté de foie gras include beef Wellington. It may also be prepared en croûte, as a mousse, truffled, with mushrooms, with steamed apples.

patent flour, a high-grade wheat flour that is free from bran (highly milled) and consists of the nutritive tissue of the grains.

patisserie or **pâtisserie** [from French *pâtisserie*], baked dessert pastry, especially **French pastry**.

Patna rice [from *Patna*, city of northeastern India, on the Ganges], a rice with a long, thin, and cylindrical grain, that originated in the Ganges valley of India.

patola [Tagalog], a dishcloth gourd (the fruit of a gourd, that has a fibrous interior used like a sponge when dried) that is eaten cooked or green (Philippines).

patty [from French *pâté*], *1.* a little pie or pasty; *2.* a small, flat cake of chopped or minced food (e.g., ground meat, for a hamburger patty). It may be a patty shell of puff pastry filled with a creamed mixture of chicken, fish, pork, lamb; *3.* a small, flat candy (e.g., of peppermint); *4.* another name for **patty shell**.

patty shell, a shell of baked puff pastry made to be filled with creamed meat, seafood, vegetables, or fruit.

paua [Maori], an abalone of New Zealand.

paupiette [French, from Italian *polpetta* "meat croquette" "little pulp," diminutive of *polpa* "pulp, flesh"], a thin slice of meat (e.g., beef, veal, turkey) or fish (e.g., sole) wrapped around a forcemeat (pork and veal, or greens, pork and ham) filling, and braised in wine and stock with herbs and aromatic vegetables.

pavlova [for Russian ballerina Anna *Pavlova*, 1882–1931], a dessert of Australian and New Zealand origin consisting of a meringue base topped with whipped cream and fruit (e.g., kiwi, passion fruit, strawberry) and served with a fruit sauce.

pawpaw, variant of **papaw**.

paysanne [from French *(à la) paysanne* "(in) peasant or rustic (fashion)," from *paysan* "peasant"], prepared (e.g., with diced root vegetables) in country or simple style. A vegetable soup (with carrots, onions, celery, tomatoes), for instance, may be paysanne.

pea, *1.* one of the rounded, smooth or wrinkled, edible, green seeds (in a green elongated pod) of a climbing leguminous vine (likewise called *pea*); this seed is used in its green immature stage as a cooked vegetable or stored in the mature dry stage (e.g., for use in porridges or soups); *2.* the seed of any of various leguminous plants that resemble the pea (e.g., black-eyed pea, chick-pea); *3.* the unopened (immature) pods of the pea plant, with their seeds.

pea bean or **navy bean**, any of several varieties of the kidney bean grown especially for its small, white seeds, nearly round in shape, which are used dried (e.g., for baking).

peach, the soft, juicy, single-seeded, sweet fruit of a low tree (likewise called *peach*) of the rose family, having yellow flesh and downy red-tinted, yellow skin, widely used as a fresh or cooked fruit, in preserves, or dried. Peaches are used for cobblers, dumplings, ice cream, pies, salads, shortcakes, as pêche melba.

peach melba, variant of **pêche melba**.

peach palm or **pejibaye**, either of two South American palms with edible fruit.

pea crab, a minute European crab, living in mussels and cockles.

peameal, meal used to coat cured meats (e.g., bacon); it is made from ground dried peas.

peanut or **goober** or **goober pea** or **earthnut** or **grassnut** or **ground pistachio** or **monkey-nut** or **pinder** or **groundnut** [French and Italian *arachide*, Spanish *cacahuate, cacahuete, maní*], the edible, nutlike, oily seed of a vine (likewise called *peanut)*. From one to three seeds are contained in a reticulated pod that ripens underground. Peanuts are roasted or baked before being eaten and are used in cooking; as peanut butter they are used in sandwiches and added to many dishes (e.g., cakes, candy, muffins, sauces, soups).

peanut brittle, a hard candy containing peanuts.

peanut butter, a smooth paste or spread made by grinding roasted and skinned peanuts.

peanut oil or **groundnut oil**, the oil pressed from peanuts, used for cooking, as a salad oil, and in margarine.

pear, the soft and juicy fruit of a tree (likewise called *pear)* of the rose family, that is usually larger at the apical end (i.e., it is round at the base and tapering toward the stem). Spiced pears can be an accompaniment to chicken, lamb, veal. Compare **ambrette** (a dessert pear).

pear Helene or **pear belle Hélène** or **poire Hélène**, a dessert made with fresh pears halved and poached in a sugar-and-water syrup, each half served on vanilla ice cream and with chocolate sauce poured over both pear and ice cream.

pearl barley, barley reduced by grinding to small, round, pearl-like pellets.

pearl hominy, hominy milled to pearl-like grains of medium size.

pearl millet, a tall cereal grass grown in the Old World for its seeds.

pearl onion, a usually pickled onion (resembling a pearl in size) used in appetizers and as a garnish.

pearl tapioca, tapioca (sense 1) formed during processing into small, round grains that swell in cooking but retain their shape.

pear tomato, a tomato with pear-shaped fruit.

peasecod [from *pease* "pea (obsolete)" + *cod* "bag, husk (obsolete)"], a pea pod.

pease porridge [from *pease* "pea (obsolete)"], another name for **pea soup**.

pease pudding or **peas pudding** [from *pease* "pea (obsolete)"], a pudding made of cooked split peas and eggs, rubbed through a sieve, boiled, with butter added, in stock or water (in cloth or mold).

pea soup or **peas porridge**, a thick purée or soup made of dried green or yellow peas. A similar soup may be prepared with black-eyed peas, black turtle beans, navy beans, or other dried peas or beans.

peas porridge, another name for **pea soup**.

peas pudding, variant of **pease pudding**.

pecan [from American French *pacane*, of Algonquian origin], the smooth, thin-shelled, oval nut of a tree (a large hickory, likewise called *pecan)* grown in Mexico and in the south of the United States. Pecans are used in buns, cakes, pies, rolls, torte.

peccary, any of several American mammals resembling pigs, ranging from Texas to Paraguay.

pechay [Spanish, from Tagalog *petsay*, from Chinese *bécài*], another name for **Chinese cabbage**.

pêche melba [from French *pêche Melba*, for Dame Nellie *Melba* (see **melba**)] or **peach melba**, half a peach (from peaches poached in vanilla-flavored syrup) filled with cream set up on a layer of vanilla ice cream (in a timbale) and coated with a raspberry puree and whipped cream. Compare **melba**, **melba sauce**.

pecorino or **pecorino cheese** [Italian "of ewes," from *pecora* "ewe; sheep"], any of various cheeses of Italian origin (e.g., Romano) made of ewe's milk. It can be grated on pasta.

pectin [from Greek *pēktos* "coagulated"], any of various substances obtained from plant tissues that yield viscous solutions with water and when combined with acid and sugar in proper concentration yield a gel which is the basis of fruit jellies.

¹**peel**, *1.* the skin, rind or outer coating of certain fruits (e.g., orange, lemon, citron); *2.* such rind candied, used as a flavoring in cookery and confectionery.

²**peel (to)**, to remove an outer layer (skin, rind).

peen-to [from Chinese *biǎn táo*, from *biǎn* "flat" + *táo* "peach"] or **flat peach**, any of various peaches with a flattened shape.

pejerrey [Spanish "silversides," "kingfish," from regional Spanish (León and certain areas of Spanish America)], any of several silversides of the South American coasts, that resemble mackerel.

pejibaye [from American Spanish *pejibaye*, *pijibay*], another name for **peach palm**.

Pekin [variant of *Peking*, obsolete romanization of *Beijing*, city in northeastern China], any of a breed (likewise called *Pekin)* of large white ducks of Chinese origin used for meat-duck production.

Peking duck, *1.* another name for **Pekin**; *2.* a Chinese dish consisting of roasted duck meat (carved into very thin slices) and strips of crispy duck skin topped with scallions and sauces (plum and hoisin) and wrapped in thin pancakes. First the skin is peeled off and eaten in a pancake brushed with the sauce, then the meat is eaten in the same way.

pekoe [from Xiamen Chinese *pek-ho*, from *pek* "white" (corresponding to Chinese *bái)* + *ho* "down" (corresponding to Chinese *háo)*], *1.* a grade of black tea made from young leaves (the leaves around the buds) that are slightly larger than those of orange pekoe; *2.* a tea of India or Sri Lanka made from leaves of about the same size.

pelamyd, a young tuna (fish).

pemmican or **pemican** [from Cree *pimihkân*, from *pimii* "grease, fat"], *1.* a concentrated food prepared by North American Indians and consisting of lean, dried strips of meat (e.g., buffalo, venison) pounded into paste, mixed with melted fat and berries; *2.* a similar food made chiefly from beef, dried fruit (e.g., raisins), and suet (with some flour and molasses or sugar), used as concentrated emergency rations (e.g., by explorers).

penuche or **panocha** [from Mexican Spanish *panocha* "raw sugar," from Spanish *panocha* "ear of maize"], a fudgelike confection of brown sugar, water or milk, and chopped nuts, sometimes also of cream and butter. Penuche can be used as icing. See also **panocha**.

peperek, another name for **sapsap** (Indonesia).

peperoni [from Italian *peperoni* "cayenne peppers"], variant of **pepperoni**.

pepino [American Spanish, from Spanish "cucumber"] or **melon pear**, a bushy plant of temperate uplands of Peru grown for its edible, melon-like, yellow fruits which have a juicy, aromatic, yellow pulp.

pepo [Latin "melon"], a berry usually with a hard rind, fleshy pulp, and numerous seeds (e.g., cucumber, melon, pumpkin, squash) that is the characteristic fruit of the gourd family.

¹**pepper**, *1.* [in sense 1, French *poivre*, Italian *pepe*, Spanish *pimienta*] a pungent product obtained from the fruit of a plant (a woody vine, likewise called *pepper*, having berrylike fruit) native to the oriental tropics (southeastern Asia), used as a condiment, consisting of the entire, dried, blackish berry (when ground whole called *black pepper*), or of the dried seeds with the shell removed (called *white pepper*), with both forms usually ground into powder before use; *2.* any of various pungent condiments obtained from other plants; *3.* [in sense 3, French *piment*, Italian *peperone*, Spanish *pimiento*] the many-seeded berry (a podlike fruit) of another plant called pepper or of similar plants, that is enclosed in a thickened integument, varies greatly in shape, size, and degree of pungency in different varieties (the milder types [also called *sweet peppers*] include the bell pepper and pimiento, and the more pungent types [also called *hot peppers*] include the bird pepper, the cherry pepper), is usually red or yellow when ripe, and includes numerous cultivated forms used in the preparation of condiments and relishes and as vegetables; *4.* any of various condiments (also called *hot pepper*; e.g., cayenne pepper, chili) made from the more pungent varieties (of pepper, sense 3). The following are all ground from red pepper pods: paprika (mildly pungent), red pepper (sharper), cayenne (the hottest of all).

²**pepper (to)**, to sprinkle or season with ¹**pepper** (senses 1 and 2).

peppercorn, a dried berry of the black pepper vine. It can be used in curry powders.

pepperdulse, a red alga with a pungent taste (Scotland).

peppermint or **lamb mint** or **American mint**, *1.* a pungent and aromatic mint (sense 1, a plant) having downy leaves that yield a pungent oil; *2.* any of several mints related to the peppermint; *3.* the oil (also called *peppermint oil)* from this plant or a preparation made from it, used as flavoring; *4.* a candy or lozenge with this flavoring. Compare **spearmint**.

peppermint oil or **peppermint**, either of two oils obtained from mints used as a flavoring agent.

peppernut [translation of German *Pfeffernuss*], another name for **pfeffernuss**.

pepper oil, an oil obtained from the fruit of black pepper; it has an odor like that of pepper and is used in flavoring

pepperoni or **peperoni** [from Italian *peperoni* "cayenne peppers, hot peppers," plural of *peperone* "hot pepper," augmentative of *pepe* "¹pepper (sense 1)"], a beef and pork sausage seasoned with pepper.

pepper plant, *1.* a plant yielding pepper; *2.* any of several pungent plants (e.g., a certain Australian plant with a pungent, edible rootstock).

¹**pepper pot**, a thick, highly seasoned West Indian stew of meat or fish with vegetables, cassareep, and other condiments.

²**pepper pot** or **Philadelphia pepper pot**, a thick soup made with vegetables and tripe or other meat, seasoned with pepper (sense 1, crushed peppercorns), and often containing dumplings.

pepper sauce or **chili vinegar**, a condiment made by steeping small hot peppers in vinegar.

pepper steak, *1.* thin-sliced steak cooked with green peppers (sweet peppers), onions, tomatoes, and soy sauce (garlic, hoisin sauce, and ginger slices may be added); *2.* another name for **steak au poivre**.

perch, *1.* any of various freshwater fishes of North America and of Europe; compare **yellow perch**; *2.* any of various similar fishes, such as the pike perch. They are lean fishes, and therefore best for boiling or steaming.

perciatelli [from Italian] or **bucatini**, long, hollow pasta. Some people use the word *perciatelli* when slightly larger than spaghetti and *bucatini* when thinner than spaghetti.

percolate (**to**), *1.* to filter, sift, cause a liquid to pass through a permeable substance in order to extract the essence; *2.* to prepare coffee in a **percolator**.

percolator, a type of coffee pot in which boiling water repeatedly bubbles up through a tube and filters back to the bottom through a perforated basket containing ground coffee beans, in order to extract their essence.

perdiz, Spanish for **partridge**.

perdrix, French for **partridge**.

periwinkle, any of various edible marine snails.

permit [from Spanish *palometa*, a kind of pompano "little dove," diminutive of *paloma* "dove"] or **great pompano**, a large pompano of the western Atlantic.

Persian date, any of several soft-fleshed dates grown in southwestern Asia.

Persian melon, a large muskmelon having unridged rind and orange-colored flesh.

persillade (adjective) [French, from *persil* "parsley"], dressed with or containing parsley (e.g., persillade potatoes). In French, a *persillade* (noun) is (1) a sauce or seasoning of minced parsley (with fines herbes, garlic, oil, vinegar, sometimes bread crumbs) used as a dressing (e.g., on sautéed eggplant, baked zucchini, saddle of lamb), and (2) cold beef slices served with this seasoning.

persimmon [Algonquian] or **possum fruit** or **possum apple** or **winter plum**, the orange-red, round fruit of any of various chiefly tropical trees (likewise called *persimmons*) of the ebony family. It is edible when fully ripe but astringent when unripe.

Peru. The following are representative dishes and products of Peru: ceviche, corbina, shrimp, shrimp stew (Spanish *chupe de camarones*), broiled fish; spitted, roasted pieces of beef heart *(anticuchos);* corn, potatoes, sweet potatoes, hearts of palm *(palmito);* pieces of chicken and pork with crushed peanuts *(carapulcra);* tamales, rice and duck; mashed potatoes with cheese, olives, corn, avocado *(causa rellena);* sweet-and-sour chicken; a dish of potatoes and tripe *(cau cau);* a dish of chicken, pork, sweet potatoes, corn, and cassava *(yuca)* cooked in a pit over hot stones *(pachamanca);* avocados *(paltas),* pineapple, bananas, oranges, papaya, cherimoya; purple corn dessert *(mazamorra morada);* a sweet made from milk condensed in a double boiler mixed with regular milk and meringue *(suspiros de limeña* "sighs of a Lima woman"). Beverage: a soft drink made from purple corn *(chicha morada).*

pesto [Italian "pounded," from *pestare* "to pound"], a green sauce characteristic of Genoese cooking made especially of fresh basil, garlic, olive oil, pine nuts, and grated cheese (typically pecorino). It is used on pasta, especially spaghetti.

petit chou, see **chou**.

petite marmite [French "small kettle"], a soup of brown stock served in a marmite; the soup can be made with a few large pieces of vegetable, fowl, or beef. Sometimes the ingredients can be quite varied: when the major meat is beef, for instance, chicken wings and gizzards may be added, as well as carrots, turnip, leeks, onion, bouquet garni. Slices of French bread are often added.

petit four [French "small oven"], a small tea cake cut in a fancy shape (e.g., squares, diamonds) from pound or sponge cake, decoratively frosted, and ornamented with sugar flowers or crystallized fruit. In French, the term is more general and this category of pastry is divided between *petits fours secs* (that include small almond-paste cakes and meringues) and *petits fours frais* (that comprises pastry-shop cakes [French pastry] of a reduced size).

petits pois [French "small peas"] or **French peas**, very small green peas.

petrale sole, a flounder of the Pacific waters of North America.

pe-tsai or **peh-tsai** [from regional Chinese pronunciation (central China) *bé cai*, corresponding to Chinese *bái cai* "white vegetable, greens"], another name for **Chinese cabbage**.

pfefferkuchen [German "peppercake"], another name for **gingerbread** (sense 1, dark molasses cake).

pfeffernuss [German "peppernut"] or **peppernut**, a small, spiced cookie made traditionally for the Christmas holidays.

pheasant, any of numerous large birds. It is prepared like chicken (e.g., smothered, roasted, poached; in the form of pâté).

Philadelphia ice cream, ice cream made from cream and flavoring, but no eggs.

persimmon

Philadelphia ice cream

Philadelphia pepper pot, another name for ²**pepper pot**.

Philippines. The following are representative dishes and products of the Philippines: rice (Pilipino *kanin)*, corn, sweet potatoes, pork, fish *(isdá)*, adobo, whole roast pig *(lechón);* stewed fish or meat *(sinigang);* noodles with fish or shrimp or meat *(pancit);* mango, papaya, banana, coconut; beef in peanut sauce *(kare kare)*.

phosphated flour, soft-wheat flour with monocalcium phosphate added (to improve the baking qualities).

phulwa butter, another name for **Indian butter**.

phyllo or **filo** [from modern Greek *phyllon* "leaf; sheet of pastry"], another name for **puff pastry** (sense 1).

piccalilli, a pickled relish of various chopped vegetables and pungent spices.

piccata [Italian "fried meat interlarded with bacon," from *piccare* "to prick"], thin slices of meat (e.g., veal) sautéed (dusted lightly with flour) and served in a lemon and butter sauce (usually with chopped parsley; often with mushrooms).

pichurim or **pichurim bean** [from Portuguese *pichurim*], one of the aromatic cotyledons (first leaves) of a tropical American tree called *Brazilian sassafras*, used as a substitute for nutmegs and as a flavoring agent.

pickerel or **pickering**, *1.* a young or small pike; *2.* any of various small fishes related to the pike.

pickering, *1.* another name for **pickerel**; *2.* another name for **sauger** (a pike perch).

¹**pickle**, *1.* a solution of brine (salt-and-water) or of vinegar, often spiced, for preserving and flavoring food (fish, meat, vegetables, fruits, eggs, oysters); *2.* an article of food (e.g., cucumber, herring) that has been preserved and flavored in a solution of brine or of vinegar.

²**pickle** (**to**), to steep in a solution of salt or vinegar for preservation or flavoring. Fruit can be pickled in syrup and vinegar.

pickle-cured, preserved in pickle (sense 1).

pickled, preserved in pickle (sense 1).

pickle-herring, a pickled herring.

pickler, a vegetable (e.g., cucumber, onion) grown for pickling, or of a suitable size or quality for pickling.

pickling cabbage, any of several cabbages especially suitable for pickling.

pickling cucumber, any of several cucumbers cultivated primarily for pickling.

picnic or **picknick** [from French *picnic* or from German *Picknick*], *1.* an excursion or outing with food provided by members of the group and eaten outdoors; *2.* the food provided for such an outing; *3.* a standard size of container for canned food; *4.* a standard size of cheddar cheese; *5.* or **picnic ham** or **picnic shoulder**, a smoked shoulder of pork with the butt removed, often boned.

pidan [from Chinese *pídàn* "covered eggs"], duck eggs preserved in a brine to which lime, ashes, and a tea infusion are added and after several months coated with rice hulls. These have been called "100-year-old eggs" and even "1000-year old eggs" (they are best when about

100-<u>days</u> old). In Chinese they are also called "pine flower eggs" (*song hua dan*).

pie, *1.* a meat or shellfish (e.g., clam) dish baked with biscuit or pastry crust; the meat is often cooked cubes of beef or lamb with gravy (compare **shepherd's pie**). Compare **potpie** (sense 1); *2.* a baked dessert consisting of a filling (e.g., of fruit or custard) in a pastry shell (in a dish or pan lined with pastry) or topped with pastry or both (in the latter case, it may be called a two-crust pie). Both the bottom crust and the top cover may be plain paste of fat and flour (with salt), usually one part fat to three parts flour, mixed to a firm dough with water and rolled thin; the bottom crust may also be made by mixing and pressing cracker crumbs or ready-to-eat cereals, sugar, and melted butter. Berry pies may have a filling of blackberries, boysenberries, gooseberries, loganberries, raspberries, strawberries; other dessert pies may have apple, apricot, blueberry, cherry, cranberry, grape, peach, pear, pecan, pineapple, raisin, rhubarb, walnut, and include chess, custard, coconut custard, meringue, mince, pumpkin, squash, streusel, sweet potato, yam pies. There are cream pies (almond, banana, butterscotch, chocolate, coconut, vanilla), chiffon pies (chocolate, lemon, lime, orange, pineapple, pumpkin, raspberry, strawberry); *3.* a split layer of cake spread with a custard, cream, jelly, or jam filling (compare **Boston cream pie, Washington pie**).

pièce de résistance [French "piece of resistance" (from the idea of "it is not easy to eat it all"], the chief dish of a meal. In French, it may also be called *plat de résistance.*

piecrust, *1.* the pastry shell of a pie; *2.* paste for pies.

pierogi or **pirogi** [Polish "dumplings," plural of *pieróg*], a meat, cheese, or vegetable turnover cooked by boiling and then panfrying.

pig, *1.* pork, the edible parts of a swine, swine flesh as food; *2.* swine, hog (a mammal).

pigeon or **rock dove**, any of a certain family of birds.

pigeon pea or **Indian pea** or **poona pea**, the small, edible, brown seed, contained in somewhat flat pods, of a tropical leguminous shrub likewise called *pigeon pea.*

pigeon plum, *1.* the edible fruit of any of several tropical American plants likewise called *pigeon plums*; *2.* the edible fruit of an African tree likewise called *pigeon plum.*

pigfish or **hogfish** [it makes a grunting sound when taken from the water], a salt-water grunt of Atlantic waters of the United States found from Long Island southward.

pig meat, pork.

pignoli or **pignolia** [from Italian *pignoli* "pine nuts," plural of *pignolo*], pine nut, the edible seed of the nut pine.

pignon [French, a certain pine nut], the nutlike seed of any of various pines.

pignut, another name for **earthnut**.

pigs' feet, the feet of swine, especially after boiling and pickling. They may also be baked, jellied, or stewed; when stewed and when baked, green beans, cabbage, or sauerkraut may be added; when jellied, onion, garlic, bay leaves, peppercorns, cloves, vinegar may be added.

pigs in blankets, or **devils on horseback**, broiled or sautéed morsels (e.g., of oysters, chicken livers). wrapped in bacon and fastened with skewers.

pigweed or **wild beet**, any of several plants of the goosefoot or amaranth families, sometimes used as potherbs and having edible seeds.

pike or **grass pike** or **great northern pike**, a freshwater bony fish of the Northern Hemisphere. It is a lean fish and therefore best for boiling and steaming. It can be served amandine, and it can also be fried.

pikelet or **crumpet**, a small, round teacake or pancake, made of fine flour, baked on a griddle (sometimes a light cake or muffin) and traditionally served on Christmas day in Great Britain.

pike perch, any of various fishes (e.g., the sauger, walleye) related to the perches that are felt to resemble pikes.

piki [from Hopi *píki*], bread made from cornmeal (especially from blue cornmeal) baked in very thin sheets on heated stones by the Indians (especially Hopi) of the southwestern United States.

pilaf or **pilaff** or **pilau** or **pilaw** [from Persian *pilav* or Turkish *pilāv* (from Persian)], a dish of Oriental origin made of rice usually combined with meat (often mutton), shellfish, fish, or vegetables, fried in oil, steamed in stock (broth), and seasoned with any of various herbs and spices (e.g., saffron, curry), and sometimes raisins.

pilchard, *1.* a fish of the herring family; *2.* any of various sardines.

pile, the quality of bread when the crumb looks silky.

pile perch, a fish of the Pacific coast of North America.

pili, or **pili nut** [from Tagalog *pilì*], the edible nut of a certain Philippine tree.

pilipili, Swahili for pepper seeds and pepper pods (especially red pepper [*pilipili hoho*] but also black pepper [*pilipili manga* "Arabian pepper"]).

piloncillo [Mexican Spanish, diminutive of Spanish *pilón* "sugar loaf"], unrefined sugar, especially when molded into cone-shaped loaves, or flat loaves, or sticks.

pilot biscuit or **pilot cracker**, biscuit hardtack served with seafood stews and chowders.

pilot bread, another name for **hardtack**.

pimento, *1.* another name for **pimiento** (sweet pepper); *2.* another name for **allspice**; *3.* a small hot pepper (as a cayenne or Guinea pepper).

pimento cheese or **pimiento cheese**, a Neufchâtel, process, or cream cheese to which ground pimientos have been added.

pimenton [from Spanish *pimentón*, augmentative of *pimiento* "sweet pepper"], another name for **Spanish paprika** (sense 2).

pimento oil or **pimenta oil** or **allspice oil**, oil obtained from allspice and used in flavoring.

pimiento [Spanish "sweet pepper," from *pimienta* "black pepper"] or **pimento** or **Turkish pepper** or **bonnet pepper**, any of various ripe, red, sweet peppers that have mild flavor and are used especially as a garnish, in salads, as a stuffing for green olives, and as a source of paprika

pimpernel, another name for **salad burnet**.

piña, Spanish for **pineapple**.

pinbone, the hipbone of a bovine.

pinbone steak, a sirloin steak that contains the pinbone (= hipbone).

pinder or **pinda** or **pindar** [from Kongo *mpinda*], another name for **peanut**.

pine (to), to shrink fish in the process of curing, to dry fish by exposure to the weather.

pineapple [French *ananas*, Portuguese *abacaxi* or *naná*, Spanish *piña*, *ananás*], the large, fleshy, edible fruit (consisting of the flowers fused into a compound whole) of a tropical American plant (likewise called *pineapple*). Dishes using pineapples include pies, meringue pies, chiffon pies, Bavarian cream, cake, coffee cake, cookies, filling, frosting, ice, ice cream, icing, salad, sauce, sherbet, upside down cake.

pineapple cheese, a cheddar type of cheese made to look like a pineapple.

pine nut or **Indian nut**, the edible seed (kernel) of any of several species of pine.

pinguin, a tropical American plant that has plum-shaped edible fruit.

pink, another name for **humpback salmon** (a small Pacific salmon).

pink salmon, another name for **humpback salmon**.

pinole [American Spanish, from Nahuatl *pinole*], *1.* a finely ground flour made from dried Indian corn (sometimes sweetened and mixed with cinnamon); *2.* any of various flours resembling pinole and ground from the seeds of other plants (e.g., mesquite beans, chia, wheat).

piñon or **pinyon** [from American Spanish *piñón*, from Spanish *piñón* "pine nut"], the nutlike, edible seed of a pine tree (called *piñon* or *piñon pine)* used especially in confectionery.

pinto bean, or **pinto** [American Spanish, from Spanish "spotted, mottled"], a mottled kidney bean, a form of the string bean that has mottled seeds.

pinyon, another name for **piñon**.

pip, the small seed of a fleshy fruit (e.g., apple, orange, pear) having several seeds.

pipi [Maori], *1.* a certain bivalve mollusk found on sandy beaches in New Zealand; *2.* a similar, edible, Australian wedge shell.

pipi kaula [Hawaiian, from *pipi* "beef rope"], beef preserved in long, sundried slices (Hawaii). Compare **jerk**.

piping hot, very hot.

pippin, any of several varieties of apple.

piquant sauce or **sauce piquante** [from French *piquant* "pungent, sharp, spicy," literally = "pricking," from *piquer* "to prick, sting"], a sauce (usually a brown sauce) with a sharp flavor (e.g., from lemon juice, vinegar, chopped capers or chopped sour pickles [for instance, gherkins], spices). Mustard and minced shallots may be added. Pork in general, especially pork chops and pigs' feet, may be served with this sauce.

piquia [from Portuguese *piquiá*, from Tupi], a South American tree bearing edible oily nuts.

pirarucu [Portuguese, from Tupi "red fish"], a fish of northern South American rivers.

pirogen or **pirogi** [from Yiddish *pirogen* "pastries," plural of *pirog*, from Russian *pirogi* "pastries," plural of *pirog*], another name for **piroshki**.

piroshki or **pirozhki** [from Russian *pirozhki* "small pastries," plural of *pirozhok* "small pastry," diminutive of *pirog* "pastry"], small pastry turnovers with meat, cheese, or vegetable filling.

pisang [Malay "banana; plantain"], another name for **plantain**.

pishpash, a rice broth or soup containing small pieces of meat (India).

Pismo clam [from *Pismo* Beach, California], an edible, thick-shelled marine clam of the southern Pacific coast of North America.

pissaladière, see under **France** *(Provence)*.

pistache [French], another name for **pistachio**.

pistachio [from Italian *pistacchio*] or **pistache** or **green almond**, the green kernel (seed) of the nut (called *pistachio nut)* of a small tree (likewise called *pistachio)* of the Mediterranean region and western Asia; this kernel is used as a flavoring substance in cookery and confectionery.

pistachio nut, see **pistachio**.

pistol prawn or **pistol shrimp** [from the snapping sound it makes with a claw], another name for **snapping shrimp**.

pistou [French, from Provençal, from *pistar*, *pestar* "to powder, pound, grind, crush"], a vegetable soup of Provençal origin served with a puree of garlic, herbs (especially powdered basil), oil, and usually cheese and often tomatoes. The puree itself is likewise called *pistou* in French and is served, for instance, stirred into sautéed eggplants or zucchini, or added to beef stew before serving.

pita, or **pita bread** [modern Greek "pie, cake"] or **pocket bread**, a thin, flat (only slightly leavened), round, soft bread that can be separated into two layers to form a pocket or pouch. Compare **falafel**.

pitahaya or **pitaya** [from Spanish *pitahaya*, from Taino *pitahaya*], the edible, juicy fruit of any of several cacti of northern Mexico and southwestern United States.

pitanga [Portuguese, from Tupi], another name for **Surinam cherry** (sense 2, the fruit of a Brazilian tree).

Pithiviers almond cake, see under **France** *(Loire valley)*.

pizza, or **pizza pie** [Italian], a baked dish of Italian (and specifically of Neapolitan) origin consisting of a usually large, shallow, open pie, made typically of flattened bread dough spread with a savory mixture (usually including tomatoes and cheese and often other toppings [e.g., one or more of the following: ground meat, garlic, anchovy, mushrooms, ham, salami, chorizo, sausage, tuna, peppers, onions, olives, seafood (for instance, shrimp, oyster), chicken]; still other ingredients may be bacon, asparagus, eggplant, oregano, sesame, thyme, basil).

plaice [from Old French *plaïs* (French *plie*)], any of various flatfishes.

plank (to), to cook and serve on a plank (a thick heavy board grooved to catch the drip). Some examples are broiled meat (e.g., steak) or fish (e.g. salmon, shad), usually with a garnish (e.g., boiled potatoes or other vegetables).

plantain [from Spanish *plátano* "plane tree; banana (plant and fruit)"] or **pisang** or **cooking banana**, the angular, greenish, starchy fruit of a banana plant (likewise called *plantain*), that when cooked is a staple food in tropical regions. In certain Spanish-speaking areas, *banana* means "banana" and *plátano* "plantain"; in Mexico, "banana" is *plátano* and "plantain" is *plátano macho*.

plat [French "plate, dish", from *plat* "flat"], a dish of food as served at table, food dressed for the table.

platano [from Spanish *plátano* "banana; plantain"], another name for both **banana** and **plantain**.

plat du jour [French "dish of the day"], a dish that is one of a restaurant's specialties and is emphasized as a feature on a particular day (and usually varies from day to day).

plate, the under portion of the forequarter of beef.

plover, any of various shore-inhabiting, wading, game birds.

pluck, a slaughtered animal's heart, liver, lungs and windpipe used for food.

plum, *1.* the smooth-skinned, fleshy fruit (with a single, hard-shelled, oblong seed) of any of several small trees likewise called *plums*. Compare **damson**, **greengage**, **prune**; *2.* a raisin when used in puddings or other desserts.

plum duff, a flour pudding with raisins or currants or prunes, boiled in a cloth bag.

plum fir or **plum-fruited yew**, a Chilean evegreen tree with an edible plumlike fruit.

plum pudding, *1.* a rich, boiled or steamed pudding made with flour or bread crumbs, raisins, currants, citron, and other fruits, suet, eggs, and spices; *2.* a pudding containing plums.

plum tomato, the oblong fruit of any of several cherry tomatoes (plants), used for salads and preserves.

poach (to), to cook (e.g., fish [for instance, trout], egg) in a simmering liquid (e.g., water, milk, bouillon, wine) kept just below the boiling point. The poaching of fish is often a preliminary to the making of a creamed fish dish, or of a chowder.

poached egg or **dropped egg**, an egg dropped from its shell and cooked in simmering water (i.e., kept just below the boiling point). The eggshell is broken and the egg slipped into the water. A poached egg may be simply served on toast, or it may be combined with English muffins, ham, and hollandaise sauce. When spinach is added to poached eggs, the dish is called eggs Florentine.

pocket bread, another name for **pita**.

pod corn or **husk corn** or **pod maize**, an Indian corn that has each kernel enclosed in a chaffy shell similar to that of other cereals (as well as the whole ear enclosed in a husk).

pohutukawa [Maori], a New Zealand variety of the sweet potato.

poi [Hawaiian or Samoan], *1.* a Hawaiian dish made of taro root which is cooked (baked) and pounded (or ground) and kneaded into a paste, moistened, and allowed to ferment before being eaten, and traditionally eaten with the fingers; *2.* a Hawaiian or Samoan food made of ripe bananas or pineapples to which coconut cream is usually added.

poire Hélène, see **pear Helene**.

poivrade [French, from *poivre* "pepper (sense 1)"], a warm peppery sauce made with pepper, salt, vinegar, and often oil. It is served, for instance, with artichokes.

poivre, French for **pepper** (sense 1). Compare **au poivre**.

poke salad, the cooked young shoots of pokeweed, that are eaten like asparagus.

pokeweed, a tall North American plant whose young shoots can be eaten as greens.

Poland. The following are representative dishes and products of Poland: carp (Polish *karp)*, herring, borsh *(barszcz)*, duck (e.g., stuffed with apples or pears), ham, pork, mushrooms, cucumbers, game, noodles; a porridge made of buckwheat groats *(kasza),* dumplings *(pierozki);* a meat (e.g., smoked pork, sausage) stew with sauerkraut *(bigos);* partridge *(kuropatwa)* in cream sauce.

polenta [Italian], a firm mush originally (and still, in Corsica) made of chestnut meal but now (in Italy) principally of cornmeal or sometimes semolina or farina. Cheese is often added.

Polish sausage, smoked sausage made of ground pork and beef with garlic.

pollack or **pollock** or **grayfish**, a northern marine food fish of the cod family.

Polonaise [from French *(à la) polonaise* "(in) Polish (fashion)"], dressed with browned butter and bread crumbs or flour (to which may be added consommé, egg yolks, lemon juice). Polonaise sauce is used for vegetables (e.g., carrots, cauliflower, green beans).

polony [alteration of *Bologna* in *Bologna* sausage], a dry, partly-cooked pork-sausage made of various ingredients (e.g., cervelat or liver).

polynee [Swedish], a tart of cookie dough, filled with meringue, often topped with a cross made of two strips of the dough.

Polynesia, see **French Polynesia**.

Polynesian chestnut or **rata**, the edible, kidney-shaped seed of a certain Polynesian tree likewise called *Polynesian chestnut.*

pomarrosa [Spanish from "fruit; apple, rose-colored"], another name for both **Malay apple** (West Indies) and **rose apple** (West Indies).

pome, a fleshy fruit having seeds but no stone (e.g., apple, pear, quince).

pomegranate [from Old French *pomme grenate* "seedy apple" (French *grenade)*], the thick-skinned fruit of a semitropical tree (likewise called *pomegranate)*, that has many seeds enclosed in a red pulp with a mildly acid flavor.

pomegranate melon, another name for **mango melon**.

pomelo [from Dutch *pompelmoes*], another name for both **grapefruit** and **shaddock** (citrus fruit).

pomfret, any of several food fishes.

pomme blanche [French "white apple"] or **pomme de prairie** [French "prairie apple"], other names for **breadroot** (a starchy root).

pompano or **pampano**, [from American Spanish *pámpano*, from Spanish *pámpano* "vine tendril; a kind of fish" or *pámpana* "vine leaf"] or **cobbler** or **cobblerfish**, any of several marine food fishes. It is a fat fish, and therefore best for broiling, baking, planking; it is often prepared en papillote.

pompelmous or **pompelmoose** [from Dutch *pompelmoes*] or **pomelo**, other names for **shaddock** (citrus fruit).

pompion berry, another name for **hackberry**.

pond apple, the edible, ovoid fruit of an evergreen tree (likewise called *pond apple*) of tropical America and of southern Florida.

pone [Algonquian], *1.* a cake of stiff cornmeal batter shaped into a thin oval by the palms of the hand and baked (often in hot ashes), fried, or boiled; *2.* coarse corn-bread made in the form of pones (sense 1, a thin cake) usually without milk or eggs; *3.* a baked dessert—pudding of grated sweet potato, milk, sugar, butter, and spices.

pont l'évêque or **Pont l'Évêque** [from *Pont l'Évêque*, town in Normandy, region of northwestern France "Bishop's Bridge"], a firm, mild, soft-centered French cheese made of whole milk.

poona pea, another name for **pigeon pea**.

poor boy, another name for a **hero** (sandwich).

poori, variant of **puri**.

pop, another name for **soda pop** (beverage).

popadam or **popadum** [from Tamil *poppaḍam*, contraction of *paruppu aḍam* "lentil cake"], a thin, wafer-like, Indian cake often eaten with curry and made of a thin strip or a ball of gluten flour (often chick-pea or lentil) or cornmeal fried in oil or other fat.

popcorn, *1.* a variety of Indian corn (Mexican Spanish *maíz palomero)* whose kernels on exposure to dry heat are popped or burst open, and form a white, starchy mass many times the size of the original kernel; *2.* these kernels of an Indian corn, after popping (Mexican Spanish *palomitas de maíz).*

popoi [Marquesan], a food of the Marquesas Islands (French Polynesia) similar to Hawaiian poi (which is made of taro root) but made of both fresh and preserved cooked and pounded breadfruit.

popover [it pops up over the rim of the baking tin], a light, puffy, quick bread shaped like a muffin, made from a thin batter of eggs, milk, and flour and subjected in the first stage of baking to such heat that steam expands it into a hollow shell.

popper, a corn variety suitable for popping (compare **popcorn**, sense 1).

poppy seed or **mohnseed**, the seed of a poppy (a plant) and especially of the opium poppy used as a food (as a topping or flavoring for baked goods) and as a chief source of poppy-seed oil.

poppy-seed oil or **poppy oil**, an oil obtained from the seeds of the opium poppy and used chiefly as food.

popsicle, a bar of sherbet (sense 1, a water ice) or of ice cream frozen on a stick.

porgy [from Portuguese and Spanish *pargo*], any of various marine fishes of the eastern and western Atlantic.

pork, the fresh or salted flesh of swine (pig, hog) when dressed for food. Pork is sold either as fresh meat or in several preserved forms (ham, sausage, bacon, headcheese); the feet are boiled and jellied; the outer hide after the hair is removed is cooked very crisp to make cracklings (sense 2), which are eaten alone or crumbled and baked into corn bread (see also **chitterlings**, that are the small intestines); its liver, heart,

209

tongue, kidney (variety meats) are also eaten. Pork can be roasted, curried, braised, in the form of chops, spareribs, patties.

pork belly, an uncured side of pork.

porkburger, *1.* a cooked patty of ground pork; *2.* a porkburger (sense 1) in a split bun.

porker or **porket**, a young pig fattened for use as food.

porkling, a piglet, a young pig.

porkpie or **pork pie**, a thick-crusted meat pie made of chopped pork, usually eaten cold.

poroporo [Maori], another name for **kangaroo apple** (New Zealand).

porridge, *1.* a soft food made by boiling meal of grains (e.g., oatmeal) or legumes (e.g., beans) in milk or water until thick (usually eaten with milk at breakfast); *2.* (obsolete) a soup of meat and vegetables often thickened with barley or other cereal.

porterhouse [archaic, a house where malt liquor (e.g., *porter* "a dark beer") is sold], a cut of beef (a large steak) taken from the thick end of the short loin, having a T-shaped bone (compare **T-bone**) and a sizeable piece of tenderloin. It is often served broiled.

Port Salut [from French *port-salut*, from *Port du Salut*, Trappist abbey in northwestern France, "Haven of Salvation"] or **Trappist cheese**, a semisoft, pressed, ripened, cow-milk French cheese made originally by Trappist monks in France.

Portugal. The following are representative dishes and products of Portugal: dried salted cod (Portuguese *bacalhau*), tunafish, lobster *(lagosta)*, octopus *(polvo)*, cabbage and potato soup *(caldo verde)*, fish soup, marinated liver *(iscas com elas)*, stuffed lamb *(carneiro recheado)*, cheeses, seafood stew *(caldeirada)*, broiled sardines *(sardinhas assadas)*, grilled squid *(lulas grelhadas)*, chicken soup *(canja de galinha*, or simply *canja)*, pork with clams *(porco com amêijoas)*, roast suckling pig *(leitão assado)*, meat stew *(cozido)*, rabbit stewed in tomato sauce *(coelho à caçadora* "rabbit in hunter fashion")*, clams in garlic sauce *(amêijoas à Bulhão Pato* [a 19th-century poet])*, lamb and kid stew *(sarapatel); an* egg yolks and sugar pudding *(ovos moles); an* egg, sugar, and almond sweetmeat *(toucinho do ceu* "bacon from heaven")*, cheese cakes *(queijadas)*, sponge cake *(pão de ló* "windward bread").

posol or **pozole** [from American Spanish *pozol*, *pozole*, from Nahuatl *pozolli* "foamy"], *1.* a thick Mexican and Central American soup made of pork, corn kernels, garlic, and hot pepper; *2.* a Mexican and Central American drink made of cornmeal, water, and sugar.

possum fruit or **possum apple**, other names for **persimmon**.

post-oak grape, the large, purplish black fruit of a tall grape (likewise called *post-oak grape*) of the United States.

potage [French, from *pot* "pot"], a thick soup of meat (e.g., ground beef) and vegetables (e.g., carrots, celery, and potatoes) cut in small pieces. It can also be made with tapioca (sense 1, preparation of cassava starch) or crayfish. Compare **pottage**, **bisque**.

potagerie, garden vegetables and herbs.

potato [from Spanish *patata*, *batata*, from Taino *batata* "sweet potato"] or earth apple or **Irish potato** or **white potato** or **murphy** (slang) or **papa**, the starchy, edible tuber (that is an enlargement of an underground stem) of a plant (likewise called *potato*) native to South America. Compare **sweet potato**. In French, a potato is *pomme de terre* "apple of earth," but on menus it is often abbreviated to *pomme*, so that *pommes* in an expression like *pommes amandine* does not mean "apples prepared or served with almonds" but "potatoes prepared or served with almonds." It may be baked, boiled, French fried, mashed, sautéed. Compare **hashed brown potatoes**.

potato ball, *1.* a small ball cut or gouged from a potato with a spoon or scoop designed for it; *2.* a potato croquette, baked (with eggs and parsley) or fried (in deep fat, with butter, grated cheese, cream, egg yolks, bread crumbs).

potato bean, another name for **yam bean** (= jicama).

potato cake, mashed potato shaped into a flattened cake, often rolled in flour, and fried. Cooked ham or salmon may be added to this cake.

potato chip or **potato crisp** or **Saratoga chip** or **Saratoga potato**, a thin slice of white potato that has been fried until crisp in deep fat and then usually salted.

potato flour or **potato starch**, a flour prepared from potatoes ground to pulp and washed free of fiber. It may be used in soups, gravies, breads, and cakes (e.g., instead of wheat flour in a sponge cake) and as a thickener in certain delicate sauces.

potato onion, another name for **multiplier onion**.

potato pancake, grated potato mixed with raw egg, and often with grated onion and spices, made into a flat cake, fried, and usually served hot with apple sauce.

pot-au-feu [French "pot on the fire"], a thick French soup in which meats (usually beef) and many vegetables (e.g., carrots, leeks, turnips, onions, celery) are simmered with rice or pasta and garnishings. It is similar to puchero.

pot cheese, another name for **cottage cheese, Dutch cheese** and **cook cheese**.

pote, regional Spanish (Asturias, Galicia) for both **olla** and **olla podrida**.

potherbs or **greens** or **table greens**, plants (usually leafy herbs) or plant parts (leaves, stems, flowers) that are cooked (boiled or steamed as a vegetable) and eaten as green vegetables (e.g., basella, chervil, chives, clary, costmary, dandelions, docks, garden orache, mint, purslane, spinach, Swiss chard) or used as seasoning.

potpie, *1.* a mixture of meat or poultry and vegetables covered with a pastry crust and baked in a pot or deep dish; *2.* a meat or poultry stew with dumplings.

potpourri [from French *pot pourri* (translation of Spanish *olla podrida* "rotten pot"), from *pot* "pot" + *pourri* "rotten"], another name for **olla podrida**.

pot roast, a piece of tough beef (from blade-bone, shoulder or chuck, round-bone, boned rump, sirloin tip) or other meat (venison, ham, bird) that is browned and then cooked by braising (i.e., not by roasting) usually on top of the stove, until tender, often with vegetables, in a covered pot.

pot-roast (**to**), to roast in a covered pot, in a small amount of water or of fat, usually on top of the stove.

pottage [from French *potage*], a thick soup or stew of vegetables and sometimes meat cooked to softness and seasoned. Compare **potage**.

poularde or **poulard** [French, from *poule* "hen, chicken"], a pullet (young hen) that has been sterilized by removing either the ovaries or a part of the oviduct, to fatten it for use as food. Compare **capon** (sense 1), which is a castrated male chicken.

poulette [French, from *poulet* "chick, pullet," from *poule* "hen, chicken"] or **poulette sauce** [from French *sauce à la poulette* or simply *sauce poulette*], velouté (i.e., a sauce with butter and chicken or veal stock) with added egg yolk.

poulp or **poulpe** [from French *poulpe* "octopus"], another name for **octopus**.

poultry [ultimately from French *poulet* "chick, pullet," from *poule* "hen, chicken"], domesticated birds raised for eggs or meat. Poultry includes chickens, turkeys, ducks, geese, squab, pigeons, guinea fowl, peafowl, pheasants. Such poultry as chicken, turkey, and duck are first cleaned and dressed and then most of them may be baked or roasted, braised, broiled, fried, stewed or fricasséed. After cooking they may be creamed and used in other made dishes, salads, and sandwiches.

pound cake [the original recipe prescribed a pound (0.45 kilogram) of each of the principal ingredients (flour, butter, sugar)], a rich, sweet, butter cake made with many eggs and about equal quantities of butter, flour, and sugar, which results in a large amount of shortening in proportion to the amount of flour used.

pour batter, batter of such consistency as to pour from a bowl or pitcher, usually made in a proportion of equal parts of flour and liquid. Distinguished from **drop batter** (made from two parts flour to one part liquid).

poussin [French], a young chicken, a small broiler.

powder, a finely ground condiment or food (e.g., curry powder).

powdered milk, or **dried milk**, dehydrated milk. Compare **evaporated milk** (which is made by evaporating some of the water).

powdered sugar, very fine sugar derived from granulated sugar by grinding, with flour added to prevent caking. Compare **confectioner's sugar** (which is finer) and **pulverized sugar**.

pozole, variant of **posol**.

prairie chicken or **prairie fowl** or **prairie grouse**, a grouse chiefly of the prairies of the central United States. It is prepared like chicken, e.g., smothered (using sour cream) or roasted.

prairie gourd, another name for **buffalo gourd**.

prairie oyster, *1.* a raw egg or egg yolk immersed in liquid (with seasoning, vinegar) and swallowed whole, especially as a palliative for a hangover; *2.* a testis of a bull calf, cooked and served as food. Compare **mountain oyster**.

prairie potato or **prairie turnip**, other names for **breadroot**.

praline [French, for Count Plessis-*Praslin*, 1598–1675, French field marshal whose cook invented the confection], a confection of nut kernels and sugar (e.g., almonds cooked in boiling sugar syrup until brown and crisp and sometimes powdered and made into a paste; or a round patty of browned sugar and pecan meats).

prawn, any of various edible crustaceans that resemble shrimp.

precook (to), to cook food in advance, either partially (before final cooking) or entirely (before reheating).

premix, a mixture, prepared beforehand, of ingredients (e.g., the dry materials for a cake batter) designed to be mixed with other ingredients (e.g., the liquid materials for a cake batter) before use.

preservative, something used to preserve, especially a substance (e.g., salt, spices, sugar) added to foods to inhibit spoilage under conditions of storage.

¹**preserve**, fruit (e.g., peaches, quince, strawberries) canned or made into jams or jellies, or cooked whole or in large pieces.

²**preserve (to)**, *1.* to prepare food (e.g., fruits, vegetables) for future use, as by canning, pickling, or salting; *2.* to treat fruit or other foods so as to prevent decay.

preserving melon, another name for **citron** (sense 1).

press (to), to squeeze out the juice.

pressed, shaped, molded, or having liquid or juices squeezed out (said, for instance, of chicken, duck, meat loaf, veal).

pressed cheese, a hard cheese (e.g., cheddar) that has been subjected to pressure (forced or squeezed into a smaller volume) to remove the whey.

pressed duck, *1.* the breast and legs of a roast duck served with a sauce prepared from juices obtained by squeezing in a press the remainder of the carcass; *2.* a dish of Chinese origin, made with steamed duck, boned, pressed, deep-fried, and served with a sauce and toasted almonds.

pressure-cook (to), to cook in a pressure cooker.

pressure cooker, an airtight metal pot, with a lid which clamps down, for quick cooking or preserving of foods by means of heated steam under pressure.

pressure saucepan, a small pressure cooker.

pretzel [from German *Brezel*], a brittle, glazed, and salted (on the outside) cracker (slender bread) made of a rope of dough often shaped like a loose knot or like a stick, and baked.

prickly pear or **devil's fig** [French *figue de Barbarie*, Italian *fico d'India*, Spanish *tuna*, *higo chumbo*] or **Barbary fig**, the round, pulpy, pear-shaped or barrel-shaped fruit of any of various cacti (likewise called *prickly pears*); compare ¹**tuna**. The leaves of these cacti, with thorns removed, are cooked in Mexico and eaten as a salad called *nopalitos* ("little nopals"); compare **nopal**. Some species of the cacti are also called **cholla**.

prime ribs, see **foreribs** (a roasting cut of beef).

printanier or **printanière** [from French *printanier* (masculine) and *printanière* (feminine) "vernal," from *printemps* "spring"], made or served with diced spring vegetables.

prix fixe [French "fixed price"], another name for **table d'hôte** (sense 3, a meal of several courses offered at a fixed price).

process cheese or **processed cheese**, a cheese made by blending several lots of cheese (e.g., green new cheese with one or more aged cheeses) by heating, stirring, and emulsifying, with water added, and often smoked or otherwise flavored.

prodigal son, another name for both **cobia** and **rainbow runner**.

profiterole [French], a miniature cream puff with a sweet (e.g., cream, ice cream, custard) or savory (e.g., cheese, purée) filling. The sweet profiterole is often covered with a chocolate cream and served warm.

prosciutto [Italian], dry-cured, spiced Italian ham. Many Italian porkers are fed chestnuts and those from Parma get whey left from the making of local cheeses. Raw ham *(prosciutto crudo)* and cooked ham *(prosciutto cotto)* are used in stuffings for tortellini and ravioli, in sauces, in risotto, in pizza. The center part of a Parma ham is the best. Prosciutto is often served with fresh figs or with slices of melon.

protective foods, foods (e.g., citrus fruits, vegetables, milk, eggs) that contain vitamins, minerals, and proteins and that guard against deficiency diseases (e.g., pellagra, scurvy).

protein milk, milk having a high protein content and low fat content.

Provençale or **Provençal** [from French *provençal* (masculine) and *provençale* (feminine) "of Provence (region of southeastern France)"], cooked with garlic, onion, olive oil, mushrooms, tomato, and herbs (e.g., frogs' legs, scallops, spinach).

Provençale sauce or simply **Provençale**, a brown sauce (onion, flour, beef stock) with tomato and garlic added. It can be used with meat, pasta, vegetables, crab.

provision tree, a tropical American tree having large fruits with edible brown seeds.

provola [Italian], a southern Italian cheese made from buffalo milk, hung in a net to cure; it is sometimes smoked.

provolette [from *provola*], a roundish cheese hung in a net to cure.

provolone or **provolone cheese** [Italian, augmentative of *provola*], an often pear-shaped southern Italian cheese, hung in a net to cure.

prune, *1.* a partially dried plum; *2.* a plum that can be dried without spoiling.

prunelle [French "sloe, wild plum"] or **prunello**, a small, dried, yellow plum, with skin and stone removed.

psoas, either of two internal muscles of the loin that connect the spinal column and the thighbone and together form the tenderloin of animals, used as food.

ptisan [Latin "peeled barley; barley water," from Greek *ptisanē* "crushed barley," from *ptissein* "to peel, crush"], an infusion, such as barley water, but also any tea or tisane.

puchero [Spanish "pot"], a Spanish or Latin American boiled dinner or stew containing beef (or veal shanks, with the bone; sometimes chicken), bacon, sausage, and various vegetables (e.g., chick-peas, carrots, turnips, zucchini, cabbage, sweet potatoes. In Mexico, fruits are often added [bananas, peaches, pears]) and spices. It is similar to **pot-au-feu**.

pudding, *1.* a sweet dessert of a soft consistency (made, for instance, with bread or rice, and flavored with apples or chocolate), usually containing flour or a cereal product (e.g., cornstarch), that has been boiled, steamed, or baked; compare **bag pudding**, **bread pudding**. A plum duff is a steamed prune-pudding; *2.* an unsweetened dish (a sausage-like preparation), made with minced meat or various other ingredients, often containing suet or having a suet crust and originally boiled in a bag but now often steamed or baked. Puddings (sense 1) include batter puddings (unsweetened), brown Betty, blancmange, cabinet pudding, corn pudding, duff, hasty pudding, Indian pudding, minute pudding, Nesselrode pudding, plum pudding, roly-poly, simnel, snow pudding, tipsy pudding.

Puerto Rico. The following are representative dishes and products of Puerto Rico: arroz con pollo, seafood, soupy rice with shrimp or chicken (Spanish *asopao*), pigeon-pea soup *(sopa de gandules)*, rice and beans *(arroz con gandules)*, tripe stew *(mondongo)*, stuffed plantains *(pasteles)*, roast suckling pig *(lechón asado)*; land crabs *(jueyes)* with rice; little pork-pies *(pastelillos)*, stewed kid *(cabrito estofado)*, paella, pickled red-grouper *(mero en escabeche)*, smothered rabbit *(conejo tapado)*; garlic and pepper sauce *(ajilimójili)* used with suckling pig; rice-flour puff with cheese *(almojábana)*, green plantains *(tostones)*; mangoes, avocados, stuffed plantains *(pionono* [from *Pío Nono* "Pius the Ninth"]); coconut custard *(flan de coco)*, bread pudding *(budín de pan)*; a dessert made with coconut milk, sugar, cinnamon and vanilla *(tembleque* "the shaky one")

puff, *1.* a light, round, hollow, inflated pastry (it rises high in baking) often filled with custard or cream; *2.* a dish that puffs in cooking (e.g., almond, cheese, crabmeat, cream, potato, sweet potato puffs).

puffball, any of various globose fungi.

puffer, any of various fishes.

puff pastry [French *pâte feuilletée*, Spanish *hojaldre, hojaldra*], *1.* or **puff paste** or **phyllo**, a pastry dough (usually composed of equal parts, by weight, of flour and butter) containing many (as many as one thousand, paper-thin) alternating layers of butter and dough, processed by repeated rolling and folding after each addition of butter, and baked at high temperature, which causes it to expand (and the layers separate from each other). It is used for pastry crust or fancy rolls. Mille-feuille, vol-au-vent, and napoleons are made with this; *2.* the light flaky pastry made from this dough.

pulasan or **pulassan** [from Malay], the fruit of an eastern Asian tree (likewise called *pulasan*), that resembles the rambutan.

pulled bread, bread pulled from the inside of a loaf, broken up into small, irregular pieces and lightly browned.

pullet [from French *poulet* "young chicken," diminutive of *poule* "hen, chicken"], a young hen, especially of the domestic chicken, usually less than one year old.

pulp [from French *pulpe*], *1.* the soft, moist part of a fruit (e.g., grape, orange); *2.* a soft mass of vegetable matter (e.g., of apples or sugarcane) from which the water has been squeezed out.

pulse, the edible seeds of certain leguminous, pod-bearing plants (e.g., beans, lentils, peas).

pulverized sugar, granulated sugar ground to reduce it to powder (usually with flour to prevent caking).

pumpernickel [German], a dark, sourish, yeast bread made from rye flour.

pumpkin, the usually large, round, pulpy, orange fruit of a trailing vine (likewise called *pumpkin*) of the gourd family, having a thick rind and numerous seeds, eaten as a vegetable and used for pies.

pumpkin bread, bread made of pumpkin and cornmeal.

pumpkinseed, the seed of the pumpkin.

punch, a sweetened, hot or cold beverage of fruit juices (e.g., apple, cranberry, lemon, orange, strawberry) and other nonalcoholic liquids (e.g., tea, ginger ale), often spiced, usually with a wine or liquor base.

pungent, of sharp flavor.

pupunha [Portuguese, from Tupi], a palm of South America that has a red edible fruit.

puree or **purée** [from French *purée* "the strained one," from Old French *purer* "to purify, strain"], *1.* a paste or thick mixture made by grinding cooked food finely or by rubbing it through a sieve or strainer, often with milk (e.g., chestnut, chicken liver, potato, split pea puree); *2.* a thick soup made of pureed vegetables.

puree (to), to boil food soft and then strain through a sieve (e.g., vegetables), to prepare in the form of a puree (sense 1, a paste).

puri or **poori** [from Hindi *puri*, from Sanskrit *purā*], a very light, puffy, flat, fried (in deep fat) wheat cake of Pakistan and northern India.

purple cane, another name for **purple raspberry**.

purple goatsbeard, another name for **salsify**.

purple granadilla, a Brazilian passionflower cultivated for its purple fruit (used for confectionery and beverages).

purple laver, an edible red alga.

purple raspberry or **purple cane**, a raspberry with purplish fruits (a hybrid between red and black raspberries).

purse crab or **coconut crab** or **palm crab** or **robber crab** or **tree crab**, a large land crab of the islands of the tropical Indian and Pacific oceans that feeds on coconuts.

purslane, a trailing plant with fleshy leaves that are eaten as a potherb and in salads.

quail quenelle quisutsch quince quelite quandong quailberry

Qatar. Kabobs, hummus; lamb and rice *(mansaf);* sweetmeats made with honey, are among the representative dishes of Qatar.

quahog or **hard-shell clam**, an edible, thick-shelled clam of the Atlantic coast of North America.

quail, any of various chickenlike birds. It is often baked, or split in halves and pan-broiled, or served warm as pâté.

quailberry, another name for **wolfberry**.

quandong or **native peach**, the round, red fruit of a small Australian tree (likewise called *quandong).*

quandong nut, the edible seed of the stone of the quandong tree.

quatre épices, see ¹**spice**.

queen crab, a large edible crab of tropical waters of the western Atlantic.

queenfish, any of several large marine fishes of the tropical Indo-Pacific.

queen olive, a variety of olive grown in the region of Seville, Spain, having large fruits that are usually cured green and are used for eating rather than as a source of oil.

Queensland cherry, the red fruit of an Australian shrub likewise called *Queensland cherry.*

Queensland nut, another name for **macadamia nut**.

queen turtle, an edible, soft-shelled, North American turtle.

quelite [Mexican Spanish, from Nahuatl *quilitl* "edible green"], potherb, any of various wild plants of Mexico and the southwestern United States, edible when tender, and cooked as greens (e.g., lamb's-quarters, purslane).

quenelle [French, from German *Knödel* "dumpling"], a poached (in boiling water or stock) usually oval dumpling of puréed or minced forcemeat (e.g., fish [often pike], fowl, game, veal), bound with eggs, served as a garnish or as a separate dish, often in a cream sauce (sometimes made with wine and lobster).

quesadilla [Mexican Spanish, from Spanish *quesadilla* "cheese pastry," diminutive of *quesada* "cheese turnover," from *queso* "cheese"], a wheat tortilla filled with a savory mixture, folded, fried in deep fat, and topped with cheese. In Mexico it is a masa (not wheat) turnover often filled with cheese, but also with pumpkin flowers, huitlacoche (a fungus that grows on Indian corn), seasoned ground beef, brains, hot-pepper strips (*rajas*), or cracklings.

quiche [French], a custard (cream and whipped eggs) pie usually having a savory filling (e.g., spinach, mushrooms, ham), baked in an unsweetened pastry shell.

quiche lorraine [French, (from *lorraine* "of Lorraine (region of northeastern France)")], a quiche containing grated cheese and crisp (fried) bacon bits.

quick bread, a bread made with a leavening agent (e.g., baking powder or baking soda and sour milk, or steam) that permits immediate baking of the dough or batter mixture (instead of the slower-acting yeast), because it expands during baking (it does not require a leavening period beforehand). Quick breads include biscuits, coffee cakes, corn breads, corn sticks, muffins, nut loaves, popovers, scones; some (pancakes, waffles) are cooked on a griddle, dumplings and brown breads are cooked by steam, doughnuts and fritters are fried in deep fat. Compare **yeast**.

quince, the aromatic, many-seeded fruit, edible only when cooked, of a tree (likewise called *quince)* of the rose family, used for marmalade, jelly, and preserves.

quinine water or **tonic water**, a carbonated beverage flavored with lemon, lime, and a small amount of quinine ["a powder obtained from certain cinchona barks," from Spanish *quina* "cinchona (tree of the madder family)," from Quechua *kina* "bark"].

quinnat salmon, another name for **king salmon**.

quinoa or **quinua** [from Spanish *quinua*, from Quechua], the seeds of a plant (likewise called *quinoa* or *quinua*) of the high Andes that are ground and widely used as food in Peru.

quisutsch, another name for **silver salmon**.

rabbit, *1.* any of various long-eared, short-tailed mammals that differ from the related hares in their burrowing habits and in having the young born naked, blind, and helpless. Rabbit is prepared like chicken (e.g., roasted); *2.* another name for **Welsh rabbit** (a cheese dish).

rabbiteye, or **rabbiteye blueberry**, a blueberry of the southern United States.

rabbitfish, a slender marine fish related to the escolar.

race, a root, especially of ginger.

race ginger, another name for **gingerroot** (the unpulverized ginger rootstock).

rack, *1.* a wholesale rib cut of lamb (sometimes of veal or pork) between the shoulder and the loin; *2.* a crown roast of lamb (compare **hotel rack**).

raclette [French "scraper," from *racler* "to scrape"], *1.* a dish of Swiss origin (from canton Valais) consisting of cheese melted over a fire and then scraped onto bread or boiled potatoes, often served with sour pickles; *2.* a firm cheese suitable for use in this dish.

radicchio [Italian "chicory"], a chicory (sense 1, plant) of a red variety with long variegated leaves used as a salad green.

radish, the pungent, thickened root of a plant (likewise called *radish*) of the mustard family, usually eaten raw as an appetizer and in salads.

raggee or **ragi** [from Hindi *rāgī*], a cereal grass of Africa and Asia, where it is cultivated for its edible grain, from which is ground a somewhat bitter flour.

ragout [from French *ragoût*, from *ragoûter* "to revive the taste"], meat (usually pieces of beef, veal, or mutton) and vegetables, well seasoned and cooked in a thick, rich, usually brown sauce. In Italian, *ragù* [from French *ragoût*] is the liquid from a meat stew (or a similar meat sauce, in English also called *Bolognese sauce*), used on pasta.

rahat lokum, see **Turkish delight**.

rainbow cactus [from its colorful flowers], a tall, spiny, cylindrical cactus of northern Mexico and the southwestern United States, having edible red fruit.

rainbow perch [from its being brilliantly striped in red, orange, and light blue], a small fish of the Pacific coast of North America.

rainbow runner or **prodigal son**, a large, blue and yellow fish.

rainbow trout, a trout of the Pacific coast of North America, that is greenish above and white on the belly and has a reddish longitudinal band and black spots.

raised, made light and high by yeast or other leaven, rather than with baking powder or baking soda. Raised doughnuts (e.g., bismarcks) are a yeast bread, fried.

raisin [French "grape"], a sweet grape of any of several varieties, dried in the sun or by artificial heat, and having a flavor quite different from that of the fresh grape. There are raisin breads, muffins, nut cakes, pies, walnut pies; raisin sauce is used for baked ham.

raisiné [French, from *raisin* "grape"], a preserve, especially of pears with quinces (with concentrated grape juice), or of grapes with quinces, cooked slowly, often in sweet wine or cider.

raisin grape, a grape of a sweet variety suitable for making raisins.

raisin-seed oil, another name for **grape-seed oil**.

rambutan [Malay, from *rambut* "hair" (the fruit is covered with long, soft spines)], the bright red, oval fruit of a Malayan tree (likewise called *rambutan*) of the soapberry family closely related to the litchi.

ramekin or **ramequin** [from French *ramequin*, from Low German *ramken* "little cream," from *ram* "cream"], a preparation of cheese made with bread crumbs, unsweetened puff paste, or eggs, baked and served in individual dishes (molds or shells). These baking dishes, too, are called *ramekins*.

ramon [from American Spanish *ramón*, from Spanish *ramón* "browse, tender shoots," from *ramo* "branch, twig"], another name fror **breadnut** (fruit).

rampion, a Eurasian plant (a bellflower) having a tuberous root used with the leaves as a salad.

ramsons, the bulbous roots of a broad-leaved Eurasian garlic (likewise called *ramson*) used in salads and relishes.

ramtil [from Hindi *rāmtil*, "dark sesame," from Sanskrit *rāma* "dark-colored" + *tila* "sesame"], a tropical African plant grown, especially in India, for its oil-rich seeds (called *Niger seeds).

rape, a plant of the mustard family. Compare **canola**.

rappini or **rapini** [from Italian *rapini* "small turnips," from *rapo* "turnip"], small plants related to the turnip, that are pulled from the soil before the development of the root and eaten as greens.

rare, (of meat, e.g., roast beef) cooked to a slight degree to retain juice and redness.

rarebit, another name for **Welsh rabbit** (a cheese dish).

rasher, *1.* a thin slice of bacon or ham to be fried or broiled; *2.* a dish of such slices.

raspberry, any of various red or black, sweet, juicy berries (borne by a shrubby plant, likewise called *raspberry*, of the rose family) that technically are aggregate fruits consisting of small drupes crowded on a fleshy receptacle and that are usually rounder and smaller than the related blackberries.

rata [Maori], another name for **Polynesian chestnut**.

ratafia [French], a small, sweet biscuit made from almond paste or flavored with a liqueur, likewise called *ratafia*, which in turn is flavored with macerated fruit or with fruit kernels or almonds.

ratatouille [French, or *ratatouille niçoise* (= "from Nice," city of southeastern France)], a stew made with eggplant, tomatoes, green peppers, zucchini, onions, and sometimes meat, seasoned with garlic and other condiments, and cooked in olive oil.

rat cheese or **rat-trap cheese**, another name for **cheddar**.

rat-tailed radish or **serpent radish**, a radish that has an inedible root but edible pods.

ravigote [French or *à la ravigote* "with ravigote sauce," from *ravigoter* "to revive, refresh"], a white (velouté) vinegar-sauce or dressing often colored green with spinach purée, spiced with minced onion, capers, a mixture of herbs (e.g., chervil, tarragon, chives), and minced hard-boiled egg, used with boiled meats (e.g., veal head) or fish.

ravioli [Italian, from regional Italian (south) *raviolo* "little turnip," from *rava* "turnip"], pasta in the form of little casings or shells of dough containing a savory filling (e.g., of chopped meat, cheese [often ricotta], cooked and seasoned vegetables [for instance, spinach]), often served with a sauce.

raw, uncooked, not subjected to heat in the course of preparation.

raw milk, milk that has not been pasteurized.

raw sugar, the yellow or brown product of sugar manufacture before refining.

raw water, water that has not been purified or distilled.

ray, any of various marine fishes (e.g., backwater).

ray-liver oil, a fish-liver oil from rays.

razor clam or **long clam**, any of numerous mollusks having a long, curved shell.

reblochon [French], a semisoft, creamy, mild-flavored, whole-milk cheese from Savoy (region of southeastern France).

réchauffé [French "warmed over"], a dish of food left from a previous meal and that has been reheated.

recipe, a formula for preparing something to be eaten or drunk, a list of the measured ingredients and often a set of directions for making such an item of food or drink.

recombined milk, milk made by combining nonfat dry milk solids with water and with cream, butterfat, or milk fat. Compare **reconstituted milk**.

reconstituted milk or **remade milk**, milk reconstituted by adding water to evaporated milk or to dry whole-milk solids.

red alga or **red seaweed**, a red or reddish alga. Compare **agar**.

red bass, *1.* another name for the **channel bass**; *2.* any of several snappers (Australia).

red cluster pepper, a small hot pepper grown for its red, extremely pungent fruits.

red cod, a reddish fish of Australia and New Zealand.

red crab, a dark red crab of the North American Pacific coast.

red crowberry, the edible red berry of a certain low shrub likewise called *red crowberry*.

red currant, the red fruit of any of various currants (sense 2) likewise called _red currants_.

red drum, another name for the **channel bass**.

red-eye (United States slang), _1._ another name for tomato **catsup** (sauce); _2._ also **red-eye gravy**, gravy made with catsup or with tomato sauce.

red flannel hash, hash made especially from beef (often corned beef), beets, potatoes, and other vegetables. It gets redder the more beets are added.

red grouper, a marine fish of the western Atlantic, that with age acquires a flesh-red color.

red herring or **highdried**, a herring cured by salting and slow smoking to a reddish color.

red hind or **cabrilla**, a grouper of the Atlantic ocean having red spots.

red-hot, _1._ a slang name for a hot dog (a frankfurter); _2._ a red candy flavored with cinnamon.

red ironwood, a small tree with an edible drupe (fleshy fruit).

red laver, any of various purple seaweeds whose stewed or pickled fronds are eaten in Europe.

red meat, _1._ meat (e.g., beef, lamb) that (unlike chicken, pork, or veal) is reddish in its raw and uncured state (compare **white meat**, sense 1); _2._ meat from a mammal as distinguished from poultry or fish.

red mombin, another name for **Spanish plum**.

red mulberry, the purple, blackberrylike fruit of a North American tree likewise called _red mulberry_.

red mullet, another name for **goatfish**.

red mustard, another name for **black mustard**.

red pepper, _1._ another name for **cayenne pepper** (hot-pepper powder); _2._ the pungent, red (at maturity), podlike fruit of any of several varieties of the pepper plant; _3._ a red or reddish sweet pepper.

red perch, another name for the **yellow perch**.

red rice, a wild rice with a red husk.

red rock-cod or **red cod**, any of several reddish or pinkish rockfishes of the North American Pacific coast.

red rockfish or **red snapper**, a large reddish or pinkish rockfish of the North American Pacific coast (chiefly California).

red salmon, another name for the **sockeye salmon**.

red seaweed, another name for **red alga**.

red shrimp, another name for the **Brazilian shrimp**.

red snapper, _1._ any of several marine fishes of tropical or semitropical waters having red or reddish bodies; _2._ another name for **red rockfish**; _3._ a silvery, blood-red fish (Australia). Red snappers are lean fish and therefore best for boiling and steaming.

red tai, a crimson Pacific Ocean porgy. In Japan, it is the symbol of the fish god.

redtail, another name for the **Brazilian shrimp**.

redware, a large, brown, leathery, edible seaweed, common off the coasts of the northern Atlantic.

red whelk, a European whelk.

reef bass, another name for **channel bass**.

reest (to), to cure (e.g., herring, bacon) by smoking (Scotland).

refried beans [translation of Mexican Spanish *frijoles refritos*] another name for **frijoles refritos**.

Reggiano or **Reggiano cheese** [Italian "from Reggio nell'Emilia (also called *Reggio Emilia)*," city of northern Italy], a high quality, Parmesan-like cheese.

reindeer, any of several large deers of arctic regions used especially in Lapland (northern Europe) as a source of food. See **venison**.

relish, *1.* a spicy or savory condiment (e.g., pickles, green tomatoes, mixed chopped vegetables [for instance, beets and corn] or fruits, horseradish sauce) served with other food (especially meat); *2.* another name for both **appetizer** and **hors d'oeuvre**.

relleno [Spanish "stuffing," from *rellenar* "to refill, stuff"], a stuffed (usually with minced meat and herbs) pepper.

remade milk, another name for **reconstituted milk**.

remoulade [from French *rémoulade*], a pungent cold sauce or dressing resembling mayonnaise but often made with cooked egg yolks and oil, and usually with chopped pickles, capers, anchovies, herbs, mustard, garlic. It is used on cold poultry, meat, and shellfish.

render (to), to melt down (e.g., suet), extract or clarify by melting (e.g., lard), over low heat.

rennet, *1.* the inner lining of the fourth compartment of the stomach of calves and other young ruminants; *2.* a dried extract of this lining, used to curdle milk; *3.* another name for **rennin**; *4.* a vegetable product used to curdle milk (e.g., steep grass).

rennin, a milk-coagulating enzyme produced from rennet (sense 1) and used in making cheeses and junkets.

Reuben, or **Reuben sandwich**, a large, grilled sandwich of corned beef slices, Swiss cheese, and sauerkraut, usually on rye bread (often a three-decker; occasionally spread with Thousand Island dressing).

rhubarb, any of several plants of the buckwheat family having long, green or reddish leafstalks that are edible when sweetened and cooked and that are used as a sauce, in pies, or in preserves.

rib, *1.* one of the paired, curved bones that stiffen the lateral walls of the body of most vertebrates; *2.* a cut of meat enclosing one or more ribs (sense 1).

ribbon candy, a thin sugar candy made in the form of a ribbon.

rib eye, the meat that lies along the outer side of the rib (of beef-cattle).

rib roast, a cut of meat for roasting containing the rib eye, one or more ribs, or parts of ribs.

¹**rice** or **arroz** (Spanish), the starchy seeds of a cereal grass (likewise called *rice)* that are cooked (boiled, steamed, or baked, in water, milk, or tomato juice) and used for food. It can also be browned, or curried. Among rice dishes: pilaf, risotto. Compare **al dente**.

²**rice (to)**, to put through a ricer.

rice bean, a bean grown in Asia for its seed.

ricer, a kitchen utensil in which soft foods (cooked or uncooked) are pressed through a perforated container to produce strings about the diameter of a grain of rice.

rice water, a drink (given chiefly to invalids) made by boiling a small amount of rice in water.

rich, containing a large or excessive proportion of fat or of tasty ingredients.

rickey, an alcoholic or nonalcoholic carbonated (with soda water) drink usually containing lime juice (or orange juice) and sugar.

ricotta [Italian "cooked again"], a whey cheese of Italian origin that resembles cottage cheese, made by repeated slow boiling. It is often used in ravioli.

rigatoni [Italian "the big furrowed ones," from *rigato* "furrowed, fluted," from *riga* "line"], hollow pasta made in short, wide, fluted (ribbed) tubes.

rijsttafel [Dutch "rice table"], an Indonesian meal consisting chiefly of rice to which are added small portions of a wide variety of accompanying dishes (spiced tidbits; e.g., meat, seafood, vegetables, chicken, fruit, eggs, curries, pickles, condiments).

rillettes [French, diminutive plural of *rille* "piece of pork"], seasoned, cooked, shredded, potted meat (e.g., pork, goose, duck, rabbit) or fish (e.g., salmon) preserved in fat.

rimas [Tagalog], another name for **breadfruit** (Philippines).

rind, a tough outer covering or layer, such as the skin of some fruits (e.g., of lemon, grapefruit, watermelon) or the coating on cheese or bacon.

ring, food in the shape of a circle (e.g., apple, onion, macaroni, noodle rings).

ringed perch or **ring perch** or **ring-tail perch**, other names for the **yellow perch**.

rinktum ditty or **rum tum ditty**, a mixture of cheese, tomato sauce, onion, egg, and seasonings (e.g., dry mustard) served on toast or crackers.

Rio [from *Rio* de Janeiro, state and city of southeastern Brazil], a Brazilian coffee.

ripe, *1.* fully grown and developed (e.g., of fruit); *2.* brought by preparation or aging to full flavor or to the best state (e.g., of cheese, venison).

risotto [Italian, from *riso* "rice"], rice cooked in meat stock and seasoned in any of various ways (e.g., with butter and grated Parmesan cheese, with saffron, with butter and tomato); mushrooms or seafood may be added, or it may first be fried with chopped onion.

rissole [French], minced meat (or fish) covered with puff pastry and usually fried in deep fat. This dish can also be baked.

rissolé [French], (of meat or vegetables [e.g., potatoes]) browned by frying at high temperature in deep fat.

river blackfish, a fish of the Murray river system of Australia.

river pear, another name for **anchovy pear**.

river perch, another name for **yellow perch**.

river prawn or **long-clawed prawn**, a large prawn of Australian rivers.

river shrimp, a freshwater shrimp of the southeastern United States.

¹**roast** (noun), *1.* a piece of meat which has been roasted. A pot roast is not really a roasted meat; it is rather braised meat (i.e., first browned in fat and then simmered); *2.* a cut of meat suitable or prepared for roasting.

²**roast (to)**, to cook by exposing to dry heat (as in an oven in a pan, or before an open fire on a spit; or by surrounding with hot embers, hot ashes, or heated stones, sand, or metals). Among meats that are roasted: beef, chicken, duck, goose, lamb, pork, turkey, veal. In French, roast potatoes are *pommes rissolées*.

³**roast** (adjective), meat that has been roasted.

roast beef, a fine piece of beef (rib roast or loin steak) that has been roasted (often served with Yorkshire pudding).

roaster, *1.* a suckling pig; *2.* a young chicken fit for roasting; *3.* any animal (e.g., rabbit) fit for roasting.

roasting ear, an ear of young, sweet corn roasted or fit for roasting in the husk, having fully developed milky grains in which the process of hardening has not begun.

rob [French, from Arabic *rubb*], thickened fruit juice of ripe fruit, obtained by evaporation over a fire and afterward sometimes mixed with honey or sugar to the consistency of syrup.

robalo [from Spanish *róbalo, robalo*], another name for **snook** (marine fish).

robber crab, another name for **purse crab**.

robusta coffee, coffee brewed from the seed (likewise called *robusta coffee*) of a robusta coffee plant (which is indigenous to central Africa but has been introduced elsewhere).

rocambole [French], the garliclike bulb of a European leek (likewise called *rocambole*), used as a seasoning.

rock, *1.* another name for **striped bass**; *2.* a stick candy with color running through and flavored with anise, clove, peppermint; *3.* another name for **rock candy**; *4.* or **rock cake**, a cookie made of firm dough (sugar, butter, eggs, flour, spices) dropped from a spoon to a greased cookie sheet or tin and that when baked retains an uneven form.

rock bass, *1.* or **rock sunfish**, a freshwater sunfish of North America; *2.* another name for **striped bass**.

rock candy or **rock**, boiled sugar crystallized in clear masses of considerable size on lightweight string.

rock cockle [the shells of these clams resemble those of cockles], any of various clams of the Pacific coast of North America.

Rock Cornish hen or **Cornish hen**, a domestic fowl produced by breeding Cornish and white Plymouth Rock strains and used especially as a roasting chicken.

rock dove, another name for **pigeon**.

rocket, another name for **arugula**.

rockfish, *1.* any of various fishes living among rocks; rockfishes include the black rockfish, the orange rockfish; *2.* another name for the **striped bass**.

rock lobster, *1.* another name for the **spiny lobster**; *2.* the flesh of the spiny lobster.

rock maple, another name for **sugar maple**.

rock melon, another name for **cantaloupe**.

rock oyster, any of various oysters occurring attached to rocks.

rock salmon, a reddish snapper of the tropical Indo-Pacific.

rock salt, *1.* common salt occurring in large, solid, rocklike masses; *2.* salt artificially prepared in large crystals or masses.

rock sunfish, another name for the **rock bass** (sense 1).

rock trout, another name for **greenling**.

rockweed, a coarse seaweed growing attached to rocks.

Rocky Mountain oyster, another name for **mountain oyster**.

roe, *1.* the eggs of a fish (black and red caviar are preserved fish eggs [e.g., sturgeon; compare **caviar**]); *2.* the egg mass of certain crustaceans (as the coral of a lobster).

roe deer, either of two small deer. Roe deer dishes include **civet**.

rohu [from Hindi *rohū*], a large Indian fish.

¹**roll**, any of various food preparations rolled up for cooking or serving (e.g., meat rolled and cooked, an egg roll), especially a small piece of yeast dough baked in any of numerous forms (e.g., a small rounded portion of bread, bialy; a cake made by rolling up sweet dough on which a filling has been spread [as a jelly roll]).

²**roll (to)**, (of dough) to place on a board and spread thin with a rolling pin (a long cylinder).

rolled oats, hulled oats steamed and then flattened by being passed between rollers.

rolled roast, a boned and rolled rib roast of beef. Compare **standing roast** (from which only the heaviest parts of the vertebrae have been removed).

rollmops [German], a fillet of herring wrapped around a gherkin or onion and skewered and then pickled in a marinade of vinegar and various spices and herbs (e.g., sliced onion, peppercorns, celery seed, bay leaves), and served as an hors d'oeuvre.

roll-up, a food preparation that is rolled up, often around a filling (as in ham roll-up).

roly-poly or **roly-poly pudding**, a dessert (a pudding, sense 1) made of rolled up sweet dough (pastry dough) spread with a filling (jam or fruit), rolled up into a cylinder shape, and baked or steamed.

Romadur [German], a cheese similar to Limburger in flavor.

romaine, or **romaine lettuce** [French "the Roman one (feminine)"], another name for **cos lettuce** (a variety of lettuce).

roman, a sea fish of southern Africa.

romana [Italian, "in Roman fashion"]. In Italian, *gnocchi alla romana* are gnocchi made with semolina.

Romania. The following are among representative dishes and products of Romania: broiled minced meat (Romanian *mititei*), minced meat in cabbage or vine leaves *(sarmale)*, pickled fish; polenta or corn flour porridge *(mămăligă)* with cheese *(cu brinză)* or other ingredients; cheese dishes, roast chicken with garlic sauce *(pui cu mujdei)*, quail, venison, wild boar, sheep, pheasant, caviar; baklava; a chopped walnut or pistachio dessert *(cataif;* called *kadaif* in Greece and Turkey, *kunafa* in Egypt).

Romano, or **Romano cheese** [from Italian *romano* "Roman, from Rome"], a hard, sharp cheese of Italian origin, of granular texture, with a blackish green rind, that is often served grated.

Romanoff [from *Romanoff* or *Romanov*, a Russian dynasty], see **noodle**.

Roman snail [it was formerly supposed to have been introduced into Britain by the Romans], a European edible snail.

roncador [Spanish "one that snores," from *roncar* "to snore"], *1.* any of several croakers of the eastern Pacific coast; *2.* any of various grunts of the Atlantic and the Pacific.

ronco [American Spanish from Spanish "hoarse"], any of several grunts of the tropical western Atlantic.

rooibos tea [from Afrikaans *rooibostee*, from *rooibos*, "red bush," the shrub from which it is made], a beverage that is made from an evergreen southern African shrub called *rooibos* in Afrikaans.

rooster and **roosterfish**, other names for **papagallo**.

root, the usually underground portion of a plant, which is often large, fleshy, and edible and sometimes is not a true root but a rhizome or tuber (e.g., carrot, radish, turnip, potato, sweet potato).

root beer, a sweetened, carbonated soft drink flavored with extracts of roots and herbs (e.g., anise, cloves, nutmeg, wintergreen).

root crop, a crop (e.g., sugar beets, sweet potatoes, turnips) cultivated for its enlarged roots.

rootstock, a rootlike, underground part of a plant.

Roquefort, or **Roquefort cheese** [from *Roquefort*-sur-Soulzon, a village in southern France, the center of manufacture of this cheese], a pungent, French blue cheese (it contains a blue mold) made from sheep's milk. It is often used in dips and dressings.

rose apple [it has a roselike fragrance] or **jambo** or **pomarrosa**, the large, fleshy fruit of a tropical tree likewise called *rose apple*.

rosefish or **redfish**, a large, bright red, marine fish of North Atlantic waters. It is a fat fish, and therefore best for broiling, baking, planking.

roselle or **Jamaican sorrel**, a tropical plant of which the immature floral bracts (leaves) are used for making tarts and jelly and an acid drink.

rosemary [from Latin *rosmarinus*, "dew of the sea"], a fragrant, evergreen, shrubby mint of southern Europe having grayish-green leaves that are used as a culinary herb.

rosette [French "small rose"], *1.* a braised or fried piece of boneless veal encircled by a skewered bacon strip; *2.* a food decoration (e.g., icing rosettes) or garnish (e.g., carrot rosettes) in the shape of a rose. In regional French (Lyons), a *rosette de Lyon* is a dry sausage.

rosolio [Italian], a liqueur made from spirits, sugar, and flavorings (e.g., with cherries, cinnamon, citron, cloves, orange-blossom water, rose petals).

roti [from Hindi *roṭī* "bread"], *1.* a thin, flat, soft cake of unleavened bread (India; West Indies); *2.* such a bread wrapped around a filling and eaten as a sandwich.

roughy, a small Australian marine fish.

rouille [French "rust," from its color], a red pepper and garlic sauce of Mediterranean French origin usually served with fish soups and stews (especially bouillabaisse).

roulade [French "roll, act of rolling"], a slice of usually stuffed meat (sometimes of fish) that is rolled, browned, and steamed or braised.

round, a cut of meat (e.g., beef) that is the hind leg, especially between the rump and the lower leg. Compare **top round**.

round steak, a lean, oval steak cut from the whole round of beef including the bone.

roux [French, from *(beurre) roux* "browned (butter)," from *roux* "reddish brown, russet"], a mixture of flour and butter or other fat cooked together, sometimes until the flour browns; it is used to thicken soups and sauces. The French speak of *roux blanc* "white roux," *roux blond* "blond roux," and *roux brun* "brown roux" according to the color, which is due to how long the butter was cooked.

rowan, a mountain ash (tree) having small pomes.

royal agaric, a certain edible mushroom.

rubberlip perch or **rubberlip sea-perch**, a medium-sized fish of the California coast (United States).

ruffed grouse [the male has a ruff (a fringe) of black feathers around the neck], a chickenlike North American grouse. Often split in halves to pan-broil with butter or bacon.

rugola, another name for **arugula**.

rumaki, a cooked appetizer made of pieces of usually marinated chicken liver wrapped together with sliced water chestnuts in bacon slices.

rump, *1.* the upper, fleshy, rounded part of the hindquarters of a quadruped mammal; *2.* a cut of meat (e.g., beef, veal) from this part, i.e. between the loin and round.

rump steak, a steak cut from the rump.

rum tum ditty, another name for **rinktum ditty**.

rusell [from Yiddish *rosel* "pickle, broth"], vinegar made of fermented (for about a month) beet juice and used during Passover. It may be employed in beet soup (borsch). With added lemon juice, salt, pepper, sugar, oil, it may be used as a salad dressing.

rush nut, another name for **chufa**.

rusk [from Portuguese or Spanish *rosca* "coil; twisted roll"], *1.* hard, crisp bread originally used on ships; *2.* a sweet or plain bread baked, sliced, and baked again until dry and crisp. It is similar to zwieback.

Russia. The following are among representative dishes and products of Russia: caviar (Russian *ikra*), borsch, sour cabbage soup *(shchi);* a meat or sturgeon soup with cabbage, olives, onions, and plenty of salt *(solyanka);* hors d'oeuvre *(zakuski*, often including caviar with blinis, smoked salmon, sturgeon in aspic, salted herring, pirozhki, crab or game salad, pickled cucumbers and mushrooms); a cold soup made of kvass (a fermented-cereal [e.g., rye bread and malt], slightly alcoholic beverage), vegetables, and meat or fish *(okroshka);* buckwheat groats *(kasha)*, pirozhki, chicken cutlets *(kotlety* or *kotletki Pozharskiy)*, fish or cabbage pie *(kulebyaka)*, roast carp *(zharennyy karp)* with porridge *(s kashoy)*, minced chicken cutlets or cutlets a la Kiev (filled with butter), sturgeon baked with cream, beef Stroganoff, dough dumplings stuffed with meat *(pel'meny);* a yeast bread made with sweet roll dough *(kulich)*. Beverage: tea.

Russian dressing, mayonnaise (or simply oil-and-vinegar) dressing with additions that give a sharp flavor and may include hot-pepper sauce, chopped pickles, or pimientos.

Russian sunflower, a large-seeded sunflower that is used as food in Russia.

Russian turnip, another name for **rutabaga**.

rusty dab, a rust-brown flatfish of the eastern coast of North America.

rutabaga [from regional Swedish *rotabagge* "baggy root"] or **Russian turnip** or **turnip cabbage** or **swede** or **Swedish turnip**, the thick, yellowish root of a plant (likewise called *rutabaga*), used as food. White it is a **turnip**, yellow it is a rutabaga. Rutabagas can be served glazed.

rye, *1.* the seeds of a cereal grass (likewise called *rye*) used for a bread flour, that is the chief ingredient of black bread; *2.* another name for rye bread.

rye and Indian, bread made of rye flour and cornmeal and in North America, in the 17th and 18th centuries, often baked in a pot or a brick oven.

rye bread, any bread made partially or entirely from rye flour (e.g., black bread, knäckebröd, pumpernickel, a light loaf often with caraway seed).

Russian turnip

rye bread

229

Saanen or **Saanen cheese** [from *Saanen*, locality in southwestern Switzerland], an Emmental-like cheese.

saba [from Tagalog *sabá*], a cooking banana (Philippines).

sabalo [from American Spanish *sábalo*, from Spanish *sábalo* "shad"] or **sabalote**, another name for **milkfish**.

sabal palmetto, another name for **cabbage palmetto** (see **cabbage tree**).

sabayon [French, from Italian *zabaione* "zabaglione"], another name for **zabaglione**.

sablefish [from *sable* "black," from *sable*, a dark brown animal] or **black cod** or **skil** or **skilfish**, a large, dark-colored marine fish of North American Pacific waters.

sabra [modern Hebrew "prickly pear"], the prickly fruit of several cacti of Palestine.

saccharin [from Latin *saccharum* "sugar"] or **gluside**, a very sweet, white, crystalline compound used as a calorie-free sweetener.

saccharine [from Latin *saccharum* "sugar"], relating to sugar.

Sacher torte [from German *Sachertorte*, from *Sacher*, name of a family of Austrian restaurant owners], a rich cake (a torte) made of chocolate, butter, eggs, confectioners' sugar, toasted bread crumbs, and spices, baked in layers, filled with cream or jam (usually apricot jam) and topped with chocolate icing. Compare **Linzer torte**.

Sacramento salmon, another name for **king salmon**.

Sacramento sturgeon, another name for **white sturgeon**.

sacred ear or **sacred earflower**, the fragrant, spicy flower of a Mexican and Central American shrub, having the shape of an ear and used by the Aztecs to flavor chocolate.

saddle, *1.* a cut of meat, consisting of both sides of the unsplit back of an animal including both loins, or the undivided loin prepared for roasting; *2.* another name for **hindsaddle**; *3.* the lower part of the back of a frog, with the hind legs.

safflower, a plant having seeds that are the source of an oil used in cooking.

safflower oil, an oil obtained from safflower seeds, used in making margarine.

saffron, a cooking spice, the deep orange, aromatic, dried stigmas (parts of the pistils of flowers) of a crocus (likewise called *saffron*) used to color and flavor food. It is the most expensive spice.

saffron plum, a buckthorn of the West Indies and Florida that bears a sweet fruit resembling a small plum.

sagamité [from Canadian French *sagamité*, of Algonquian origin], *1.* hulled Indian corn; *2.* a thin porridge (gruel, mush) made by boiling hulled corn.

sage, the aromatic, grayish-green leaves of a certain mint (likewise called *sage*), used as a cooking herb, especially in flavoring meats, and as a seasoning.

sage cheese, a cheese similar to cheddar, flavored with chopped sage leaves (preferably freshly chopped tender leaves, not dried ones).

sage oil, an oil obtained from the leaves of the sage and used in flavoring.

sage tea, a beverage prepared by infusion of sage leaves.

saging [Tagalog], another name for **banana** (Philippines).

sago [from Malay *sagu* "sago palm"], a dry, granulated or powdered starch prepared from the trunks of a sago palm, used in Asia as a thickening agent in foods (e.g., in puddings).

sago palm, any of various palm trees yielding sago.

saguaro or **sahuaro** or **suwarro** [from Mexican Spanish *saguaro*], the edible red fruit of a very large cactus (likewise called *saguaro*) occurring in desert regions of northern Mexico and southwestern United States.

sailfish, a fish having a large fin on the back. Compare **Atlantic sailfish**.

saimin, a Hawaiian noodle soup.

saint-honoré [possibly from French *(rue) Saint-Honoré*, a Paris street], French for a cake decorated with small cream puffs and whipped cream, glazed with sugar. Compare **croquembouche**.

Saint-John's-bread, a carob pod (also called *carob bean*, or simply *carob*) or its pulp.

Saint Kitts and Nevis. The following are among representative dishes and products of Saint Kitts and Nevis: aubergine soup, peanut soup, pot roast, ¹**pepper pot** (with cassareep), pork stew, lamb stew, curry with meat or poultry or fish or shellfish (e.g., spiny lobster, curried conch), chutney (mango or green papaya), coconut pie, lime pie, sweet cassava-bread, banana, coconut, mango, passion fruit. Beverage: pineappleade.

Saint Lucia. The following are among representative dishes and products of Saint Lucia: rice, fish, pork, chicken pilaf, curried goat, codfish and green bananas (known locally as *salt fish and green figs*), souse and green bananas (known locally as *souse and green figs*), sweet cassava-bread.

Saint Vincent and the Grenadines. The following are among representative dishes and products of Saint Vincent and the Grenadines: arrowroot, chicken, pilaf, arrowroot custard.

safflower

Saint Vincent and the Grenadines

sake [Japanese "liquor"], a Japanese beverage made from fermented rice.

salad [from French *salade*, from Latin *sal* "salt"], *1.* a dish consisting of green, leafy, usually raw vegetables or herbs (e.g., celery, chicory, endive, escarole, lettuce, romaine, spinach, watercress; sometimes white, like cabbage) often with tomatoes, cucumbers, or radishes and which are tossed about until marinated, and served with a dressing; *2.* a cold dish of meat, chicken, fish (e.g., salmon, tuna), shellfish (e.g., crabmeat, lobster, shrimp), eggs, fruits (e.g., apple, avocado, cranberry, grape, grapefruit, melon, orange), pasta (e.g., macaroni), nuts, cheese (e.g., cottage), or usually cooked vegetables (e.g., artichoke, bean, beet, carrot, celery root, spinach) alone or in various combinations, that are sliced, cut in pieces, shredded, or minced, usually prepared with mayonnaise or other dressing; there are also hot salads (e.g., hot potato salad). See also **Caesar salad**, **chef's salad**, **coleslaw**, **Waldorf salad**.

salad bar, a self-service counter with many salad makings and dressings.

salad burnet or **garden burnet** or **pimpernel** or **burnet**, a European burnet (sense 1) sometimes eaten as salad.

salad dressing, a sauce, a savory liquid or semisolid food (e.g., French dressing [sense 1], mayonnaise, oil and vinegar or lemon juice). In uncooked dressings, the ingredients are stirred or shaken together. Cooked dressings are made with milk and butter (to replace the oil) and may be thickened with a starch (e.g., rye, tapioca, or wheat flour) as well as egg. A boiled dressing is essentially a custard or cream sauce with vinegar and seasonings added. Salad dressings include catsup, chiffonade, garlic, Roquefort, Russian, sour cream, vinaigrette dressings.

salade niçoise, see under **France** *(Provence)*.

salading, vegetables or herbs for salad.

salad oil, a vegetable oil suitable for salad dressing.

salad plate, a salad mixture served as a main dish.

salak, the pear-shaped, pineapple-flavored fruit (a hard stone enclosed in a firm white pulp) of a thorny Philippine palm likewise called *salak* and cultivated for this fruit.

salal, a small shrub of the heath family found on the Pacific coast of North America and bearing edible, dark purple berries called *shallons*.

salami [Italian "sausages," plural of *salame*, from *sale* "salt"], a spiced and salted sausage that originated in Italy, made usually of minced pork but also of pork and beef in various proportions, either air-dried, hard, and of good keeping qualities or fresh, soft, and requiring refrigeration.

salangane [French, from Malay *sarang* "nest"], any of several swifts producing edible nests (called in French *nids d'hirondelles*, "swallow [rather than swift] nests"). Compare **bird's nest**.

salep or **saleb** [from French or Spanish *salep*, from regional Arabic *saḥlab*], the starchy or mucilagenous meal ground from dried tubers of various Old World orchids used for food (similar to tapioca).

Salisbury steak [for J.H. *Salisbury*, 19th-century English nutritionist], ground beef mixed with egg, milk, bread crumbs, and various seasonings, formed into a large patty, and broiled or fried. Compare **hamburger** (sense 2).

Sally Lunn [for *Sally Lunn*, 18th-century English baker], a slightly sweetened, yeast-leavened tea cake, baked as a thin loaf or as muffins, and often eaten hot with butter.

salmagundi [from archaic French *salmigondis*], a salad plate consisting of chopped meat, anchovies, hard-cooked eggs, and onions (sometimes also pickled vegetables, olives, radishes, endive, watercress), often arranged in rows for contrast, on lettuce, and served with vinegar and oil. Herring salmagundi is called *herring gundy* in the United States Virgin Islands.

salmi or **salmis** [from French *salmis*, short for *salmigondis*], *1.* a ragout of partly roasted game (e.g., guinea fowl, partridge, woodcock) stewed in a rich sauce; *2.* leftover game or domestic duck or goose reheated in a rich brown sauce; *3.* a sauce of butter, vinegar, brown sugar, and various spices, served with wild fowl.

salmon or **lax**, any of various large fishes of northern waters, having a pinkish flesh, eaten either fresh or cured and smoked. It is a fat fish and therefore best for broiling, baking, planking. In addition to salmon steak, salmon can be eaten in the form of canapés, loaf, marinated (with dill and pepper), mousse, pâté, salad, scalloped, simmered (in fish stock, seasoned with shallots), soufflé. Compare **Atlantic salmon**.

salmonberry, the edible, salmon-colored, raspberrylike fruit of a large prickly shrub (likewise called *salmonberry*) of western North America.

salmon trout, any of various salmonlike fish.

salsa [Spanish "sauce," from Latin *salsa* "salted (feminine)"], a spicy sauce of tomatoes, onions, and hot peppers. It may range from the mild through pungent and hot to very hot. Mexican salsas are often added to soups, are used to enliven any of the dry soups, and are eaten with plain meat or fish and added to tacos (rolled up tortillas).

salsify [from French *salsifis*] or **vegetable oyster** or **oyster plant** or **purple goatsbeard**, the long, tapering, edible taproot of a European plant (likewise called *salsify)*, eaten as a vegetable.

salsilla, a tropical American plant with roots that, especially in the West Indies, are boiled and used as a substitute for potatoes.

¹**salt** (noun), a colorless or white crystalline compound consisting chiefly of sodium chloride, extensively used to season or preserve food (e.g., fish, meat). It is abundant in nature and is obtained from deposits in the earth or by evaporation of seawater. Compare **table salt**.

²**salt** (to), *1.* to add salt to, season with salt; *2.* to preserve or cure food (e.g., fish, meat) with salt or in a salt solution.

³**salt** (adjective), *1.* tasting of salt (this is one of the four basic taste sensations; the others are bitter, sour, and sweet) or containing salt (e.g., salt butter); *2.* cured or seasoned with salt (e.g., salt beef); *3.* preserved in salt or a salt solution (e.g., salt mackerel).

salt horse, salted meat (e.g., beef, pork).

saltimbocca [Italian "it jumps into your mouth"], thin scallops of veal prepared with sage leaves, slices of raw or cooked ham, and sometimes cheese and served in a wine or an anchovy sauce or with croutons of fried bread.

saltine, a thin, crisp cracker usually sprinkled with coarse salt.

233

salt junk, dried salted beef (cured or preserved with salt).

salt pork, fat pork, especially from the belly, back, or side, cured in salt or brine.

salt-rising bread, a bread made of coarse flour, water or milk, and salt, in which leavening (rising) is produced by allowing a salted batter, held over from a previous baking, to rise before mixing with additional flour and liquid.

saltwater muskellunge or **saltwater pike**, another name for the **great barracuda**.

saltwater taffy, a pulled candy made from white sugar (and water, corn syrup, butter) and variously flavored (with oil of peppermint, or oil of orange, lime, or wintergeen, or oil of cassia or cinnamon, or oil of anise, or grated chocolate; nuts, fruits, or coconut can be added) and colored.

sambal [Malay], a southeastern Asian condiment consisting chiefly of raw vegetables and fruit (e.g., onions, cucumbers, peanuts, quinces, peppers, pickles, grated coconut, pineapple) but also of salt fish, or fish roe, prepared with spices, vinegar, soy sauce, sugar, and eaten especially with curry and rice.

samosa [Hindi], a turnover, a triangular patty shell, usually filled with meat.

samovar [Russian "self-boiler," from *samo-* "self-" + *varit'* "to boil"], a metal (usually copper) urn with a spigot at its base (and a central tube for live charcoal) used, especially, in Russia to boil water for tea.

samp, *1*. a coarse hominy; *2*. a porridge (a boiled cereal) made from coarse hominy.

sampaloc [from Tagalog *sampalok*], another name for **tamarind** (Philippines).

sand blackberry or **knee-high blackberry**, a thorny blackberry plant of the eastern United States having sweet fruit.

sand dab, any of several small fishes of Pacific waters resembling the flounders.

sand food, a low plant of the Colorado desert (United States) having edible stems and tubers resembling sweet potatoes.

sand grape or **sugar grape**, a wild grape (a shrub) of the southeastern United States having sweet dark fruit.

sandia [from Spanish *sandía*], another name for **watermelon**.

sandkruiper [from Afrikaans *zand kruiper*, "sand creeper"], any of various small rays of sandy, shallow seas.

sand pear, a Chinese pear (tree) having, in some strains, edible fruit.

sandwich [for John Montagu, 1718-1792, 4th Earl of *Sandwich*, English diplomat for whom sandwiches were made so that he could stay at the gambling table without interruptions for meals], *1*. two or more slices of bread or a split roll, often buttered, with a fairly thin layer (e.g., of meat, chicken, cheese, grilled cheese, eggs, fish [e.g., tuna], nuts, jam, crabmeat, shrimp, a savory mixture) placed between them. Compare **club sandwich**, **hamburger** (sense 3), **hot dog**, **western sandwich**. Sandwiches are sometimes broiled or toasted; *2*. a sandwich (sense 1) lacking a top covering of bread.

San Pedro fish [for Point *San Pedro*, California], another name for **opah**.

santol [from Tagalog *santól*] or **wild mangosteen**, a southeastern Asia tree sometimes grown for its red acid fruits used in preserves and pickles.

Santos or **Santos coffee** [for *Santos*, São Paulo state, Brazil, main port for shipping coffee from Brazil], Brazilian coffee produced chiefly in the southeastern state of São Paulo.

sapodilla or **sapotilla** [from Spanish *zapotillo*, diminutive of *zapote* "sapodilla," from Nahuatl *tzapotl*] or **sapota** or **sapote** or **nispero** or **zapote** [from Spanish *zapote* "sapodilla," from Nahuatl *tzapotl*] or **chico** [from Mexican Spanish *chico*, short for *chicozapote*, from Nahuatl *xicotzapotl*], the sweet, russet fruit of an evergreen tree (likewise called *sapodilla,* or **dilly**) of tropical America. The tree's latex yields chicle.

sapsago [from German *Schabziger*], a hard green cheese made from skim-milk curd, colored and flavored with dried powdered leaves of sweet clover.

sapsap or **peperek**, a small, slimy-bodied fish (Philippines).

sapucaia nut or **paradise nut**, the oily, edible seed of various trees called *sapucaias*, especially of Brazil and Guyana, that resemble Brazil nuts.

Saratoga chip or **Saratoga potato** [for *Saratoga* Springs, New York], another name for **potato chip**.

Saratoga chop, a rolled and skewered shoulder chop of lamb.

sardelle [German] or **sardel** [Yiddish] another name for **sardine**.

sardine [French, from Latin *sardina*], *1.* any of various small or half-grown herrings or related fishes, often canned in oil; *2.* any of various, unrelated, small fishes that are similarly processed. Compare **sild**, **sprat**.

sarepta mustard [for *Sarepta*, region near Volgograd, southern Russia], a Russian mustard (plant) that is the source of a brownish mustard (condiment).

sarsaparilla [from Spanish *zarzaparrilla*, from *zarza* "bush" + *parrilla* "little vine," diminutive of *parra* "vine"], *1.* the dried roots (used as a flavoring) of any of several tropical American plants (likewise called *sarsaparilla); 2.* a sweet soft drink flavored with sarsaparilla (sense 1).

sarson [from Hindi *sarsō*], an Indian colza (rape seed).

sashimi [Japanese], a Japanese dish consisting of thinly sliced raw fish served as an appetizer with a sauce for dipping.

saskatoon, the sweet, dark-purple fruit of a shrub (likewise called *saskatoon)* of northwestern North America.

sassafras [from Spanish *sasafrás*], the dried, aromatic bark of the root of a North American tree (likewise called *sassafras)* used as a flavoring agent.

sate, see under **Malaysia**.

satsuma or **satsuma orange** [from *Satsuma*, region of Japan (in southern Kyushu)], the medium-sized, largely seedless fruit of any of several mandarin trees (likewise called *satsumas).*

sauce [French, from Latin *salsa* "salted (feminine)," from *sal* "salt"], any flavorful soft or liquid dressing or relish served as an accompaniment to food (e.g., meat or fish stock or milk or cream thickened with flour

or other starch, usually flavored with a concentrate [as from roast meat], seasoned with condiments or spices, and used for meat, fish, egg, and vegetable dishes). Such sauces include aioli, allemande, béarnaise, béchamel, Bordelaise, brown sauce, cream sauce, dressing (sense 1), gravy, hollandaise, mayonnaise, Mornay, mousseline, piquant sauce, Provençale, ravigote, rouille, roux, suprême (sense 1), tomato sauce, velouté, vinaigrette, white sauce; see also **garnish**; compare **Newburg**; *2.* a flavored, sweetened mixture served as a topping with a dessert (e.g., water, milk, cream, or fruit juice [for instance, lemon, orange] with sugar and other ingredients [for instance, butterscotch, chocolate, coconut], and thickened with flour or other starch or with eggs; or eggs and butter without other liquid); *3.* stewed or puréed, sweetened fruit (e.g., cooked fresh fruit [as apple, cherry, peach, pear, plum; even rhubarb, which is no fruit] or cooked dried fruit [as apricot, apple, fig, pear, peach, prune, raisin] eaten with other food or as a dessert). White sauce, cream sauce, and gravy are basic sauces (sense 1) to which many kinds of seasonings and flavorings may be added; they consist primarily of a liquid, such as water, meat juices, or milk thickened with flour (the flour may be mixed first with heated butter or fat; then the resulting product is called a roux) or with cornstarch. In the United States, Chinese dishes are thickened with cornstarch, in China with rice starch or other starches. A plain white sauce with simple seasonings is often used for vegetables, such as potatoes, peas, carrots, celery. Egg yolks may be used to thicken the liquid in making some cream sauces. Certain sauces are traditionally used with certain foods; e.g., cranberry or orange-currant for roast duck, lamb, ham, chicken; tartar for fried or broiled fish, scallops, shrimp; raisin for baked ham; mint for roast lamb; horseradish for ham loaf or tongue; tart applesauce for roast pork or duck. For vegetables such as asparagus, broccoli, Brussels sprouts, spinach, string beans, broiled mayonnaise can be used; for broccoli, cauliflower, lima beans, hot Thousand Island dressing; for cooked celery, green and wax beans, shredded carrots or beets, drawn butter; carrots, cauliflower, green beans, can be dressed Polonaise; a crumb sauce for asparagus, cauliflower. In the case of desserts (sauce, sense 2), a butterscotch or chocolate sauce is used for ice cream and frozen desserts; a creamy, or a lemon, orange, or raspberry sauce for steamed puddings, cakes, or shortcakes; a cream, raspberry, caramel, mint sauce for fruits.

sauce béarnaise, see **béarnaise**.

sauce bordelaise, see **Bordelaise**.

sauce espagnole, see **espagnole**.

sauce piquante, see **piquant sauce**.

sauerbraten [German "sour roast meat"], oven-roasted or pot-roasted beef (e.g., chuck or rump) marinated before cooking in a vinegar solution with peppercorns, garlic, onions, and bay leaves. Parsnip, carrots, cloves, and juniper berries may be added. It is often served with boiled potatoes and sweet-and-sour red cabbage. The gravy can be dark roux made with some of the marinade.

sauerkraut [German "sour cabbage"] or **kraut**, chopped or shredded cabbage that is salted and slightly fermented in a pickling brine (with juniper berries) made of its own juice. Is often served with spareribs or sausage.

sauger or **gray pike** or **pickering**, a small North American pike perch (fish).

saurel, another name for **jack mackerel**.

sausage [from French *saucisse*, from Latin *salsus* "salted"] or **wurst** [German], *1.* finely minced and seasoned meat, especially pork, often extended (e.g., with cereal or milk solids), usually stuffed into casings of prepared (cleaned and scraped) animal intestine or of synthetic material, which are tied shut at both ends to form a unit or at intervals to form links, and is used cooked or cured; *2.* a link or patty of sausage. Sausages include bologna, cervelat, country sausage, liver sausage, mortadella, Polish sausage, salami, saveloy. Compare **chitterlings** (that are cooked intestines of hog).

sausage bull, a bull suitable for producing meat for sausage or similar products.

sausage meat, meat minced and spiced to be used in sausages or as a stuffing.

¹**sauté**, a sautéed dish.

²**sauté** (**to**), to fry lightly (to brown) in very little fat in a shallow, open pan (a skillet) on top of the range. Distinguished from **deep-fry** (to cook by immersing in a deep pan of fat). A fine distinction may be made between *sauté* and *fry:* a food is sautéed —quickly fried in a little very hot fat— as a preliminary to further cooking in a different way (e.g., the first step in preparing a French onion soup is the sautéing of the onions; liquid and other ingredients are then added, and the soup is finished by simmering; or meat may be sautéed before it is made into a casserole dish). Compare ¹**stir-fry**.

sautéed, fried in very little fat. Veal, rabbit, potatoes may be sautéed.

savarin [French, from Anthelme Brillat-*Savarin*, 1755–1826, French gastronomist], a yeast-cake baked in a ring mold, covered with nuts and fruit (e.g., almonds, citron), and soaked in a rum or kirsch syrup. Often garnished with cream.

saveloy [from French *cervelas*, from Italian *cervellata* "Milanese sausage, pig's brains," from *cervello* "brain"], a cooked, seasoned, smoked pork (meat and brains) sausage. Sometimes served with a vinaigrette. Compare **cervelat**.

¹**savory** (adjective), *1.* appetizing, agreeable to the senses of taste or smell, especially by reason of effective seasoning; *2.* piquant, pungent, or salty to the taste, not sweet.

²**savory** (noun), a cooked or uncooked dish of stimulating flavor (e.g., anchovies on toast) served usually at the end of dinner instead of a dessert but sometimes as an appetizer (hors d'oeuvre) before the meal.

³**savory** (noun), the leaves of either of two aromatic herbs (mints) also called, respectively, *summer savory* (well-suited for chowders, sausages, stuffings, and summertime vegetables) and *winter savory* (good with roast meats, stews, lentils), used (sparingly) as seasoning; the names have nothing to do with growing patterns; the winter variety tastes sharper and is more resinous than the summer.

237

savoy [from French *(chou de) Savoie* "(cabbage of) Savoy (region of southeastern France)"], *1.* or **Savoy cabbage** or **milan cabbage**, a variety of the common cabbage having a compact head of wrinkled and curled leaves; *2.* a spinach having wrinkled leaves.

Savoy cake [from *Savoy*, region in southeastern France], *1.* or **Savoy finger** or **Savoy biscuit**, another name for **ladyfinger**; *2.* a large sponge cake often baked in a mold or cut in fancy shape.

Sbrinz, a hard cheese from Switzerland, suitable for grating.

scabbard fish, any of several narrow-bodied, silvery, marine fishes of Pacific waters.

scald (to), *1.* to wash (swine or poultry) with boiling or hot water in order to remove hair or feathers or to wash fruits or vegetables with boiling water in order to loosen their skin (e.g., a tomato before peeling it); *2.* to heat (e.g., milk or another liquid) to a temperature just short of the boiling point, often in the top of a double boiler. Milk used to be scalded for making bread dough (to kill bacteria) and is scalded in making custards (to shorten the cooking time). Compare **blanch** (sense 2), **parboil**.

scallion, another name for any of the following: **shallot**, **leek**, **green onion**. It can be served as scallion pancake.

¹**scallop** [from French *escalope* "thin slice of meat"], *1.* a muscle (the adductor muscle) of any of various marine mollusks (likewise called *scallops)*, cooked and served as food. Scallops are often served fried or in a casserole; French fried seafood may include scallops and oysters, shrimp, clams; *2.* a scallop (the mollusk; see sense 1) shell, or a similarly shaped dish, used for baking and serving seafood; *3.* a thin, boneless slice of meat (e.g., veal).

²**scallop (to)** [from the former use of a large *scallop* (the mollusk; see sense 1) shell as an individual baking dish] or **escallop (to)**, to bake food, usually cut in pieces, in a casserole or a baking dish with milk or in a sauce, usually covered with seasoned bread or cracker crumbs. Scalloped foods are, like foods prepared au gratin, covered with bread crumbs and baked in the oven; the two terms therefore practically mean the same (when a distinction is made, it is that au gratin dishes include grated cheese). Potatoes or oysters, or, to make a dessert, apples, peaches, rhubarb, with sugar and crumbs, can be scalloped.

scallopini or **escallopine** or **escalope** or **scaloppine** [from Italian *scaloppine*, plural of *scaloppina* "thin slice of meat," from French *escalope* "thin slice of meat"], small, thinly sliced pieces of veal or other meat, sautéed or coated with flour and fried.

scampi [Italian, plural of *scampo*, a European lobster], large shrimps, especially as used in Italian cooking, usually prepared with a garlic-flavored sauce. Often fried.

scarlet hamelia, a tropical American shrub having edible fruit and scarlet flowers.

scarlet runner or **scarlet runner bean** or **fire bean**, a tropical American, climbing bean plant having scarlet flowers and long pods containing edible red-and-black seeds.

scarlet strawberry, another name for **Virginia strawberry**.

scarola or **scarole** [from Italian *scarola, scariola*], variants of **escarole** (i.e., another name for **endive** in either of its first two meanings).

scarus [Latin, from Greek *skaros*], a parrot fish of the Mediterranean highly esteemed today and also by the ancient Romans.

scented tea, tea having a scent or odor because it was packed with flowers or fired with flowers; especially, another name for **jasmine tea**.

schmierkase [from German *Schmierkäse*, from *schmieren* "to smear, spread" + *Käse* "cheese"], another name for **cottage cheese**.

schnecken [German "snails," plural of *Schnecke*], sweet cinnamon rolls made of dough cut in a coil shape (the yeast-leavened dough is rolled up like a jelly roll, cut into crosswise slices, and baked cut side down) like that of a snail shell.

schnitz [German "slice, cut"], sliced dried apples or other fruit.

schnitz and knepp, a dish of dried apples and dumplings, sometimes boiled with smoked ham.

schnitzel [German "cutlet," literally = "shaving, chip, small slice," diminutive of *Schnitz* "slice, cut"], a thin cutlet of veal fried lightly in butter, variously seasoned and garnished. Compare **Wiener schnitzel**.

schnitz un knepp [from Pennsylvania German *schnitz un gnepp*], another name for **schnitz and knepp**.

schoolmaster, another name for **black snapper**.

schwartzbrot or **schwarzbrot** [from German *Schwarzbrot* "black bread"], another name for **black bread**.

scone, *1*. a round, soft, doughy pastry; *2*. originally, in Scotland, a thin cake of oatmeal, cut into usually triangular shapes, and baked on a griddle.

scorpion fish, a certain marine fish.

scorzonera [from Spanish *escorzonera* "black salsify"], the root of a plant (likewise called *scorzonera*, or *black salsify); see **black salsify**.

Scotch broth, a soup made from mutton or beef, vegetables, and pearl barley.

Scotch egg, a hard-boiled egg wrapped in sausage meat (or cooked ham), covered with bread crumbs, and fried. It may be served on croutons. Some cooks make a forcemeat with the meat and mashed anchovies, in oil.

Scotch woodcock, a savory dish consisting of a buttered toast spread with anchovy paste and topped with soft scrambled egg.

scotsman, a brilliantly colored, southern African, marine fish.

scouse, another name for **lobscouse**.

scrambled eggs, eggs fried with the yolks and whites mixed together. When whites and yolks are stirred together while cooking they can be called *country-style scrambled eggs*. The eggs can also be *first* beaten slightly, usually with a little milk and *then* stirred while cooking.

scrapple, a seasoned mush of pork scraps made by boiling cornmeal with condiments and herbs in the liquid in which bones and meat (usually pork) have been boiled. The mush is allowed to set in a mold and is served sliced and fried.

scraps, cracklings (sense 1, crisp pieces of rendered animal [e.g., pork, whale, fish] fat).

Scripture cake [from *Scripture* "the books of the Bible"], a fruit cake

scarola
—————
Scripture cake

239

made of ingredients mentioned in the Bible and whose recipe refers to the pertinent biblical passages.

¹**scrod**, *1.* a young cod or haddock, especially one split and boned for cooking, and then fried or boiled; *2.* a fillet cut from the meat just ahead of the tail of one of these fishes.

²**scrod** (**to**), to split or fillet a fish, or tear it in small pieces, for cooking.

sculpin, any of various fishes, especially a scorpion fish of California coastal waters.

scungilli [from regional Italian (Neapolitan) *scungilli* "conchs, seashells," plural of *scungillo*], *1.* the meat of a conch cooked and used as food (often served with a seasoned sauce); *2.* pasta in the shape of conch shells.

scup, a porgy of western Atlantic waters used as a panfish.

sea bass, any of various marine fishes. Sea bass can be served broiled or Basque style or Pompadour style.

sea beef, *1.* the flesh of a porpoise or whale used as food; *2.* a chiton used as food; *3.* beef pickled for use on shipboard.

sea biscuit, another name for **hardtack**.

sea blite, a plant that grows on the sea shore, in salt marshes, and has leaves sometimes used as potherbs.

sea bob, a small shrimp that is commonly used dried.

sea bread, another name for **hardtack** (sea biscuit).

sea bream, any of various marine fishes.

sea buckthorn, a Eurasian maritime shrub having orange-red edible berries.

sea cabbage, another name for **sea kale** (a potherb).

sea carp, another name for **morwong**.

sea catfish, any of various marine fishes, a few of which are used as food.

sea clam, another name for **surf clam**.

sea crayfish or **sea crawfish**, another name for **spiny lobster**.

sea-ear, another name for **abalone**.

seafood, marine fish (e.g., cod, pompano, salmon, tuna) and shellfish (compare **shellfish**) used as food. Seafood can be served French fried, or a la Newburg (see **Newburg**), or in a zarzuela.

sea grape or **seaside grape** or **seaside plum**, a tropical American tree of the buckwheat family, that inhabits sandy shores and bears grape-like clusters of purplish, edible berries.

sea kale, a European plant of the mustard family having long-stalked, cabbagelike leaves used as a potherb.

seakale beet, a beet grown for its edible foliage.

sea lamprey, a large lamprey of northern Atlantic waters sometimes used as food.

sea lettuce or **green sloke**, any of various green seaweeds having leaflike fronds sometimes eaten as salad.

sea mullet, a bluish-green fish of the Australian coasts.

sea orache, an edible seacoast plant (an orache) that grows on wasteland, found in Europe and used as a substitute for spinach.

sear (**to**), to cook (to brown) quickly the surface of a piece of meat.

sea salt, salt obtained by the evaporation of seawater.

sea scallop, another name for **giant scallop**.

seaside grape or **seaside plum**, other names for **sea grape**.

season (to), to enhance the flavor of food by adding salt, spices, herbs, or other flavorings (savory ingredients).

seasoned, made savory with condiments.

seasoning, an ingredient (e.g., condiment, spice, flavoring) added to food to flavor it.

sea squab, the tail of a puffer fish (the ovaries and liver are very poisonous) when served as food.

seatron [from *sea* + *citron*], a confection made from a kelp, often in syrup.

sea trout or **whitling**, any of various trouts or chars that live in the sea but migrate to fresh water to spawn.

sea urchin or **urchin**, any of various echinoderms (marine animals) having a soft body enclosed in a spine-covered shell. It may be served au beurre blanc.

seaweed, any of numerous marine algae (e.g., kelp, dulse, sea lettuce, gulfweed, rockweed) used for food.

sebesten, *1.* the fruit of a tree (likewise called *sebesten*) used in India for pickles; *2.* the white fruit of the geiger tree.

Seder, a Jewish Passover service including a ceremonial dinner held in commemoration of the exodus from Egypt.

sedge root, a sedge (a marsh plant) with an edible root, especially a **chufa**.

seed, the grains of plants, used for sowing and as food.

seedcake, a sweet cake (e.g., a pound cake) or cookie containing spicy (aromatic) seeds, such as sesame or caraway. Shaved citron and grated lemon rind can be added.

seedless orange, another name for **navel orange**.

seer or **seerfish** [from Portuguese *serra* "saw"], any of several large fishes of southeastern Asian seas, resembling mackerels.

sego lily or **sego**, the edible bulb of a plant of western North America likewise called *sego lily* or *sego*.

sela, rice heated before milling (Myanmar).

self-rising flour, a commercially prepared mixture of flour, salt, and a leavening agent (e.g., baking powder). It is used, for instance, in making pancakes, biscuits.

seltzer, or **seltzer water** [from German *selterser (Wasser)* "(water) of Selters," from Nieder *Selters*, a district near Wiesbaden, Germany, locality of the springs], *1.* a mineral water from Nieder Selters containing much free carbon dioxide; *2.* soda water (artificially carbonated water).

semiscald (to), to dip fowl for less than a minute in water heated to a temperature just short of the boiling point.

semisoft, (of cheese) easily cut though firm.

semmel [German], a bread roll with a crisp crust.

semolina [from Italian *semolino*, diminutive of *semola* "bran"], *1.* the purified middlings (gritty, coarse particles) of durum or other hard wheat used especially for pasta (e.g., spaghettis, macaroni, noodles); *2.* coarse middlings (cracked wheat) used for polenta, breakfast cereal, couscous, or puddings.

semsem [from Arabic *simsim*], another name for **sesame**.

Senegal. The following are among representative dishes and products of Senegal: seafood (e.g., crayfish, rice with fish *(tiéboudienne)*, rice with chicken *(yassa)*. Beverage: an herb tea *(citronelle)*.

senvy [from French *sénevé* "wild mustard," from Latin *sinapi* "mustard"], another name for mustard seed.

separated milk, milk from which the cream has been extracted (with a separator, an appliance that whirls the milk round).

sergeant or **sergeant fish** [so called from the stripes on the fins] or **lemon-fish**, another name for both **cobia** and **snook** (fishes).

serpent cucumber or **serpent melon**, other names for the **snake melon**.

serpent radish, another name for **rat-tailed radish**.

serpolet [French], another name for **wild thyme**.

serum, another name for **whey**.

service [ultimately from Latin *sorbus*], the edible fruit of a service tree.

serviceberry, another name for **Juneberry**.

service tree, or simply **service**, either of two Old World trees having edible fruit (called *service*).

sesame [from Latin *sesamum*, from Greek *sēsamon*] or **ginjelly** or **jinjili** or **oily bean** or **oily grain** or **semsem** or **simsim** or **teel** or **til** or **ajonjoli** or **benne**, the small, flat seeds of an herb (likewise called *sesame*), used as food (as a flavoring agent) and as a source of oil.

sesame oil or **ginjelly oil** or **teel oil** or **til oil**, an edible oil obtained from sesame seeds (used, for instance in margarine).

seven-top turnip or **Italian kale**, an herb that bears leaves that are used for greens and in salads.

seviche [from American Spanish *cebiche, ceviche, seviche*], variant of **ceviche**.

Seville orange, another name for **sour orange**.

sey, a cut of beef (Scotland), see **backsey, foresey**.

Seychelles. The following are among representative foods of Seychelles: breadfruit (Creole *friyapen* [from French *fruit à pain*]), bananas, cassava, coconuts, mangoes, fish, pork, chicken, bats, pasta, rice.

shad, any of several fishes related to the herrings. They are fat fishes, and therefore best for broiling (e.g., a broiled steak), baking, planking.

shadberry, the fruit of the shadbush (= the Juneberry shrub).

shaddock [for Captain *Shaddock*, English ship commander who brought the seed from the East Indies to Barbados in 1696] or **pomelo** or **pompelmous**, the large, yellow, thick-rinded citrus fruit of a tropical tree (likewise called *shaddock*), related to the grapefruit.

shad trout, the common weakfish.

shagbark hickory, a North American hickory having sweet nuts with a hard shell.

shaggymane, or **shaggymane mushroom**, or **horsetail agaric**, an edible mushroom having shaggy white scales covering the cap.

shake, a beverage in which the ingredients are mixed by shaking. It may be a milk shake, or it may be made without milk.

shallon, the dark purple fruit of the salal (a shrub).

shallot [from French *échalote*] or **eschalot** or **scallion** or **ciboule**, a plant closely related to the onion, cultivated for its edible bulb used in seasoning.

shallow-fry (to), see ²**fry**.

shama millet [from Hindi *sāmā*, *śāmā*, from Sanskrit *śyāmāka* "millet"], a tropical Asiatic cereal cultivated in India, yielding a millet-like grain.

shank, a cut of meat from the upper or the lower part of the leg of a steer, calf, sheep, or lamb. It may be served braised.

shark, any of numerous, chiefly marine, fishes that include the largest existing fishes; their flesh is in some cases used as food. Compare **dogfish**.

sharkfin soup, see **soupfin shark**.

sharklet, a small or young shark.

shashlik [Russian, of Turkic origin], another name for **kabob**.

shea butter or **kanya butter** or **karite butter** (or **oil**), a fat obtained from the seeds (nuts) of the shea tree, used as food.

shea butter tree, another name for **shea tree**.

shea nut, the seed of the shea tree.

shea-nut oil, another name for **shea butter**.

shea tree or **shea butter tree** or **shea** [from Bambara *si*] or **karite**, a tropical African tree of the sapodilla family having fruits that contain a nut that yields an edible fat called *shea butter*.

sheefish, another name for **inconnu**.

sheep, any of various ruminant mammals related to the goats raised in many breeds, specifically one long domesticated for its edible flesh (the flesh of a young sheep is called *lamb*; of an older one, *mutton*).

sheepberry or **nannyberry** or **wild raisin**, the blue-black, edible berry of a North American shrub likewise called *sheepberry*.

sheepnose, any of various apple trees with fruit having four salients at the blossom end.

sheepshead or **sheephead** [it has broad incisor teeth that suggest those of a sheep], a large fish of the Atlantic and Gulf coasts of the United States, with massive head and forepart.

shell bean, the edible seed of any of various beans (plants, likewise called *shell beans*) grown primarily for their seeds. Distinguished from **snap bean** (which is grown for its pods).

shellfish, any aquatic animal having a shell, especially an edible mollusk (e.g., clam, mussel, oyster, scallop) or crustacean (e.g., crab, lobster, shrimp). All these animals are used in soups and chowders; crabs, lobsters, and shrimps are boiled and the meat used, as are the other shellfish, in salads and with sauces. In addition, oysters, clams, and mussels are often served raw with cocktail sauce (they may also be steamed, roasted, fried, or made into a soup); clams are steamed and served in their shells, live lobsters are split and baked or broiled; clams, oysters, scallops, and shrimps are fried. Scallops can be served in a casserole.

shepherd's pie, a meat pie (cooked cubes of beef or lamb with gravy) baked in a crust of mashed potatoes.

sherbet [from Turkish *şerbet*, from Persian *sharbat*, from Arabic *sharbah* "a drink"], *1.* a sweet-flavored (e.g., with lemon, orange, pineapple, raspberry, strawberry) water ice to which milk, egg white, or gelatin has been added before freezing; *2.* a cold drink made of sweetened, diluted, fruit juice; *3.* or **sherbet powder**, a preparation, especially of bicarbonate of soda, tartaric acid, and sugar, variously flavored, for making an effervescent drink.

ship biscuit or **ship bread**, another name for **hardtack**.

shirr (**to**), to bake eggs removed from the shell, until set. "Shirred" potatoes (the same verb being applied to something other than eggs) are grated raw, then dropped into hot white-sauce, poured into a baking dish and baked uncovered.

shish kebab or **shish kabob** [from Turkish *şiş kebabı*, from *şiş* "skewer, spit" + *kebap* "roast meat"], kabob (often lamb) broiled and served with condiments (e.g., onions, tomatoes, green peppers, and oregano) on skewers. Often served with pilaf.

shoestring potatoes [they are narrow and long, somewhat like a shoestring], long, slender (very thin) strips cut from a raw potato (preferably a mature baking potato) and fried in deep fat.

shogoin turnip, a turnip grown for its leaves, that are used as a potherb.

shoofly pie or **shoofly cake**, a pie having a filling consisting of layers of molasses and brown sugar, and a crust of crumbs made by mixing flour, butter, and sugar. It is a brown-and-white crumb cake (which is baked until the molasses bubbles up through the layer of crumbs).

shore dinner, a dinner consisting mainly of seafood.

short, crisp, friable, crumbling readily, containing shortening (e.g., pastry).

shortbread, a thick cookie made of flour, a small amount of sugar, and a large amount of butter or other shortening.

shortcake [the cake is rich in *short*ening], *1.* a crisp, light, and often unsweetened biscuit, cookie, or teacake with the texture of pastry (frequently served with fruit or whipped cream as a dessert); *2.* a dessert made of rich biscuit-dough cooked in a cake, or of sponge cake, and served hot after being split in layers, buttered, and spread with sweetened, especially fresh, fruit (e.g., strawberries, raspberries, peaches), often topped with cream; *3.* a luncheon dish consisting of a rich biscuit split and covered with a meat mixture (e.g., chicken, ham, turkey).

shorten (**to**), to add fat (shortening) to dough (e.g., a pastry dough) in order to make it tender and flaky (crumbly).

shortening, an edible fat (e.g., butter, lard, margarine, vegetable oil) used to make cake or pastry light or flaky.

short loin, a portion of the hindquarter of beef immediately behind the ribs (club, porterhouse, and T-bone steaks are cut from it).

short ribs, a cut of beef containing lower ribs (that do not attach to the sternum).

shoulder, a cut of meat (e.g., lamb, mutton, pork) consisting of the upper foreleg and adjoining parts (and including more or less of the neck and chest).

shovelfish [so called from the shape of its head], another name for **paddlefish**.

shoyu [from Japanese *shōyū*], another name for **soy** (sense 1, brown sauce).

shred (to), to cut or tear into long narrow strips.

shredded wheat, a breakfast cereal made from cooked wheat.

Shrewsbury cake [from *Shrewsbury*, city in western England], a short, sweet biscuit (flat, round, and crisp) baked in wafers.

shrimp or **camarón** (Spanish), any of various crustaceans, many species of which are edible. Shrimps are served with hot sauces, with a cold tomato sauce, or in salad with mayonnaise or boiled dressing. They can also be served in the form of bisque, canapés, gumbo; creole, curried, French fried, supreme. Velvet shrimp puffs consist of minced shrimp cooked with egg whites and chicken purée.

shrub [from Arabic *sharāb* "beverage, alcoholic drink"], a beverage made by adding acidulated (with lemon juice) fruit juice (e.g., raspberry) to iced water or sparkling water (with sugar).

Sichuan pepper, see **five-spice powder**.

siddha, rice soaked in water and boiled before milling.

side dish, a food served separately along with the main course.

side meat, bacon or salt pork, usually from the side of a pig.

sierra [Spanish "saw"], any of several large fishes related to the mackerel.

sieva bean or **butter bean** or **civet bean**, the flat, edible seed of a bean plant (likewise called *sieva bean)* of tropical America that is closely related to the lima bean.

sild [Norwegian "herring"], a young herring other than a sprat, that is canned as a sardine in Norway.

silk snapper, a West Indian snapper, similar to the red snapper (sense 1).

silver bream, any of several fishes.

silver hake, a hake of the northern Atlantic coast of the United States.

silver herring, the menhaden, especially when processed and canned for food.

silver perch, any of several silvery fishes similar to perch.

silver salmon or **coho** or **hoopid salmon** or **quisutsch**, a rather small salmon, originally of Northern Pacific waters.

silversides, any of various small fishes with a silvery stripe along each side of the body.

silver squeteague or **bastard trout** or **bastard weakfish**, a weakfish of the Atlantic coast of North America that is silvery below.

simmer (to), to cook gently in a liquid at a uniform heat below the boiling point (or just at that point), on top of the range. "Boiled" meat and eggs are really simmered; so are fruits that are to be kept whole. Stock is made by cooking meat, poultry, fish, vegetables, and seasonings in water at simmering temperature. Compare [2]**fricassee**.

simmer down (to), to reduce the liquid volume by simmering.

simnel [ultimately from Latin *simila* "wheat flour"], *1.* or **simnel cake**, a fruited cake resembling a plum pudding, containing currants, that is covered with a flour paste and first boiled and then baked, and traditionally eaten on Mothering (mid-Lent) Sunday; *2.* a rich fruit cake sometimes coated with almond paste and baked for mid-Lent, Easter, and Christmas; *3.* or **simnel bread**, a bun or a crisp bread or biscuit made of fine wheat flour

simsim [Arabic], another name for **sesame**.

Singapore. The following are among representative dishes and products of Singapore. Some of the seafood used: fish (e.g., pomfret, tuna, snapper); shellfish (e.g., lobster, crayfish, prawns, squid); steamed or fried seafood (e.g., seabass; crabs). Some of the tropical fruits found there: duku, durian, jackfruit, lychee, mango, mangosteen, papaya, rambutan, starfruit, watermelon.

These are the different cuisines of Singapore: Chinese, Indian, Malay/Indonesian, and Nonya or Peranakan (the Peranakans are a people who stem from marriages between early Chinese settlers [men, now called *Babas*] and local Malay women [now called *Nonyas*] as early as the 15th century).

Within Peranakan food are a noodle dish served in a spicy coconut gravy *(laksa);* a blend of fish, coconut milk, hot-pepper paste, *galangal*, and herbs wrapped in a banana leaf *(otak-otak);* chicken pieces and black nuts *(buah keluak);* a soup containing duck, tomatoes, green peppers, salted vegetables, and preserved sour plums simmered together *(itek tim)*.

singkamas or **sincamas** [from Tagalog, from Mexican Spanish *jícama*, from Nahuatl *xicama*], another name for **yam bean**.

sinker, a slang word for **doughnut**.

sippet, a small piece of toast or bread soaked in gravy, milk, or broth, or fried, especially for garnishing.

sirloin [from French *surlonge* "over loin"], a cut of meat, and especially of beef but also of lamb, from the part of the hindquarter just in front of the round.

sirop [French "syrup"], *1.* a syrup of concentrated fruit juice (or fruit extract, or aromatic substances), sugar, and water; *2.* a drink made from this syrup. Among the fruit or plants used: pomegranates, red currants, raspberries, lemon, black currants, mint.

sirup, variant spelling of **syrup**.

skewer, a long metal or wooden pin used to secure or suspend meat while roasting or to hold small pieces of meat and vegetables for broiling. Compare **brochette**, **spit**.

skewering, cooking on skewers.

skil or **skilfish**, another name for **sablefish**.

skilligalee or **skilly**, a thin, watery broth or porridge (a gruel), usually of oatmeal.

¹**skim (to)**, to remove floating cream from milk.

²**skim** (adjective), *1.* having the cream removed; *2.* made of skim milk (e.g., skim cheese).

³**skim** (noun), something that has been skimmed, as skim milk.

skim milk or **skimmed milk**, milk from which the cream has been removed.

skink, a soup made of the skin or hock (cut of meat from the leg, just above the foot) of beef.

skipjack, or **skipjack tuna**, a fish of warm seas, related to the tuna (fish).

skirret, an Old World plant having a sweetish, edible, tuberous root.

skirt, *1.* the diaphragm or midriff of a butchered animal, used for food; *2.* a flank of beef.

skirt steak, a strip of beef cut from the plate, that is usually broiled.

skyr [from Icelandic *skyr*], *1.* sour curdled milk; *2.* a dish (a dessert) prepared from curdled milk, or from sweet and sour cream with sugar.

slake, or **slake kale**, another name for **sloke**.

slapjack, another name for **pancake**.

slaw, another name for **coleslaw**.

slice (to), to cut one or more thin, flat pieces.

slim cake, a kind of plain cake used in Ireland.

sloe, the tart, plumlike fruit of the blackthorn, used especially for preserves.

sloke or **sloak** or **slake**, any of various edible seaweeds.

sloppy joe, ground beef cooked in a thick sauce (butter, minced onions, chopped green peppers; chopped mushrooms may be added) and usually served on a toasted bun.

Slovakia. The following are among representative dishes and products of Slovakia: mutton-and-pork roast (Slovak *perkelt);* smoked sausages cooked in bread; mushrooms; mushroom soup *(mrvenica)*, carp, dumplings *(knedlíky)*, cheese, geese, pastries.

small fruit, the table fruit (e.g., strawberry, raspberry, currant) of a low-growing plant.

smallmouth buffalo, a buffalo fish smaller than the bigmouth buffalo.

smash, a soft drink made of crushed or squeezed fruit (e.g., cherry).

smearcase or **smiercase** [from German *Schmierkäse*, from *schmieren* "to smear, spread" + *Käse* "cheese"], another name for **cottage cheese**.

smear dab, a brown, mottled flatfish (a flounder) of the coasts of northern Europe.

smelt, any of various small fishes that resemble the trouts and have delicate flesh. It is often fried.

Smithfield ham [from *Smithfield*, town in southeastern Virginia (United States)], uncooked ham, dry-cured and cold-smoked with special care, and then aged by hanging in a dry room, a Virginia ham produced in or near Smithfield, Virginia.

smoke (to), to preserve (cure) meat (e.g., ham) or fish (e.g., salmon) by exposure to the aromatic smoke of burning hardwood, usually after pickling in salt or brine.

smolt, a young salmon or sea trout.

smorgasbord [from Swedish *smörgåsbord*, from *smörgås* "(open-faced) sandwich, bread and butter" (from *smör* "butter" + *gås* "goose," from a fancied resemblance of lumps of butter to geese) + *bord* "table"], a meal featuring a variety of foods and dishes (e.g., hors d'oeuvres, smoked and pickled fish, sausages, hot and cold meats, cheeses, salads, relishes), served buffet-style.

smørrebrød or **smorrebrod** [from Danish *smørrebrød*, from *smør* "butter" + *brød* "bread"], a Danish hors d'oeuvre (e.g., a slice of meat or fish) served on buttered bread (an open sandwich).

smother (to), *1.* to cook (e.g., cabbage, chicken, pheasant) in a covered pan or pot with little liquid over low heat; *2.* to serve food covered thickly with other food cooked or uncooked.

Smyrna fig, a fig originally grown near Smyrna (former name of Izmir, city of western Turkey).

snack, a light meal.

snail [Frenc *escargot*, Spanish *caracol*], any of various mollusks characteristically having an enclosing spiral shell.

snake, any of various limbless reptiles having a long, tapering body.

snake eggplant, an eggplant with long curled fruit.

snake gourd, *1.* another name for **snake melon**; *2.* a gourd with long, twisted fruits.

snake mackerel, a long, marine fish related to the escolar.

snake melon or **serpent cucumber** or **serpent melon** or **snake gourd**, a long, wavy melon that resembles a cucumber.

snap bean [when the crisp pod is broken in pieces before cooking, it makes a snapping sound] or **string bean** or **green bean**, one of the pods of a bean (plant), cooked as a vegetable while young and tender and before the seeds have become enlarged. Distinguished from **shell bean** (a plant grown for its seeds rather than for its pods).

snapper, any of various large fishes of warm seas, resembling bass (especially the red snapper).

snapping shrimp or **pistol shrimp**, any of various small shrimps that make a snapping sound with one of their claws.

snapping turtle or **snapping terrapin**, any of several large, New World, freshwater turtles that seize their prey with a snap of their powerful jaws.

snook [from Dutch *snoek* "pike, snook"] or **robalo** or **sergeant**, any of several large marine fishes of warm seas, resembling pikes.

snow, a dessert made of beaten egg whites, sugar, and fruit (e.g., apple) pulp.

snow apple, see **Fameuse**.

snowball, *1.* shaved or chipped ice molded into a ball and covered with fruit or other syrup; *2.* any other dish or confection having the appearance of a ball of snow.

snow crab, either of two crabs of the northern Pacific Ocean.

snow pea or **mange-tout** or **sugar pea**, a variety of pea with flat pods that are eaten with the seeds they contain. Compare **edible-podded pea**.

snow pear, a European variety of pear used especially for making pear cider. The fruit is hard but mellowed by exposure to snow.

snow pudding, a kind of pudding made whitish and fluffy by the addition of beaten egg whites and gelatin. It often contains sugar.

sockeye, or **sockeye salmon** or **red salmon**, a small salmon of northern Pacific coastal waters.

soda, *1.* another name for **soda water**; *2.* another name for **soda pop**; *3.* another name for **ice-cream soda** (a refreshment made from soda water, ice cream, and sometimes flavoring).

soda biscuit, *1.* a breadlike biscuit leavened with sodium bicarbonate and sour milk or buttermilk; *2.* another name for **soda cracker**.

soda bread, a quick bread leavened with sodium bicarbonate and buttermilk or sour milk.

soda cracker or **soda biscuit**, a thin, usually square cracker leavened slightly with sodium bicarbonate.

soda pop [called *pop* from the sound made by opening the container], or

soda or **pop**, a beverage (a soft drink) consisting of soda water, flavoring, and a sweet syrup.

soda water or **club soda** or **carbonated water**, a beverage consisting of unflavored water combined with carbon dioxide gas (and therefore effervescent [= bubbling]), used in various drinks (nonalcoholic and alcoholic). Compare **Vichy water**.

sodium bicarbonate or **sodium acid carbonate** or **baking soda**, a crystalline compound used in making baking powders and carbonated beverages (including artificial mineral water).

sodium glutamate, another name for **monosodium glutamate**.

sofkee [American Indian (southeastern United States)], a thin mush or gruel made of cornmeal.

soft, (of a beverage) containing no alcohol. Compare **soft drink**.

soft-boiled, (of an egg) boiled only a short time so that the yolk has a soft consistency.

soft clam, another name for **soft-shelled clam**.

soft corn or **flour corn** or **squaw corn**, an Indian corn having kernels composed of soft starch.

soft crab, another name for **soft-shell crab**.

soft custard, custard cooked in a double boiler (not baked) used as a sauce over fruit or cake or served in sherbet glasses. Among the dishes made with soft custard: floating island.

soft drink, a nonalcoholic, usually carbonated, beverage, especially soda pop.

¹**soft-shell** (adjective), (used, e.g., of a crab) having a soft or unhardened shell, especially as a result of recent shedding.

²**soft-shell** (noun), another name for both **soft-shell crab** and **soft-shell clam**.

soft-shell clam or **soft-shelled clam** or **long-neck clam** or **long clam** or **soft clam**, a clam of the eastern coast of North America having a thin, brittle, elongated shell; it is chiefly eaten steamed.

soft-shell crab or **soft-shelled crab**, a marine crab of eastern North America, that has recently shed its shell and has a very soft new one. Distinguished from **hard-shell crab** (that has not recently shed its shell and therefore has the shell rigid [fully hardened]).

soft wheat, a wheat with soft kernels that yield a weak flour especially suitable for pastry and breakfast foods. These kernels are high in starch but low in gluten. Distinguished from **hard wheat** (which is suited for bread and pasta).

soja or **soja bean** [from Dutch *soja*], another name for **soybean**.

solar salt, a salt from sea water evaporated in the sun.

soldier prawn, an Australian deep-water prawn.

sole [French, from Latin *solea* "sandal; a flatfish (from its shape)"], any of various, chiefly marine, flatfishes resembling the flounders. Filets of sole are often prepared bonne femme or amandine.

soluble coffee, an easily dissolved powder produced by dehydration from strong coffee and used for the quick preparation of coffee.

¹**sop**, *1.* a piece of bread or other food dipped or soaked in a liquid before being eaten; *2.* the liquid into which food is dipped before being eaten.

²**sop** (**to**), to dip or soak in a liquid.

sopaipilla or **sopapilla** [from South American Spanish *sopaipilla*, diminutive of Spanish *sopaipa* "fritter soaked in honey," from *sopa* "sop, food soaked in milk"], a fritter, a square of deep-fried dough looking like a little fat pillow, often sweetened (with syrup or sprinkled with sugar and cinnamon) and eaten as dessert.

sorb [from French *sorbe* "fruit of the service tree"], the fruit of any of various trees (likewise called *sorbs*) related to the apples and pears, such as the service tree or the rowan.

sorbet [French, from Italian *sorbetto*, from Turkish *şerbet*, from Persian *sharbat*, from Arabic *sharbah* "a drink"], a fruit-flavored ice similar to a frappé and having a mushy consistency, served as a dessert or between courses as a palate refresher. It can be flavored with lemon or with herbs (e.g., rosemary, lavender).

sorghum [from Italian *sorgo*], *1.* an Old World grass several varieties of which are cultivated as grain or as a source of syrup; *2.* syrup produced by evaporating from stems of any sorgo the juice, which resembles cane sugar; *3.* the seeds of grain sorghum (sense 1) used as cereal.

sorgo [Italian] or **sweet sorghum**, any of various sorghums (sense 1) grown for the sweet juice in their stems from which sugar and syrup are made.

sorgo syrup, syrup made of sorghum.

sorrel, *1.* any of various plants having acid-flavored leaves sometimes used as salad greens; *2.* any of various docks and their leaves used as a potherb; *3.* or **Jamaican sorrel**, or **roselle** [American Spanish *jamaica*], a flower whose reddish sepals are used in the West Indies and Mexico to make a beverage (American Spanish *agua de jamaica* or *agua de flor de jamaica*), in Jamaica with the addition of allspice and ginger.

sorva [from Portuguese *sôrva*, from Latin *sorba*, plural of *sorbum* "serviceberry"], another name for **couma**.

souari nut, the large, nutlike seed of a South American tree (called *souari* or *souari nut*) used as food and as a source of cooking oil.

soubise, or **soubise sauce** [from French *soubise*, for Charles de Rohan, Prince de *Soubise*, 18th-century French nobleman, from *Soubise*, village in western France], a white or brown sauce containing onions or onion purée (strained onions) and melted butter, and used, for instance, on meats.

souchong, any of several Chinese black teas made from the larger leaves of the shoot.

¹**soufflé** (noun) [French "blown, puffed up"], a light, fluffy main dish or a dessert, made from a white sauce, egg yolks and beaten egg whites, seasonings, and added ingredients (e.g., minced meat, minced seafood [e.g., clams, codfish, salmon, tuna], cheese, vegetables [e.g., broccoli, corn, tomatoes], fruit [e.g., orange], chocolate) and baked until puffed up. Sweet soufflés are made with the addition of sugar, and sometimes served with fruit sauces. Compare **mousse** (sense 3).

²**soufflé** (**to**), to cause food to puff up in baking.

³**soufflé** (adjective), puffed up, made light and fluffy by beating and baking (e.g., crackers, mashed potatoes, omelette).

soufflé potatoes [translation of French *pommes de terre soufflées*], *1.* mashed potatoes with egg yolks, beaten egg whites, butter, and seasonings baked in an oven until puffed up; *2.* thinly sliced potatoes fried in deep fat of moderate temperature and then in fat of high temperature until puffed up.

soul cake, a sweet bun traditionally eaten on All Souls' Day (2 November) in England.

soul food, or simply **soul** [from *soul* "characteristic of Black Americans or of their culture"], food traditionally eaten by Blacks of the southern United States (for instance, catfish, chitterlings, collards, corn bread, ham hocks, hogs' jowls).

soup [from French *soupe*], a liquid food, especially with a meat, fish, or vegetable stock as a base (compare **stock**); it may be clear or thickened to the consistency of a thin puree or it may have milk or cream added, and often contains pieces of solid food (e.g., bread slices [which can also be toasted or fried], fowl, meat [e.g., mutton, oxtail], pasta, fish, shellfish [e.g., crab, lobster, shrimp], cheese, mushroom, or vegetables [e.g., cabbage, carrot, celery, corn, garlic, leeks, lima beans, onions, potatoes, rice, spinach, split peas, tomato, turnips]) as well as salt, pepper, herbs, and served either hot or cold. Soups include bisque, borsch, bouillon, broth (sense 2), chowder, consommé, ¹**cream** (sense 2), gumbo (sense 2), julienne, madrilene, minestrone, mulligatawny, oyster stew, potage, pottage, vichyssoise.

soupbone, a shin, knuckle (e.g., veal), or other bone suitable for making soup stock.

soupfin shark or simply **soupfin**, any of several sharks whose fins when boiled form gelatin used in making a certain Chinese soup (called *sharkfin soup*, made with clear chicken [or meat] soup).

¹**sour**, having a taste characteristic of that produced by acids; sharp, tart, or tangy, as lemons or vinegar. This is one of the four basic taste sensations; the others are bitter, salt, and sweet. Compare ¹**tart**.

²**sour (to)**, *1.* to become sour; *2.* to make sour.

sour ball, a round and tart piece of hard candy. Compare **acid drop**.

sour-cake, a sour leavened cake of oatmeal or rye, made of fermented dough.

sour cherry, the edible, soft-fleshed, tart fruit of a tree likewise called *sour cherry*.

sour cream, *1.* cream that has soured naturally by the action of lactic acid bacteria, and is used in baking certain breads and cakes; *2.* a thick, artificially soured cream (by the addition of a culture of lactic acid bacteria that produce lactic fermentation).

sourdough, a leaven consisting of dough in which fermentation is active, used in making bread.

sourjack, another name for **jackfruit** (sense 1).

sour milk, soured milk, milk made sour or that became sour.

sour milk cheese, another name for **cottage cheese**.

sour orange or **bitter orange** or **Seville orange** or **chinotto**, the fruit of a citrus tree (likewise called *sour orange*), having somewhat bitter pulp and used especially in making marmalade (also for beverages).

soursop or **guanabana,** the large fruit (greenish outside, white inside, with black seeds) of a small tropical American tree (likewise called *soursop*) of the custard apple family.

sour-sweet [translation of French *aigre-doux*], sweet and sour at the same time (e.g., molasses, oranges).

¹**souse,** *1.* pickled food, especially pork trimmings (feet, ears, and head of a pig), fish, or shellfish chopped, seasoned, cooked, and molded for slicing; *2.* the liquid used in pickling, brine.

²**souse (to),** to steep in a mixture, as in pickling.

South Africa. The following are among representative dishes and products of South Africa: lobster tails, simmered, and served on noodles or rice; corn on the cob *(mealies)*, steaks, sausages (Afrikaans *boerewors)*, fish, shellfish (e.g., oysters), grilled meat *(braai vleis);* curried minced beef *(bobotie)*, served with rice; biltong; curried kabob *(sosatie)*, salted ribs of mutton *(sout ribbetjie)*, tangerine, lemon, figs, pineapple, papaya, avocado, melon, orange, apples, pears, peaches.

southern pea, another name for **cowpea.**

souvlakia [from modern Greek *soublakia*, plural of *soublaki*, from the diminutive of *soubla* "spit, skewer"], another name for **shish kebab.**

sowbelly, salted side of pork.

sowens [from Scottish Gaelic *sùgan* "liquid of which sowens are made," from *sùgh* "juice"], a slightly fermented porridge made from oat husks and siftings. Compare **flummery** (sense 1).

soy or **shoyu** [from Japanese *shōyū* "soy (sense 1)"] or **soja** or **soja bean,** *1.* or **soy sauce,** a dark, salty oriental condiment for fish and other foods (especially Chinese and Japanese dishes), consisting of a liquid sauce made by subjecting boiled beans (especially soybeans) or beans and roasted wheat flour to fermentation and then to digestion in brine; *2.* or **soy pea,** or **soya,** another name for **soybean.**

soybean or **soya bean,** or simply **soya** [from Dutch *soja*, from Japanese *shōyū* "soy (sense 1)"], the edible seed of a leguminous Asiatic plant (likewise called *soybean*), that yields oil, flour, and meal.

soybean milk or **soya milk,** soybean flour or finely ground meal suspended in water (soaked and squeezed) and used as a substitute for milk (in any recipe). Some cooks sweeten it, with dextrose or honey.

soybean oil or **soya oil** or **soya-bean oil** or **soy oil,** an oil obtained from soybeans and used as food.

soy flour or **soybean flour,** a fine, hull-free soybean meal. It is used together with all-purpose flour in many recipes (instead of just wheat flour).

soymilk, a milk substitute based on soybeans.

spadefish, any of several marine food fishes widely distributed in warm seas.

spaetzle or **spätzle** [from German *Spätzle*, from regional German (Alemannic) "little sparrow," diminutive of *Spatz* "sparrow; dumpling"], a small dumpling (in the shape of a string or a lump) cooked by running batter made of eggs, milk, flour, and salt through a coarse colander into boiling water. When cooked, spaetzle are used as additions to gravy, goulash, or other stews.

spaghetti [Italian, plural of *spaghetto* "little string," from *spago* "cord, string"], a pasta made in long, solid strings of small diameter but larger than vermicelli or than spaghettini, cooked by boiling (like macaroni and noodles), and served with different sauces (see a list under **pasta**).

spaghettini [Italian, diminutive of *spaghetti*, plural of *spaghetto* "little string," from *spago* "cord, string"], a thin variety of spaghetti (but vermicelli are even thinner).

spaghetti squash, an oval winter squash with flesh that once cooked is similar in texture to spaghetti.

Spain. The following are among the most important regions of Spain from the gastronomical point of view (certain cities in the region that are outstanding for their food are shown in parentheses): Andalusia (Seville, Málaga), Aragon (Zaragoza), Asturias (Oviedo), Cantabria (Santander, Bilbao), Castile (Madrid, Toledo), Catalonia (Barcelona), Galicia (Santiago), Valencia (Alicante, Jijona, Valencia).

Some representative dishes and products of these regions are:

Andalusia. Gazpacho, oxtail soup, anchovies, fried fish, almond-and-garlic soup (Spanish *ajo blanco*).

Aragon. Simmered pieces of chicken with tomato *(pollo a la chilindrón).*

Asturias. Bean soup *(fabada)*, olla *(pote)*, roast suckling lamb or kid, pork tripe *(mondongo de cerdo)*, nougat *(turrón)*, cakes made from must *(mostillo).*

Cantabria. Biscayan codfish *(bacalao a la vizcaína)*, or codfish stew *(bacalao al pil-pil)*, olla podrida, baby eels *(angulas)*, hake in green sauce *(merluza en salsa verde)*, broiled bonito, grilled sea-bream *(besugo a la parrilla)*, squid in their own "ink" *(chipirones* [or *maganos*] *en su tinta)*, anchovy tart *(tarta de anchoa)*, lobster *(abacanto* or *bogavante)*, stuffed peppers.

Castile. Meat stew *(cocido)*, tripe *(callos)*, partridge stew *(perdiz estofada);* an omelet combining eggs, potatoes, onions, sausage *(tortilla española)*, roast lamb *(lechazo al horno* or *asado de cordero)*, olla podrida, chorizo, blood sausage *(morcilla)*, snails, roast suckling pig *(lechón asado)*, fowl stew *(pepitoria)*, minced-lung stew *(chanfaina)*, porridge *(gachas)*, marzipan *(mazapán)*, egg-yolk sweets *(yemas).*

Catalonia. Sausage *(butifarra)*, snails, lobster, cuttlefish; mixed fish fry (Catalan *suquet de piex)* in olive oil, to be eaten with sops of bread; partridge with cabbage, zarzuela.

Galicia. Olla podrida *(pote)*, shellfish casserole *(caldeirada marinera)*, blood sausage *(morcilla)*, empanadas (especially with shellfish), scallops *(vieiras).*

Valencia. Paella.

Food found in other regions, or in several regions: snacks of seafood or meat *(tapas* or *aperitivos);* an omelet combining eggs, potatoes, onions, sausage *(tortilla española)*, garlic soup *(sopa de ajo)*, fish (e.g., eels; baby eels [*angulas*]), shellfish (e.g., squid, clams), roast suckling pig *(cochinillo asado)*, olla podrida *(cocido)*, meat stew *(ropa vieja,* "old clothes"), cheeses, grapes, peaches, oranges, honey; sweets: rice and milk *(arroz con leche)*, custard *(natillas)*, French toast *(torri-*

jas), fried flour-and-milk *(leche frita)*, nougats *(turrones)*, whipped-cream-filled cake roll *(brazo de gitano*, "gypsy's arm").

spam, a canned meat of spiced pork products.

spanakopita [from modern Greek *spanakópēta*, from *spanaki* "spinach" + *pēta*, *pita* "pie"], a traditional Greek pie of spinach, feta cheese, and seasonings (spring onions, olive oil, parsley, dill), baked in phyllo (puff pastry). It is usually baked in small individual puffs.

Spanish chestnut or **marron** or **French chestnut** or **European chestnut** or **sweet chestnut**, the nutritious nut borne by a large tree likewise called *Spanish chestnut*. Compare **marron**.

Spanish cream, a molded dessert (a boiled custard) made of eggs, caramelized sugar, milk, and gelatin. The center may be filled with whipped cream; the top may be sprinkled with shredded toasted almonds or crushed nut brittle.

Spanish mackerel, any of various sea fishes related to the mackerels.

Spanish omelet, an omelet served with a sauce (folded in or poured over the top) containing chopped tomato, onion, and green pepper. In Spain, an omelet is called *tortilla*. For the Mexican tortilla (cornmeal pancake), see **tortilla**.

Spanish onion, a mild-flavored, large-bulbed, yellow-skinned onion.

Spanish oyster plant or **Spanish salsify**, a tall thistle (prickly-leaved) of southwestern Europe grown for its edible roots which resemble those of salsify (and are used as them), for its foliage which is eaten like that of the cardoon, and for its flowers which are used as a substitute for saffron.

Spanish paprika, *1.* another name for **pimiento** (a sweet pepper with mild flavor); *2.* a mild seasoning (a paprika) made from pimientos.

Spanish pear, another name for **avocado**.

Spanish plum or **red mombin**, the red, edible fruit (resembling a plum) of a tropical American hog plum (a tree, likewise called *Spanish plum)*.

Spanish potato, another name for **sweet potato**.

Spanish rice, a dish consisting of rice cooked with chopped onions, green pepper, tomatoes, and spices.

Spanish salsify, another name for **Spanish oyster plant**.

Spanish sauce, another name for **brown sauce**.

spanspek [Afrikaans, from *spaanspek* "Spanish bacon,"], a moderately sweet muskmelon cultivated in southern Africa.

spareribs, a cut of pork consisting of the ribs and breastbone separated from the bacon strip (i.e., with most of the meat trimmed off). It can be served baked, barbecued, roast, with sauerkraut.

sparkling water, another name for **soda water** (beverage with carbonic acid gas).

sparkling wine, an effervescent (= bubbling) table wine. Compare **table wine**.

sparling, *1.* a European smelt; *2.* a young herring.

¹**spatchcock**, a freshly killed fowl split, dressed, and grilled immediately.

²**spatchcock (to)**, to prepare and cook a fowl for eating as a spatchcock.

spätzle, variant of **spaetzle**.

spearmint or **garden mint** or **lamb mint** or **lamb's mint**, an aromatic mint grown for use in flavoring and for its aromatic oil, also used as flavoring. It resembles peppermint but has slender, interrupted spikes.

spearmint oil, an oil obtained from spearmint, used in flavoring.

speckled hind, a certain large grouper of the Florida coast.

speckled perch, another name for **black crappie**.

speckled trout or **speckle trout**, another name for the **brook trout**, and for any of several other trouts.

spelt or **starch corn**, a hardy wheat having spikelets that contain two light-red kernels.

Spencer roll, beef trimmed from the ribs and rolled (used for a roast or for short steaks).

¹**spice**, any of various aromatic and pungent vegetable products (e.g., all-spice, cinnamon, cloves, cumin, ginger, mace, nutmeg, pepper) used to season or flavor foods (e.g., cakes, cookies, curries, pickles, sauces, soups, vegetables, infusions, marinades, chutneys). Some spices are toasted to concentrate the flavor. Cooking spices are often used in combination, as in garam masala; in France, the following mixture is used, called *quatre épices* "four spices": cinnamon, cloves, nutmeg, pepper; see also **five-spice powder**. Spices and herbs are condiments (which include horseradish, oregano, paprika, parsley, saffron, vanilla). In Asia, flowers used to flavor foods and foods flavored with flowers include lotus salad, rose soup, fried chrysanthemums, magnolias to garnish fish filets, jasmin with squids. In Argentina, they use lilac, lillies, cotton flower. Other flowers that can be used minced include azaleas, carnations, jacaranda, marigold (in certain salads), pansies, violets. Spices that are used with certain foods include anise (seeds), used in cookies, breads, honey, soufflés, tea; fenugreek (seeds), in pickles, curry, chutney, and imitation maple extract; saffron (flower stigmas), in risotto, paella, Mediterranean soups like bouillabaisse; cinnamon (bark), in desserts, chocolate, cookies, fruit, hot chocolate, coffee, tea; cardamom seeds, in curries, gingerbread, cakes, Turkish coffee; coriander (seeds), in vegetables, soups, sauces, infusion; black mustard (seeds), in curries and Dijon mustard; white mustard, in American mustard and some English mustards; allspice (seeds), in marinades, pickles, broths, sauces (with orange and butter) for pork and duck; sassafras (bark), in tea.

²**spice (to)**, to season with spices.

spice nut, a small spiced cookie.

spicy, having the characteristics of spice, such as flavor and aroma.

spiedino [Italian, "little skewer," from *spiedo* "skewer, spit, spear"], *1.* a dish of meat rolled around a filling, batter-dipped, and cooked on a skewer; *2.* batter-dipped slices of bread and mozzarella, cooked on a skewer and served with an anchovy sauce.

spinach [French *épinards*, Italian *spinaci*, Spanish *espinaca*], an Asian plant (a potherb) of the goosefoot family grown for its edible leaves which are eaten as a vegetable. It may be used as greens (salad), or served creamed, Provençale, in a soup (cream), timbales.

spinach beet, a beet that lacks a fleshy root and is used as a potherb.

spinach mustard, another name for **tendergreen**.

spiny lobster or **(cape) rock lobster** or **langouste** or **crayfish** or **sea cray-**

fish or **thorny lobster**, any of various edible marine crustaceans distinguished from the true lobster by lacking the large pincers (they have an unenlarged first pair of legs and claws) characteristic of true lobsters, and by the spiny carapace. It may be served à l'américaine, au court-bouillon, au gratin. Compare **Cape crayfish**.

spirit vinegar, another name for **vinegar**.

spit, a pointed, usually metal, slender, rod for holding meat and other foods (that are impaled) stationary or revolving while cooking before or over a fire. Compare **skewer**, **brochette**.

spitchcock, an eel split open or cut up in pieces and grilled or fried.

split pea, a dried, hulled pea in which the cotyledons (the first pair of leaves of a seed plant) usually split apart. Split peas are used, for instance, for making soup, pudding.

splittail, a California margate (fish).

split-tail perch, either of two margates (fishes) of the Pacific coast of North America.

sponge, *1.* dough that is leavened or in the process of being leavened; *2.* a dessert (e.g., sponge cake) made light by the incorporation of air usually through addition of whipped egg whites, or of gelatin whipped after it has jelled.

sponge cake or **diet loaf**, a light cake made of flour, sugar, beaten eggs, and flavoring (e.g., lemon and vanilla, pineapple), but containing no shortening. Distinguished from **butter cake** (that is made with shortening).

sponge finger, another name for **ladyfinger**.

sponge mushroom, another name for **morel**.

spoon bread or **batter bread**, soft, custardlike bread made of cornmeal with or without added rice and hominy and mixed with milk (or buttermilk), eggs, shortening, and leavening to a consistency that it must be served from the baking dish with a spoon. It is often served in place of mashed potatoes.

spot, a small croaker of the Atlantic coast of the United States, esteemed as a panfish, that has a dark spot behind the shoulders.

spotted cat or **spotted catfish**, a black-spotted catfish of the southeastern United States regarded as superior to most catfishes as food.

spotted dog, a suet pudding containing currants or raisins.

spotted grunter, a large grunter of the Indian Ocean.

spotted sea trout, a weakfish of the southeastern coasts of the United States.

sprat or **brisling**, *1.* a small European herring of northeastern Atlantic waters related to the common herring; *2.* any of various similar fish, such as a young herring. Compare **sardine**.

¹**spread**, a food (e.g., anchovy, butter, cheese, deviled meat, fruit, jam, jelly, lobster Newburg, peanut butter, sardine) used or made for use to spread on bread or crackers. See also **dip**.

²**spread (to)**, to cover bread or crackers with a thin layer.

sprig, a small shoot or twig of a plant (e.g., of parsley).

spring chicken [it was formerly available only from spring hatchings], a young table fowl having tender meat (used for broiling or frying).

springer, *1.* a fryer, a young chicken that is smaller than a roaster but larger than a broiler; *2.* an Atlantic Ocean salmon that in the *spring* returns to fresh water.

springerle [from regional German (Alemannic) "hare," diminutive of *springer* "jumper"], a thick hard cookie that is usually flavored with anise and has an embossed design and that is eaten particularly during the Christmas season in German-speaking countries.

spring herring, another name for **alewife** (fish).

spring lamb, the meat of a market lamb (likewise called spring lamb) born in late winter or early spring and sold before July.

spring onion, another name for **Welsh onion.**

spring roll, an egg roll or a similar appetizer of Oriental cuisine.

spring salmon, another name for **king salmon.**

sprinkles or **jimmies,** rod-shaped bits of variously flavored (often chocolate-flavored) candy sometimes sprinkled (scattered) on pastry and ice cream.

sprout, a young plant growth, such as a bud or shoot from a seed or a root.

sprouts, another name for **Brussels sprouts.**

spumoni or **spumone** [from Italian *spumone* "big foam," augmentative of *spuma* "foam, froth"], an Italian frozen dessert of ice cream containing fruits, candied fruits, nuts, or candies, often with egg whites or whipped cream added. In Italy, a *spumone* is also a light cake, made with egg whites or whipped cream.

spun sugar or **cotton candy,** a confection resembling floss or fluff, made from sugar boiled to the long-thread stage. The threads may be used as a garnish or heaped upon a stick as a candy.

spur pepper, another name for **hot pepper.**

squab, a fledgling bird, and, specifically, a young (about four weeks old), unfledged pigeon. It can be prepared as a casserole or broiled; dishes using squab include a Chinese minced-squab soup.

squab chicken, a young chicken suitable for an individual serving.

squash, the fleshy, edible fruits of any of various plants of the gourd family grown as vegetables. The summer squashes include zucchini, that can be prepared Provençale; the winter squashes include acorn, banana, Danish, Hubbard, spaghetti squashes.

squawberry or **squawbush** [from *squaw* "an American Indian woman"] or **lemonade bush,** a sumac (a plant) of western North America, with edible fruit.

squaw corn [from *squaw* "an American Indian woman": it was much grown by American Indians], another name for **soft corn.**

squid [Italian *calamaro,* Spanish *calamar* or (when small) *chipirón*] or **calamary** or **calamar,** any of various ten-armed marine mollusks. They secrete a dark, inky fluid and are often served in their own "ink." Compare **octopus** (that has eight arms).

squirrel, any of certain rodents. It can be prepared like other wild game animals. Compare **Brunswick stew.**

squirting cucumber, a vine of the gourd family, of the Mediterranean region, having oblong fruit that bursts from the peduncle (stalk) when ripe and forcibly ejects the seeds and juice.

Sri Lanka. Some representative dishes and products of Sri Lanka are: curries served with boiled rice, seafood, vegetarian dishes, coconut, pineapple, mangosteen, mango, papaya, rambutan. Beverage: tea.

stag, *1.* a young, adult, male domestic fowl, a market fowl which is less tender than a fryer but still suitable for roasting; *2.* the adult male of various deer; *3.* an animal (especially a pig) castrated after reaching maturity.

standing roast, a rib roast from which only the heaviest parts of the vertebrae have been removed. Compare **rolled roast** (which is boned).

star anise or **star aniseed** [so called from the shape (an eight-point *star*) of the fruit] or **Chinese anise** or **aniseed star**, the dried, anise-scented fruit of an aromatic tree (called *star anise)* of eastern Asia, used as a spice in Oriental cooking. The brown pod is one of the traditional ingredients in **five-spice powder** (a seasoning).

star anise oil or **star aniseed oil** or **anise oil**, an oil obtained from star anise and used as a flavoring agent.

star apple or **star plum** [so called from the starlike figure formed by the carpels (central female organs of a flower) in cross section] or **caimito**, the greenish-purple fruit of an evergreen tropical American tree (likewise called *star apple)* of the sapodilla family (it is not the same fruit as the starfruit or carambola).

starch, a nutrient carbohydrate from plants. It is found chiefly in the seeds, fruits, tubers, and roots, notably in corn, potatoes, wheat, and rice.

starch corn, another name for **spelt**.

starch syrup, a syrup (especially corn syrup) made from starch.

starfruit [its cross section has the shape of a five-pointed star], another name for **carambola** (it is not the same fruit as the star apple or caimito).

star plum, another name for **star apple**.

starry flounder, a large flatfish of both coasts of the northern Pacific Ocean.

¹**steak**, *1.* a slice of meat cut from a fleshy part of a beef carcass (usually cut thick and across the muscle grain) and usually broiled or fried; *2.* a similar slice of a specified meat (e.g., ham, veal, leg steak of lamb); *3.* a thick slice of a large fish (e.g., halibut, swordfish) cut across the body; *4.* a dish suggesting beefsteak, especially a cake of ground meat (broiled or fried) prepared for cooking or for serving in the manner of a steak (compare **hamburger** [sense 2], **Salisbury steak**).

²**steak (to)**, to cut large fish into steaks (e.g., halibut, swordfish) across the body.

steak au poivre [from French *au poivre* "with pepper"], a steak (preferably a tender, aged cut of beef) that has had coarsely crushed black pepper pressed into it before cooking (or rather the steaks should be pressed into the pepper), and is served with a seasoned sauce (butter, Worcestershire sauce, lemon juice). It is sometimes flambéed.

steak Diane, a beefsteak fried with seasonings (especially Worcestershire sauce), served with a seasoned butter sauce (often flambéed with cognac).

steak tartare [from French *tartare* "Tartar"], highly seasoned ground beef eaten raw as an appetizer. Often mixed with onion and raw egg.

steam (to), to cook food (e.g., vegetables, fish, puddings) by direct exposure to steam (as in a steamer or a pressure cooker) or in a vessel surrounded by steam (as in a double boiler). Steaming is used in the preparation of foods which burn easily (e.g., fish and most vegetables). Steamed puddings are desserts prepared in steamers or in double boilers.

steenbras [Afrikaans, from *steen* "stone" + *brasem* "bream"], any of several southern African marine, food fishes.

steep (to), to soak in a liquid at a temperature just under the boiling point (as for softening or extracting a flavor).

steepgrass, a butterwort (herb with fleshy leaves) used like rennet (i.e., to curdle milk).

steer, a bull castrated before sexual maturity and raised for beef.

sterlet [from Russian *sterlyad'*], a small sturgeon found in the Black Sea and adjacent waters, used as food and as a source of caviar.

¹**stew**, chunks of meat or seafood, usually with vegetables and herbs, prepared by stewing (simmering slowly) in liquid (e.g., water, milk, stock). In the case of meat stews, vegetables, which require less time for cooking, are added when the meat is partially done. Some stews (e.g., oyster) are made with more liquid, so they are eaten as soup. Stews include beef, Irish (usually lamb), oxtail, oyster, puchero.

²**stew (to)**, to cook (e.g., beef, chicken, lamb, prunes, tomatoes) in a little liquid over a gentle fire without boiling, i.e., by simmering in a heavy covered pot, often with the addition of spices or flavoring.

stewed, cooked by stewing (e.g., chicken, prunes, tomatoes).

stick candy or **sugar-stick**, candy molded in the shape of rods.

sticking-piece, a cut of coarse beef from the lower part of the neck.

Stilton or **Stilton cheese** [from *Stilton*, in eastern England, where it was originally sold], a blue-veined cheese (it has a blue-green mold) with wrinkled rind, made of whole cows' milk enriched with cream.

stirabout, a porridge of Irish origin, consisting of oatmeal or cornmeal boiled in water or milk and stirred during cooking.

¹**stir-fry (to)**, to fry meat (e.g., shredded beef) or vegetables (e.g., bean sprouts, onions, celery) rapidly on high heat in a lightly oiled pan (such as a wok) while stirring and tossing them in the pan continuously. It is the most popular method of Chinese cooking. Compare ²**sauté**.

²**stir-fry**, a dish of something stir-fried.

stir off (to), *1.* to boil down syrup so the sugar is separated from the molasses; *2.* to **sugar off**.

stock, the liquid in which meat (or meat and bones, e.g., a shin, veal knuckle), fish (including fishbones), poultry (e.g., chicken with bones), or vegetables have been simmered and which is used as a base for soup, gravy, sauce, or stew. Brown stock is the water in which beef (e.g., marrow bones [cracked] and shin) has been cooked; white stock is the water in which chicken, other fowl, or veal has been cooked. The water in which ham or pork bones have been cooked is often used for pea and bean soups. Brown stock is generally used for bouillon, white stock or chicken stock for consommé. Suitable bones for a soupstock include shin and knuckle. Beef, veal, chicken, and fish stocks are those most frequently called for. When a stock is strained, seasoned, and served as a clear soup, it is either a bouillon or a consommé. Compare **broth**.

stocker, a young animal (e.g., a steer or heifer) to be kept until matured or fattened before killing.

stockfish, fish (e.g., cod, haddock, hake, ling) cured by being split and dried in the open air, on wooden racks, without salt.

stock melon, another name for **citron** (sense 1).

stock pea, another name for **soybean**.

stodge, a heavy, substantial, filling food (e.g., oatmeal, stew).

stollen [from German *Stolle* "post, support"], a sweet yeast bread of German origin containing fruit (e.g., citron, raisins) and chopped nuts, usually made in a long oval loaf.

stone crab [Spanish *cangrejo moro*] or **moro crab**, a large edible crab.

stone parsley, a Eurasian plant (a slender herb) having aromatic seeds used as a condiment.

store cheese [it is a staple article stocked in grocery *stores*], another name for **Cheddar cheese**, used especially of sharp cheddar.

straight flour, flour recovered from bolted (= sifted) wheat meal.

Strasbourg goose [from *Strasbourg*, city, northeastern France], a goose fattened in such a way as to enlarge the liver for use in pâté de foie gras.

straw [it is shaped like a straw (dry stem of a cereal grass)], a short, narrow strip of pastry.

strawberry, a juicy, edible, usually red fruit of any of certain low-growing plants of the rose family. Dishes using strawberries include creams, glazes, ices, ice creams, milk shakes, mousses, pies, sherbets, shortcakes, tortes.

strawberry bass, another name for **black crappie**.

strawberry guava, *1.* the fruit of a subtropical shrub (likewise called *strawberry guava*), used either fresh or preserved; *2.* another name for **feijoa** (fruit).

strawberry pear, the red, slightly acid fruit of a West Indian cactus likewise called *strawberry pear*.

strawberry perch, another name for **black crappie**.

strawberry raspberry, a low bramble grown for its red fruits.

strawberry tomato or **ground-cherry**, the sweet, yellowish fruit, enclosed in a husk, of a North American plant likewise called *strawberry tomato*.

strawberry tree or **madrona**, a small European evergreen tree of the heath family, with fruit resembling strawberries.

streusel [German "something strewn, sprinkling"], a crumblike mixture of fat (e.g., melted butter), sugar, and flour and sometimes chopped nuts and spices (e.g., cinnamon) that is used as topping with filling for cake (especially for coffee cake).

streuselkuchen [German "streusel cake"], a coffee cake baked with a topping of streusel.

string bean [it has stringy fibers on the lines of separation of the pods], another name for **snap bean**.

stripe, another name for **striped bass**.

striped bass or **rockfish** or **rock bass** or **rock**, a fish of North American coastal waters, having dark longitudinal stripes along its sides.

striped perch, any of various striped fishes resembling perch.

stroganoff [for Count Paul *Stroganoff*, 19th-century Russian diplomat], said, postpositively, of beef or chicken sliced thin and cooked in a sauce of consommé, sour cream, onion, mushrooms, and condiments (e.g., mustard).

strömming [Swedish, from *ström* "stream"], a small herring found in the Swedish lakes and in the Baltic Sea.

strongbark or **strongback**, a small tree with edible berries from which a beverage is made.

strudel [German "whirlpool"], a kind of pastry made from a thin sheet of dough rolled up with any of various fillings (e.g., apple) and baked.

stuff (to), to prepare meat or vegetables (e.g., cabbage, green peppers) for cooking or eating by filling or lining with a **stuffing**. In French, "stuffed" is *farci* following masculine nouns (plural *farcis)*, *farcie* for feminine (plural *farcies)*.

stuffing, a seasoned mixture put in the cavity of meat, vegetables, eggs, or of sausage casings, especially a mixture for poultry, made of bread, onion, celery, and condiments (e.g., sage, thyme, or marjoram, with pepper and salt). The major chopped, diced, or crumbled component for meats and poultry may be apple, chestnut, giblet, mushroom, orange, oyster, sausage. Peppers may be stuffed with ground beef.

stum, another name for **must**.

stumpknocker, a small sunfish of the southeastern United States used as a panfish.

sturgeon, *1.* any of various large fishes of the Northern Hemisphere, having edible flesh and whose roe is made into caviar; sturgeons are fat fish, and therefore best for broiling, baking, planking; *2.* fresh or cured sturgeon flesh. Compare **isinglass**.

subgum [from Cantonese *sahp-gám* "mixture; assorted"], a dish of Chinese origin prepared with a mixture of vegetables (e.g., water chestnuts, mushrooms, and peppers).

submarine sandwich or simply **submarine** [so called from its shape], other names for **hero** (sandwich).

succade, fruit candied (crystallized) or preserved in syrup, a preserve or confection made from fruit.

succory, another name for **chicory** (the plant).

succotash, a mixture of lima beans or shell beans and kernels of green Indian corn cooked (baked or simmered) together (with salt, pepper, butter, cream).

sucker, any of numerous North American freshwater fishes related to carp but with thick soft lips adapted for feeding by suction.

sucking (adjective), very young; not yet weaned.

suckling (noun), a young, unweaned animal.

sucrose [from French *sucre* "sugar"], a sweet sugar that occurs in most land plants, especially in the juices, fruits, and roots, is used widely as a sweetener, and is obtained commercially especially from sugarcane, sugar beets, or maple.

Sudan. Some representative dishes and products of the Sudan are: kabobs; a boiled bean dish (Arabic *ful*), falafel (sense 1, in Arabic also called *ta'miyya*), steaks, wheat, millet, peanuts.

suet, the fatty tissue of cattle and sheep, particularly the comparatively hard fat about the kidneys and loins, used in cooking.

suet pudding, a boiled or steamed sweet pudding made with chopped suet, flour (the usual proportion is one part suet to two of flour), bread crumbs, raisins, and spices (e.g., grated nutmeg, ground ginger, mixed spices). Candied lemon peel, molasses, sugar, grated carrots may be added.

sugar, a sweet, crystallizable material that consists wholly or essentially of sucrose, is obtained from sugarcane and sugar beet, and less extensively from sorghum, maples, and palms, and is used as a sweetener of other foods.

sugar apple, another name for **sweetsop**.

sugar beet, a form of the common beet, a white-rooted beet grown for the sugar in its roots.

sugarberry, a hackberry with sweet fruits.

sugar candy, hard candy made from pure sugar clarified and concreted or crystallized.

sugarcane or **cane**, a stout, tall grass widely grown in warm regions as a source of sugar.

sugarcoat (**to**), to coat food (e.g., almonds) with sugar or candy.

sugar corn, another name for **sweet corn**.

sugar-cured, (of meats) cured with a preparation of sugar, salt, and nitrate.

sugared, *1*. containing sugar, sweetened with sugar; *2*. covered with sugar, sugarcoated (e.g., almonds).

sugar grape [it has sweet fruit], another name for **sand grape**.

sugar grass, any sorghum (sense 1) grown chiefly for the sweet juice in its stem; especially sorgo.

sugarhouse, *1*. a sugar refinery; *2*. a building where maple sap is boiled and maple syrup and maple sugar are made.

sugarhouse molasses [from *sugarhouse* "sugar refinery"], a viscid syrup (thin molasses) remaining after refining of sugarcane; this syrup drains from the sugar-refining molds.

sugarloaf, pure concentrated sugar molded into a solid cone.

sugar maple or **hard maple** or **rock maple**, a maple tree of eastern North America having sap that is the chief source of maple syrup and maple sugar.

sugar off (**to**), to complete the process of boiling down maple sap to yield maple syrup and maple sugar.

sugar on snow, a delicacy made by pouring hot maple syrup on snow or ice.

sugar palm, any of various palms yielding sugar.

sugar pea, another name for both **edible-podded pea** and **snow pea**.

sugar pear, *1*. another name for **Juneberry**; *2*. a sweet variety of pear.

sugarplum, sweetmeat, a small piece of sugary candy usually in the form of a ball or disk.

sugar-stick, another name for **stick candy**.

sugar vinegar, vinegar made from the waste juice of sugar manufacture.

sukiyaki [Japanese "slice", "broil, roast"], a Japanese dish consisting of sliced meat, soybean curd, onions, bamboo shoots, and other vegetables fried together in soy sauce, sake and sugar, usually at the table.

sultana, a small, sweet, pale yellow, seedless raisin of a grape (likewise called *sultana*) grown chiefly in Asia Minor.

sulze [German "calf's-foot jelly, brine"], another name for **calf's-foot jelly**.

summer sausage or **dry sausage**, dried or smoked uncooked sausage (e.g., cervelat, Thuringer) that keeps well in warm weather without refrigeration.

summer savory, a mint used in cookery for the flavoring of meats, soups, stuffings, salads, or other dishes. Compare ³**savory, winter savory**.

summer squash, any of several varieties of squash used as a vegetable while immature (e.g., zucchini, cocozelle) and before hardening of the seeds and rind (shortly after being picked rather than kept for storage). Compare **winter squash**.

sunberry, another name for **wonderberry**.

sundae, a dish of plain ice cream served with toppings such as syrup, fruits, nuts, or whipped cream.

sunfish, any of various fishes having brightly colored bodies.

sunflower, any of several plants having flowers that produce edible seeds rich in oil.

sunflower oil or **sunflower-seed oil**, an oil expressed from the seeds of the sunflower and used in foods.

sunny-side up, (of an egg) fried on one side only.

supari [from Hindi *supārī*], another name for **betel nut**.

suprême [French "supreme, highest in quality"], *1.* or **sauce suprême**, a white sauce (a velouté) made of chicken stock and cream; *2.* a made dish of game, meat (e.g., veal; liver), fish (e.g., sole, tuna), or chicken dressed with a sauce suprême; *3.* a dessert served in a suprême or supreme (a tall sherbet glass).

surette [French "sourish," diminutive of *sur* "sour"], a tropical American tree having edible, yellow, acid berries.

surf and turf [underlying idea: "from sea and land"], seafood and steak served as a single course; the Curaçao version is called *sea and turf* or *mar y tierra* [Spanish "sea and land"].

surf clam or **hen clam** or **sea clam**, any of various large, surf-dwelling clams, common in the United States on the sandy coasts of the Atlantic.

surimi, imitation shellfish made from fish paste.

Surinam cherry [from *Surinam*, now *Suriname*, country of northern South America] or **Florida cherry** or **pitanga**, *1.* the aromatic fruit of a Barbados cherry (a West Indian shrub); *2.* the spicy, red fruit of a Brazilian tree (likewise called *Surinam cherry*), that resembles a cherry.

Suriname. Some representative dishes and products of Suriname are: pork chop and potato casserole; rijsttafel, meat grilled on spits (Indonesian *sate*), fried plantains (Indonesian *pisang goreng*), seasoned fried chicken *(ayam kuning* "yellow chicken"), peanut *(katjang* "bean") soup and sauces; chicken soup *(soto ayam; soto* = "soup, broth"), roti (sense 2) with a variety of fillings.

sushi [Japanese], cold rice dressed with vinegar, formed into any of various shapes (e.g., small cakes), and topped or wrapped with garnishes (e.g., bits of raw fish or shellfish).

Suwannee chicken [from *Suwannee,* river in Georgia and Florida], an edible river-terrapin.

suwarro, variant of **saguaro.**

swamp apple or **honeysuckle apple,** a slightly acid, edible gall on the swamp azalea (a shrub of the heath family).

swamp blackberry, a dewberry of the eastern United States.

swamp blueberry, another name for **highbush blueberry.**

swan potato [from *swamp potato*] or **swamp potato,** one of several plants having tubers used as food.

Sweden. Some representative dishes and products of Sweden are: smörgåsbord; open-faced sandwich (Swedish *smörgås),* dairy products, cabbage soup *(vitkålsoppa),* fish (e.g., pike, salmon, smoked eel, young herring [*sill*]); hard, flat, rye bread *(knäckebröd),* fish puddings, herring salads, meat balls made with cream *(köttbuller),* pastries.

Swedish meatball, see **meatball.**

swedish turnip or **swede turnip,** or simply **swede** [it was introduced (into Scotland) from Sweden], other names for **rutabaga.**

¹**sweet,** *1.* having a sugary taste, containing a sugar, indicating one of the four basic taste sensations (the others are: bitter, salt, and sour); *2.* not pungent, mildly seasoned (e.g., pickles).

²**sweet,** a food (e.g., candy, preserve) having a high sugar content; in the plural, **sweets:** *1.* a sweet dish served at the end of a meal, dessert (e.g., preserves, confections); *2.* candy.

sweet almond, the edible, sweet seed of a tree likewise called *sweet almond.*

sweet-and-sour, seasoned with a sauce containing sugar and vinegar or lemon juice (e.g., red cabbage, shrimp, tongue).

sweet balm, another name for **lemon balm.**

sweet basil, a species of basil.

sweet bay, another name for **laurel** (tree and its aromatic leaves).

sweet bean, another name for **honey locust.**

sweetbread [French: *ris de veau*], the thymus or the pancreas of a young animal (e.g., a calf) used for food; compare **beef bread** (which is the pancreas of a mature beef). It may be served au gratin, creamed, baked, pan-fried.

sweet calabash, a West Indian passionflower with edible apple-like fruit, yellow when ripe, with black seeds and a thick rind.

sweet cassava, a cassava with roots that are used as a vegetable.

sweet cherry or **black cherry** or **American cherry,** the sweet, edible fruit of a tree likewise called *sweet cherry.*

sweet chervil or **aniseroot,** a tall sweet-cicely with sweet, anise-flavored, aromatic roots.

sweet chestnut, another name for **Spanish chestnut.**

sweet chocolate, chocolate that contains added sugar.

sweet cicely, any of various plants (e.g., sweet chervil) having aromatic roots.

sweet cider, unfermented cider.

sweet clover, a legume having three-parted leaves.

sweet corn or **sweet maize** or **sugar corn**, a variety of Indian corn with kernels that are sweet when young (they contain a high percentage of sugar) and that is the common edible corn.

sweet cup, any of various passionflowers or their fruits.

sweet-curd, (of cheese) made of curd formed with rennet from cow's milk.

sweeten (to), to make sweet.

sweetener, a substance that sweetens.

sweetfish, another name for **ayu**.

sweet herbs, fragrant herbs grown for culinary purposes (e.g., basil, marjoram, mint, rosemary, sage, [3]savory, thyme).

sweet lemon, any of various lemons having fruit with a sweet though somewhat insipid pulp.

sweet maize, another name for **sweet corn**.

sweet marjoram, a species of marjoram (aromatic herb). Wild marjoram is another name for **oregano**.

sweetmeat, any sweet food or dainty of the confectionery or candy kind, prepared with sugar or honey (e.g., sugar-covered nuts, sugarplums, bonbons, balls or sticks of candy, preserves), especially a candied or crystallized fruit.

sweet oil, olive oil or some other mild, edible oil (e.g., rape oil).

sweet orange or **common orange**, the fruit of an orange tree (likewise called *sweet orange*), with a relatively thin skin and a sweet, juicy, edible pulp.

sweet orange oil, another name for **orange oil**.

sweet pepper or **bell pepper** [the fruit is bell-shaped] or **green pepper** [the fruit is red when ripe but often eaten green] or **bullnose pepper**, any of various large fruits of a plant likewise called *sweet pepper*, characterized by mild flavor (distinguished from **hot pepper**, which is pungent). Frequently served stuffed.

sweet-pickle (to), to cure meat by soaking in a solution of salt and sugar with sometimes the addition of spice.

sweet plum, another name for **Burdekin plum**.

sweet potato or **kumara** [New Zealand] or **Spanish potato** or **yellow yam** or **batata** (Spanish) or **camote** (Spanish), the large, thick, sweet, tuberous root of a tropical American vine (likewise called *sweet potato)*, that is eaten cooked as a vegetable, or is used in pies. It may be baked, candied, French fried, mashed, sautéed. Compare **yam**.

sweet roll, another name for both **coffee roll** and **bun**.

sweetroot, another name for **licorice** (sense 1).

sweets, see [2]**sweet**.

sweetsop or **anon** or **custard apple** or **sugar apple** [Spanish *anona, chirimoya*], the sweet, pulpy fruit of a tropical American tree of the custard apple family.

sweet sorghum, another name for **sorgo**.

sweet tangle, a large seaweed having fronds that contain much sugar and are used in preparing a syrup.

sweetwood, another name for **licorice** (sense 1).

sweetwort, a sweet-flavored wort, an unfermented malt infusion, the infusion of malt before the hops are added in the manufacture of beer.

swiftlet, a swift of eastern Asia that produces the nest used in bird's nest soup.

swine, any of various animals that constitute the family that includes pigs, hogs, and boars.

Swiss, or **Swiss cheese** [from *Swiss* "of Switzerland," from French *suisse* "Swiss"] or **Emmental** [from German *emmentaler (Käse)* "Emmental (cheese)," from *Emmental*, valley of Switzerland, from *Emme* river], a hard cheese originally produced in Switzerland characterized by large holes that form during ripening. Compare **Gruyère cheese** (which has small holes).

Swiss chard, another name for **chard**.

Swiss cheese, see **Swiss**.

Swiss roll, another name for **jelly roll**.

Swiss steak, a slice of round or shoulder steak into which flour is pounded on both sides and which is then braised, smothered in onions, tomatoes, and other vegetables, and usually served with a seasoned sauce.

switchel, a beverage made of water with molasses or sometimes honey or maple syrup, and usually flavored with ginger and vinegar; occasionally rum is added.

Switzerland. The country can be divided gastronomically in four sections according to language (certain cantons in each section that are outstanding for their food are shown in parentheses): French-speaking (Fribourg, Geneva, Neuchâtel, Valais, Vaud), German-speaking (Basel, Bern, a part of Graubünden or Grisons, Luzern, Zürich), Italian-speaking (Ticino), Romansh-speaking (a part of Graubünden or Grisons).

Some representative dishes and products of these regions are:

French-speaking. Hot melted cheese dishes (fondue, râclette), sausages; dried, paper-thin, sliced meat (German *Bindenfleisch*), cold meats (e.g., smoked ham, sausages, pâtés), tripe, crayfish au gratin, fish (e.g., trout, baby perch, pike).

German-speaking. Roasts, sausages, fried potatoes *(Rösti);* ham, sausage and beef with sauerkraut *(Bernerplatte),* veal in cream sauce *(Geschnetzeltes);* fruit and nuts with yogurt and oats *(bircher Müsli),* pastry (e.g., one with pears, hazelnuts, almonds, and raisins [*Birnbrot* "pear bread"]).

Italian-speaking. Spaghetti, ravioli, risotto, polenta, perch, osso buco, zabaglione.

Romansh-speaking. Dried, paper-thin, sliced meat (German *Bindenfleisch*).

Food found in other regions, or in several regions: cheeses and other dairy products, fondue bourguignonne, ramekins.

sword bean, a twining tropical plant grown in the Orient, bearing large flat pods having red or pink seed, both pods and seed being used for food.

swordfish, a very large marine fish having a long, swordlike extension of the upper jaw. It may be served Cajun style or the steaks may be broiled.

sycamore or **sycomore** [from Latin *sycomorus*, from Greek *sykomoros*] or **sycamore fig** or **sycomore fig**, a fig tree of Africa and Asia Minor that has sweet fruit similar to the common fig.

syllabub or **sillabub**, *1.* a dessert (a sweetened drink or topping) that is made by beating to a froth milk or cream sometimes with added egg whites, occasionally further thickened with gelatin; it is flavored with wine or liquor and when thin served as a drink or when thick poured over cake or fruit; *2.* a drink or dessert made with milk or cream mixed with wine, cider, or other acid so as to form a curd.

Syria. Some representative dishes and products of Syria are: assorted hors d'oeuvre (Arabic *mazza*), kabobs, roast mutton *(mashwi* "roast"), meat balls *(kubbah)*, roast stuffed lamb *(kharuf mashwi)*, rice; stuffed (with ground meat or rice) grape or cabbage leaves; hummus; salad with tomatoes, ground wheat, mint, and parsley *(tabule)*, crushed wheat *(burghul)*, tahini, olives, yogurt, pastries (e.g., baklava, halvah).

Syrian juniper, an evergreen tree of Asia Minor and Greece with an edible fruit.

syrup or **sirup** [from French *sirop*, from Arabic *sharab* "drink; wine; coffee; syrup"], *1.* a thick, sweet, sticky liquid, consisting of a sugar base, flavorings (e.g., chocolate, lemon, vanilla) and water; *2.* the concentrated juice of the sugar cane just prior to crystallization of the sugar; *3.* the juice of a fruit or plant boiled with sugar until thick and sticky.

Szechuan [from *Szechuan* (now *Sichuan*), province in China], of a style of Chinese cooking that is spicy, oily (usually with hot sesame oil), and peppery. This style has a fine balance of flavors, except that hot pepper is added freely.

Szechuan pepper or **Sichuan pepper**, see **five-spice powder**.

sycamore
———————
Szechuan pepper

talo **tzimmes** **turbinado** **tahini** **teiglach** **trepang** **tournedos**

tabasco [from *Tabasco*, state in southeastern Mexico], *1.* a pungent condiment sauce prepared from hot peppers and vinegar; *2.* a pungent hot pepper (e.g., a bird pepper) suitable for the preparation of tabasco sauce.

tabbouleh or **tabouli** [from Arabic *tabbula*], a salad of Lebanese origin consisting chiefly of cracked wheat, tomatoes, fresh mint, parsley, onions, and olive oil. It is served cold.

table d'hôte [French "host's table"], *1.* a communal table for guests at a hotel or restaurant; *2.* a meal (as in a hotel) served to all guests at a stated hour and a fixed price; *3.* or **prix fixe**, a meal of several courses (e.g., appetizer, entree, dessert, and beverage) offered at a fixed price in a restaurant or hotel. Distinguished from **a la carte** (in which each dish has a separate price).

table greens, another name for **potherbs**.

table jelly, another name for **jello**.

table salt or **common salt**, a refined mixture of salts, chiefly sodium chloride, suitable for use in cooking and at the table as a seasoning.

tablespoon or **tablespoonful**, *1.* enough to fill a tablespoon (a large spoon used for eating soups and serving foods); *2.* a household cooking measure equal to one level tablespoon (sense 1) or 15 milliliters (more precisely, 14.784) or 3 teaspoons or ½ a fluid ounce or 4 fluid drams.

table sugar, granulated white sugar.

tablet, a small flat or flattish patty or lozenge of candy.

tablet tea, *1.* a small brick of choice tea; *2.* a small compressed tablet of tea dust (for making one cup). Compare **brick tea**.

table wine, an unfortified wine averaging 12% alcohol by volume and usually suitable for serving with a meal. It may be red (e.g., Burgundy, claret) or white (e.g., Rhine wine, sauterne). Compare **dessert wine**, **sparkling wine**.

tabouli, tabule, see **tabbouleh**.

taco [Mexican Spanish, from Spanish *taco* "bung; drink of wine; snack (pieces of cheese or ham)], a tortilla (pancake of unleavened cornmeal) that is rolled

268

around, or folded over, a filling, as of a mixture of seasoned meat, cheese, and shredded lettuce. It is often fried before serving.

taffy, a sweet, chewy candy made usually of molasses or brown sugar boiled until very thick (caramelized) and then pulled with the hands or by machine until the candy is porous and light-colored, is glossy and holds its shape.

tagliarini [Italian, from *tagliare* "to cut, trim"], a pasta in flat ribbon form.

tagliatelle [Italian, from *tagliate* "cut (feminine plural)," past participle of *tagliare* "to cut, trim"] or **fettuccine** (*fettuccine* is the word used in the area of Rome for what elsewhere in Italy is called *tagliatelle*), pasta in the shape of noodles (narrow strips).

tahini [from regional Arabic *ṭaḥīna*, from *ṭaḥana* "to grind"], a smooth paste made from sesame seeds mixed with spicy seasonings; as a sauce, it is used in various Middle Eastern dishes.

tall blueberry, another name for **highbush blueberry**.

tallote [from Mexican Spanish *talayote*, a kind of gourd, from Nahuatl *tlalayotli*, "earth gourd"], another name for **chayote** (a squashlike fruit).

tallow, a mixture of the whitish, nearly tasteless, solid, rendered fat of cattle and sheep, used in edibles (e.g., margarine).

talmouse [archaic French], an often triangular pastry shell with a filling of cheese.

talo [Samoan], another name for **taro**.

tamale [Mexican Spanish *tamales*, plural of *tamal* "tamale," from Nahuatl *tamalli* "steamed cornmeal dough"], a Mexican dish of cornmeal dough, with a seasoned cooked meat or other filling (e.g., hot pepper, vegetable, beans, cheese) rolled up in it, wrapped in corn husks (sometimes in banana leaves), and steamed or boiled. Compare **masa**.

tamara, a spice or condiment, used especially in Italy; it is a mixture of cinnamon, cloves, coriander seeds, aniseed, and fennel seeds ground together.

tamari [Japanese], a soy sauce prepared with little added wheat.

tamarillo, see **tree tomato**.

tamarind or **tamarindo** [from Portuguese or from Spanish *tamarindo*, from Arabic *tamr hindī*, "Indian date," from *tamr* "dried date" + *hindī* "of India"] or **sampaloc** (Philippines), the fruit of a tropical Old World tree (likewise called *tamarind*), consisting of a long, brown pod with seeds embedded in an edible, acid pulp often used for preserves. The red-striped, yellow flowers of the tree are eaten in India. Indian cooks use the pulp as Americans use lemon juice; it is a primary ingredient in Worcestershire sauce; the pulp or soaking water is used in Asian recipes, particularly relishes, chutneys, and curries.

tampala, a potherb native to the Orient, grown for its tender stems.

tamure [Maori], a snapper (fish) of Australia and New Zealand.

tandoor [from Hindi *tandūr*, *tannūr*, from Persian *tanūr*, from Arabic *tannūr*], a jar-like clay or earthenware oven used in northern India and Pakistan, in which food (e.g., kabobs, marinated chicken, chapatis, nans) is cooked over charcoal.

tandoori [from Hindi *tandūri*, from *tandūr* (see previous entry)], cooked in a tandoor.

tangelo [from *tangerine* + *pomelo*] or **ugli**, the fruit, having a winkled rind and an acid, orange pulp, of a hybrid citrus tree (likewise called *tangelo*) that is a cross between a tangerine and a grapefruit.

tangemon [from *tangerine* + *lemon*], the fruit of a hybrid citrus tree (likewise called *tangemon*) that is a cross between the tangerine and the lemon.

tangerine [from French *Tanger* "Tangier," city of northern Morocco] or **mandarin**, or **mandarin orange** or **kid-glove orange**, the fruit of a small, spiny citrus tree (likewise called *tangerine*) of southeastern Asia, that has an easily-peeled, deep-orange skin and sweet, juicy pulp.

tangleberry, another name for **dangleberry**.

tangor [from *tangerine* + *orange*], the easily-peeled fruit of a hybrid citrus tree (likewise called *tangor*) that is a cross between the mandarin orange and the sweet orange.

tanguingue or **tanguigue** [from Tagalog *tanguingi*], a Spanish mackerel (a large mackerel of the Indo-Pacific).

tania or **tannier**, any of several plants of the arum family having edible, farinaceous roots (e.g., taro, yautia).

tansy, *1.* a plant native to the Old World, having pungent, aromatic juice sometimes used as a flavoring; *2.* a cake or pudding flavored with tansy (sense 1).

Tanzania. The following are among representative dishes and products of Tanzania: a cornmeal porridge (Swahili *ugali*), poultry and lamb served with pilipili sauces, dishes prepared with coconut milk.

tapas [Spanish, plural of *tapa*, "cover, lid"], hors d'oeuvre or snacks served with drinks in Spanish bars.

tapioca [Portuguese or Spanish, from Tupi *typyóca*], *1.* a usually granular preparation of cassava starch used as a food (especially in puddings and as a thickening in liquid food [e.g., soups]); *2.* a dish (as pudding, cream, pie) containing tapioca (sense 1).

tapioca fish, another name for **escolar**.

taro or **tara** [from Tahitian or from Maori *taro*] or **dasheen** or **talo** or **eddo**, the large, edible, starchy, tuberous rootstock of a tropical plant (likewise called *taro; also eddo)* of the Pacific islands (but cultivated throughout the tropics), of the arum family, that serves as a food staple. For a dish of young taro leaves, see **luau** (sense 2). See also **poi** (sense 1).

tarragon [French *estragon*], the narrow leaves of an aromatic herb (likewise called *tarragon)* native to Eurasia, used as a flavoring (e.g., in making pickles, mustard, vinegar). Chicken can be prepared with tarragon (French *poulet à l'estragon).*

tarragon oil, an aromatic oil obtained from tarragon and used as a flavoring material.

¹**tart**, agreeably acid (sour) or pungent to the taste (as a cranberry). Compare **sour**.

²**tart** [from French *tarte*], a small pie or pastry shell, usually without a top crust, containing jelly, jam, custard, or fruit (e.g., apple, coconut). Tarts include Banbury, fanchonette, Josephine, Coventry tartlet.

tartaric acid, a strong acid, found in plants and especially in fruits (e.g., grapes, mountain ash), used in effervescent (= bubbly) beverages and baking powders, in desserts and candies.

tartar sauce or **tartare sauce** [from French *sauce tartare*], a sauce made principally of mayonnaise and chopped pickles (but also with the addition of olives, capers, parsley, onion, spices, chopped herbs, mustard) and usually served with fried or broiled fish, scallops, shrimp.

tartar steak, see **steak tartare**.

tartine [French, from *tarte* "²tart"], a slice of bread (sometimes toasted) spread with butter and usually preserves or jam.

tartlet, a small tart (e.g., a Coventry tartlet).

tasajo [Spanish], jerked meat, especially jerked beef (preserved in long, sun-dried slices).

taste, *1.* the power of perceiving flavor; *2.* the sense that perceives and distinguishes the sweet, sour, bitter, or salty quality of a dissolved substance; *3.* any of these four qualities as perceived by the sense of taste.

Taunton turkey [from *Taunton*, city of southeastern Massachusetts], another name for **alewife** (fish).

tautog, a dark-colored fish of the wrasse family, found along the North American Atlantic coast.

T-bone or **T-bone steak**, a small beefsteak (a thick porterhouse steak) taken from the thin end of the short loin and containing a T-shaped bone and a small piece of tenderloin, usually served broiled.

tea [from regional Chinese (Xiamen) *t'e*, from Chinese *chá* "tea"], *1.* an aromatic, slightly bitter, hot beverage made by steeping tea leaves (see **tea**, sense 2) in boiling water (or by pouring fresh boiling water over tea leaves or tea bags and straining off after some five minutes). Flower-scented teas have flower petals added (jasmine is the most popular; gardenia and magnolia are also used); *2.* the dried leaves of a shrub (likewise called *tea*) of eastern Asia prepared by various processes and in various stages of growth. The leaves are classed in different types according to method of manufacture (e.g., green tea, black tea, oolong) and according to size (e.g., orange pekoe, pekoe, souchong, congou); for instance, pekoe has leaves larger than orange pekoe; *3.* any of various beverages made by steeping the leaves of certain other plants; *4.* light refreshments usually including tea (sense 1, the beverage) with bread and butter sandwiches, crackers, cookies, served in the afternoon.

tea bag, a small, porous bag holding enough tea leaves for an individual serving of the beverage.

tea ball, a hollow, perforated metal ball (often made of silver) that holds tea leaves and is immersed in hot water when brewing tea in a teapot or a cup.

tea biscuit, any of various plain cookies or biscuits served with afternoon tea.

tea bread, a kind of light (sweetened) bread or bun eaten with tea.

tea cake, *1.* a light, flat cake, sometimes made with raisins; *2.* another name for **cookie**.

tea-seed oil or **tea oil**, an edible oil resembling olive oil obtained from the seeds of the sasanqua or tea-oil tree.

teaspoon or **teaspoonful**, *1.* enough to fill a teaspoon (a small spoon used

271

for eating soft foods and stirring beverages); *2.* a household cooking measure equal to one level teaspoon (sense 1) or 5 milliliters (more precisely, 4.928) or ⅓ tablespoon or ⅙ fluid ounce or 1⅓ fluid drams.

teel oil, another name for **sesame oil**.

teff or **teff grass** [from Amharic *ṭef*], an African cereal grass grown for its grain which yields a white flour of good quality.

teiglach or **teiglech** [from Yiddish *teyglekh*, diminutive of *teyg* "dough"], a confection consisting of small pieces of dough cooked briefly in a mixture of honey, brown sugar, and nuts, then cooled and rolled into balls.

teju [from Portuguese *tejú, teiú*], any of several large South American lizards hunted for their flesh.

telinga potato [from *telinga* "sepoy, Indian soldier in the British army," from Tamil *telinkam* "Telugu country," from the employment of Telugus as sepoys], another name for **yam**.

Tellicherry pepper [from *Tellicherry*, seaport in Tamil Nadu state, southeastern India], a superior grade of Indian pepper.

tempeh [from Javanese *témpé*], an Asian (especially Indonesian) foodstuff made by fermenting soybeans with a rhizopus (mold fungus) and deep-frying them in fat.

tempura [from Japanese *tenpura* "fried food"], a Japanese dish of vegetables or shrimp (or other seafood, or chicken) dipped in batter and fried in deep fat.

tench, a Eurasian freshwater fish.

tendergreen or **spinach mustard**, a mustard whose foliage and root crown are used as a vegetable.

tenderize (**to**), to make meat tender by applying a process or substance (e.g., a plant enzyme, for instance papain) that breaks down connective tissue without impairment of flavor or nutritive quality.

tenderizer, a device or substance, such as a plant enzyme (e.g., papain), applied to meat to make it tender.

tenderloin or **undercut**, a fillet, a strip of tender meat (e.g., beef, pork) consisting of a large internal muscle (called *psoas*) of the loin (it is the tenderest part) on each side of the vertebral column. Compare **chateaubriand**, **filet mignon**, **porterhouse**, **tournedos**.

tenpounder, a large fish of warm seas, whose body resembles that of a herring.

teosinte [from Mexican Spanish *teosinte, teocinte*, from Nahuatl *teocintli*, from *teotl* "god" + *cintli* "dried ears of corn"], a tall annual grass of Mexico and Central America related to Indian corn and sometimes regarded as ancestral to it.

tepary bean, an edible bean (seed) borne by a vine (likewise called *tepary bean*) of northern Mexico and the southwestern United States.

terfez [from French *terfesse, terfèze*, from Tuareg *tarfest, tĕrfest*, from Arabic *tirfās, tirfāsh* "truffle"], the edible fruit of a fungus of Old World desert regions, resembling a truffle.

teriyaki [Japanese "glaze", "broil, grill"], a dish of Japanese origin consisting of skewered and broiled (or grilled) slices of marinated (in a seasoned soy sauce) meat, shellfish, or chicken.

teel oil

teriyaki

termite [from Latin *termit-*, stem of *termes* "a worm that eats wood"] or **white ant**, any of various soft-bodied, superficially antlike, social insects.

terrapin [Algonquian], any of various aquatic, edible, North American turtles.

terrine [French "an earthenware dish, and its contents," from *terre* "earth"], *1.* a usually earthenware dish in which foods are cooked and served, tureen; *2.* a mixture of chopped meat (e.g., duck pâté, pâté de foie gras, boar), fish (e.g., smoked eel), or vegetables cooked and served in a terrine (sense 1).

tetrazzini [for Luisa *Tetrazzini*, 1874–1940, Italian opera singer (coloratura soprano)], prepared (e.g., chicken, veal, turkey, seafood [for instance, tuna, shrimp, clams]) with pasta (e.g., spaghetti, macaroni) and a white sauce (chicken broth, flour, chicken fat) seasoned with sherry (or dry white wine) and served au gratin (or with grated cheese).

Tex-Mex [from *Texan* + *Mexican*, or from *Texas* + *Mexico*], of the Texan variety of Mexican cuisine.

textured vegetable protein, protein obtained from some vegetables (especially soybeans), but given a texture that resembles meat, and used as a substitute for, or added to, meat.

Thailand. The following are among representative dishes and products of Thailand: rice (Thai *kao* [e.g., fried rice with chunks of meat *(kao pad)*]), curries *(kang ped* [e.g., chicken curry *(kang ped kai)* with coconut milk; fish curry and vegetables, in banana leaves *(hor mok pla)*]), fish (e.g., fried or steamed *plakapong* served with sweet-and-sour ginger-sauce), prawns (e.g., fried prawns [*kung tod*]), crisp noodles *(mi krob)* with shrimp; sweet-and-sour beef *(preaw wan nua)*, curried beef *(kang ped nua)*, grapefruit, mangoes, pineapple, papaya, rambutan, mangosteen; fried chicken *(kai yang)*, fried crab *(poo cha);* skewered chicken or pork, served with a sauce of coconut milk, mashed peanuts, and curry; fried mackerel *(pla too)*, stir-fried mixed vegetables *(pak ruam mit)*, a sauce made from salted shrimp or fish *(nam pla);* a dessert of noodles in coconut milk *(salim)*, lotus seeds in syrup; coconut cream *(sankhaya)*, coconut custard or pudding (served in the shell). Beverage: green tea.

tharfcake [from Middle English *tharf* "unleavened"], a flat, circular cake made of unleavened flour or meal dough (oat, rye, or barley) rolled thin and baked (England). When flavored with butter and molasses it becomes a parkin.

theezan tea, a shrubby Chinese plant with edible fruit and with leaves that are sometimes used in place of tea.

theine [from French *théine*, from *thé* "tea," so called from its occurrence in tea], another name for **caffeine**.

Thermidor, see **lobster Thermidor**.

thimbleberry, any of several American raspberries or blackberries with fruit shaped like a thimble.

thorn locust, another name for **honey locust**.

thorny lobster, another name for **spiny lobster**.

thorny locust, another name for **honey locust**.

thousand-headed cabbage, another name for **Brussels sprouts**.

Thousand Island dressing [from *Thousand Islands*, group of islands in the Saint Lawrence river, partly in New York state (United States) and partly in Ontario (Canada)], a dressing consisting of mayonnaise with chili sauce (or catsup) and seasonings (e.g., chopped pimientos, green peppers, and onion). Chives, paprika, pickles, minced olives, cream, may also be added. It is used, for instance, on wedges of lettuce, or, hot, on broccoli, cauliflower, lima beans.

three thorn acacia, another name for **honey locust**.

throat sweetbread, another name for **thymus**.

thrumwort, another name for **carambola** (= starfruit).

Thuringer or **Thüringer**, or **Thüringer sausage** [from German *Thüringerwurst*, from *Thüringer* "Thuringian" (from *Thüringen* "Thuringia," region of central Germany) + *Wurst* "sausage"], a mildly seasoned summer sausage.

thyme [from French *thym*], the leaves of any of several pungent, aromatic herbs (mints) likewise called *thyme*.

thyme oil, a fragrant oil obtained from various thymes and used as a flavor in foods.

thymus or **throat sweetbread**, a glandlike structure present in the young of most vertebrates, situated at the base of the neck. Compare **sweetbread**.

ti [Polynesian or Austronesian], a woody plant having thick sweet roots that are used as food.

tidbit, a pleasing or choice morsel or delicate bit of food.

tiger, a large grunt (fish) of the Indian Ocean.

tiger flathead, a large flathead (fish) of eastern Australia.

tigernut, another name for **chufa**.

tiger shrimp, a large shrimp of the Indian and Pacific oceans.

tikor [from Hindi *tīkhur*], a starch or arrowroot made from the tubers of an eastern Asian herb likewise called *tikor*.

til or **teel** [from Hindi *til*, from Sanskrit *tila*], another name for **sesame**.

tilapia, an African fat, flat-bodied, freshwater fish. From Africa it has been introduced elsewhere.

tilefish, any of several marine fishes.

Tillamook or **Tillamook cheese** [from *Tillamook*, town and county in Oregon, northwestern United States], a sharp cheddar cheese.

til oil, another name for **sesame oil**.

til seed, the seed of sesame.

Tilsit or **Tilsiter** [from *Tilsit*, city of western Russia], a semisoft cheese made with whole or skim milk and having flavor that ranges from mild to sharp.

timbale [French "kettledrum," from the shape of the mold], *1.* a creamy mixture of minced food (e.g., of chicken, meat, ham, lobster or other shellfish, fish, pasta, cheese, vegetables [for instance, spinach]), often mixed with eggs, crumbs, and liquid, baked in a tall drum-shaped pastry mold or in individual molds or cups; *2.* a small pastry shell fried on a timbale iron (a round and high iron mold) and filled with a cooked timbale mixture (sense 1) or served with fruit sauce; *3.* a drum-shaped, iron mold.

tip, a portion of beef cut from between the sirloin and the round and used for grilling or for roasting.

tipsy cake [from *tipsy* "staggering from the effects of liquor"], a sponge layer cake over which wine or brandy has been poured, with custard or preserves between the layers (or served with custard sauce), frosted with whipped cream, and decorated with toasted almonds.

tipsy pudding [from *tipsy* "staggering from the effects of liquor"], stale sponge cake over which wine (especially sherry) has been poured; it is served with boiled custard.

tiramisu [Italian "pull me up"], a dessert somewhat like a light trifle, consisting of sponge cake (or ladyfingers) dipped in a coffee-marsala mixture, then layered with mascarpone and grated chocolate. It is similar to zuppa inglese.

tisane [French, from Latin *ptisana* "peeled barley; barley water," from Greek *ptisanē*, "crushed barley," from *ptissein* "to peel, crush"], an infusion, originally of barley but now usually of dried leaves or flowers (e.g., linden blossoms, chamomile, rose hips, maté, mints, sages, thymes, orange blossoms, lemon blossoms, cherry stems) drunk as a beverage or for its mildly medicinal effects. Tisanes may also be made from bark (e.g., sassafras) and from seeds (e.g., anise, fennel). Compare ptisan.

toad-in-the-hole, meat (usually sausage), baked in batter.

¹**toast** (**to**), to make the surface of (e.g., bread, a sandwich, cheese) crisp, hot, and brown by the action of direct heat (by placing it close to a fire or in a toaster or in an oven).

²**toast**, *1.* sliced bread browned on both sides by heat; it is used plain, with butter, jam, marmalade, in sandwiches, and as a base for serving fish, meat, eggs, vegetables in a sauce; *2.* food prepared with toasted bread (compare **French toast**, **melba toast**, **milk toast**).

tocusso [from Amharic *tokusso*], a grass grown in Ethiopia for its edible seeds (a kind of millet) (used in a dark heavy bread).

toddy [from Hindi *tāṛī* "juice of the palmyra palm"], *1.* the fresh or fermented sap of several tropical Asian palm trees, used as a beverage; *2.* a usually hot drink consisting of brandy or other liquor (e.g., rum, whiskey) combined with hot water, sugar, and spices (e.g., cinnamon, cloves, nutmeg) and often garnished with fruit (e.g., a slice of lemon).

toddy palm, another name for **jaggery palm**.

toffee or **toffy** [from *taffy*], *1.* a hard but chewy candy, made by boiling usually brown sugar (or molasses) and butter together (pecans or almonds may be added); *2.* another name for **butterscotch** (sense 1, hard candy).

tofu [from Japanese *tōfu*, from Chinese *dòu fù* "bean curdled"], another name for **bean curd**.

toheroa [Maori], a large marine mollusk of New Zealand.

tomalley [from Carib *tumali* "sauce of lobster or crab livers"], the liver of the lobster, that turns green when boiled.

tomatillo [Spanish, "little tomato," diminutive of *tomate* "tomato"], the small, pale green or purplish fruit of a Mexican ground-cherry (likewise called *tomatillo*), resembling a small tomato.

tomato, [from Spanish *tomate*, from Nahuatl *tomatl*] or **gold** or **golden apple** or **love apple**, the large, rounded, red, fleshy fruit of a plant (likewise called *tomato*) that is a New World herb of the nightshade family. Tomatoes can be stewed, broiled, fried, baked, stuffed, and used in canapés, salads, bouillon, soufflé, casserole, dressing, omelet, soup (including cream of tomato, and clam chowder), juice, served with vinaigrette.

tomato sauce, a sauce made with tomatoes and usually onions, garlic, and olive oil; basil may be added. It is often served with spaghetti and in general with pasta.

tomcod or **tommycod**, either of two small fishes of northern waters, related to the cod.

tong [Afrikaans "tongue; flatfish"], a large southern African flatfish.

tongue, the flesh of the tongue (process of the floor of the mouth) of an animal (e.g., ox, calf, sheep, hog) used as food. It is a variety meat.

tonic water, another name for **quinine water**.

topinambour [French], another name for **Jerusalem artichoke**.

top milk, the upper layer of milk in a container.

topping, a sauce, frosting, or garnish placed on top of a food for flavor or decoration. Toppings used on pies and other desserts include bread crumbs, fruit, fudge, ice cream, meringue, nuts, whipped cream; fudge topping may be put on a sundae.

top round, a cut of meat, as a roast or steak, from the inner part of a round of beef.

top smelt, a silversides (a fish) of the North American Pacific coast.

torrone [Italian, from Spanish *turrón*, from *turrar* "to roast, toast"], a candy made of honey and toasted almonds (or pistachios, hazelnuts). Compare **nougat**.

torsk [Scandinavian (e.g., Danish and Swedish *torsk*)], another name for **codfish**.

torta [Spanish "cake"] or **tourte** [French "round pie with a savory filling"], an often round open pie with a base of bread or biscuit dough and sweet (e.g., fruit, cream) or savory filling. In Spain, a *torta* is a cake, but in Mexico it is a split roll with avocado, beans, and one of the following: ham, cheese, chicken.

torte [German], a cake or pastry made with many eggs, sugar, and often dry bread crumbs (not too finely ground) or chopped (or grated) nuts (e.g., almonds, pecans, hazelnuts, walnuts) in place of flour and baked in a large flat form, being sometimes filled with jam (or dates and nuts, or custard cream, or cheese, or marzipan) and usually covered with a rich frosting (e.g., chocolate, meringue, mocha, caramel). It may also have a whipped cream or fruit sauce garnish. Compare **Linzer torte**, **Sacher torte**.

tortellini [Italian, plural of *tortellino*, diminutive of *tortello*, from *torta* "cake"], pasta of noodle dough cut in rounds, folded around a savory filling (e.g., of meat, cheese, vegetables, shrimp), formed into rings, and boiled.

tortilla [American Spanish, from Spanish "omelet," diminutive of *torta* "cake"], a round, thin, soft pancake of unleavened cornmeal (or of wheat flour), usually baked on a griddle, eaten hot with a topping or filling that may include ground meat, shredded chicken, beans, cheese, and any of various sauces. It is characteristic of Mexican cookery. In Mexico, when food is rolled in a tortilla, the resulting combination is called *taco*. Compare **enchilada, masa, taco.**

tortoise [from French *tortue* "turtle"], any of various terrestrial turtles.

tortoni or **biscuit tortoni**., an ice cream made of heavy cream, often with minced almonds and chopped maraschino cherries, and sometimes with other flavoring ingredients (e.g., macaroons, vanilla, raspberries).

toss (to), to mix lightly, usually with a fork and spoon, until covered with a dressing or until the elements are thoroughly combined, without mashing the ingredients.

tossed salad, a salad made of greens (e.g., lettuce) often with added vegetables (e.g., sliced tomato or cucumber, radishes, chopped olives) tossed in an oil dressing. Vinegar or lemon juice may be added, as well as sardines, anchovies, cheese. Compare **Caesar salad**.

tostada [Mexican Spanish, from Spanish "toasted, roasted (feminine)"], a tortilla fried in deep fat.

totoaba or **totuava** [from Mexican Spanish *totuaba*], a large weakfish of the Gulf of California.

totora [Quechua or Aymara], a South American cattail (a marsh plant); its young shoots are used as food.

tournedos [French, from *tourner* "to turn" + *dos* "(the) back"], a fillet of beef usually cut from the tip of the tenderloin and often encircled by a strip of bacon, suet, or salt pork for quick cooking.

tourte [French], another name for **torta** (open pie).

tous-les-mois, starch from the rootstocks of edible canna.

Trappist cheese, another name for **Port Salut** (a cow-milk cheese).

traveler's-tree or **traveler's palm**, a tree of Madagascar having leaves whose petioles (stems) contain large amounts of watery sap and yield a refreshing drink.

treacle or **golden syrup**, *1.* molasses (sense 1, sugar syrup); *2.* a blend of molasses (sense 1, sugar syrup), invert sugar, and corn syrup used as syrup at the table.

tree crab, another name for **purse crab**.

tree ear, any of several brown, ear-shaped fungi used in Chinese cooking.

tree milk, the milky juice of an eastern Asian plant used for food.

tree onion, any of several garden onions cultivated for early salad onions.

tree tomato or **tamarillo** [from *tomatillo*], the egg-shaped, reddish, edible fruit of a South American shrub (likewise called *tree tomato* or *tamarillo)* of the nightshade family, somewhat resembling a tomato in flavor.

tref [from Yiddish *treyf*], ritually unfit according to Jewish dietary laws. Opposite of **kosher**.

trehala [ultimately from Persian *tīghāl*], a sweet, edible substance constituting the pupal (= of the pupa stage of an insect, that occurs between the larva and the imago) covering of an Old World beetle.

trepang [from Malay *tĕripang*] or **bêche-de-mer** [from French *bêche-de-mer*, "caterpillar of the sea; spade of the sea"], any of several large sea cucumbers that are taken mostly in the southwestern Pacific and are

boiled, dried, and smoked and used especially in the Orient for making soup.

trevally, an Australian food fish.

trifle ["something of little substance"], *1.* a dessert of many varieties typically including plain or sponge cake, spread with jam (e.g., raspberry) or jelly, sprinkled with crushed macaroons (or with vanilla wafers), soaked in sherry, rum, or brandy, and topped with custard and whipped cream; *2.* a dessert (e.g., of soft fruit) served with custard and whipped cream. It is similar to zuppa inglese and to tiramisu.

trifoliate orange, a Chinese orange tree with small, acid fruits.

triggerfish, any of various fishes of warm seas.

trillado [American Spanish, from Spanish "threshed"], coffee beans dried in the sun.

Trinidad and Tobago. The following are among representative dishes and products of Trinidad and Tobago: pork and beef casserole *(sancoche* [from American Spanish *sancocho* "meat stew," from Spanish *sancocho* "half-cooked food"]), ¹callaloo, roti, meat pancakes *(pasteles)*, crabmeat, oysters, curries (e.g., prawn, beef, chicken, shrimp, kid, potato), wild duck, pork souse, ¹pepper pot (with cassareep), salt codfish cakes *(accras)*, salt codfish salad *(buljol)*, split-pea fritters *(phulouri)*, chicken pilaf, crab pilaf, split-pea puree *(dal)*, split-pea stuffed bread *(dal puri)*, avocado, sapodilla, mangoes, pineapple, bananas, mango chutney, coconut bread, cornmeal *(coo-coo)* with okra, cornmeal pone, lime soufflé, pumpkin buns.

tripe, the light-colored, rubbery, stomach tissue of a ruminant (especially of the ox) used as food. Plain tripe is from the walls of the paunch or rumen (first compartment of the stomach), honeycomb tripe is from the walls of the reticulum (second compartment; it has hexagonal cells which make it resemble honeycomb). In Spain, *callos a la madrileña* ("Madrid tripe") is tripe with sausage.

tripletail, a large marine fish having fins that extend backward and resemble extra tails.

triticale [from Latin *triticum* "wheat" + *secale* "rye"], a hybrid between wheat and rye, that has rich protein content.

trompillo [Spanish] or **white horse nettle**, a nightshade of the New World with a roundish berry used to curdle milk.

tropical almond, another name for **Malabar almond**.

tropical apricot, another name for **mammee**.

trotter, the foot of a pig (sometimes of a sheep) prepared as food.

trou normand [French "Norman hole"] or **normand**, a sorbet served between courses as a palate refresher (to separate the flavors). In French, *faire le trou normand* ("to make the Norman hole") means to drink a glass of wine or liquor between two courses (which is deemed to increase eating capacity).

trout or **trucha** (Spanish) or **truite** (French), any of various fishes (e.g., brown trout), mostly smaller than salmons and many restricted to cool, fresh waters, usually having a speckled body and well-flavored flesh. Trouts are often served meunière or au bleu.

trub, another name for **truffle** (subterranean fungus).

trucha, Spanish for **trout**.

truffle [French] or **trub**, *1.* the usually dark and rugose fruiting body of any of various subterranean fungi (likewise called *truffles*). Truffles grow at a depth of about 80 centimeters, on the roots of certain trees, chiefly oaks (dogs and hogs are trained to find truffles by the scent). Pâté de foie gras and turkey are often prepared with truffles; *2.* a candy made of grated chocolate, butter (cream may be added), and sugar shaped into balls and coated with cocoa, macaroon crumbs, or chopped nuts (e.g., hazelnuts).

truffled, cooked, stuffed, or garnished with truffles (sense 1).

truite, French for **trout**.

truss (to), to arrange for cooking by binding or skewering the wings or legs of a fowl close to the body (or by tying other meat) so that the fowl will hold its shape.

try out (to), to render, to melt by frying (e.g., lard, oil) in order to separate (e.g., fat from membrane).

tsamba or **tsampa** [from Tibetan *tsampa*], flour made from parched, ground barley (or wheat), that is the chief cereal food (cooked as porridge [often mixed with yak-milk butter] or in tea) in and near Tibet (region of southwestern China, called Xizang in Chinese).

tsimmes, another name for **tzimmes**.

tuber, a short, swollen, usually underground stem of a plant (e.g., the potato or the Jerusalem artichoke).

tub sugar, soft maple sugar that is run into tubs for storage.

tuckahoe, *1.* the edible rootstock of either of two arums of the United States; *2.* or **Indian bread**, the large sclerotium (a part of a fungus, that holds reserve food material) of a subterranean fungus.

tucum or **tucuma** [from Portuguese *tucumã*, from Tupi *tucumá*], any of various Brazilian palms with seeds that yield oil.

tucunaré [Portuguese, from Tupi], any of various South American riverfishes that resemble bass.

tufoli, pasta shells or cases, small but large enough for stuffing (e.g., with meat, cheese). They are usually served without a sauce so the subtlety of the stuffing and the excellence of the pasta can be fully appreciated.

tule potato or **tule root** [from Mexican Spanish *tule* "bulrush," from Nahuatl *tollin*], another name for **wapatoo**.

tullibee [from Canadian French *toulibi*], any of several whitefishes of North America.

¹**tuna** [Spanish, from Taino], the edible fruit of any of several tropical American prickly pears likewise called *tunas* (compare **nopal**).

²**tuna** [American Spanish, from Spanish *atún*, from Arabic *tūn*, from Latin *thunnus*] or **tuna fish** or **ahi** (Hawaiian), the flesh of any of various large marine fishes (likewise called *tuna*, but also *tunny*), often commercially canned or processed. The fish is fat and therefore best for broiling, baking, planking. Tuna may be served as burgers, casserole, salad, supreme.

Tunis [from *Tunis*, formerly Tunisia, one of the Barbary States in North Africa, where the breed originated], a sheep of a breed likewise called *Tunis*.

Tunisia. The following are among representative dishes and products of Tunisia: couscous, roast mutton (Arabic *mashwi*, "roast"); a dish of peppers, tomatoes, onions, and eggs *(shakshuka);* olives, dates, bananas, pomegranates, grapes, oranges, dried figs, honey cakes, baklava; Turkish delight. Beverage: sweet mint-tea.

tunny [from French *thon* or Italian *tonno*], another name for ²**tuna** (the fish).

turban shell, any of numerous marine snails with a spiral shell.

turban squash, any of various winter squashes having fruit shaped somewhat like a turban.

turbinado or **turbinado sugar** [American Spanish], partially refined, granulated, pale-brown cane sugar that has been washed (in a centrifuge) and dried.

turbot [French], *1.* a large European flatfish having a compressed, disk-shaped body; *2.* any of various other flatfishes. Turbots may be served as broiled filets.

tureen [from French *terrine* "an earthenware dish," from *terre* "earth"], a deep and usually covered bowl or dish used for serving cooked foods (e.g., soup, stew, egg, sauce). Compare **terrine** (sense 1).

turkey [short for *turkey-cock* "male turkey, gobbler," originally applied to the guinea fowl (with which the American bird was later mistakenly identified) supposed to have been first imported by the Portuguese from Africa by way of Turkish territory, from *Turkey*, country], a large North American bird. Turkey, like duck and goose, is almost always stuffed and roasted whole, although the smoked meat is also served; turkey can also be broiled, pan-fried, served a la king, and made into cream pie or hash. The liver, heart, and gizzard, called giblets, are often cooked and served either separately or chopped and added to gravy.

Turkey. The following are among representative dishes and products of Turkey: hot and cold hors d'oeuvre (Turkish *meze*), that may include (a) thin sheets of puff pastry (called *yufka* in Turkish) filled with ground meat or cheese and fried crisp *(börek)*, (b) a variety of salads made from such ingredients as beans, cucumbers, tomatoes, yogurt, eggplant, olives, garlic, and parsley, (c) rice-stuffed vine leaves *(yaprak* ["leaf"] *dolması)*, (d) poached chicken in walnut puree *(çerkez tavuğu,* "Circassian chicken"), (e) a pickled-and-salted tuna dish *(lakerda)*, (f) sheep's milk cheese *(beyaz peynir,* "white cheese"), (g) pickled anchovies *(hamsi tursu)*, (h) mussels cooked in the shell with rice, onions, raisins, and olive oil *(midye dolması);* other dishes: chicken or turkey stuffed with pilaf *(iç pilav* ["inside pilaf"], which is rice cooked with currants, pine nuts, and spices); swordfish kabob *(kiliç şiş* [*şiş* = "spit"]); roast pieces of lamb on a spit *(kebap);* pieces of lamb roasted on a vertical spit *(döner kebap)*, meatballs *(köfte)*, meatballs grilled on a spit *(şiş kebap)*, rice, lamb, eggplant *(patlıcan;* e.g., grilled, fried [*patlıcan kızartması*]; stuffed with rice and pine nuts; one stuffed-eggplant dish is called *imam bayıldı,* "the priest fainted"); okra, zucchini, fish (e.g., stuffed with raisins and pine nuts; grilled bluefish [*lüfer*], in a little olive oil, with parsley, coriander, and lemon wedges; other fish: sea bass, turbot, bonito, plaice), fish roe salad *(tarama)*, stuffed tomato *(domates dolması)*, stuffed lamb *(kuzu dolması)*, figs, grapes, peaches, apricots, melon, watermelon, yogurt, baklava, Turkish delight *(rahat lokum)*, breast of chicken prepared as a dessert with milk and sugar *(tavuk göğsü)*, shredded wheat stuffed with nuts in syrup *(tel kadayıf)*, rose jam *(gül receli)*.

Turkey fig [from *Turkey*, country], *1.* a common cultivated fig; *2.* in Australia, the prickly pear.

Turkey wheat [from *Turkey*, country], another name for **Indian corn** [Italian *granturco*, "Turkish grain"].

Turkish coffee, powdered coffee in a thin sugar syrup.

Turkish delight, a candy of Turkish origin consisting of jellylike or gummy cubes (made of glucose and corn flour) dusted with sugar, often perfumed with orange-blossom or rose water, sometimes with chopped almonds or pistachios added. In Turkish, it is called *rahat lokum* ["rest morsels" or "calmness bites"].

Turkish pepper, *1.* another name for **pimiento**; *2.* a paprika (sense 1) made from pimiento.

Turkish walnut, another name for **English walnut**.

turmeric, the clean, boiled, sun-dried, and usually powdered, aromatic rootstock of a plant (likewise called *turmeric*, or *curcuma*) of eastern Asia, of the ginger family, used as a condiment (e.g., in curry powder, in pickling) and as a yellow dye.

turnip, the root of a plant (likewise called *turnip*) of the mustard family, cooked and eaten as a vegetable. Yellow it is a **rutabaga**, white it is a turnip. Compare **turnip tops**.

turnip bean, another name for **yam bean**.

turnip cabbage, another name for both **kohlrabi** and **rutabaga**.

turnip radish or **turnip-rooted radish**, any of several radishes with roundish roots.

turnip-rooted celery or **turnip celery**, another name for **celeriac**.

turnip-rooted chervil, the edible, spindle-shaped tuber of a European plant likewise called *turnip-rooted chervil*.

turnip tops or **turnip greens**, the young leaves of the turnip boiled as greens.

turnover or **pasty**, a small, triangular or semicircular filled pastry (sense 3) made by folding half of the crust (square or circular piece of dough) over the other half. The filling may be, for instance, fruit (e.g., apple), preserves, chicken. Compare **samosa**.

turrón, see **nougat**.

turtle [from French *tortue*, from Late Latin *tartarucha* "of Tartarus (feminine)," from Greek *Tartaros* "Tartarus, the infernal region," from the turtle's having been regarded as an infernal creature], any of various reptiles. Compare **terrapin**.

tutti-frutti [Italian "all fruits"], *1.* a confection, especially ice cream, containing a variety of chopped, usually candied, fruits; *2.* a flavoring simulating the flavor of many fruits.

tutu [Maori], a New Zealand shrubby tree with a juicy, black, edible receptacle (but the dry fruit enclosed by this receptacle contains a poisonous seed).

TV dinner [so called from its saving a person from having to interrupt television viewing to prepare and serve a meal], a quick-frozen, packaged, ready-to-serve meal (e.g., of meat, potatoes, and a vegetable) that requires only heating (e.g., in an oven) before it is served.

twelfth-cake or **twelfth-night cake** [from *Twelfth-night*, which is both the evening of 6 January (Twelfth-day or Epiphany, twelve days after Christmas), marking the end of medieval Christmas festivities, and the evening before (5 January) Twelfth Day], a large cake prepared for Twelfth-night festivities, that contains a bean or a coin. The person finding the bean or coin in his piece was declared monarch for the evening (or ruler of the feast). Compare **galette**.

twist, *1*. bread or another bakery product for which the dough was twisted or formed by winding before baking; *2*. a strip or sliver of citrus peel twisted above or dropped into a drink in order to flavor it with the expressed oils.

twister, a twisted cruller or doughnut.

tyee, a king salmon (= quinnat salmon), especially when of large size.

tzimmes or **tsimmes** [from Yiddish *tsimes* "vegetable or fruit stew"], a stew or casserole of a sweetened combination of vegetables or vegetables and dried fruit, sometimes with meat (usually with carrots and one or two of the following: potatoes, prunes, apples, dried apricots and pears, sweet potatoes and apples).

udo [Japanese], a Japanese plant, of which the blanched young shoots are cooked and eaten as a vegetable and in salads.

ugli, another name for **tangelo** (a citrus fruit).

uintjie [from Afrikaans *euntjie*, *uintjie*], the edible corm (underground stem base) of various plants, that when boiled tastes like a chestnut (southern Africa).

Ukraine. The following are representative dishes and products of Ukraine: cabbage borsch; dumplings with meat, curds, cabbage, potatoes, cherries, strawberries; chicken croquettes à la Kiev (see **chicken Kiev**); fish, cucumbers, dark breads, sauerkraut, sour cream. Beverage: tea.

uku [Hawaiian], a grayish snapper of Hawaiian seas.

ulaula [from Hawaiian *'ula'ula*], any of several snappers.

ullucu [from American Spanish *ulluco*, *olluco*, from Quechua *ullucu*], an Andean (Ecuador, Peru) plant having tuberous roots which are used in place of potatoes.

ulua [Hawaiian], any of several large cavallas (fish) of Hawaiian waters.

umble pie [from *umbles* "the entrails of an animal"], another name for **humble pie**.

umbles or **nombles** or **numbles** ["certain edible viscera"], the internal parts of an animal (usually of a deer, but also of a hog, a sheep) used as food. Compare **giblet** (which is the viscera of a fowl).

uncooked, not cooked, raw.

undercook (to), to cook insufficiently.

undercut, another name for **tenderloin** (of beef).

underdo (to), to cook inadequately or lightly.

underdone, (of food, especially beef) rare, not thoroughly cooked, cooked for a comparatively short or an insufficient time.

United Kingdom. One way of dividing the United Kingdom gastronomically is to speak of three main regions—England, Scotland, and Wales, although England could in turn be divided into five areas—northern, central, southern, eastern, and western. The following are representative dishes and products of the three main regions of the United Kingdom:

United States

Uzbekistan

England. Roast beef with Yorkshire pudding, steak and kidney pie, Lancashire hot pot, Cornish pasty, cheeses; fried or grilled Dover sole; plaice, bream, halibut, turbot, salmon, herring, oxtail soup, trout, York ham, grouse, shrimps, tripe; fish-and-chips, roasts, steaks, turkey, oysters, crab, lobster, scallops, sausages, farmed venison, lamb with mint sauce, duck, goose, asparagus, plums, apples, cherries, plum pudding, trifle. Beverage: tea.

Scotland. haggis, Scotch broth, finnan haddie, porridge, kipper, oatcakes, beef, game, salmon, preserves, scones. Beverage: tea.

Wales. lamb, mutton, salmon, trout, cheese, lobster, crayfish, crab, bass, herring, mackerel, cockles.

United States. The following are representative dishes and products of the United States: hot dogs, hamburger (sense 3, sandwich), pizza, shellfish (e.g., shrimp, crab, lobster, abalone), fish (e.g., trout, salmon, halibut), clam chowder, baked beans, Virginia ham, ears of corn, steaks, chops, spareribs, leg of lamb, bacon and eggs, ham and eggs, fowl (e.g., southern fried chicken, roast turkey), New Orleans gumbo, [2]creole jambalaya, hominy grits, wild rice, barbecues, sweet potatoes, doughnuts, cheese cake, pecan pie, apple pie.

United States Virgin Islands. The following are representative dishes and products of the United States Virgin Islands: herring salmagundi (called locally *herring gundy)*, asparagus, curries, meat pie, coconut, fish, okra.

upland cress, another name for **winter cress**.

upside-down cake, a single-layer cake baked with its batter covering a close arrangement of pieces of fruit (e.g., pineapple slices, apricot halves) in a syrup at the bottom of the pan, then served with the fruit side up.

urchin, another name for **sea urchin**.

urd or **urd bean** [from Hindi *urd*, *urad*], the edible, blackish seed of a bean (likewise called *urd)* native to India, grown in warm regions, closely related to the **mung bean**.

Uruguay. The following are representative dishes and products of Uruguay: beef (e.g., boiled dinner [Spanish *puchero*], grilled [*asado a las brasas*], roast, barbecued in its own hide [*asado con cuero*], grilled steak [*churrasco*]), barbecued pig, grilled chicken, meat pie, meat roasted on a spit *(asado);* beef that is roasted or grilled is usually accompanied with a sauce called *chimichurri* made of vinegar, oil, onion, garlic, parsley, and other herbs (e.g., thyme, marjoram); a stew of small pieces of meat, Indian corn, squash, potatoes, and sometimes rice, peaches, pears, raisins *(carbonada);* assorted grilled meats *(parrillada)* including chorizo, blood sausage, variety meats; grilled fish, lobster; milk jam-like sweet *(dulce de leche);* sponge cake with cream, meringue, and peaches *(chajá).* Beverage: mate.

Uruguay potato, the tuber (fleshy underground stem or root) of a South American plant (likewise called *Uruguay potato)*, resembling the common potato.

Uzbekistan. The following are representative dishes and products of Uzbekistan: pilaf (Uzbek *plov)*, mutton, kabob, mutton soup *(shurpa)*, steamed meat-pies *(manty)*, meat and onion pies *(samsa).*

284

Valencia orange, or simply **Valencia** [from *Valencia*, province of eastern Spain], a certain sweet orange.

vanaspati [Sanskrit "forest tree; soma plant (a leafless vine)," "lord of the forest"], a vegetable fat (a kind of ghee) used in India as a butter substitute.

vanilla [from Spanish *vainilla* "vanilla (fruit and plant)," "small pod," diminutive of *vaina* "pod, sheath," from Latin *vagina* "sheath; vagina"], *1.* or **vanilla bean**, the aromatic seed-pod (a long capsular fruit) of any of various tropical American orchids (likewise called *vanillas); 2.* a flavoring extract used in confections, made by soaking powdered vanilla pods in a mixture of water and grain alcohol (or prepared synthetically).

vanille [French] *1.* another name for **vanilla** (sense 2); *2.* or **vanille ice**, vanilla ice cream.

vanillin, a substance used in flavoring, that is extracted from vanilla beans (or produced synthetically).

vanillon [French, from *vanille* "vanilla"], any of various coarse vanillas of inferior flavor and aroma, that are obtained especially from uncultivated vanilla vines.

variety meat or **fancy meat**, meat (e.g., beef, lamb, pork, veal) taken from a part of a slaughter animal other than skeletal muscles, usually including organ meats (e.g., liver, heart, brains, lungs, tripes, spleen, kidneys) and various other structures (e.g., tongues, ears, thymus, pancreas, skin, oxtail), or a processed meat product (e.g., sausage) that does not consist chiefly of skeletal muscle.

veal, the flesh of a young calf. Its variety meats are chiefly heart, kidney, tongue. Veal may be sautéed, braised, roasted, pressed, cordon bleu; veal dishes include chops, cutlets, steaks, casserole, daube, stuffed breast, supreme, tetrazzini, veal birds.

veal bird, a thin slice of veal, rolled around stuffing, stewed. In Italian this dish, with bacon stuffing, is called *uccelli scappati* "birds that escaped." Compare **bird**, sense 2.

veal cutlet

---

vegetable

286

veal cutlet, a thin slice from a leg of veal cut into small portions (often pounded) and fried (or braised) plain or breaded. When fried Italian style, cheese and chopped tomatoes (skinned and seeded) can be added.

veal scallopini, see **scallopini**.

vegeburger [from *vege*table or *vege*tarian + -*burger*], *1.* a patty of vegetable protein used as a meat substitute; *2.* a sandwich containing such a patty.

vegetable, an edible part (e.g., leaves, seeds, roots, stems, flowers) of a usually herbaceous plant likewise called *vegetable* (e.g., bean, cabbage, potato, turnip), usually eaten, cooked or raw (most vegetables may be eaten raw), during the main part of a meal rather than as a dessert. Vegetable juices are served as cocktails and used for sauces, jellied salads, and in made dishes.

Many vegetables (e.g., asparagus tips, whole beets) are boiled (simmered) or steamed (and oven steamed), then dressed in various ways (e.g., with sauces, garnishes, herbs [e.g., chopped parsley]); those that are good baked include artichokes, beets, onions, potatoes, squash, sweet potatoes. Cooked vegetables are used in soups and salads, reheated in a sauce, broiled or pan-fried. Other methods for cooking vegetables: pressure cooked, fried, French fried, shallow fried, sautéed, braised, broiled; some ways to serve them: au gratin, buttered, creamed, scalloped.

Vegetables include (with specific ways to serve them —only some of the possibilities— including main dishes) artichoke (including casserole), asparagus, beans, beets (including Harvard beets), broccoli (casserole, soufflé), Brussels sprouts, cabbage (scalloped, hot cabbage slaw, panned, celery cabbage [Chinese]), carrots (ring, in cream, baked shredded), cauliflower (with cheese, casserole), celery (Chinese, creole, with water chestnuts), chard, corn (custard = corn pudding; scalloped, sauté, corn patties, soufflé, oven-roasted corn on cob, corn-tomato casserole), cucumbers (baked, in sour cream consommé), eggplant (broiled, fried, stuffed), green or wax beans, greens (chicory, collards, dandelion greens, escarole, lettuce, mustard greens, romaine, spinach [timbales, sprite, creamed, Provençale], watercress; tops of: beet, kale, kohlrabi, radish, turnip), Jerusalem artichokes, kohlrabi, lima beans (including succotash), mushrooms (although frequently these organisms are no longer classified in the plant kingdom, and therefore are not technically vegetables; stuffed, in cream), okra, onions (green: scallions, shallots, chives; leeks; garlic) [including French fried, sautéed, caramel cream, creamed, glazed, escalloped, stuffed baked], parsnips (glazed baked), peas (in cream), peppers (sweet, not hot) [sautéed], potatoes (boiled, parsleyed, creamed, au gratin, browned, broiled, cottage fried, lyonnaise, hashed browned, sautéed potato balls, pancakes, French fried, chips, baked, mashed, mashed potato cakes, puff, duchesse, puffed, scalloped, shirred), pumpkin, rutabagas (puff, glazed), salsify, sauerkraut (with spare ribs), spinach, squash (summer, winter, zucchini) [Provençale], sweet potatoes (baked candied, skillet candied, puff), tomatoes (the tomato, though botanically a fruit, is usually eaten as a vegetable; stewed, broiled, fried, baked, stuffed), turnips (puff, glazed).

Dried vegetables include beans, peas, lentils, peanuts.

Vegetables retain their color and nutritive value better if cooked quickly (not over-long) and in a small amount of water; they come in four basic classes of pigment: yellow-to-orange (carrots, rutabagas, sweet potatoes), red-to-purple-to-blue (beets, cabbage, eggplant), green (broccoli, green beans, peas, spinach), white (cauliflower, onions, turnips).

Seasonings that can be added (sparingly) to certain vegetables: asparagus (dill), beets (basil, savory, thyme), broccoli (oregano), cabbage (oregano), carrots (bay leaf, mint, thyme), cucumbers (dill), eggplant (basil, sage), green beans (dill, marjoram, savory, thyme), greens (dill), lentils (oregano), lima beans (sage), mushrooms (marjoram, rosemary, savory), new potatoes (dill, mint), onions (basil, sage, thyme), peas (marjoram, mint, rosemary, savory), potatoes (bay leaf), salsify (savory), spinach (marjoram, mint, rosemary), squash (basil, rosemary), stewed tomatoes (bay leaf), tomatoes (basil, oregano, sage), zucchini (marjoram).

Sauces used for vegetables include almond or cashew, bread crumbs, butter, cheese, egg, hollandaise, mushroom, parsley, tartare.

Garnishes used with vegetables include chopped toasted almonds, cashews, or peanuts; bread-crumb sauce; grated cheese; croutons; crumbled crisp bacon bits or crisp cereals or cheese crackers or potato chips; quartered or sliced hard-cooked eggs, sieved hard-cooked eggs or yolks; lemon slices or wedges; French-fried onions, minced green onion tops or chives; paprika; parsley; green pepper rings or strips, pimiento strips.

vegetable butter, *1.* any of various vegetable fats that resemble butter or lard, especially in consistency, yielded by some plants, as the cacao bean, coconut, nutmeg, shea; *2.* another name for **avocado**.

vegetable egg, *1.* another name for **eggplant**; *2.* the fruit of the marmalade tree.

vegetable fat, a fat obtained naturally or manufactured from plants.

vegetable marrow or **marrow squash** or simply **marrow**, any of various smooth-skinned, elongated summer squashes (e.g., zucchini, cocozelle).

vegetable oil, any of various oils obtained from plants (usually from seeds or nuts) used in food products.

vegetable orange, another name for **mango melon**.

vegetable oyster, another name for both **salsify** and **black salsify**.

vegetable pear, another name for **chayote**.

vegetable plate, a main course consisting of various vegetables, cooked separately but served on one plate.

vegetable rennet, a plant that has the power of coagulating milk (e.g., butterwort [a plant with fleshy leaves]).

[1]**vegetarian** (noun), one who practices vegetarianism.

[2]**vegetarian** (adjective), *1.* relating to vegetarianism; *2.* consisting wholly of vegetables, fruits, and sometimes eggs or dairy products.

vegetarianism, the practice of living on a diet made up only of vegetables and plant products (e.g., fruits, grains, nuts), and sometimes also of eggs or dairy products, usually for health or moral reasons.

vell, a calf stomach used in making rennet.

velouté, or **velouté sauce** [from French *velouté* "velvety," from *velours* "velvet"], a thick white sauce made with flour, butter, and a chicken or veal stock. It may also include cream or egg yolks. It may be served on asparagus, chicken, fish, game, tomatoes, wild mushrooms. Veloutés include allemande, béchamel, Bercy, Mornay, Normande, poulette, ravigote, suprême.

velvet tamarind, or **black tamarind**, a tree of West Africa with velvety black pods containing a pulp that is macerated in water to form a beverage or is chewed to relieve thirst.

Venezuela. The following are representative dishes and products of Venezuela: hors d'oeuvre (regional Spanish *pasapalos*), including tortillas with cheese *(cachapita)*, dough rolls with cheese *(tequeño)*, cracklings tamale *(hallaquita)*, small chicken-and-meat empanada, and green plantains with garlic *(tostones);* tamales in banana leaves *(hallacas)* with olives, capers, chick-peas; meat (or fish) and cassava stew *(sancocho);* black beans with shredded beef, onion, tomato, rice, and fried banana *(pabellón criollo);* scrambled eggs with tomato, onion, and garlic *(pericos);* oxtail soup *(sopa de rabo de res);* beans *(caraotas)*, avocados, rice, corn; shellfish (e.g., oysters, clams, lobster, shrimps), fish (e.g., pargo [sense 2], red snapper); corn bread *(arepa)* with black beans, filled with cheese, chicken, or fish; kid; cake with meringue and coconut *(bienmesabe,* "it tastes well to me"), cooked dried fruit *(abrillantados).*

venison, the flesh of a deer (moose, elk; reindeer), used for food. Venison dishes include **civet**. Venison is cooked like beef, well done but not overcooked, and often served with wild-plum jelly. Deer loin may be prepared with plums.

Venus's-ear, another name for **abalone**.

verdolaga [Spanish], a common purslane.

verjuice [from French *verjus*, from *vert jus* "green juice"], the sour juice of green or unripe fruit (e.g., grapes, apples) or of crab apples, formerly much used in cooking. Grape verjuice is used in preparing Dijon mustard.

vermicelli [Italian "little worms," plural diminutive of *verme* "worm"], wheat flour pasta made into long, solid strings, thinner than spaghetti.

vermilion rockfish, a reddish rockfish of the Pacific coast of North America.

Vermont snakeroot, another name for **wild ginger**.

Véronique or **Veronique** [from French *Véronique*, a feminine given name corresponding to English *Veronica*], prepared or garnished (e.g., sole, trout, chicken) with grapes (usually white and seedless).

vetch, the small, edible, dark brown seed of a Eurasian twining, leguminous plant likewise called *vetch*.

viajaca [from Cuban Spanish *viajaca*, *biajaca*, from Carib *diahaca*], a small Cuban freshwater fish.

vi apple, or simply **vi** [Tahitian], another name for **otaheite apple**.

vichyssoise [French "of Vichy (feminine)," from *Vichy*, city of central France], a thick, creamy, strained-potato soup, flavored with pureed leeks or onions, and cream, chicken stock, and seasonings, and usually served cold.

Vichy water or simply **Vichy** or **vichy** [from *Vichy*, city of central France], *1.* a soda water, a natural, sparkling, mineral water from the springs at Vichy; *2.* a natural, sparkling, mineral water resembling this.

Vienna sausage [from *Vienna*, capital of Austria] or **wienerwurst**, a small sausage resembling a frankfurter, in a thin casing usually having the ends cut off, often served as an hors d'oeuvre.

Viet Nam. The following are representative dishes and products of Viet Nam: rice, shrimp chips (Vietnamese *phong tôm*), egg roll *(cha giò)*, with crab, pork, vegetables; omelet with pork and shrimps *(cha tôm)*, fish; fish paste *(nước mắm)* used as a condiment; beef, pork, chicken, duck, crabs, peas, corn; soya-bean curd *(đâu phụ)*, potatoes, yams, peas, bamboo shoots. Beverage: tea.

vinaigrette [French, from *vinaigre* "sour wine"] or **spirit vinegar** or **vinaigrette sauce** or **vinaigrette dressing**, a cold sauce or dressing made typically of vinegar and oil flavored with finely chopped onions, parsley, herbs, and other seasonings (e.g., salt, pepper), and used especially on cold meats or fish, and on salads and other raw vegetables.

vindaloo [ultimately from Portuguese *vinho de alho* "wine and garlic sauce," from *vinho* "wine" + *de* "of, from" + *alho* "garlic"], a curried dish of Indian origin made with meat or shellfish (or fish, or poultry) in a sauce of garlic, wine or vinegar, and spices.

vinegar [from French *vinaigre* "vinegar," "sour wine," from *vin* "wine" + *aigre* "sour"], a sour liquid used as a condiment or a preservative (e.g., for ¹capers, gherkins, onions), that is obtained by fermentation of dilute alcoholic liquids (e.g., cider, malt beer, wine) beyond the alcohol stage, and is often seasoned, especially with herbs (e.g., tarragon).

vinegar pie, a pie consisting of a filling of flour, water, vinegar, and butter, sweetened with brown sugar and baked in a pastry shell.

vine peach, another name for **mango melon.**

Virginia ham [from *Virginia*, state of the eastern United States], a dry-cured, lean, hickory-smoked, and aged ham with dark red meat, especially from a peanut-fed razorback hog.

Virginia oyster [from *Virginia*, state of the eastern United States], the common oyster of the Atlantic coast of North America.

Virginia sarsaparilla, another name for **wild sarsaparilla.**

Virginia strawberry, or **scarlet strawberry**, a North American plant having sweet, scarlet fruit.

vitelline [from Latin *vitellus* "yolk; little calf," from *vitulus* "calf"], the yolk of an egg.

viznaga, variant of **bisnaga.**

vol-au-vent [French "flight in the wind"], a light, baked, pastry shell (made of puff paste) filled with a ragout or a creamy mixture of meat, fowl, game, or seafood, in a sauce, often with mushrooms or quenelles. Compare **timbale** (sense 1).

wokas   wineberry

waterzooi   whelk

wapatoo

wheatmeal

watermelon

wafer, a thin, crisp cake, cracker, or candy.

waffle, a light, crisp pancake-batter cake baked in a waffle iron.

waffle iron, a cooking utensil having two hinged, indented metal plates that shut upon each other and impress a grid pattern (square, round, or oval surface projections) into waffle batter (= pancake batter, compare **pancake**) as it bakes.

wahoo, a large, tropical, marine mackerel.

Waldorf salad [from *Waldorf*-Astoria Hotel, New York City, where it was originally served], a salad made typically of diced raw apples, celery, and walnuts mixed with mayonnaise. Often the apples are used with the red skin on.

walleye or **walleyed pike** or **gray pike**, a large freshwater fish of North America, having large, prominent eyes, and related to the perches.

walleye pollack, a large, dark, food fish of the northern Pacific related to the pollack. It has large, staring eyes.

walnut [from Old English *wealhhnutu* "Welsh nut, foreign nut"], the ridged or corrugated nut of the round, sticky fruit of any of several trees likewise called *walnuts*. Dishes using walnuts include cakes and pies, Waldorf salad.

walnut oil, an oil obtained from English walnuts, used in foods.

walrus, a large marine mammal of Arctic regions, related to the seal (another marine mammal, of cold regions).

wapatoo or **duck potato** or **muskrat potato** or **tule potato**, either of two plants having edible tubers.

warabi [Japanese], a brake (fern, a flowerless plant) whose young fronds are eaten in Japan.

ware, potatoes suitable for table use.

warehou [Maori], a sea bream of Australia and New Zealand.

wasabi [Japanese], a condiment that is prepared (grated) from the thick, pungent, greenish root (likewise called *wasabi*) of an herb (likewise called *wasabi*) of the mustard family, is similar in flavor and use to horseradish, and is eaten with fish and other food.

washed-curd cheese, cheddar cheese in which the curd is washed before being pressed into forms.

Washington clam [from *Washington*, state of the northwestern United States], a butter clam.

Washington pie [for George *Washington*, 1732–1799, first president of the United States (1789-1797)], a layer cake with a filling of jam, fruit jelly, cream, custard, or chocolate.

water, a clear, colorless, nearly odorless and tasteless liquid that descends from the clouds as rain.

water bath, see **double boiler**.

water biscuit or **winter cracker**, a cracker or biscuit made of water and flour, sometimes with added salt and shortening.

water buffalo or **carabao**, a large buffalo of Asia and Africa, often domesticated.

water chestnut or **Jesuits' nut** or **Jesuits' waternut** or **ling**, *1.* or **water caltrop**, the edible, nutlike fruit of a floating, aquatic plant likewise called *water chestnut; 2.* the edible tuber (corm) of a Chinese sedge (likewise called *water chestnut)* used in Oriental cookery.

water chinquapin or **yockernut**, the edible, nutlike seed of a North American aquatic plant (likewise called *water chinquapin)* related to the lotus and the water lilies, that has the flavor of a chinquapin.

water cracker, another name for **water biscuit**.

watercress or **well cress**, any of several cresses growing in freshwater ponds and streams and having pungent leaves used especially in salads or as a potherb.

water hickory, a hickory of the southern United States having rather bitter nuts.

water ice, a dessert made from sweetened, flavored, finely crushed ice. Compare **sherbet** (sense 1).

water lily, any of various aquatic plants.

watermelon [French *pastèque*, Spanish *sandía*], the large, oblong or roundish fruit of a vine (likewise called *watermelon)* native to tropical Africa, having a hard, green rind and sweet, watery, reddish flesh.

water oat or **water rice**, other names for **wild rice**.

water tree, any of several chiefly tropical plants with fluids (e.g., sap, or water stored in the roots) that are used as an emergency source of drinking water (Africa, Australia, Sri Lanka).

waterzooi [from Flemish *waterzooi*, from *water* + *zooi* "quantity of cooked food"], a stew, of Belgian origin, of chicken or fish and vegetables (cut in long strips or diced) served with a sauce of seasoned stock thickened with cream (crème fraîche) and egg yolks, or the sauce may be in the stew.

wax bean or **butter bean** or **waxpod bean**, a variety of string bean having yellow pods. When mature enough, they can be used as **snap beans**.

wax gourd or **Chinese watermelon**, the fleshy, edible fruit, resembling a pumpkin, of a tropical Asiatic plant likewise called *wax gourd*. It is used for pickles.

waxpod bean, another name for **wax bean**.

waxy corn or **waxy maize**, an Indian corn with grains that look waxy when cut; the grains are used for desserts and as a replacement for tapioca (sense 1).

weakfish [from Dutch *weekvis* "soft, tender (weak) fish"; from its tender flesh], any of several marine fishes of North American Atlantic waters.

Weddell seal [for English navigator James *Weddell*, 1787–1834], an Antarctic seal valued for its flesh and blubber.

wedding cake or **bridecake**, an elaborately decorated and tiered cake made for the celebration of a wedding. It is often a dark, unleavened fruited cake, or a light fruited cake, or a white butter cake, and heavily frosted.

weenie or **wienie** or **wiener** [short for *wienerwurst* (German) "Vienna sausage,"], another name for **frankfurter**.

weever, any of several marine fishes having venomous spines, and eyes looking upward.

well cress, another name for **watercress**.

well-done, (of a steak or roast) cooked thoroughly.

Welsh onion or **spring onion**, an Asiatic onion grown for its leaves which are used in seasoning and its slender bulbs which are used as early green onions.

Welsh rabbit or **Welsh rarebit** or **rabbit** or **rarebit**, a dish made of melted and often seasoned cheese, milk, or cream, seasonings, and sometimes ale, served hot over toasted bread or crackers. Compare **golden buck**.

Wensleydale [from *Wensleydale*, locality in Yorkshire, England], *1*. a cylindrical, pale, soft cheese, blue-veined after curing; *2*. a flat-shaped, white cheese eaten fresh before curing

western, another name for **western sandwich**.

western omelet or **Denver omelet**, an omelet (beaten egg) cooked usually with diced or minced ham, chopped green pepper, and onion.

western sand cherry, the large, sweet fruit of a dwarf shrub of the western United States likewise called *western sand cherry*.

western sandwich or **Denver sandwich**, a sandwich having a western omelet as a filling.

West Indian cherry [from *West Indian* "of the West Indies (the islands bordering the Caribbean)"], another name for **Barbados cherry**.

West Indian locust, a tropical American tree with pods that contain an edible pulp.

Westphalian ham [from *Westphalia* (German *Westfalen*), region of western Germany], a ham smoked with juniper brush.

whale, any of various marine mammals.

whale oil, oil obtained from the blubber (fat) of whales, used in making margarine.

whapuku [Maori], a large marine fish of New Zealand.

wharf fish, another name for **cunner** (marine fish).

wheat, a cereal grain (of any of various cereal grasses likewise called *wheat)* ground to produce a fine white flour used in breadstuffs and in pasta products (e.g., macaroni, noodles, spaghetti).

wheat bread, a bread made of a mixture of flours (white and whole wheat); distinguished from bread made wholly of one or of the other flour.

wheat cake, a pancake made of wheat flour.

wheat germ, the embryo or germ of the wheat kernel separated before milling for use as a cereal or food supplement.

wheat-germ oil, an oil obtained from wheat germ.

wheatmeal, a meal or flour obtained by grinding the entire wheat berries.

wheel [from its resembling a *wheel* (solid disk) in shape], a round, flat cheese.

whelk, any of various large marine snails.

whey or **serum**, the thin, watery part of milk which separates from the thicker or more coagulable part (curd, sense 1) after coagulation, especially in the process of making cheese.

whiff, a name for various flatfishes or flounders related to the turbot.

¹**whip (to)**, to beat (e.g., eggs, cream) into a froth or foam, usually with a whisk, fork, or other utensil, to increase volume by incorporating air.

²**whip**, a dessert made by whipping a portion of the ingredients (e.g., cream, egg whites, ice cream, gelatine) with sugar and often with fruit (e.g., prune) or fruit flavoring.

whipped, (of cream) beaten until light and frothy.

whipped cream, cream beaten until light and frothy.

whipping cream, a cream suitable for whipping, containing from 30 to 36% butterfat (compare **coffee cream**, which contains from 18 to 30%).

white or **egg white**, the light-colored, clear, semifluid mass of albuminous material surrounding the yolk of an egg (e.g., of a hen or duck), used beaten or unbeaten.

white ant, another name for **termite**.

whitebait, *1.* the young of any of several European herrings or of the sprat; *2.* any of various other small fishes. These fishes (senses 1 and 2) are usually served fried.

whitebark, another name for **blueberry ash**.

white bass or **barfish**, a North American freshwater fish of the Great Lakes and the Mississippi Valley.

whitebill, a West Indian sardine.

white biskop, a silvery biskop (fish).

white bread, bread of a light color made from finely sifted white and especially bleached wheat flour. Compare **whole-wheat flour**.

white cake, a butter cake in which the egg whites but not the yolks are used (e.g., Lady Baltimore cake). Distinguished from **gold cake** (in which the yolks but not the whites are used).

white chocolate, a confection of cocoa butter, sugar, and milk solids.

white crappie or **white perch**, a crappie (fish) used as a panfish.

whitefish, any of various freshwater fishes that resemble the salmon and trout. They are fat fishes and therefore best for broiling, baking, planking; they are also served as fillet amandine.

white ginger or **Cochin ginger**, the rootstock of ginger, dried and scraped; distinguished from **black ginger** (which is unscraped).

white hake, a hake of the northwestern Atlantic.

white horse nettle, another name for **trompillo**.

white ironwood, a tree of Florida and the West Indies having edible berries.

white meat, *1.* a meat (e.g., veal, pork, rabbit) that is light in color (unlike beef or lamb, which are red), especially when cooked (compare **red meat**, sense 1); *2.* meat of those parts (e.g., breast, wings) of poultry (chicken, turkey, pheasant) that are light-colored when cooked (compare **dark meat**).

white-meat tuna, *1.* another name for **albacore**; *2.* the canned flesh of albacore.

white mustard [from the pale color of its seeds] or **kedlock**, a mustard plant grown for its pale yellow seeds that yield mustard (the condiment) and mustard oil (compare **black mustard**).

white of egg, another name for **white**.

white pepper, a pungent condiment (a spice) consisting of the fruit of a pepper (plant of eastern Asia) ground after the black husk has been removed (compare ¹**pepper**, sense 1; **black pepper**).

white perch, *1.* a small, silvery bass of the Atlantic coast and freshwater ponds of North America; *2.* another name for **white crappie**.

white potato, another name for **potato**.

white pudding, *1.* a light-colored sausage made with a mixture of meat (e.g., heart, liver, lungs, or muscle) ground with beef suet or pork fat, blended with bread crumbs, herbs, onion, and spices; *2.* a light-colored sausage made with a mixture of oatmeal and suet flavored with onion, salt, and pepper.

white rice, rice from which the hull and bran have been removed by milling.

white sapota or **white sapote**, a Mexican and Central American tree of the rue family, grown for its yellow-green, round, pulpy, edible fruit.

white sauce, a sauce in which the thickening agent (e.g., flour) has not been browned, which consists essentially of a roux (flour and butter), with milk, cream, or stock (or a combination of these) with seasoning and which is used as basis for other sauces (e.g., béchamel; cheese, cream, cucumber, egg, Mornay, mushroom, ravigote, seafood sauces; velouté). Distinguished from brown sauce.

white sea-bass, a large, gray and silvery croaker related to the Atlantic weakfishes.

white shrimp, another name for **lake shrimp**.

white stock, soup stock made from veal, chicken, or pork (without colored seasonings), often used in white sauce.

white stumpnose, a southern African sea bream that resembles the silver bream.

white sturgeon or **Sacramento sturgeon**, a sturgeon of the North American west coast.

white sugar, sugar that in bulk appears white.

white walnut, another name for **butternut**.

white wheat, a wheat with pale kernels that are suitable for pastry flour.

white yam or **winged yam**, a yam (sense 1) grown in Australasia and Polynesia for its white-fleshed roots that are eaten cooked with coconut milk or baked or boiled.

whiting, any of various marine fishes. They are lean fishes and therefore best for boiling and steaming.

whitling, **another** name for **sea trout**.

whole, containing all its natural constituents, all the elements properly belonging, deprived of nothing by refining or otherwise processing (as used in the next few entries).

whole milk, milk from which no constituent has been removed, unskimmed.

whole meal, another name for **whole-wheat flour**.

whole wheat, *1.* made from the entire wheat-kernels, including the bran (e.g., flour); *2.* made from whole-wheat flour (e.g., bread).

whole-wheat flour or **entire wheat flour** or **graham flour** or **whole meal**, flour that is ground from the entire grain of the wheat and contains all the constituents of the wheat kernels (including a large part of the bran).

whortleberry or **whort** or **whortle** or **frawn**, a sweet, blackish blueberry from a shrub likewise called *whortleberry*.

wiener [short for *wienerwurst*], see **weenie**.

wiener schnitzel [German "Vienna cutlet"], a thin, breaded, veal cutlet, variously seasoned, usually served with a garnish (e.g., anchovy fillets, capers, a fried egg, lemon wedges). Compare **schnitzel**.

wienerwurst [German "Vienna sausage," from *wiener* "of Vienna"], another name for both **Vienna sausage** and **frankfurter**.

wig, a bun or cake flavored with spices and caraway seeds.

wild basil or **dog mint**, an aromatic herb.

wild beet, *1.* another name for **pigweed**; *2.* a primrose of the United States, sometimes used as a potherb.

wild boar, an Old World wild hog. Wild-boar dishes include civet, ham, terrine.

wild chestnut, *1.* the nut of a shrub of southern Africa (likewise called *wild chestnut*), that is edible when roasted; *2.* the edible, black seed of a southern African tree.

wild date, a Spanish-bayonet (a plant) of southern California with edible fruit.

wild duck, an undomesticated duck. Can be served roasted.

wild ginger or **Vermont snakeroot**, an aromatic plant resembling common ginger.

wild licorice, a North American herb related to the true licorice (sense 1), having a sweet root that is the source of flavoring extracts.

wild mango, an African tree with a yellow fruit that somewhat resembles the mango. Compare **dika** and **dika bread**.

wild mangosteen, another name for **santol**.

wild marjoram, another name for **oregano** (sense 1).

wild peanut, another name for **hog peanut** (a vine).

wild prune, the red fruit of a southern African tree (likewise called *wild prune*), resembling a cherry.

wild raisin, another name for **sheepberry**.

wild rice or **Indian rice** or **water oat** or **water rice**, the grain of a tall aquatic grass (likewise called *wild rice)* of northern North America. It can be served boiled.

wild sago, another name for **coontie** (a plant).

wild sapodilla, another name for **dilly** (sense 2).

wild sarsaparilla or **wild spikenard** or **Virginia sasparilla,** a North American herb of the ginseng family, having aromatic roots used as a substitute for sarsaparilla (sense 1). This plant is characterized by one long-stalked leaf.

wild succory, another name for **chicory** (sense 1, plant).

wild thyme or **creeping thyme** or **serpolet,** a thyme (herb) that spreads by creeping stems.

Wiltshire, or **Wiltshire cheese** [from *Wiltshire*, county of southern England], an English cheese similar to Derby.

Wiltshire bacon [from *Wiltshire*, county of southern England], bacon from a Wiltshire side (of a hog).

Wiltshire side [from *Wiltshire*, county of southern England], lateral half of a lean hog carcass with legs cut off.

windberry, another name for **mountain cranberry.**

wine, the fermented juice of fresh grapes, usually containing from 10 to 15% alcohol by volume, used as a beverage and in cooking. Compare **dessert wine, sparkling wine, table wine.**

wineberry, a raspberry of China and Japan having red, acid fruits.

wine grape, a grape used in making wine (distinguished from raisin grape).

winged bean, the edible, four-winged pod of an Asian legume (likewise called *winged bean)* grown in warm regions.

winged pea, a European plant having a four-winged, edible pod.

winged yam, another name for **white yam.**

winter apple, a late-ripening apple that will keep during the winter.

winter cabbage, any of several cabbages that can survive the winter in the open if they are in mild-weather regions.

winter cauliflower, another name for **broccoli.**

winter cress or **land cress** or **upland cress,** any of several cresses grown for winter salad.

winter flounder, a brown flounder of the northwestern Atlantic.

wintergreen, *1.* or **mountain tea,** a small evergreen shrub common in eastern North America with a bright-red berry-like fruit (called *checkerberry)* and aromatic leaves that yield an oil used as a flavoring; *2.* an oil or flavoring obtained from the leaves of this plant; *3.* the flavor of wintergreen oil.

winter lettuce, another name for **endive.**

winter melon, *1.* a muskmelon having sweet, light-colored flesh, but lacking a musky aroma (e.g., casaba); *2.* a large, white-fleshed melon that is the fruit of an Asian vine and is used especially in Chinese cooking.

winter onion, any of various onions that persist from year to year and are used for early salad onions.

winter pear, a pear that ripens late and keeps well in winter.

winter plum, another name for **persimmon** (fruit, and tree).

winter savory, a European mint grown for its leaves that are used for seasoning roast meats, stews, lentils. See [3]**savory**; compare **summer savory.**

winter squash, any of various squashes or pumpkins that can be stored for several months, such as the acorn squash, banana squash, buttercup squash, Hubbard squash, turban squash, used as table vegetables. Compare **summer squash**.

wirrah, an Australian saltwater fish that is greenish brown with blue spots.

witch or **witch flounder**, a flounder of the northern Atlantic resembling the lemon sole (a flatfish).

witchetty grub or simply **witchetty**, any of several large, white, Australian grubs that are larvae of moths; the grubs infest roots and stem of the witchetty bush (an Australian acacia), from which they are extracted for use as food.

witloof [Dutch "white foliage"], another name for both **chicory** (sense 1, plant) and **endive** (in all three senses, especially as the crown of foliage of chicory used as a salad green).

wok [from Cantonese *wohk*], a bowl-shaped cooking utensil used especially in stir-frying, in the preparation of Chinese food.

wokas, the dried and roasted seeds of a western American spatterdock (a water lily) likewise called *wokas*.

wolfberry or **quailberry**, a shrub of western North America, of the honeysuckle family, grown for its white berries.

wolf herring, a large fish of the western Pacific Ocean.

wonderberry or **sunberry**, the edible, black fruit of the black nightshade (a certain weed that yields berries).

wonton [from Cantonese *wàhn-tan*], *1.* in Chinese cookery, a noodle-dough dumpling filled with spiced minced pork, usually served boiled in soup, or fried; *2.* soup containing such dumplings.

wood almond, the edible seed of a West Indian woody vine likewise called *wood almond*.

wood apple, the acid, hard-rinded, orange-like fruit of a small tree (likewise called *wood apple*) of southeastern Asia.

woodchuck or **groundhog**, a marmot (a certain rodent) of northern North America.

woodcock, a certain game bird.

wood snail, a European edible snail.

Woolton pie [for early 20th-century English businessman Frederick James Marquis, 1st Baron *Woolton*], a vegetable pie.

Worcestershire sauce or **Worcester sauce** [from *Worcestershire*, former county of western England, where it was originally made], a pungent sauce of soy, vinegar, garlic, tamarind pulp, and spices.

wort, an infusion of malt (compare **sweetwort**).

wrasse, any of numerous, chiefly tropical, marine fishes (e.g., cunners).

wurst [German], another name for **sausage**.

xarque [from Portuguese *xarque*, from Spanish *charque*, *charqui*], another name for **charqui**.

yak, a large, long-haired ox of the mountains of central Asia, that is a source of flesh and milk.

yakitori [Japanese "grilled chicken"], bite-sized, marinated chicken (including liver and other parts of the giblets; sometimes beef or seafood) pieces grilled on a small bamboo skewer. The sauce in which it is marinated consists chiefly of soy sauce, sugar, powdered ginger, and crushed garlic.

yam [from earlier *iname*, from Portuguese *inhame* or Spanish *ñame*, of West African origin] or **telinga potato**, *1.* the large, edible, starchy, tuberous root of any of various plants (climbing vines likewise called *yams)* growing in tropical climates, used as a staple food in those areas; *2.* a sweet potato having reddish-orange flesh, that remains moist when baked (southern United States). Yams can be cooked the same way as sweet potatoes, i.e., baked, candied, French fried, mashed, sautéed.

yam bean or **jicama** or **singkamas** or **singkamas** or **singcamas** or **turnip bean**, a tropical, twining plant of the bean family, with tuberous roots (the pods are eaten too) resembling turnips, which are eaten raw as a salad or cooked. When yam beans are not available, some cooks replace them in salads with tart cooking apples (peeled, cored, and chopped). One Mexican jicama-salad includes beets and oranges.

yangtao [from Chinese *yáng-táo*], a Chinese woody vine with fruits like gooseberries.

yard-long bean [from the pod measuring up to one yard (30 to 90 cm)], another name for **asparagus bean**.

yautia [from American Spanish *yautía*, from Taino], the starchy, edible tubers of any of several plants (likewise called *yautia)* of the arum family, chiefly of tropical America, that are cooked and eaten like yams or potatoes.

yeast, *1.* a surface froth or sediment that occurs especially in saccharine liquids (e.g., fruit juices), that consists largely of cells of a fungus, and is used as a leaven in baking; *2.* a commercial preparation, either in powdered or compressed form (moist cakes, dry cakes, or granules), containing yeast cells and inert material such as meal, and used as a leavening agent or as a dietary supplement. Yeast bread is distinguished from quick bread (which is made with a different, and faster-acting, leavening agent). For yeast breads, see ¹**bread**.

yellow-banded hussar, an Australian snapper (fish) with a broad yellow band along each side.

yellowbelly, any of several flatfishes of New Zealand.

yellow granadilla, another name for **Jamaica honeysuckle**.

yellow grunt, a ²grunt (fish) of yellow color, found in Western Atlantic waters.

yellow jack, a silvery and yellowish marine fish of Western Atlantic and Caribbean waters.

yellow mackerel, another name for **blue runner** (fish).

yellow melilot, another name for **yellow sweet clover**.

yellow nut grass, another name for **chufa**.

yellow perch or **red perch** or **ringed perch** or **river perch**, a North American, freshwater, yellowish fish of the perch family.

yellow sweet clover or **yellow melilot**, a yellow-flowered sweet clover with aromatic leaves sometimes used as a flavoring agent.

yellowtail, any of various fishes having a yellowish tail.

yellow yam, another name for a **sweet potato**.

yerba maté [from American Spanish *yerba mate* "herb maté (beverage)"], another name for **maté**.

yerba santa [from Mexican Spanish *yerba santa, hierba santa* "holy herb"], an evergreen shrub of Mexico and California whose aromatic leaves are used as seasoning.

yockernut, another name for **water chinquapin**.

yogurt or **yoghurt** [from Turkish *yogurt*], a fermented, slightly acid, semisolid food (with the consistency of custard) made of whole or skimmed cow's milk and milk solids (often sweetened or flavored with fruit) to which cultures of two bacteria have been added that curdle the milk. Compare **leben**.

yolk, the yellow, roundish mass of the egg of a bird or reptile, that is surrounded by the white.

Yorkshire pudding [from *Yorkshire*, area of northern England], a pudding of popover batter, made of eggs, flour, and milk, that is baked in the drippings of meat, especially of roast beef, and is usually served with roast beef.

youngberry [for B.M. *Young*, United States fruit grower who developed it around 1900], the large, sweet, dark-red fruit of a hybrid (a bramble related to the boysenberry and the loganberry) between a blackberry and a dewberry.

yuca, another name for **cassava** (sense 1).

Yugoslavia. The following are representative dishes and products of Yugoslavia: grilled minced meat (Serbian *cevapcici*), roast pork; puff pastry filled with egg, cheese, meat, spinach; cabbage or grape leaves or zucchini stuffed with minced meat *(punjena tikvica);* skewered chunks of lamb or pork or veal *(raznjici)*, cheeses; fish (e.g., red mullet, mackerel, trout).

ziti zeppole zucchini zingel zarzuela zieger Z zabaglione

zabaglione or **zabaione** [from Italian *zabaione, zabaglione*] or **sabayon**, a whipped, semiliquid dessert consisting of a mixture of egg yolks, sugar, and wine (usually Marsala) or fruit juice, beaten over hot water (in a double boiler) until thick and light and often served, warm or cold, in a sherbet or parfait glass or as a sauce on fruit (e.g., raspberries), ice cream, or cake.

Zaire, see **Congo**.

zakuska (plural *zakuski*) [from Russian *zakuska*, from *zakusit'* "to have a snack," from *za* "for, behind" + *kus* "morsel, bit"], another name for **hors d'oeuvre** (especially when served before a Russian meal). Compare **Russia**.

Zambia. The following are representative dishes and products of Zambia: maize, sorghum, beans, groundnuts; maize-meal *(nshima);* tiger fish *(ncheni).*

Zante currant [from *Zante*, island of the Ionian group, in southwestern Greece (Greek *Zákinthos)*], a small, seedless grape or raisin.

¹**zap**, a pungent or zestful quality, liveliness.

²**zap (to)**, to make pungent.

zapota gum [from Spanish *zapote* "sapodilla"], another name for **chicle**.

zarzuela [Spanish], a Spanish made-dish consisting of several kinds of fish and shellfish with a sauce.

zebra, or **zebra fish** [from *zebra* "mammal with dark and whitish stripes," from Portuguese *zebra* "wild ass"], any of several barred (striped) fishes.

zeppole [Italian], a ring-shaped doughnut of Italian origin made from deep-fried cream-puff dough. In Sicily, zeppole are rice croquettes.

zest [from French *zeste* "orange or lemon peel (used as flavoring)"], a piece of the peel or of the thin outermost part of the rind of an orange or lemon used as flavoring (e.g., for creams, cakes).

zieger [German], a cheese made from whey.

Zimbabwe. The following are representative dishes and products of Zimbabwe: a maize-meal (sometimes made not of maize but of ground rice or sorghum) porridge *(sadza)*, which is often served with a peanut butter sauce that includes tomato and onion; in addition to this sauce, *sadza* may also be served with a meat (beef, chicken, lamb) curry, or with dried meat (beef or venison biltong —*chimukuyu*). Vegetarians eat it instead with fried vegetables such as cabbage, curly kale, beans, or pumpkin leaves; the peanut butter sauce is optional. Aside from this porridge, the following are eaten: *mufushwa* (sun-dried, blanched green vegetable leaves [cowpea or curly kale], with peanut butter sauce and tomato), *jakarasi* (brisket with green vegetable leaves [broccoli or curly kale or cabbage], with peanut butter sauce and tomato), *kapenta* (a certain fish, dried, fried with tomato and onion [preferably shallots]). Other fish include trout, bream, tiger fish, black bass. Goat and oxtail are frequent.

zingel [German], a small, elongated, freshwater, European perch found in the Danube and its tributaries.

ziti [Italian], medium-sized tubular pasta (wider than macaroni). In Italian, smaller ziti are called *mezzi ziti* "half ziti".

zucchini [Italian, plural of *zucchino* "small gourd," diminutive of *zucca* "gourd"] or **green squash**, the cylindrical, elongated, usually dark-green fruit of a variety of summer squash (likewise called *zucchini*). Zucchini are often served Provençale (sautéed with onion, garlic, and salad oil) or fried, or used in ratatouille.

zuppa inglese [Italian "English soup"], a dessert consisting of sponge cake and custard or pudding that is covered with cream, garnished with fruit, and usually flavored with rum. It is similar to trifle and to tiramisu.

zwieback [German "twice baked"], a type of usually sweetened bread enriched with eggs and baked first as a loaf and later sliced and toasted until crisp. It is similar to **rusk** (in senses 1 and 2).

Basic Five-Language Gastronomy Dictionary

PART 1

English	French	German	Italian	Spanish
almond	amande	Mandel	mandorla	almendra
anchovy	anchois	Anchovis	acciuga	anchoa
angler	lotte de mer	Seeteufel	lofio	pejesapo
apple	pomme	Apfel	mela	manzana
apricot	abricot	Aprikose	albicocca	albaricoque, chabacano
artichoke	artichaut	Artischocke	carciofo	alcachofa
asparagus	asperge	Spargel	asparago	espárrago
aubergine	aubergine	Aubergine	melanzana	berenjena
avocado	avocat	Avokado	avocado	aguacate
bacon	lard	Speck	carnesecca	tocino
bake	cuire (au four)	backen	cuocere al forno	cocer en horno, hornear
baked	cuit au four	gebacken	cotto al forno	cocido en horno, horneado
banana	banane	Banane	banana	plátano
barley	orge	Gerste	orzo	cebada
bass	perche	Barsch	pesce persico	lobina
baste (to)	arroser	mit Fett übergiessen	ungere	humedecer mientras se cuece
batter	pâte	Teig	pasta	batido, masa
bean	haricot	Bohne	fagiolo	frijol, judía, fríjol
bean (string)	haricot vert	grüne Bohne	fagiolino	judía verde, ejote
beat (to)	battre, fouetter	schlagen	battere	batir
beef	boeuf	Rindfleisch	manzo	vaca, res
beer	bière	Bier	birra	cerveza

English	French	German	Italian	Spanish
beet	betterave	rote Rübe	barbabietola	remolacha, betabel
berry	baie	Beere	bacca	baya
beverage	boisson	Getränk	bibita	bebida
bilberry	myrtille	Heidelbeere	mirtillo	arándano
blackberry	mûre	Brombeere	mora	mora, zarzamora
blanch (by scalding)	mettre dans l'eau bouillante	blanchieren	scottare nell'acqua bollente	poner en agua hirviendo
blend (a)	mélange	Mischung	miscela	mezcla
blend (to)	mélanger	mischen	mescolare	mezclar, incorporar
blueberry	myrtille	Heidelbeere	mirtillo	arándano
boil (to)	boullir	kochen	bollire	hervir
bone	os	Knochen	osso	hueso
brain	cervelle	Hirn	cervello	sesos
braise (to)	braiser, cuire à l'étouffée, cuire à l'étuvée	schmoren	brasare	cocer a fuego lento en olla tapada
bran	son	Kleie	crusca	salvado
bread	pain	Brot	pane	pan
breakfast (a)	petit déjeuner	Frühstück	(prima) colazione	desayuno
broad bean	fève	Saubohne	fava	haba
broil (to)	griller	auf dem Rost braten	arrostire in graticola	asar sobre ascuas o en parrillas
broth	bouillon, potage	Brühe	brodo	caldo
brown (to)	rissoler	anbraten	rosolare	dorar, tostar ligeramente
brush	enduire au pinceau	bürsten	ungere con pennello	untar con brocha
Brussels sprouts	choux de Bruxelles	Rosenkohl	cavolini di Brusselle	coles de Bruselas
butter	beurre	Butter	burro	mantequilla
cabbage	chou	Kohl	cavolo	col

English	French	German	Italian	Spanish
cake	gâteau	Kuchen	torta	torta, pastel
candy	bonbon	Süssigkeit	dolci	dulce
cantaloupe	melon	Melone	melone	melón
capon	chapon	Kapaun	cappone	capón
carp	carpe	Karpfen	carpa	carpa
carrot	carotte	Mohrrübe, Karotte	carota	zanahoria
cattle	bétail	Vieh	bestiame	ganado
cauliflower	chou-fleur	Blumenkohl	cavolfiore	coliflor
celery	céleri	Sellerie	sedano	apio
cereal	céréale	Getreide, Zerealie	cereale	cereal
cheese	fromage	Käse	formaggio	queso
cherimoya	chérimolia	Chirimoya, Honigapfel	annona	chirimoya
cherry	cerise	Kirsche	ciliegia	cereza
chestnut	marron, chataîgne	Kastanie	castagna	castaña
chickpea	pois chiche	Kichererbse	cece	garbanzo
chicken	poulet	Huhn	pollo	pollo
chocolate	chocolat	Schokolade	cioccolata	chocolate
chop (a)	côtelette	Kotelett	costoletta	chuleta
chop (to)	hacher	(zer)hacken	tagliare	picar
cinnamon	cannelle	Zimt	cannella	canela
citrus fruit	agrume	Zitrusfrüchte	agrumi *(pl.)*	fruto cítrico
clam	palourde	Venusmuschel	vongola	almeja
clementine	clémentine	Clementine	mandarancio	naranja clementina
clove	clou de girofle	(Gewürz)Nelke	chiodo di garofano	clavo (de olor, de especia)
coat (to)	enduire	bestreichen	coprire	cubrir
cock, rooster	coq	Hahn	gallo	gallo

English	French	German	Italian	Spanish
cocoa	cacao	Kakao	cacao	cacao
coconut	noix de coco	Kokosnuss	cocco	coco
cod	morue	Kabeljau	merluzzo	bacalao
coffee	café	Kaffee	caffè	café
cold (adj.)	froid	kalt	freddo	frío
cold cuts	charcuterie	Aufschmitt	salumi	fiambres
cook (to)	(faire) cuire	kochen	cuocere	cocer
corbina	corbeau de mer	Adlerfisch	corvina	corvina
core (to)	enlever le coeur	entkernen	togliere il torsolo	despepitar, descorazonar
corn (maize)	maïs	Mais	granturco	maíz
courgette	courgette	Zucchini	zucchina, zucchino	calabacín, calabacita
crab	crabe	Krebs	granchio	cangrejo
cream	crème	Sahne	panna	nata, crema
croaker	ombrine	Umberfisch	ombrina	corvina
crumb	miette	Krume	briciola	migaja
crumble (to)	effriter	zerkrümeln	polverizzare	desmenuzar
crush (to)	écraser	zerquetschen	schiacciare	machacar
cube (to)	couper la surface en carreaux	gitten artig einschneiden	quadrettare	escaquear la superficie
cucumber	concombre	Gurke	cetriolo	pepino
cup	tasse	Tasse	tazza	taza
custard	crème au lait et aux oeufs	Eierrahm, Vanillepudding	crema di latte e uova	crema pastelera, natillas, flan
custard apple	anone	Zimtapfel, Rahmapfel	annona	anona, [chirimoya]
cut (to)	couper	schneiden	tagliare	cortar
cuttlefish	seiche	Tintenfisch	seppia	calamar
dandelion	pissenlit	Löwenzahn	radichiella	diente de león
date	datte	Dattel	dattero	dátil
deer	cerf	Hirsch	cervo	ciervo

English	French	German	Italian	Spanish
dessert	dessert	Nachtisch	dolce	postre
dice (to)	couper en cubes	würfeln	tagliare in cubetti	cortar en cubos
dinner (a)	dîner	Abendessen	pranzo	comida
dip (a)	sauce	Dip	salsa	moje, mojo, salsa
dish (food)	mets	Gericht	piatto	plato, platillo
dredge (to)	saupoudrer	bestäuben	cospargere	polvorear
dressing	sauce	Salatsosse	condimento	salsa, aderezo
drink (a)	boisson	Getränk	bibita	bebida
drink (to)	boire	trinken	bere	beber
dry (adj.)	sec, sèche	trocken	secco	seco
duck	canard	Ente	anitra	pato
duckling	caneton	Entchen	anatroccolo	anadino, patito
ear (of corn)	épi	Maiskolben	pannocchia, spiga	mazorca, espiga
eat (to)	manger	essen	mangiare	comer
eel	anguille	Aal	anguilla	anguila
egg	oeuf	Ei	uovo (m.) (*pl.* uova, *f.*)	huevo
eggplant	aubergine	Aubergine	melanzana	berenjena
endive (broad-leaved)	scarole	Chicorée	indivia	escarola, endibia de hoja ancha
endive (curly-leaved)	chicorée frisée	Endivien	cicoria	achicoria rizada, endibia de hojaizada
English (adj.)	anglais	englisch	inglese	inglés, inglesa
fat (the)	graisse	Fett	grasso	grasa, manteca
fennel	fenouil	Fenchel	finocchio	hinojo
fig	figue	Feige	fico	higo
fish	poisson	Fisch	pesce	pescado
flounder	flet, carrelet	Flunder	passera di mare	lenguado
flour	farine	Mehl	farina	harina
flower	fleur	Blume	fiore	flor

English	French	German	Italian	Spanish
fork	fourchette	Gabel	forchetta	tenedor
fowl	volaille	Geflügel	pollo	pollo
French	français	französisch	francese	francés, francesa
fried	frit	frittiert	fritto	frito
frog	grenouille	Frosch	rana	rana
fruit	fruit	Frucht; Obst	frutto (m.) (pl. frutta, f.)	fruta
fry (to)	frire	frittieren	friggere	freír
game	gibier	Wild	selvaggina, cacciagione	caza
garlic	ail	Knoblauch	aglio	ajo
garnish (to)	garnir	garnieren	guarnire	decorar
German	allemand	deutsch	tedesco	alemán, alemana
ginger	gingembre	Ingwer	zenzero	jengibre
glass	verre	Glas	bicchiere	vaso
goat	chèvre	Ziege	capra	cabra
goose	oie	Gans	oca	ganso
grain (cereal)	grains	Getreide	cereale	grano
grape	raisin	Traube	uva	uva
grapefruit	pamplemousse, pomélo	Pampelmuse, Grapefruit	pompelmo	toronja, pomelo
grate (to)	râper	reiben	grattugiare	rallar
gravy	sauce	Bratensauce	sugo	salsa
grease	graisse	Fett	grasso	grasa, manteca
green bean	haricot vert	grüne Bohne	fagiolino	judía verde, ejote
grill (to)	griller	auf dem Bratrost braten	cuocere in graticola	asar sobre ascuas o en parrillas
ground (adj.)	haché, moulu, pilé	gemahlen	macinato	molido
guava	goyave	Guave	guaiava	guayaba
guinea fowl	pintade	Perlhuhn	faraona	gallina de Guinea, pintada

English	French	German	Italian	Spanish
hake	merluche	Seehecht, Kummel	merluzzo	merluza
halibut	flétan	Heilbutt	rombo	hipogloso
ham	jambon	Schinken	prosciutto	jamón
hare	lièvre	Hase	lepre	liebre
hazelnut	noisette	Haselnüss	nocciola	avellana
head	tête	Kopf	testa	cabeza
heart	coeur	Herz	cuore	corazón
hen	poule	Henne	gallina	gallina
herb	herbe	Kraut	erba	hierba
herring	hareng	Hering	aringa	arenque
hog	porc	Schwein	maiale	puerco
honey	miel	Honig	miele	miel
horse	cheval	Pferd	cavallo	caballo
horseradish	raifort	Meerrettich	cren, rafano	rábano picante
hot	chaud	heiss	caldo	caliente
ice	glace	Eis	ghiaccio	hielo
ice cream	glace	(Speise)Eis	gelato	helado
Indian corn	maïs	Mais	granturco	maíz
Italian	italien, italienne	italienisch	italiano	italiano
jam	confiture	Marmelade	marmellata	mermelada
jelly	gelée	Gelee	gelatina	jalea
juice	jus	Saft	succo	jugo, zumo
kid	chevreau	Zicklein	capretto	cabrito
kidney	rognon	Niere	rognone	riñón
knead (to)	pétrir	kneten	impastare	amasar
knife	couteau	Messer	coltello	cuchillo
lamb	agneau	Lamm	agnello	cordero
lamb chop	côtelette d'agneau	Lammkotelett	costoletta d'agnello	chuleta de carnero
lard	saindoux	Schmalz	lardo	manteca

English	French	German	Italian	Spanish
lark	alouette	Lerche	allodola	alondra
leaf	feuille	Blatt	foglia	hoja
leek	poireau	Lauch, Porree	porro	puerro, poro
leg	jambe	Bein	gamba	pierna
leg of lamb	gigot d'agneau	Lammkeute	coscia d'agnello	pierna de cordero
lemon	citron	Zitrone	limone	limón [amarillo]
lemonade	citronnade	Limonade	limonata	limonada
lentil	lentille	Linse	lenticchia	lenteja
lettuce	laitue	(Kopf)Salat	lattuga	lechuga
lime	lime, citron vert	Limette	cedro	limón [verde]
liver	foie	Leber	fegato	hígado
loaf	pain	Laib	pane	hogaza
lobster	homard	Hummer	aragosta	langosta, bogavante
lunch (a)	déjeuner	Mittagessen	(seconda) colazione	almuerzo, comida
macaroni	macaron	Makkaroni	maccherone	macarrones
mackerel	maquereau	Makrele	sgombro	caballa, escombro; pejerrey
mandarin	mandarine	Mandarine	mandarino	mandarina
mango	mangue	Mango	mango	mango
marzipan	massepain	Marzipan	marzapane	mazapán
mash (to)	mettre en purée	pürieren	ridurre in polpa	hacer puré
meal	repas	Mahlzeit	pasto	comida
meat	viande	Fleisch	carne	carne
melon	melon	Melone	melone	melón
melt (to)	fondre	schmelzen	fondere	derretir
menu	carte	Speisekarte	lista (delle vivande)	menú
milk	lait	Milch	latte	leche
milk products, dairy products	laitages, produits laitiers	Milchprodukte	latticinio, latticino (*pl.* latticini)	productos lácteos

English	French	German	Italian	Spanish
mince (to)	hacher menu	feinhacken	tritare	picar fino
mint	menthe	Münze	menta	menta
molasses	mélasse	Melasse	melassa	miel de caña, melaza
mushroom	champignon	Pilz	fungo	seta, hongo, champiñón
mussel	moule	Miesmuschel	cozza	mejillón
mustard	moutarde	Senf	senape	mostaza
mutton	mouton	Hammelfleisch	carne di montone	carnero
napkin	serviette	Serviette	tovagliolo	servilleta
noodle	nouille	Nudel	tagliatella	fideo, tallarín
nut	noix	Nuss	noce	nuez
nutmeg	muscade, noix muscade	Muskatnuss	noce moscata	nuez moscada
oats	avoine	Hafer	avena	avena
octopus	poulpe, pieuvre	Seepolyp	piovra	pulpo
oil	huile	Öl	olio	aceite
olive	olive	Olive	oliva	aceituna
olive oil	huile d'olive	Olivenöl	olio d'oliva	aceite de oliva
onion	oignon	Zwiebel	cipolla	cebolla
orange	orange	Orange, Apfelsine		arancia naranja
oven	four	Backofen	forno	horno
ox	boeuf	Ochs	bue (pl. buoi)	buey
oyster	huître	Auster	ostrica	ostra
pan (frying)	poêle	Pfanne	padella	sartén
panfry (to)	frire à la poêle	in der Pfanne braten	friggere in padella	freír en sartén
papaya	papaye	Papaya	papaia	papaya
parboil (to)	cuire à demi	leicht kochen	sbollentare	hervir brevemente, medio cocer, sancochar
pare (to)	éplucher, peler	schälen	pelare, sbucciare	mondar, pelar
parsley	persil	Petersilie	prezzemolo	perejil

English	French	German	Italian	Spanish
pasta	pâtes	Teigwaren	pasta	pasta
pea	petit pois	Erbse	pisello	guisante, chícharo
peach	pêche	Pfirsich	pesca	melocotón, durazno
peanut	cacahuète	Erdnuss	arachide	maní, cacahuate
pear	poire	Birne	pera	pera
peel (to)	peler, éplucher	schälen	sbucciare, pelare	pelar
pepper (green vegetable)	poivron	Paprika	peperone	pimiento
pepper (seasoning)	poivre	Pfeffer	pepe	pimienta
perch	perche	Barsch	pesce persico	perca, percha
pickle (to)	mariner	einmachen	marinare	escabechar
pie	tarte	Obstkuchen	torta	pastel
pig	cochon	Schwein	porco	cerdo
pigeon	pigeon	Taube	piccione	paloma
pike	brochet	Hecht	luccio	lucio
pineapple	ananas	Ananas	ananas, ananasso	piña
pine nut, piñon, pinyon	pignon	Pinienkern	pinolo, pinocchio, pignuolo, pignolo	piñón
pistachio	pistache	Pistazie	pistacchio	pistacho
plate	assiette	Teller	piatto	plato
plum	prune	Pflaume	prugna	ciruela
pomegranate	grenade	Granatapfel	melagrana	granada
pork	porc	Schweinefleisch	maiale	cerdo
pork chop	côtelette de porc	Schweins-rippchen	costoletta di maiale	chuleta de cerdo
potato	pomme de terre	Kartoffel	patata	papa, patata
poultry	volaille	Federvieh	pollame	aves de corral
pour (to)	verser	einschenken	versare	verter
prawn	crevette	Garnele	gambero	gamba
preserve (a)	confiture	Marmelade, Konfitüre	conserva	compota, mermelada

English	French	German	Italian	Spanish
press (to)	presser	zerdrücken	spremere	prensar, comprimir
prune	pruneau	Backpflaume	prugna secca	ciruela pasa
pudding (dessert)	pudding, pouding	Pudding	budino	pudín, budín
pumpkin	courge	Kürbis	zucca	calabaza
purée (to)	cuire et écraser	pürieren	fare un passato	hacer puré
quail	caille	Wachtel	quaglia	codorniz
quince	coing	Quitte	cotogna	membrillo
rabbit	lapin	Kaninchen	coniglio	conejo
radish	radis	Rettich	ravanello	rábano
raisin	raisin sec	Rosine	uva secca	pasa
raspberry	framboise	Himbeere	lampone	frambuesa
ray	raie	(Glatt)rochen	razza	raya
reindeer	renne	Renntier	renna	reno
render (to)	fondre	schmelzen	fondere	derretir
rhubarb	rhubarbe	Rhubarber	rabarbaro	ruibarbo
rib	entrecôte, côte	Rippe	costola	costilla
rice	riz	Reis	riso	arroz
roast (a)	rôti	Braten	arrosto	asado
roast (to)	rôtir	braten	arrostire	asar
roastbeef	rosbif	Rinderbraten	rosbif, manzo arrosto	rosbif
roasted	rôti	gebraten	arrostito	asado
rock lobster (spiny lobster)	langouste	Languste	aragosta	langosta
roll (bread)	petit pain	Brötchen	panino	panecillo
roll (to)	étendre au rouleau	ausrollen	stendere col matarello	alisar o estirar con rodillo
root	racine	Wurzel	radice	raíz
rye	seigle	Roggen	segale	centeno
sage	sauge	Salbei	salvia	salvia

English	French	German	Italian	Spanish
salad	salade	Salat	insalata	ensalada
salmon	saumon	Lachs, Salm	salmone	salmón
salt	sel	Salz	sale	sal
sandwich	sandwich	belegtes Brot, Sandwich	sandwich	emparedado
sardine	sardine	Sardine	sardina	sardina
sauce	sauce	Sauce	salsa	salsa
saucer	soucoupe	Untertasse	sottotazza	platillo
sausage	saucisse	Wurst	salsiccia	salchicha
sauté (to)	sauter	anbraten	soffriggere	saltear, sofreír en poco aceite o manteca
sawfish	scie (de mer)	Sägefisch	pesce sega	pez sierra
scald (to)	échauder	blanchieren	scaldare sino all'ebollizione	escaldar, poner en agua hirviendo
scallop	pétoncle, peigne, coquille Saint-Jacques	Kammmuschel	pettine	venera
scorzonera	scorsonère	Schwarzwurzel	scorzonera	escorzonera
scrambled eggs	oeufs brouillés	Rührei	uova strapazzate	huevos revueltos
scrape (to)	racler	schaben	raschiare	raspar
sea bass	loup	Roter Grouper	spigola, branzino	mero
seafood	fruits de mer	Meeresfrüchte	frutti di mare	pescado y mariscos
sear (to)	brûler la surface	(scharf) anbraten	bruciacchiare	quemar la superficie
sheep	mouton	Schaf	pecora	oveja
shellfish	coquillage, crustacé	Schaltier	mollusco, crustaceo, frutti di mare	crustáceo, molusco
shoulder	épaule	Schulter	spalla	hombro
shred (to)	couper en bandes	klein schneiden	sbrindellare	cortar en tiras
shrimp	crevette	Krabbe	scampo, gamberetto	camarón

English	French	German	Italian	Spanish
sift (to)	passer au tamis	sieben	stacciare	cerner
simmer	mijoter	schmoren	bollire a fuoco lento	cocer a fuego lento por abajo del punto punto de ebullición
skate	raie	Rochen	razza	raya
slice (a)	tranche	Schnitte	fetta	rebanada
slice (to)	couper en tranches	zerschneiden	affettare	rebanar
smoked	fumé	geräuchert	affumicato	ahumado
snail	escargot	Schnecke	lumaca	caracol
soak (to)	tremper	durchnässen	impregnare	empapar
soft	mou (f.: molle)	weich	soffice	blando
sole	sole	Seezunge	sogliola	lenguado
soup	soupe	Suppe	minestra	sopa
sour	aigre	sauer	agro	agrio
spaghetti	spaghetti	Spaghetti	spaghetti	espagueti
Spanish	espagnol	spanisch	spagnolo	español
spice	épice	Gewürz	spezia	especia
spinach	épinards	Spinat	spinaci	espinaca
spiny lobster (rock lobster)	langouste	Languste	aragosta	langosta
spoon (tablespoon)	cuillère à soupe	Esslöffel	cucchiaio	cuchara
spoon (teaspoon)	cuillère à thé	Teelöffel	cucchiaino	cucharita
sprinkle (to)	saupoudrer	bestreuen	spruzzare, aspergere	polvorear
squash	courge	Kürbis	zucca	calabaza
squid	calmar	Calamari	calamaro	calamar
squirrel	écureuil	Eichhörnchen	scoiattolo	ardilla
starch	fécule	Stärke	amido	almidón
steak	bifteck	Steak	braciola, bistecca	biftec, lonja de carne

English	French	German	Italian	Spanish
steam (noun)	vapeur	Dampf	vapore	vapor
steam (to)	cuire à la vapeur, à l'étuvée	dämpfen	cuocere a vapore	cocer al vapor
steep (to)	infuser	in heissen Wasser ziehen lassen	macerare in acqua bollente	macerar, vaciar agua hirviendo sobre
stew (noun)	ragoût, fricassée	Schmorgericht	stufato, umido	estofado
stew (to)	cuire en ragoût, à la casserole, mijoter	schmoren	cuocere a fuoco lento	cocer a fuego lento
stir (to)	remuer	rühren	mescolare	revolver
strain (to)	filtrer	durchseihen	passare	colar
strawberry	fraise	Erdbeere	fragola	fresa
string bean	haricot vert	grüne Bohne	fagiolino	judía verde, ejote
stuffed	farci	gefüllt	riempito	relleno
sugar	sucre	Zucker	zucchero	azúcar
supper	souper	Abendbrot	cena	cena
sweetbread	ris de veau	Kalbsmilch	animelle	mollejas, lechecillas
sweet pepper	poivron doux	Paprika	peperone	pimiento morrón
wine	cochon	Schwein	maiale	marrano
table	table	Tisch	tavola	mesa
tablespoon	cuillère à soupe	Esslöffel	cucchiaio	cuchara
tail	queue	Schwanz	coda	cola
tangerine	mandarine	Mandarine	mandarino	mandarina
tarragon	estragon	Estragon	artemisia	estragón
tea	thé	Tee	tè	té
teaspoon	cuillère à thé	Teelöffel	cucchiaino	cucharita
tender	tendre	zart, weich	tenero	tierno
thigh	cuisse	Schenkel	coscia	muslo
tip (gratuity)	pourboire	Trinkgeld	mancia	propina
toast (bread)	pain grillé	geröstete Brotschnitte	pane tostato	tostada

English	French	German	Italian	Spanish
tomato	tomate	Tomate	pomodoro	tomate, jitomate
tongue	langue	Zunge	lingua	lengua
trout	truite	Forelle	trota	trucha
tuna	thon	Thunfisch	tonno	atún
turbot	turbot	Steinbutt	rombo	rodaballo
turkey	dindon	Truthahn	tacchino	pavo
turnip	navet	Rübe	navone	nabo
turtle	tortue	Schildkröte	tartaruga	tortuga
variety	assortiment	Auswahl	assortimento	surtido
veal	veau	Kalbfleisch	vitello	ternera
veal chop	côtelette de veau	Kalbskotelett	costoletta di vitello	chuleta de ternera
vegetable	légume	Gemüse	verdura	hortaliza, verdura, legumbre
vine	vigne	Weinstock	vite	vid
vinegar	vinaigre	Essig	aceto	vinagre
violet	violette	Veilchen	violetta	violeta
walnut	noix	Walnuss	noce	nuez
warm	chaud	warm	caldo	caliente
warm (to)	chauffer	wärmen	riscaldare	calentar
water	eau	Wasser	acqua	agua
watermelon	pastèque, melon d'eau	Wassermelone	anguria	sandía
whale	baleine	Walfisch	balena	ballena
wheat	blé	Weizen	grano, frumento	trigo
wine	vin	Wein	vino	vino
wing	aile	Flügel	ala	ala
witloof chicory	chicorée witloof	Zichorie	cicoria belga	achicoria witloof
woodcock	bécasse	Waldschnepfe	beccaccia	becada, chocha
yeast	levain	Hefe	lievito	levadura
zucchini, courgette	courgette	Zucchini	zucchina, zucchino	calabacín, calabacita

PART II

Index français

abricot = apricot
agneau = lamb
agrume = citrus fruit
aigre = sour
ail = garlic
aile = wing
alouette = lark
allemand = German
amande = almond
ananas = pineapple
anchois = anchovy
anglais = English
anguille = eel
anone = custard apple
arroser = baste
artichaut = artichoke
asperge = asparagus
assiette = plate
assortiment = variety
aubergine = aubergine,
  eggplant
avocat = avocado
avoine = oats
baie = berry
baleine = whale
banane = banana
battre = beat
bécasse = woodcock
bétail = cattle
betterave = beet
beurre = butter
bière = beer
bifteck = steak
blé = wheat
boeuf = beef, ox
boire = drink

boisson = beverage, drink
bonbon = candy
bouillir = boil
bouillon = broth
braiser = braise
brochet = pike
cacahuète = peanut
cacao = cocoa
café = coffee
caille = quail
calmar = squid
canard = duck
caneton = ducking
cannelle = cinnamon
carotte = carrot
carpe = carp
carrelet = flounder
carte = menu
céleri = celery
céréale = cereal
cerf = deer
cerise = cherry
cervelle = brain
champignon = mushroom
chapon = capon
charcuterie = cold cuts
chataîgne = chestnut
chaud = hot, warm
chauffer = warm
chérimolia = cherimoya
cheval = horse
chèvre = goat
chevreau = kid
chicorée frisée = endive
chicorée witloof = witloof
  chicory

chocolat = chocolate
chou = cabbage
chou-fleur = cauliflower
choux de Bruxelles =
  Brussels sprouts
citron = lemon
citron vert = lime
citronnade = lemonade
clémentine = clementine
clou de girofle = clove
cochon = pig, swine
coeur = heart
coing = quince
concombre = cucumber
confiture = jam, preserve
coq = cock
coquillage = shellfish
coquille Saint-Jacques =
  scallop
corbeau de mer = corbina
côte = rib
côtelette = chop
couper = cut
courge = pumpkin, squash
courgette = courgette,
  zucchini
couteau = knife
crabe = crab
crème = cream
crevette = prawn, shrimp
crustacé = shellfish
cuillère = spoon
cuire = bake, cook
cuisse = thigh
datte = date
déjeuner = lunch

317

Index français

dessert = dessert
dindon = turkey
dîner = dinner
eau = water
échauder = scald
écraser = crush
écureuil = squirrel
effriter = crumble
enduire = coat
entrecôte = rib
épaule = shoulder
épi = ear
épice = spice
épinards = spinach
éplucher = pare, peel
escargot = snail
espagnol = Spanish
estragon = tarragon
étouffée = braise
étuvée = braise, steam
farci = stuffed
farine = flour
fécule = starch
fenouil = fennel
feuille = leaf
fève = broad bean
figue = fig
filtrer = strain
flet = flounder
flétan = halibut
fleur = flower
foie = liver
fondre = melt, render
fouetter = beat
four = oven
fourchette = fork
fraise = strawberry
framboise = raspberry
français = French
fricassée = stew
frire = fry
frit = fried
froid = cold

fromage = cheese
fruit = fruit
fruits de mer = seafood
fumé = smoked
garnir = garnish
gâteau = cake
gelée = jelly
gibier = game
gigot = leg
gingembre = ginger
glace = ice, ice cream
goyave = guava
grains = grain
graisse = fat, grease
grenade = pomegranate
grenouille = frog
griller = broil, grill
haché = ground
hacher = chop
hareng = herring
haricot = bean
haricot vert = green bean,
    string bean
herbe = herb
homard = lobster
huile = oil
huître = oyster
infuser = steep
italien = Italian
jambe = leg
jambon = ham
jus = juice
lait = milk
laitages = dairy products
laitue = lettuce
langouste = rock lobster,
    spiny lobster
langue = tongue
lapin = rabbit
lard = bacon
légume = vegetable
lentille = lentil
levain = yeast

lièvre = hare
lime = lime
lotte de mer = angler
loup = sea bass
macaron = macaroni
maïs = corn, Indian corn,
    maize
mandarine = tangerine,
    mandarin
manger = eat
mangue = mango
maquereau = mackerel
mariner = pickle
marron = chestnut
massepain = marzipan
mélange = blend
mélasse = molasses
melon = cantaloupe, melon
melon d'eau = watermelon
menthe = mint
merluche = hake
mets = dish
miel = honey
miette = crumb
mijoter = simmer, stew
morue = cod
mou = soft
moule = mussel
moulu = ground
moutarde = mustard
mouton = mutton, sheep
mûre = blackberry
muscade = nutmeg
myrtille = blueberry,
    bilberry
navet = turnip
noisette = hazelnut
noix = nut, walnut
noix de coco = coconut
nouille = noodle
oeuf = egg
oeufs brouillés = scrambled
    eggs

oie = goose
oignon = onion
olive = olive
ombrine = croaker
orange = orange
orge = barley
os = bone
pain = bread, loaf
pain grillé = toast
palourde = clam
pamplemousse = grapefruit
papaye = papaya
parsley = persil
pastèque = watermelon
pâte = batter
pâtes = pasta
pêche = peach
peigne = scallop
peler = pare, peel
perche = bass, perch
petit déjeuner = breakfast
petit pain = roll
petit pois = pea
pétoncle = scallop
pétrir = knead
pieuvre = octopus
pigeon = pigeon
pignon = pine nut
pilé = ground
pintade = guinea fowl
pissenlit = dandelion
pistache = pistachio
poêle = pan
poire = pear
poireau = leek
pois chiche = chickpea
poisson = fish
poivre = pepper
poivron = pepper
pomélo = grapefruit
pomme = apple
pomme de terre = potato
porc = pork, hog

potage = broth
pouding = pudding
poule = hen
poulet = chicken
poulpe = octopus
pourboire = tip
presser = press
prune = plum
pruneau = prune
pudding = pudding
queue = tail
racine = root
racler = scrape
radis = radish
ragoût = stew
raie = ray, skate
raifort = horseradish
raisin = grape
raisin sec = raisin
râper = grate
remuer = stir
renne = reindeer
repas = meal
rhubarbe = rhubarb
ris de veau = sweetbread
rissoler = brown
riz = rice
rognon = kidney
rosbif = roastbeef
rôti = roast, roasted
rôtir = roast
saindoux = lard
salade = salad
sandwich = sandwich
sardine = sardine
sauce = gravy, sauce, dip,
    dressing
saucisse = sausage
sauge = sage
saumon = salmon
saupoudrer = sprinkle,
    dredge
sauter = sauté

scarole = endive
scie = sawfish
scorsonère = scorzonera
sec = dry
seiche = cuttlefish
seigle = rye
sel = salt
serviette = napkin
sole = sole
son = bran
soucoupe = saucer
soupe = soup
souper = supper
spaghetti = spaghetti
sucre = sugar
table = table
tarte = pie
tasse = cup
tendre = tender
tête = head
thé = tea
thon = tuna
tomate = tomato
tortue = turtle
tranche = slice
tremper = soak
truite = trout
turbot = turbot
vapeur = steam
veau = veal
verre = glass
verser = pour
viande = meat
vigne = vine
vin = wine
vinaigre = vinegar
violette = violet
volaille = poultry, fowl

Deutsches Verzeichnis

Aal = eel
Abendbrot = supper
Abendessen = dinner
Adlerfisch = corbina
Ananas = pineapple
anbraten = brown, sauté,
  sear
Anchovis = anchovy
Apfel = apple
Apfelsine = orange
Aprikose = apricot
Artischoke = artichoke
Aubergine = aubergine,
  eggplant
Aufschmitt = cold cuts
ausrollen = roll
Auster = oyster
Auswahl = variety
Avokado = avocado
backen = bake
Backofen = oven
Backpflaume = prune
Banane = banana
Barsch = bass, perch
Beere = berry
Bein = leg
bestäuben = dredge
bestreichen = coat
bestreuen = sprinkle
Bier = beer
Birne = pear
blanchieren = scald, blanch
Blatt = leaf
Blume = flower
Blumenkohl = cauliflower
Bohne = bean
Braten = roast
braten = roast
Bratensauce = gravy

Brombeere = blackberry
Brot = bread
Brötchen = roll
Brühe = broth
bürsten = brush
Butter = butter
Calamari = squid
Chicorée = endive
Chirimoya = cherimoya
Clementine = clementine
Dampf = steam
dämpfen = steam
Dattel = date
deutsch = German
Dip = dip
durchnässen = soak
durchseihen = strain
Ei = egg
Eichhörnchen = squirrel
Eierrahm = custard
einmachen = pickle
einschenken = pour
Eis = ice; ice cream
Endivien = endive
englisch = English
Entchen = duckling
Ente = duck
entkernen = core
eonschenken = pour
Erbse = pea
Erdbeere = strawberry
Erdnuss = peanut
essen = eat
Essig = vinegar
Esslöffel = tablespoon
Estragon = tarragon
Federvieh = poultry
Feige = fig
feinhacken = mince

Fenchel = fennel
Fett = fat
Fett = grease
Fisch = fish
Fleisch = meat
Flügel = wing
Flunder = flounder
Forelle = trout
französisch = French
frittieren = fry
frittiert = fried
Frosch = frog
Frucht = fruit
Früstück = breakfast
Gabel = fork
Gans = goose
Garnele = prawn
garnieren = garnish
gebacken = baked
gebraten = roasted
Geflügel = fowl
gefüllt = stuffed
Gelee = jelly
gemahlen = ground
Gemüse = vegetable
geräuchert = smoked
Gericht = dish
Gerste = barley
Getränk = beverage, drink
Getreide = grain, cereal
gewürz = spice
Glas = glass
Granatapfel = pomegranate
Grapefruit = grapefruit
grüne Bohne = green bean,
  string bean
Guave = guava
Gurke = cucumber
hacken = chop

Hafer = oats
Hahn = cock, rooster
Hammelfleisch = mutton
Hase = hare
Haselnüss = hazelnut
Hecht = pike
Hefe = yeast
Heidelbeere = bilberry,
  blueberry
Heilbutt = halibut
heiss = hot
Henne = hen
Hering = herring
Herz = heart
Himbeere = raspberry
Hirn = brain
Hirsch = deer
Honig = honey
Honigapfel = cherimoya
Huhn = chicken
Hummer = lobster
Ingwer = ginger
italienisch = Italian
Kabeljau = cod
Kaffee = coffee
Kakao = cocoa
Kalbfleisch = veal
Kalbsmilch = sweetbread
kalt = cold
Kammmuschel = scallop
Kaninchen = rabbit
Kapaun = capon
Karotte = carrot
Karpfen = carp
Kartoffel = potato
Käse = cheese
Kastanie = chestnut
Kichererbse = chickpea
Kirsche = cherry
Kleie = bran
kneten = knead
Knoblauch = garlic
Knochen = bone

kochen = cook, boil
Kohl = cabbage
Kokosnuss = coconut
Konfitüre = preserve
Kopf = head
Kotelett = chop
Krabbe = shrimp
Kraut = herb
Krebs = crab
Krume = crumb
Kuchen = cake
Kummel = hake
Kürbis = squash, pumpkin
Lachs = salmon
Laib = loaf
Lamm = lamb
Lammkeute = leg of lamb
Languste = rock lobster,
  spiny lobster
Lauch = leek
Leber = liver
Lerche = lark
Limette = lime
Limonade = lemonade
Linse = lentil
Löwenzahn = dandelion
Mahlzeit = meal
Mais = corn, maize,
  Indian corn
Maiskolben = ear
Makkaroni = macaroni
Makrele = mackerel
Mandarine = tangerine,
  mandarin
Mandel = almond
Mango = mango
Marmelade = jam, preserve
Marzipan = marzipan
Meeresfrüchte = seafood
Meerrettich = horseradish
Mehl = flour
Melasse = molasses
Melone = cantaloupe, melon

Messer = knife
Miesmuschel = mussel
Milch = milk
mischen = blend
Mischung = blend
Mittagessen = lunch
Mohrrübe = carrot
Münze = mint
Muskatnuss = nutmeg
Nachtisch = dessert
Nelke = clove
Niere = kidney
Nudel = noodle
Nuss = nut
Obst = fruit
Obstkuchen = pie
Ochs = ox
Oistazie = pistachio
Öl = oil
Olive = olive
Olivenöl = olive oil
Orange = orange
Pampelmuse = grapefruit
Papaya = papaya
Paprika = pepper
Perlhuhn = guinea fowl
Petersilie = parsley
Pfanne = pan
Pfeffer = pepper
Pferd = horse
Pfirsich = peach
Pflaume = plum
Pilz = mushroom
Pinienkern = pine nut
Pistazie = pistachio
Porree = leek
Pudding = pudding
pürieren = mash, purée
Quitte = quince
Rahmapfel = custard apple
reiben = grate
Reis = rice
Renntier = reindeer

Deutsches Verzeichnis

Rettich = radish
Rhubarber = rhubarb
Rinderbraten = roastbeef
Rindfleisch = beef
Rippe = rib
Rochen = skate, ray
Roggen = rye
Rosenkohl = Brussels
  sprouts
Rosine = raisin
rote Rübe = beet
Rübe = turnip
Rührei = scrambled eggs
rühren = stir
Saft = juice
Sägefisch = sawfish
Sahne = cream
Salat = salad, lettuce
Salatsosse = dressing
Salbei = sage
Salm = salmon
Salz = salt
Sardine = sardine
Saubohne = broad bean
Sauce = sauce
sauer = sour
schaben = scrape
Schaf = sheep
schälen = peel, pare
Schaltier = shellfish
Schenkel = thigh
Schildkröte = turtle
Schinken = ham
schlagen = beat
Schmalz = lard
schmelzen = melt, render
schmoren = simmer, braise,
  stew
Schmorgericht = stew
Schnecke = snail
schneiden = cut

Schnitte = slice
Schokolade = chocolate
Schulter = shoulder
Schwanz = tail
Schwarzwurzel = scorzonera
Schwein = hog, pig, swine
Schweinefleisch = pork
Seehecht = hake
Seepolyp = octopus
Seeteufel = angler
Seezunge = sole
Sellerie = celery
Senf = mustard
Serviette
sieben = sift
Spaghetti = spaghetti
spanisch = Spanish
Spargel = asparagus
Speck = bacon
Speisekarte = menu
Spinat = spinach
Stärke = starch
Steak = steak
Steinbutt = turbot
Suppe = soup
Süssigkeit = candy
Tasse = cup
Taube = pigeon
Tee = tea
Teelöffel = teaspoon
Teig = batter
Teigwaren = pasta
Teller = plate
Thunfisch = tuna
Tintenfisch = cuttlefish
Tisch = table
Tomate = tomato
Traube = grape
trinken = drink
Trinkgeld = tip
trocken = dry

Truthahn = turkey
Umberfisch = croaker
Untertasse = saucer
Vanillepudding = custard
Veilchen = violet
Venusmuschel = clam
Vieh = cattle
Wachtel = quail
Waldschnepfe = woodcock
Walfisch = whale
Walnuss = walnut
warm = warm
wärmen = warm
Wasser = water
Wassermelone = watermelon
weich = soft, tender
Wein = wine
Weinstock = vine
Weizen = wheat
Wild = game
würfeln = dice
Wurst = sausage
Wurzel = root
zart = tender
zerdrücken = press
Zerealie = cereal, grain
zerkrümeln = crumble
zerquetschen = crush
zerschneiden = slice
Zichorie = witloof chicory
Zicklein = kid
Ziege = goat
Zimt = cinnamon
Zimtapfel = custard apple
Zitrone = lemon
Zitrusfrüchte = citrus fruit
Zucchini = courgette,
  zucchini
Zucker = sugar
Zunge = tongue
Zwiebel = onion

Indice italiano

acciuga = anchovy
aceto = vinegar
acqua = water
affettare = slice
affumicato = smoked
aglio = garlic
agnello = lamb
agro = sour
agrumi = citrus fruit
ala = wing
albicocca = apricot
allodola = lark
amido = starch
ananas = pineapple
anatroccolo = duckling
anguilla = eel
anguria = watermelon
animelle = sweetbread
anitra = duck
annona = cherimoya,
  custard apple
arachide = peanut
aragosta = lobster
arancia = orange
aringa = herring
arrostire = roast
arrostito = roasted
arrosto = roast
artemisia = tarragon
asparago = asparagus
aspergere = sprinkle
assortimento = variety
avena = oats
avocado = avocado
bacca = berry
balena = whale
banana = banana
barbabietola = beet
battere = beat

beccaccia = woodcock
bere = drink
bestiame = cattle
bibita = beverage, drink
bicchiere = glass
birra = beer
bistecca = steak
bollire = boil
braciola = steak
brasare = braise
briciola = crumb
brodo = broth
bruciacchiare = sear
budino = pudding
bue = ox
burro = butter
cacao = cocoa
cacciagione = game
caffè = coffee
calamaro = squid
caldo = hot, warm
cannella = cinnamon
cappone = capon
capra = goat
capretto = kid
carciofo = artichoke
carne = meat
carnesecca = bacon
carota = carrot
carpa = carp
castagna = chestnut
cavallo = horse
cavolfiore = cauliflower
cavolini di Brusselle
cavolo = cabbage
cece = chickpea
cedro = lime
cena = supper
cereale = cereal, grain

cervello = brain
cervo = deer
cetriolo = cucumber
chiodo di garofano = clove
cicoria = endive
cicoria belga = witloof
  chicory
ciliegia = cherry
cioccolata = chocolate
cipolla = onion
cocco = coconut
coda = tail
colazione (prima) = breakfast
colazione (seconda) = lunch
coltello = knife
condimento = dressing
coniglio = rabbit
conserva = preserve
coprire = coat
corvina = corbina
coscia = thigh
cospargere = dredge
costola = rib
costoletta = chop
cotogna = quince
cozza = mussel
cren = horseradish
crusca = bran
crustaceo = shellfish
cucchiaino = teaspoon
cucchiaio = tablespoon
cuocere = cook
cuore = heart
dattero = date
dolce = dessert
dolci = candy
erba = herb
fagiolino = green bean,
  string bean

fagiolo = bean
faraona = guinea fowl
farina = flour
fava = broad bean
fegato = liver
fetta = slice
fico = fig
finocchio = fennel
fiore = flower
foglia = leaf
fondere = melt, render
forchetta = fork
formaggio = cheese
forno = oven
fragola = strawberry
francese = French
freddo = cold
friggere = fry
fritto = fried
frumento = wheat
frutti di mare = seafood, shellfish
frutto = fruit
fungo = mushroom
gallina = hen
gallo = cock
gamba = leg
gamberetto = shrimp
gambero = prawn
gelatina = jelly
gelato = ice cream
ghiaccio = ice
granchio = crab
grano = wheat
granturco = corn, maize, Indian corn
grasso = fat, grease
grattugiare = grate
guaiava = guava
guarnire = garnish
impastare = knead
impregnare = soak
indivia = endive

inglese = English
insalata = salad
italiano = Italian
lampone = raspberry
lardo = lard
latte = milk
latticinio = milk products
lattuga = lettuce
lenticchia = lentil
lepre = hare
lievito = yeast
limonata = lemonade
limone = lemon
lingua = tongue
lista = menu
lofio = angler
luccio = pike
lumaca = snail
maccherone = macaroni
macerare = steep
macinato = ground
maiale = pork, hog, swine
mancia = tip
mandarancio = clementine
mandarino = tangerine, mandarin
mandorla = almond
mangiare = eat
mango = mango
manzo = beef
marinare = pickle
marmellata = jam
marzapane = marzipan
mela = apple
melagrana = pomegranate
melanzana = aubergine, eggplant
melassa = molasses
melone = cantaloupe, melon
menta = mint
merluzzo = cod, hake
mescolare = stir, blend

miele = honey
minestra = soup
mirtillo = bilberry, blueberry
miscela = blend
mollusco = shellfish
montone = mutton
mora = blackberry
navone = turnip
nocciola = hazelnut
noce = nut, walnut
noce moscata = nutmeg
oca = goose
olio = oil
oliva = olive
ombrina = croaker
orzo = barley
osso = bone
ostrica = oyster
padella = pan
pane = bread, loaf
pane tostato = toast
panino = roll
panna = cream
pannocchia = ear (of corn)
papaia = papaya
passare = strain
pasta = pasta, batter
pasto = meal
patata = potato
pecora = sheep
pelare = peel, pare
pepe = pepper
peperone = pepper
pera = pear
pesca = peach
pesce = fish
pettine = scallop
piatto = dish; plate
piccione = pigeon
pignuolo = pine nut
pinolo = pine nut
piovra = octopus

pisello = pea
pistacchio = pistachio
pollame = poultry
pollo = chicken, fowl
polverizzare = crumble
pomodoro = tomato
pompelmo = grapefruit
porco = pig
porro = leek
pranzo = dinner
prezzemolo = parsley
prosciutto = ham
prugna = plum
prugna secca = prune
quadrettare = cube
quaglia = quail
rabarbaro = rhubarb
radice = root
radichiella = dandelion
rafano = horseradish
rana = frog
raschiare = scrape
ravanello = radish
razza = ray, skate
renna = reindeer
riempito = stuffed
riscaldare = warm
riso = rice
rognone = kidney
rombo = halibut, turbot
rosbif = roastbeef
rosolare = brown
sale = salt
salmone = salmon
salsa = sauce, dip

salsiccia = sausage
salumi = cold cuts
salvia = sage
sandwich = sandwich
sardina = sardina
sbollentare = parboil
sbrindellare = shred
sbucciare = peel, pare
scampo = shrimp
schiacciare = crush
scoiattolo = squirrel
scorzonera = scorzonera
secco = dry
sedano = celery
segale = rye
selvaggina = game
senape = mustard
seppia = cuttlefish
sgombro = mackerel
soffice = soft
soffriggere = sauté
sogliola = sole
sottotazza = saucer
spaghetti = spaghetti
spagnolo = Spanish
spalla = shoulder
spezia = spice
spiga = ear (of corn)
spinaci = spinach
spremere = press
spruzzare = sprinkle
stacciare = sift
stufato = stew
succo = juice
sugo = gravy

tacchino = turkey
tagliare = cut, chop
tagliatella = noodle
tartaruga = turtle
tavola = table
tazza = cup
tè = tea
tedesco = German
tenero = tender
testa = head
tonno = tuna
torta = cake, pie
tovagliolo = napkin
tritare = mince
trota = trout
umido = stew
ungere = baste
uova strapazzate = scrambled eggs
uovo = egg
uva = grape
uva secca = raisin
vapore = steam
verdura = vegetable
versare = pour
vino = wine
violetta = violet
vite = vine
vitello = veal
vongola = clam
zenzero = ginger
zucca = pumpkin, squash
zucchero = sugar
zucchina, zucchino = courgette, zucchino

Índice español

aceite = oil
aceituna = olive
achicoria = endive
aderezo = dressing
agrio = sour
agua = water
aguacate = avocado
ahumado = smoked
ajo = garlic
ala = wing
albaricoque = apricot
alcachofa = artichoke
alemán = German
almeja = clam
almendra = almond
almidón = starch
almuerzo = lunch
alondra = lark
amasar = knead
anadino = duckling
anchoa = anchovy
anguila = eel
anona = custard apple
apio = celery
arándano = blueberry,
  bilberry
ardilla = squirrel
arenque = herring
arroz = rice
asado = roast; roasted
asar = broil, grill, roast
atún = tuna
avellana = hazelnut
avena = oats
azúcar = sugar
bacalao = cod
ballena = whale
batido = batter
batir = beat

baya = berry
beber = drink
bebida = beverage, drink
becada = woodcock
berenjena = aubergine,
  eggplant
betabel = beet
biftec = beefsteak
blando = soft
bogavante = lobster
budín = pudding
buey = ox
caballa = mackerel
caballo = horse
cabeza = head
cabra = goat
cabrito = kid
cacahuate = peanut
cacao = cocoa
café = coffee
calabacín = courgette,
  zucchini
calabacita = courgette,
  zucchini
calabaza = pumpkin,
  squash
calamar = cuttlefish, squid
caldo = broth
calentar = warm
caliente = hot, warm
camarón = shrimp
canela = cinnamon
cangrejo = crab
capón = capon
caracol = snail
carne = meat
carnero = mutton
carpa = carp
castaña = chestnut

caza = game
cebada = barley
cebolla = onion
cena = supper
centeno = rye
cerdo = pork, pig
cereal = cereal
cereza = cherry
cerner = sift
cerveza = beer
chabacano = apricot
champiñón = mushroom
chícharo = pea
chirimoya = cherimoya,
  custard apple
chocolate = chocolate
chocha = woodcock
chuleta = chop
ciervo = deer
ciruela = plum
ciruela pasa = prune
clavo = clove
cocer = cook
coco = coconut
codorniz = quail
col = cabbage
cola = tail
colar = strain
coles de Bruselas = Brussels
  sprouts
coliflor = cauliflower
comer = eat
comida = dinner, lunch,
  meal
compota = preserve
comprimir = press
conejo = rabbit
corazón = heart
cortar = cut

326

corvina = corbina, croaker
costilla = rib
crema = cream
crema pastelera = custard
crustáceo = shellfish
cubrir = coat
cuchara = tablespoon
cucharita = teaspoon
cuchillo = knife
dátil = date
decorar = garnish
derretir = melt, render
desayuno = breakfast
descorazonar = core
desmenuzar = crumble
despepitar = core
diente de león = dandelion
dorar = brown
dulce = candy
durazno = peach
ejote = green bean, string
  bean
empapar = soak
emparedado = sandwich
endibia = endive
ensalada = salad
escabechar = pickle
escaldar = scald
escaquear la superficie =
  cube
escarola = endive
escombro = mackerel
escorzonera = scorzonera
espagueti = spaghetti
español = Spanish
espárrago = asparagus
especia = spice
espiga = ear (of corn)
espinaca = spinach
estofado = stew
estragón = tarragon
fiambres = cold cuts
fideo = noodle

flan = custard
flor = flower
frambuesa = raspberry
francés = French
freír = fry
fresa = strawberry
frijol, fríjol = bean
frío = cold
frito = fried
fruta = fruit
gallina = hen
gallina de Guinea = guinea
  fowl
gallo = cock
gamba = prawn
ganado = cattle
ganso = goose
garbanzo = chickpea
granada = pomegranate
grano = grain, cereal
grasa = fat, grease
guayaba = guava
guisante = pea
haba = broad bean
harina = flour
helado = ice cream
hervir = boil
hielo = ice
hierba = herb
hígado = liver
higo = fig
hinojo = fennel
hipogloso = halibut
hogaza = loaf
hoja = leaf
hombro = shoulder
hongo = mushroom
horneado = baked
hornear = bake
horno = oven
hortaliza = vegetable
hueso = bone
huevo = egg

huevos revueltos = scram-
  bled eggs
incorporar = blend
inglés = English
italiano = Italian
jalea = jelly
jamón = ham
jengibre = ginger
jitomate = tomato
judía = bean
judía verde = green bean,
  string bean
jugo = juice
lamb = cordero
langosta = lobster, rock
  lobster, spiny lobster
leche = milk
lechecillas = sweetbread
lechuga = lettuce
legumbre = vegetable
lengua = tongue
lenguado = flounder, sole
lenteja = lentil
levadura = yeast
liebre = hare
limón [amarillo] = lemon
limón [verde] = lime
limonada = lemonade
lobina = bass
lonja de carne = steak
lucio = pike
macarrones = macaroni
macerar = steep
machacar = crush
maíz = corn, maize,
  Indian corn
mandarina = tangerine,
  mandarin
mango = mango
maní = peanut
manteca = fat, lard, grease
mantequilla = butter
manzana = apple

Índice español

marrano = swine
masa = batter
mazapán = marzipan
mazorca = ear (of corn)
mejillón = mussel
melaza = molasses
melocotón = peach
melón = cantaloupe, melon
membrillo = quince
menta = mint
menú = menu
merluza = hake
mermelada = jam, preserve
mero = sea bass
mesa = table
mezcla = blend
mezclar = blend
miel = honey
miel de caña = molasses
migaja = crumb
moje = dip
mojo = dip
molido = ground
mollejas = sweetbread
molusco = shellfish
mondar = pare, peel
mora = blackberry
mostaza = mustard
muslo = thigh
nabo = turnip
naranja = orange
nata = cream
natillas = custard
nuez = nut, walnut
nuez moscada = nutmeg
ostra = oyster
oveja = sheep
paloma = pigeon
pan = bread
panecillo = roll
papa = potato
papaya = papaya
pasa = raisin

pasta = pasta
pastel = cake, pie
patata = potato
patito = duckling
pato = duck
pavo = turkey
pejerrey = mackerel
pelar = peel, pare
pepino = cucumber
pera = pear
perca = perch
percha = perch
perejil = parsley
pescado = fish
pez sierra = sawfish
picar = chop
picar fino = mince
pierna = leg
pimienta = pepper
pimiento = pepper
pintada = guinea fowl
piña = pineapple
piñón = pine nut
pistacho = pistachio
plátano = banana
platillo = saucer; dish
plato = dish, plate
pollo = chicken, fowl
polvorear = sprinkle,
   dredge
pomelo = grapefruit
poro = leek
postre = dessert
prensar = press
propina = tip
pudín = pudding
puerco = hog
puerro = leek
pulpo = octopus
queso = cheese
rábano = radish
rábano picante = horse-
   radish

raíz = root
rallar = grate
rana = frog
raspar = scrape
raya = ray, skate
rebanada = slice
rebanar = slice
relleno = stuffed
remolacha = beet
reno = reindeer
res = beef
revolver = stir
riñón = kidney
rodaballo = turbot
rosbif = roastbeef
ruibarbo = rhubarb
sal = salt
salchicha = sausage
salmón = salmon
salsa = gravy, sauce,
   dip, dressing
saltear = sauté
salvado = bran
salvia = sage
sancochar = parboil
sandía = watermelon
sardina = sardine
sartén = pan
seco = dry
servilleta = napkin
sesos = brain
seta = mushroom
sofreír = sauté
sopa = soup
surtido = variety
tallarín = noodle
taza = cup
té = tea
tenedor = fork
ternera = veal
tierno = tender
tocino = bacon
tomate = tomato

toronja = grapefruit
torta = cake
tortuga = turtle
tostada = toast
trigo = wheat
trucha = trout
uva = grape

vaca = beef
vapor = steam
vaso = glass
venera = scallop
verdura = vegetable
verter = pour
vid = vine

vinagre = vinegar
vino = wine
violeta = violet
zanahoria = carrot
zarzamora = blackberry
zumo = juice

From Hippocrene's Cookbook Library

Americas

A TASTE OF HAITI

Mirta Yurnet-Thomas & The Thomas Family

With African, French, Arabic and Amerindian influences, the food and culture of Haiti are fascinating subjects to explore. From the days of slavery to present times, traditional Haitian cuisine has relied upon staples like root vegetables, pork, fish, and flavor enhancers like *Pikliz* (picklese, or hot pepper vinegar) and *Zepis* (ground spices). This cookbook presents more than 100 traditional Haitian recipes, which are complemented by information on Haiti's history, holidays and celebrations, necessary food staples, and cooking methods. Recipe titles are presented in English, Creole, and French.

180 pages • 5½ x 8½ • 0-7818-0927-4 • $24.95hc • (8)

FRENCH CARIBBEAN CUISINE

Stéphanie Ovide
Preface by Maryse Condé

This marvelous cookbook contains over 150 authentic recipes from the French islands of Guadeloupe and Martinique. Favorites such as Avocado Charlotte, Pumpkin and Coconut Soup, Fish Crêpes Saintoise, and Fish Court Bouillon will beckon everyone to the table. The author has spent many hours traveling, researching, and cooking all over the French islands to give her readers a real taste and appreciation of what French Creole cuisine is about.

The book would not be complete without its chapter on favorite drinks, featuring the famous Ti Punch. Also included are an extensive glossary of culinary terms that will familiarize home cooks with various exotic fruits, vegetables, and fish, as well as a list of websites that specialize in Caribbean products and spices.

232 pages • 6 x 9 • 0-7818-0925-8 • $24.95hc • (3)

COOKING WITH CAJUN WOMEN: RECIPES AND REMEMBRANCES FROM SOUTH LOUISIANA KITCHENS

Nicole Fontenot

In this treasury of Cajun heritage, the author allows the people who are the very foundations of Cajun culture to tell their own stories. They visited Cajun women in their homes and kitchens and gathered over 300 recipes as well as thousands of narrative accounts. Most of these women were raised on small farms and remember times when everything (except coffee, sugar, and flour) was homemade. They shared traditional recipes made with modern and simple ingredients.

376 pages • 6 x 9 • 0-7818-0932-0 • $24.95hc • (75)

A TASTE OF QUEBEC, SECOND EDITION

Julian Armstrong

First published in 1990, *A Taste of Quebec* is the definitive guide to traditional and modern cooking in this distinctive region of Canada. Now revised and updated, this edition features over 125 new recipes and traditional favorites, along with highlights on up-and-coming new chefs, the province's best restaurants, notes of architectural and historical interest, and typical regional menus for a genuine Quebecois feast. With photos illustrating the people, the cuisine, and the land sprinkled throughout, this is *the* food lover's guide to Quebec.

200 pages • 8-page color insert • 7³/₄ x 9³/₈ • 0-7818-0902-9 • $16.95pb • (32)

ARGENTINA COOKS!

Shirley Lomax Brooks

Argentine cuisine is one of the world's best-kept culinary secrets. The country's expansive landscape includes tropical jungles, vast grasslands with sheep and cattle, alpine lakes and glacier-studded mountains. As a result, a great variety of foods are available—game, lamb, an incredible assortment of fish and seafood, exotic fruits and prime quality beef. This cookbook highlights recipes from Argentina's nine regions, including signature recipes from Five Star chefs, along with the best of collections from the author and other talented home chefs.

298 pages • 6 x 9 • 0-7818-0829-4 • $24.95hc • (85)

CUISINES OF PORTUGUESE ENCOUNTERS

Cherie Hamilton

This fascinating collection of 225 authentic recipes is the first cookbook to encompass the entire Portuguese-speaking world and explain how Portugal and its former colonies influenced each other's culinary traditions. Included are dishes containing Asian, South American, African, and European spices, along with varied ingredients like piripiri pepper, coconut milk, cilantro, manioc root, bananas, dried fish, seafood and meats. The recipes range from appetizers like "Pastel com o Diabo Dentro" (Pastry with the Devil Inside from Cape Verde), to main courses such as "Frango à Africana" (Grilled Chicken African Style from Mozambique) and "Cuscuz de Camarão" (Shrimp Couscous from Brazil), to desserts like "Pudim de Côco" (Coconut Pudding from Timor). Menus for religious holidays and festive occasions, a glossary, a section on mail-order sources, a brief history of the cuisines, and a bilingual index will assist the home chef in creating meals that celebrate the rich, diverse, and delicious culinary legacy of this old empire.

378 pages • 6 x 9 • drawings • 0-7818-0831-6 • $24.95hc • (91)

ART OF SOUTH AMERICAN COOKERY

Myra Waldo

This cookbook offers delicious recipes for the various courses of a typical South American meal, with specialties from all countries. Dishes show the expected influence of Spanish and Portuguese cuisines, but are enhanced by the use of locally available ingredients.

272 pages • 5 x 8½ • 0-7818-0485-X • $11.95pb • (423)

ART OF BRAZILIAN COOKERY

Dolores Botafogo

In the 40 years since its original publication, *The Art of Brazilian Cookery* has been a trusted source for home chefs through the decades. This authentic cookbook of Brazilian food, the first of its kind to be published in the U.S., includes over 300 savory and varied recipes and begins with a vivid historical-geographic and culinary picture of Brazil.

240 pages • 5½ x 8¼ • 0-7818-0130-3 • $11.95pb • (250)

OLD HAVANA COOKBOOK

Cuban Recipes in Spanish and English

Cuban cuisine, though derived from its mother country, Spain, has been modified and refined by locally available foods like pork, rice, corn, beans and sugar, and the requirements of a tropical climate. Fine Gulf Stream fish, crabs and lobsters, and an almost infinite variety of vegetables and luscious, tropical fruits also have their places on the traditional Cuban table. This cookbook includes over 50 recipes, each in Spanish with side-by-side English translation—all of them classic Cuban fare and old Havana specialties adapted for the North American kitchen. Among the recipes included are: Ajiaco (famous Cuban Stew), Boiled Pargo with Avocado Sauce, Lobster Havanaise, Tamal en Cazuela (Soft Tamal), Quimbombó (okra), Picadillo, Roast Suckling Pig, and Boniatillo (Sweet Potato Dulce), along with a whole chapter on famous Cuban cocktails and beverages.

123 pages • 5 x 7 • line drawings • 0-7818-0767-0 • $11.95hc • (590)

Asia and Middle East

THE INDIAN SPICE KITCHEN:
Essential Ingredients and Over 200 Authentic Recipes

Monisha Bharadwaj

This richly produced, wonderfully readable cookbook, written by the food consultant to the celebrated London restaurant, Bombay Brasserie, takes you on an unforgettable culinary journey along the spice routes of India with over 200 authentic recipes and stunning color photographs throughout. Simple step-by-step recipes, all adapted for the North American kitchen, allow the home chef to create delicious foods with precious saffron, aromatic tamarind, and delicately fragrant turmeric, mustard and chilies.

The recipes are arranged by featured ingredient in a full range of soups, breads, vegetarian and meat dishes, beverages and desserts. Among those included are "Lamb with Apricots," "Cauliflower in Coconut and Pepper Sauce," and "Nine Jewels Vegetable Curry." This cookbook includes historical and cultural information on each ingredient, facts on storing and preparation, medicinal and ritual uses, and cooking times and serving suggestions for all recipes.

240 pages • 8 x 10¼ • color photographs throughout • 0-7818-0801-4 • $17.50pb • (513)

AFGHAN FOOD & COOKERY
Helen Saberi

This classic source for Afghan cookery is now available in an updated and expanded North American edition! This hearty cuisine includes a tempting variety of offerings: lamb, pasta, chickpeas, rice pilafs, flat breads, kebabs, spinach, okra, lentils, yogurt, pastries and delicious teas, all flavored with delicate spices, are staple ingredients. The author's informative introduction describes traditional Afghan holidays, festivals and celebrations; she also includes a section "The Afghan Kitchen," which provides essentials about cooking utensils, spices, ingredients and methods.

312 pages • 5½ x 8¼ • illustrations • $12.95pb • 0-7818-0807-3 • (510)

IMPERIAL MONGOLIAN COOKING:
Recipes from the Kingdoms of Genghis Khan
Marc Cramer

Imperial Mongolian Cooking is the first book to explore the ancient culinary traditions of Genghis Khan's empire, opening a window onto a fascinating culture and a diverse culinary tradition virtually unknown in the West.

These 120 easy-to-follow recipes encompass a range of dishes—from Appetizers, Soups and Salads to Main Courses (Poultry & Game, Lamb, Beef, Fish & Seafood), Beverages and Desserts. Among them are "Bean and Meatball Soup," "Spicy Steamed Chicken Dumplings," "Turkish Swordfish Kabobs," and "Uzbek Walnut Fritters." The recipes are taken from the four *khanates* (kingdoms) of the empire that include the following modern countries: Mongolia, Chinese-controlled Inner Mongolia, China, Bhutan, Tibet, Azerbaijan, Kyrgyzstan, Tajikistan, Turkmenistan, Uzbekistan, Kazakhstan, Georgia, Armenia, Russia, Poland, Ukraine, Hungary, Burma, Vietnam, Iran, Iraq, Afghanistan, Syria and Turkey. The author's insightful introduction, a glossary of spices and ingredients, and list of sample menus will assist the home chef in creating meals fit for an emperor!

211 pages • 5½ x 8½ • 0-7818-0827-8 • $24.95hc • (20)

ALL ALONG THE RHINE
Recipes, Wines and Lore from Germany, France, Switzerland, Austria, Liechtenstein and Holland
Kay Shaw Nelson

This wonderful collection of over 130 recipes spans the range of home cooking, from Appetizers, Soups, Main Courses, and Side Dishes, to Desserts and Beverages. Among the recipes included are traditional favorites and signature dishes from the six countries: "Cheese Fondue," "Balzers Split Pea-Sausage Stew," "Alpine Sauerkraut Soup," "Bratwurst in Beer," and "Pears in Red Wine."

Each chapter covers the culinary history and winemaking tradition of a different Rhine country. The literary excerpts, legends and lore throughout the book will enchant the reader-chef on this culinary cruise down one of the world's most famous rivers.

230 pages • 5½ x 8½ • b/w photos • 0-7818-0830-8 • $24.95hc • (89)

THE SCOTTISH-IRISH PUB & HEARTH COOKBOOK
Kay Shaw Nelson

From hearty, wholesome recipes for family dinners, to more sophisticated and exotic dishes for entertaining with flair, this book is the perfect source for dining the Celtic way! In this collection of 170 recipes of the best of Scottish and Irish pub fare and home cooking, you'll find old classics like Corn Beef 'N Cabbage, Cock-A-Leekie, Avalon Apple Pie, and Fish and Chips, and new recipes as well: Tobermory Smoked Salmon Pâté, Raisin Walnut Porridge, and Skibbereen Scallop-Mushroom Pie. Each chapter begins with entertaining stories, legends, and lore about Celtic peoples, traditions, customs, and history.

260 pages • 5½ x 8½ • b/w photos/illustrations • 0-7818-0741-7 • $24.95hc • (164)

COOKING IN THE FRENCH FASHION
Recipes in French and English
Stéphanie Ovide
Illustrated by Maurita Magner

France is renowned for its contributions to worlds of cuisine and fashion, and this cookbook captures the essence of both!

Featuring 38 bilingual recipes, *Cooking in the French Fashion* offers unique insight into the art of contemporary French cuisine. Popular recipes—both traditional and contemporary—are all adapted for the modern North American kitchen. Sample such stylish delicacies *Blanquette de veau* (Veal Blanquette), *Artichauts vinaigrette* (Artichokes with Vinaigrette

Sauce), *Gigot d'agneau aux flageolets* (Leg of Lamb with Flageolets) and *Mousse au chocolat* (Chocolate Mousse) among many others.

With the illustrator's enchanting fashion sketches throughout, *Cooking in the French Fashion* is the perfect gift for any cook, novice or gourmand, who wants to learn more about the French palate, culture and language.

93 pages • 5 x 7 • 0-7818-0739-5 • $11.95hc • (139)

TASTE OF ROMANIA
Expanded Edition
Nicolae Klepper

Here is a real taste of both Old World and modern Romanian culture in a unique cookbook that combines over 140 traditional recipes with enchanting examples of Romania's folklore, humor, art, poetry and proverbs. Contains recipes such classic favorites as Lamb Haggis, Mamaliga, Eggplant Salad, Fish Zacusca, and Mititei Sausages. This comprehensive and well organized guide to Romanian cuisine also includes a section on Romanian wines and an index in Romanian and English.

335 pages • 6 x 9 • b/w photos and illustrations • 0-7818-0766-2 • $24.95 hardcover • (462)

POLISH HERITAGE COOKERY, ILLUSTRATED EDITION
Robert and Maria Strybel

Over 2,200 authentic recipes!
Entire chapters on dumplings, potato dishes, sausage-making, babkas and more!
American weights and measures
Modern shortcuts and substitutes for health-conscious dining
Each recipe indexed in English and Polish

"An encyclopedia of Polish cookery and a wonderful thing to have!"
—Julia Child, *Good Morning America*

"Polish Heritage Cookery is the best [Polish} cookbook printed in English on the market. It is well-organized, informative, interlaced with historical background on Polish foods and eating habits, with easy-to-follow recipes readily prepared in American kitchens and, above all, its fun to read."
—*Polish American Cultural Network*

915 pages • 6 x 9 • 16 pages color photographs • 0-7818-0558-9 • $39.95hc • (658)

TASTES & TALES OF NORWAY
Siri Lise Doub
This cookbook offers more than 100 recipes, as well as historical accounts, local customs, and excerpts from Norwegian folk songs, traditional blessings, poetry, and mythology.
288 pages • 5½ x 8½ • $24.95hc • 0-7818-0877-4 • (341)

THE BEST OF SCANDINAVIAN COOKING: DANISH, NORWEGIAN AND SWEDISH
Shirley Sarvis & Barbara Scott O'Neil
This exciting collection of 100 recipes includes such tempting dishes as Norwegian Blueberry Omelet, Danish Butter Cake, Swedish Pancakes with Ligonberries, as well as a section entitled "A Smørrebrød Sampling," devoted to those open faced Danish sandwiches.
142 pages • 5½ x 8¼ • 0-7818-0547-3 • $9.95pb • (643)

ICELANDIC FOOD & COOKERY
Nanna Rögnvaldardóttir
In 165 recipes, this cookbook explores the evolution of Icelandic cuisine over the last two centuries. Modern trends include making use of the wonderful fresh fish and shellfish in Icelandic waters, as well as local wild herbs.
158 pages • 5½ x 8½ • 0-7818-0878-2 • $24.95hc • (12)

THE BEST OF FINNISH COOKING
Taimi Previdi
The Finnish-born author has compiled a delicious array of recipes for every occasion, all adapted for the American kitchen.
242 pages • 5½ x 8½ • 0-7818-0493-0 • $12.95pb • (601)

Prices subject to change without prior notice. **To purchase Hippocrene Books** contact your local bookstore, call (718) 454-2366, or write to: HIPPOCRENE BOOKS, 171 Madison Avenue, New York, NY 10016. Please enclose check or money order, adding $5.00 shipping (UPS) for the first book, and $.50 for each additional book.